DRA-MATIC DE-SIGN

IN THE CHESTER CYCLE

A scene from *The Holkham Bible Picture Book* (fol. 36) depicting the Marys kissing the resurrected Christ.

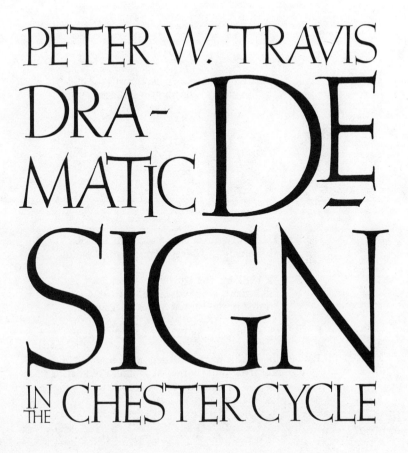

PETER W. TRAVIS

DRA-
MATIC DE-
SIGN

IN THE CHESTER CYCLE

The University of Chicago Press • Chicago and London

Peter W. Travis is associate professor of
English at Dartmouth College.

The University of Chicago Press, Chicago 60637
The University of Chicago Press, Ltd., London

© 1982 by The University of Chicago
All rights reserved. Published 1982
Printed in the United States of America

88 87 86 85 84 83 82   1 2 3 4 5

Publication of this work has been made possible in part
by a grant from the Andrew W. Mellon Foundation.

Library of Congress Cataloging in Publication Data

Travis, Peter W.
    Dramatic design in the Chester cycle.

    Bibliography: p.
    Includes index.
    1. Chester plays. 2. Mysteries and miracle-
plays, English—History and criticism. 3. English
drama—To 1500—History and criticism. I. Title.
PR644.C4T7   822'.0516   81-13047
ISBN 0-226-81164-6   AACR2

To my father and mother

Contents

Contents

Acknowledgments

While a graduate student at the University of Chicago, I was fortunate to be in the presence of three teachers deeply committed to the study of medieval drama. In his course on the subject, Jerome Taylor realized with such rigor his own high standards of criticism that they remain for me an unattainable ideal. Alan Nelson's critical reappraisals of the dramatic records proved the need to consider anew the staging history of each cycle. David Bevington, a most generous advisor, persuaded me of the value of continuing research in the field. This book, both in its inception and its development, is indebted to the influence of these three men.

Various parts of the book were given initial public exposure at the Medieval Institute conferences held annually at Western Michigan University. Under the general guidance of Clifford Davidson, the conferences' drama sections were ideal occasions for presenting, exchanging, and encouraging new ideas. Among the many like-minded scholars whom I first met at these conferences, three have been of very special assistance. Lawrence Clopper, of Indiana University, is responsible for bringing Chester's dramatic records to their present state of order; my second chapter could not have been written without his careful editing of these primary materials. Kathleen Ashley, of the University of Southern Maine, has written the best article-length study of the Chester cycle; my fifth chapter would have been radically different without it. Theresa Coletti, of the University of Maryland, has in my judgment written the best study on the cultural backgrounds of medieval English drama; my final

Acknowledgments

chapter builds extensively on her original research. Many other scholars of medieval drama have contributed to the progress of this book, by sharing their own work and scrutinizing mine; I prefer not to list them here but rather to recognize the contributions of each at the appropriate time in the text itself.

While lecturing at University College, London, I profited from the counsel of several scholars healthily skeptical of my American critical excesses. I would especially like to thank John McGavin, David Daniell, and David Mills. The majority of the book's gestation took place in the sympathetic environment of Dartmouth College. My thanks to the college itself for financial support, and to Ralph Cryesky and the staff of Baker Library, whose attentiveness to my needs was well-nigh saintly. My own department of English has been unusually appreciative of the difficulties of my labors. Peter Saccio was especially helpful in descrying the argumentative forms potential in my early work. David Kastan, who over the years scribbled thousands of marginal notes, has been an invaluable friend. Alan Gaylord, a teacher and colleague of the highest integrity, saved the finished manuscript from innumerable solecisms. In addition I am grateful to Penelope Walton, whose tracing of fol. 16 of *The Holkham Bible Picture Book* serves as the book's frontispiece; to Douglas Andrews, who uncomplainingly tracked down hundreds of citations I managed to foul up over the years; to Dorothy Beck, who helped with indexing; and to Arthur Mann, who has offered personal support for a very long time.

Even after the longest days, my wife June managed to make the center hold. Her strong will and good humor brought us through. And I have to hand it to our sons—Sean, Jared, and Matthew—who also kept the faith, certain that life, the book once done, would be an everlasting holiday.

Introduction

In the past fifteen years, two major works in the field of medieval drama scholarship have succeeded in bringing to belated maturity the study of the English plays of Corpus Christi. V. A. Kolve's *The Play Called Corpus Christi* (1966) identifies and explores many of the major themes and strategies to be found in the four extant cycles—Wakefield, York, N-Town, and Chester. Complementing Kolve's brilliant work, Rosemary Woolf's *The English Mystery Plays* (1972) offers a more detailed historical and literary analysis of all four cycles, scrutinizing and comparing nearly every episode in every play. After the publication of these two classics, it seemed reasonable at the time to anticipate several studies of continuing scholarship each of which would examine in detail the major dramatic designs of a single cycle. But with the possible exception of John Gardner's highly idiosyncratic *The Construction of the Wakefield Cycle* (1974), no such works have appeared. Rather, the few pertinent book-length studies recently published have tended to take one of three critical tacks. Either they offer a specialized interpretation of the development of English medieval drama;[1] or they examine one dramatic technique (such as typology)[2] or one dramatic element (such as poetry)[3] within a single cycle; or they return to the cycles' historical records to reinvestigate evidence of the ways the plays were originally performed.[4] Despite the important contributions of these recent works, what seemed the most important next step after Woolf's study has, surprisingly, not yet been taken. That step was to be a thorough examination of the dramatic designs of a single cycle—a study based firmly upon all prior scholarship and advancing that scholarship by the rigorous application of a newly defined "dramatic aesthetic." This present study of the Chester cycle is such an attempt. In addition, because it is the first critical book to examine the craft of the Chester cycle in all of its twenty-four pageants, it can for the moment claim to be unique in its field.

Any extended study of a Corpus Christi cycle will inevitably be fraught with structural problems if it intends to offer both a theoretical analysis as well as a "close reading" of the entire dramatic work. Because the cycles are history plays of such length, plays whose primary significance resides largely in the immediate experience of the dramatized events themselves, each cycle may be richly appreciated by tracing in detail its dramatization of Christian history from beginning to end. But because it is clear that the cycle authors designed their plays to accord with certain theoretical models, each cycle should also be fully analyzed in light of its own cluster of theological, historical, and artistic precepts. How to integrate these two critical allegiances—how to sustain one's "high thematic" arguments while offering an ongoing detailed description—is a problem which has troubled most critical studies of these plays. Kolve, for instance, arranges each of his chapters around a single major theme: lifting lines and episodes here and there from among the plays, he normally overlooks the discrete integrity of individual pageants (and cycles) for the sake of illuminating the general designs shared by all four cycles. Woolf, on the other hand, sacrifices the development of any overarching argument in order to examine (in a running commentary from Creation to Doomsday) every choice made by each playwright at each dramatic moment. Notwithstanding these two implicit warnings, it is my intention in this study to integrate both levels of critical activity, and to balance in each chapter an appreciation of Chester's dramatic presentation of sequential events with an understanding of the theoretical constructs which give shape to those events. To accomplish this objective, I will rely heavily upon "dramatic design" as a critical term applicable to nearly every level of the playwright's craft.

"Dramatic design" in this study means three interrelated things: structure, strategy, and "idea." The dramatic design of an individual pageant, in other words, is revealed in its principles of structural unity, in its affective relationship with its viewers, and in those theoretical models which determine its shape. These interrelated concepts pertain to an understanding of the craft of the playwright on three different levels: they will be applied to each of Chester's twenty-four pageants, to each of its six pageant-groups, as well as to the cycle as a whole. A straightforward description of a pageant's structure will serve throughout as the study's basic critical unit. But because (unlike its structure) a pageant's strategy and idea can be fully understood only in terms of that larger dramatic environment of which it is an integral part, the six chapters examining the finished design of the cycle (Chapters 3 through 8) will each focus upon one of Chester's six pageant-groups. The workaday obligation of these chapters will therefore be to define the dramatic design (structure, strategy, and idea) of individual pageants; to define concurrently the ways those pageants are part of the dramatic design of their pageant-group; and to define as well the place of that group in the dramatic design of the complete cycle. In addition, each of these six chapters has one further charge: to explore one major issue essential to an understanding of the entire cycle, an issue illustrated best by the pageants under immediate consideration. Thus each chapter studying the finished form of the cycle will be distinct in its thematic focus. Chapter 3 will focus upon the dramatic hermeneutics of Old Testament time; Chapter 4 will explore the relationship between "comic" dramatic structures and liturgical celebrations; Chapter 5 will define the nominalist foundations of Chester's "neo-Romanesque" aesthetic; Chapter 6 will trace the ritual rhythms of the Passion *agon;* Chapter 7 will integrate the "credal" designs of the cycle; and Chapter 8 will show how Chester defines its own meaning as a semiotic system. It is important therefore to recognize from the outset that these six chapters, while using essentially the same critical apparatus, will nevertheless examine their material in quite different ways because of their unique thematic concerns.

It is important to recognize from the outset what this book does not intend to do. It does not intend to apply a wealth of newly discovered nondramatic "primary" texts to the Chester cycle. Medieval drama scholarship does not suffer from a paucity of such texts; but it could profit from the application of a few carefully selected texts (some of them the most "standard") to very specific passages in certain plays. Nor does this study intend to offer a sustained "theatrical" analysis of the entire cycle, even though one of its major interests is the cycle's rhetorical-dramatic strategies. Matters such as stage-blocking, costume design, acting styles, and stage machinery will normally be left to the side as subjects appropriate to a full "dramaturgic" study by a scholar grounded in the field of theater arts. In addition, this study does not intend to deal primarily with Chester's dramatic records (although these are considered at some length); nor with its place in the development of medieval dramatic traditions (although these are mentioned); nor with the multitude of scenic analogues found in the graphic arts (although some are brought to bear on specific episodes). In other words, this present study—a multileveled formal, rhetorical, and thematic analysis of Chester's dramatic designs focusing upon six different major issues—is in its own terms an adequately balanced and sufficiently ambitious undertaking. However, were that undertaking only such as has been described to this point, it could rightly be criticized as a hermetic and self-referential exercise, its critical precepts and techniques generated entirely from that play under its consideration. Therefore, to widen the study's critical scope, and to enrich our understanding of the Chester cycle in terms of, and as part of, its cultural environment, two chapters precede the formal analysis of the finished play. Chapter 1 first defines the spirit and shapes of several late medieval celebrations of Corpus Christi, and then finds in the play of Corpus Christi (as a dramatic genre) a number of general precepts whose specific realizations in Chester will define that cycle as a unique variant of a dramatic type. Chapter 2 traces the history of Chester's development in order to discover those unifying principles (theological, historical, and aesthetic) which may have obtained and may have changed at various stages of the cycle's career. Together, Chapters 1 and 2 raise and define all the general precepts and problems that will serve as critical foci in the ensuing chapters. Although each prepares for what is to follow, Chapters 1 and 2 each have a self-contained argument. In fact, all eight chapters of this study are designed so that they may be read, if need be, in isolation as independent essays. But because part of each of these eight chapters also contributes to the progress of an overarching argument, it is recommended that they be read in the order presented. Like the Chester cycle itself, their argument is designed as a sequential experience which begins as it ends—by meditating upon the meaning of the image of the Body of God.

1

Medieval Celebrations of Corpus Christi: A Formal Analysis

The popular success of several recent productions of the English Corpus Christi cycles has shown how readily a modern audience, with little prior knowledge of medieval conventions, can appreciate the dramatic integrity of these "ancient" plays. In certain regards it would seem desirable here to emulate these stage productions by simply beginning (as they do) at the cycle's dramatic beginning, with God the Father creating his world ex nihilo. But in a book-length study of the Chester cycle, some preliminary understanding of the plays' cultural milieu is absolutely necessary—both as an introduction to the imaginative "register" of the cycle's original viewers, and as a way of arriving at those kinds of questions which may legitimately be asked of this kind of drama. An inquiry into the imaginative context which created and gave shape to these plays, however, is no small matter. It could easily consist of a history of dramatic, artistic, and musical developments from the twelfth to the sixteenth century; or a history of major changes in philosophical and theological thought within the same span of time; or a history of certain religious movements, such as that of the Franciscans, and the aesthetics they made popular; or a history of craft guilds and lay religious confraternities; or a history of all these things and of several others. The design of this chapter, however, is much more limited: I wish to represent a few relevant cultural features by focusing upon one important late medieval phenomenon and upon certain ways that phenomenon was honored. This phenomenon is the eucharistic Host. The modes of its celebration I will discuss are the rite of the Roman Mass (as practiced in the late Middle Ages), the Feast of Corpus Christi, the Corpus Christi procession, and the Corpus Christi play.

As several historians have noted, the rather sudden appearance in the late twelfth century of the belief that the eucharistic Host actually contained the living body of Christ was one indication that a major shift in Western religious thought was taking place. This growing veneration of the sacramental wafer, a veneration later given full expression through a variety of artforms, marked in its own way a new understanding of the relationship of things natural to things divine:

It was as though Europe had become populated with doubting Thomases eager to thrust their fingers into the very wounds of Christ. To an extraordinary degree the new eucharistic cult was empirical in temper, permitting the constant seeing and handling of God. The elevation of the consecrated host first appeared at Paris between 1196 and 1208; the reservation of the host for adoration became so common that the altar, hitherto conceived as a table, came to be thought of as normally supporting a tabernacle or monstrance; the dogma of transubstantiation was defined in 1215; the feast of Corpus Christi was instituted in 1264; and the first procession in honor of the host was held in 1279. Superficially the new piety might seem to be a development and expansion of the traditional sacramentalism, and as such a buttressing of the older symbolic and mediate view of nature. But, as the more conservative Eastern Church suspected, this was a sacramentalism of a new flavor, suffused with a spirit alien to that of the first Christian millennium. It seemed almost that the Latin Church, in centering its devotion upon the actual physical substance of its deity, had inadvertently deified matter.[1]

The Host's elevation in significance from commemorative symbol to corporeal container of the Deity was a shift in value paralleled by a revalorization of other things in the world of experience. Not only, in the spirit of St. Francis, was nature in the late Middle Ages allotted a quite high degree of spiritual reality (containing a quintessential substance some philosophers called *hyle*), but religious art (seen less rarely now as a flawed and untrustworthy image) was sometimes defended by apologists as if it were an icon that deserved veneration

2

in its own right because it participated fully in the sacred reality it represented. How far such liberal notions could go, however, and how much free rein orthodox belief could allow the heterodox imagination, were matters of considerable debate. This late medieval propensity to secularize the sacred, the closely related tendency to sacralize the secular, and the tension inherent in these two movements are all to be found in the new veneration of the eucharistic Host.

The degree to which the secular and the sacred could be allowed to interpenetrate was an issue that normally moved, as it were, on a vertical plane: its theoretical resolution involved defining the perfect vertical design, from high to low, of God's great chain of being. But I am more concerned here with the way this interpenetration of sacred and secular was expressed on a horizontal plane. One reason I have chosen to analyze the late medieval celebration of the Mass and the Corpus Christi feast, procession, and play is that all four were formal, sacred *actions* realized in human performance. Rather than an abstract philosophic debate, or a protracted social movement, or a religious creed or a novel aesthetic, these are activities whose choreographed movements were meant to project the perhaps otherwise inexpressible spiritual movements of the cultic community. Just as God remained throughout the Middle Ages the most sacred point atop the vertical chain of being, so the sacred point on the horizontal plane remained the center, that *axis mundi* of religious celebration from which God's energy was felt to emanate and toward which all worshipers wished to be returned. To trace in these four celebrations of the Eucharist the movement of spiritual energy—both "centripetally" toward and "centrifugally" away from this sacred center—will help to define their distinctive forms as sacred actions, as well as the needs and values they all expressed.

I have also chosen to examine these celebrations, dramatic and nondramatic, because they raise questions concerning the interpretive vocabulary proper to their kind. These questions are in part the creation of the late medieval temperament itself. How (for instance) a sacrament differed from a symbol, a symbol from an icon, an icon from an image, an image from a mirror, and so on, were matters involving the perceived relationship of the sacred, the natural, and the artistic worlds whose resolutions depended in no small part upon the range and restraint of each beholder's religious imagination. But these problems of vocabulary also derive in part from modern literary criticism, and its habit of applying to postmedieval drama terms that have been appropriated from the world of religious celebration. Such terms as "ritual" and "sacramental" and "iconic" are often useful in describing elements in postmedieval drama because they are understood to be true only metaphorically (cf. the Protestant devaluation of the Eucharist). But when these terms, and other standard critical locutions like "realism" and "illusion" and "suspended disbelief" are applied to medieval drama, problems arise, for contiguous to this drama is ritual itself. Conservatively defined, Christian ritual (unlike drama) offered a re-presentation (rather than representation) of Reality (rather than reality), not through the techniques of illusion, but through its own powers of canonized magic. It is a temptation to try to offer at the outset similar prescriptive and conservative definitions of all the terms necessary to this study, but such a list of rigidly defined meanings, I believe, would succeed only in distorting and simplifying the richness of the world we are entering. Therefore, in the following pages I will rely upon a general understanding of these and related critical terms, and will then try to uncover their appropriate significance within the context of late medieval ritual and dramatic practice.

It is possible that some suggestions of historical development may be discovered in this chapter: the twelfth century may be seen to be "represented" by the innovations in the Mass I will discuss; the Feast of Corpus Christi, although proclaimed for the universal church in 1311, was a thirteenth-century conception; the Corpus Christi procession was added to the feast during the fourteenth century; and the English Corpus Christi play is normally understood as a fifteenth-century phenomenon. But in fact the least of my interests here lies in offering a balanced, objective, and heavily documented study of gradual historical development and counterdevelopment. Rather, I intend to range freely over these centuries, combining things early and late, "lerned" and "lewed," sacred and secular, leaving to later chapters whatever complex historical matters need detailed study.

My interests are thus primarily formal: I wish to define these four celebrations of the Eucharist in order to understand precisely what the Corpus Christi play had in common with the rest, and what elements made it distinctive as drama. My interests are also affective or

4

psychological: in order to define the play's formal elements, that is, it is necessary to understand how the play was perceived and how it manipulated its viewers. I will allow myself the luxury of only one historical claim made at the outset—in response to the assumption that the English cycles, as "realistic" vernacular drama, were somehow always striving to move away from Latin church drama, which in its turn had striven to move away from the rites of the liturgy. On the contrary, I would suggest that this drama always "moved" in both directions at once. The late Middle Ages would not have sought a deeper interpenetration of the sacred and the secular had there not been an increasing fear of the disengagement of the divine from everyday life. In the same way, late medieval religious drama stretched in both directions—out toward the people and back toward ritual—because it knew its viewers feared that their world was in constant danger of being separated even further from the world of their Savior. Like the eucharistic Host itself, late medieval drama attempted a far-reaching unification of the sacred and the secular, of Christ and the community of his faithful.

I

The impetus which led to the initial formation of the Corpus Christi feast came from a humble source, a thirteenth-century Augustinian nun named Juliana of Liége. Troubled by the recurring dream of a moon in partial eclipse, she came to understand the radiant moon as a symbol of Christ's glorious Body, his church, and the dark shadow as a figure lamenting the absence of a special feast in honor of the Blessed Sacrament. This vision, along with her interpretation of its allegorical import, she conveyed to Robert of Thourette, bishop of Liége: in 1226 Robert instituted a local feast after Juliana's wishes. In 1264 Pope Urban IV, a former subordinate of Robert, attempted to institute a Corpus Christi feast for the whole church. But the *Festum Eucharistiae* was not universally acclaimed until more than a century after its original conception when, finally reconfirmed in 1311 by Pope Clement V, it was rapidly embraced by the dioceses of the Western church.[2]

Juliana's adoration of the Sacrament was shared by Christians in the Middle Ages well before the institution of the feast. As Christ was

5

the spiritual center of their religious beliefs, so the eucharistic wafer served as mystical center of their religious lives. The pure magic of the Sacrament evoked the simplest forms of religious feeling—faith, wonder, and adoration. Even to the *simpliciores,* the significance of the consecrated Host was clear. No works of art depicting Christ, no cathedral paintings, statues, or icons, could quite match the power which emanated from the Host: whereas those were images of the Son of God worthy of veneration because they were reflections of a higher Reality, the Sacrament was that Reality itself, the living Body of the Lord who had died on the cross for man's salvation. In the presence of this miraculous transubstantiation, believers responded with a feeling of profound awe.

The veneration felt for the Blessed Sacrament was heightened, protracted, and dramatized by a manner of celebrating the Mass peculiar to the late Middle Ages. Originally conceived by the primitive church as a communal ritual shared almost equally by the celebrant, the deacons, and the faithful, the Mass during the Middle Ages gradually shifted from a public form of communion to a more private celebration of the mysteries of the faith. The consecrated wine and eucharistic wafer, symbols of the unity of the whole Christian family in Christ, were rarely offered to the laity after the tenth century, and the direct sharing of Christ's mystical body could be experienced only vicariously in the celebrant's partaking of the bread and wine. The innovation of silent prayers, which the priest uttered softly to himself, and the displacement of the sacramentary by the *Missale Plenum,* allowing the priest to serve as lector, succeeded in distancing the Mass even further from the people, as well as from the deacons, whose former importance in the celebration of the mysteries had symbolized the sharing of the public at large. The erection of the rood screen between nave and choir formed a logical and visible conclusion to this centripetal movement of the Mass, so that the laity found themselves no longer participants in, but spectators of, a distant and rather arcane rite.[3]

In conjunction with and as a consequence of this growing emphasis upon the Mass as arcane mystery, other changes occurred which created for the viewers a new understanding of the rite's significance. In the high Middle Ages, the Mass increasingly came to be seen as a form of sacred drama, a disguised or symbolic mimesis of Christ's life, of the expectations of his coming, the central deeds of his ministry, his Passion, Resurrection, and Ascension. Numerous exegetes maintained that a vast compendium of correspondences existed between the story of Christ and the performers, words, gestures, sacraments, and sacramentals of the Mass itself. The first movement, for instance, from Introit to the Gospel, exegetes often interpreted as depicting the expectations of Christ's coming to earth (the *Gloria* stands for the angels' song announcing the Nativity, the reading represents the prophecy of John, and so on); the second part of the Mass, from the Offertory to the *Pater Noster,* represented Christ's Passion and burial (the *Unde et memores* opens the Passion, the *Nobis quoque peccatoribus* symbolizes the centurion's confession, etc.); and the last movement dramatized Christ's triumph (the commingling of the Host and consecrated wine marks the return of his soul to his body, the Kiss of Peace represents the disciples' joy on hearing of the Resurrection, and the blessing of the congregation is equated with Christ's blessing his disciples before the Ascension). Opening with prophecies of Christ's Nativity, the "historical drama" of the Mass concluded with a vision of the New Jerusalem and a celebration of Christ's return to his father.[4]

When this sort of allegorical practice was applied to every nuance of the Mass, and a number symbolism further explained the repeated gestures of the performers and a color symbolism their vestments, the Mass was divested of much of its ritual economy and density of significance. "Less and less did the spoken word project its own contents," writes Josef Jungmann; "one concentrated rather on the alternation between the loud and the soft tones of prayer. The meaning of the ceremonies was often a synthetic one, abstracting entirely from the course of the sacred action, and giving a fixed significance to each repeated ceremony just as a fixed significance was given to the visible appurtenances."[5]

It has been clear to most scholars of the Gothic Mass that a mimetic drama never actually occurred at the altar[6] but rather in the minds of the observers, who were obliged to draw from memory the narrative events which the ritual evoked, and subjectively to connect each scriptural action with its symbolic counterpart. The important point is not that this allegorical interpretation was fanciful or invalid, but that it apparently answered a profound need and for centuries

7

influenced both the felt experience of the Mass and its mode of celebration. Congregations waited expectantly to glimpse any gestures which could correspond to the familiar scriptural story. Celebrants, in turn, exaggerated some gestures and added others to commemorate the sufferings of Christ. During the Consecration, for instance, the priest raised his eyes imploringly to heaven, and after the elevation of the Host he extended his arms as if in the agony of crucifixion. With the addition of numerous kisses (which generally signified the love of the disciples for Christ) and of protracted sighs (signifying their lamenting his death), the Mass was conceived as a disguised drama mimetic of the sacred past, as well as a ritual enactment in the absolute present.

The deepening interest in the Mass as a "dramatic" spectacle helped prompt another innovation in its celebration. Traditionally, at the ritual center of the Mass, the priest had lifted the bread breast-high as he blessed it; he then replaced it on the altar and turned immediately to the consecration of the chalice. But the growing belief in the Sacrament as the real Body of Christ, and not a symbol, along with an essential need to see each "dramatic" gesture clearly, made it imperative that this moment in the Mass not be missed by anyone. So, in the late twelfth century, most celebrants in Europe accepted *hoc est enim corpus meum* as the actual consecration of the species, and then elevated the Host full-reach above their heads for all to see and adore. The gesture was announced by the ringing of a bell (another twelfth-century innovation), and in some places the elevation was repeated, for many believed they had not properly heard Mass unless they had seen the Sacrament. An English Reformation critic, Thomas Becon, recorded that if the Host is not clearly visible, "the rude people of the countrey in diverse partes of England will crye out to the priest: houlde up Sir John, houlde up. Heave it a little higher."[7]

The elevation of the Host, coming as it does immediately after the Consecration, is a gesture of unusual significance. It was not a traditional part of the Mass as ritual, nor is it properly part of the Mass as "drama" (despite the attempts of a few allegorists to equate the elevation with the elevation of Christ on the cross).[8] It is rather a self-contained gesture performed for the sake of the audience alone, a brief hiatus in the action where visible proof is proffered to the

8

congregation of the Real Presence. This is neither primarily ritual nor primarily drama. For lack of a better term, it should perhaps be defined as pure "spectacle": a simple and wordless gesture where the belief of the congregation is evoked and expressed in a moment of ocular communion.

Instituted in the primitive church as an active, familiar, and tactile concelebration by the faithful,[9] the Mass by the end of the twelfth century had developed into a privileged rite and a pseudodrama which the audience no longer directly participated in, but viewed from a distance. It had consequently become a highly visual ceremony, and whatever communion took place could be effected only by an imaginative meditation upon the enacted spectacle. Formerly a *eucharistia*, a feast for the body, the Mass was now an *epiphania*, a feast for the eyes. This new emphasis upon an ocular rather than a participatory communion evoked a variety of responses, ranging from a simple faith in witness of Christ's presence to an imaginative recreation of the central elements of Christian history. The spectrum of responses to the Mass, and the needs they expressed, were fully manifested elsewhere in the late Middle Ages: specifically, in the Corpus Christi feast, the Corpus Christi procession, and the Corpus Christi play. The devotion to the Eucharist as the supreme sacrament, the need shared by both "lerned" and "lewed" for a dramatic projection of Christian history, and the communal joy evoked by the spectacle of the elevated Host were central among the emotions gratified on Corpus Christi day.

The thinking responsible for the formation of one of these ceremonies, the Corpus Christi procession, has gone unrecorded. A council of church authorities convened in Paris in 1323 decided that the procession had been created "by a sort of inspiration," and decreed that the forms it might assume were best left to the discretion of "the clergy and the people" of the various dioceses in Europe.[10] The purpose of the procession, however, is clear. Wherever it was celebrated, the procession served as an extension of the climax of the Mass into the world of everyday reality. The Host consecrated at the Mass was carried in a ceremony of solemn joy through the byways and past the sacred places of the town, sometimes into the far reaches of the countryside, and then finally returned to the church altar. By processing from the grounds of the church through the secular streets, the congregants were expressing the adoration they felt for the Sacrament in their daily lives, and displaying the ideal effect Christ's presence had on their own society. That effect was symbolized by the formal ranks of the procession (clerical orders, mayor, town council, religious guilds, craft guilds, and so on): a linear arrangement of the community which served as an image of the ideal hierarchy a society achieves with Christ as its king.[11]

The express effect of this procession was similar to that of the early Mass, and, to a lesser degree, of the Gothic Mass: both were forms of devout action where a harmonious rapport between the human order and the divine was gained. The procession differed from the Mass in that it lifted from the Mass and magnified in isolation the elevation of the Host. The elevation, I have noted, was a simple and wordless gesture where the belief of the congregation was evoked and expressed in a moment of ocular communion. The procession was a similar spectacle, only it ceremonially protracted that moment and mobilized its effect, displaying the Sacrament to the adoring community and the adoring community to themselves.

Lacking the symbolic, archetypal density of the Mass, the procession clearly remained a "ceremony," not a ritual, a wordless display of a single religious "stance," rather than a verbal, melodic rite performed within a traditional structure. The emotion it expressed did not change, as did the emotions of the Mass: the solemn joy to which the ritual of the Mass built remained the durable and steady emotion contained by the procession from beginning to end. Yet as a sacred action created by the people, for their edification, and celebrated within their midst, the Corpus Christi procession offered to the feast day a societal expression of the spiritual communion which the feast was instituted to honor.

The Feast of Corpus Christi expressed its devotion to the Sacrament by quite different means. Working within a traditional liturgical framework, those who selected the readings for the feast, and for its office and Mass, chose excerpts from patristic writings which analyzed the symbolism of the Eucharist. A majority of these readings raised and answered certain theological questions which pertained to the mysteries immediately related to the Sacrament: how does the bread become the Body of Christ, how does the Word become one with the flesh, how did the Wisdom of God become the Son of Man, and how does the partaking of the Sacrament render the faithful one with Christ? In emphasizing the theophanic mystery of the Sacrament, the wondrous union of the human, natural, and divine, these texts also insist that the union of like particles from nature in the eucharistic wine and wafer symbolizes the social unification of men on earth. *Ex multis namque granis unus panis conficitur et ex multis racemis vinum confluit* (thus out of many grains is made one bread and out of many grapes flows together one wine); in like manner—the feast proclaims—under the power of the Holy Spirit men must come together into one race united in Christ.

The partaking of the Sacrament as a commemoration of the original paschal feast with the disciples is also emphasized in the readings. But Christ's command *hoc facite in meam commemorationem* is used to such advantage that the Sacrament is seen to commemorate all the wonders of Christ's life: his miraculous conception, the marvels of his ministry, the drama of his Passion, Resurrection, and Ascension. In answering the central questions concerning the mystery of the Sacrament, the original authors of the feast (Aquinas is thought to have been one of its compilers) discovered analogies and proofs which expanded even beyond the reaches of Christ's life, and extended to the beginning and end of Christian time. Thus, an excerpt from the works of Ambrose argues that the instantaneous creation of Christ in the consecrated wafer is proved valid by the prototypical example of God's creation of heaven and earth. Another reading, drawn from the pseudo-Isidore, offers the traditional understanding that the paschal feast was prefigured in Melchisedec's offering of bread and wine, and that the power of Moses' wand which drew forth water from a rock is the same which the celebrant invokes as he consecrates the bread and wine as the body and blood of Christ. Additional texts, from the works of Augustine, Cyprian, John Chrysostom, and others, allude to further miracles in the Old Testament, then to Pentecost, and finally, in the Postcommunion, to the ultimate reaches of sacred history, in the argument that the eucharistic feast is a prefiguration of the final messianic feast at the Last Judgment.[12]

The Feast of Corpus Christi thus derives much of its theological unity from the polysemous nature of the Sacrament itself. As the sacrament of Christ's Body, and the sacrificial food of the eucharistic feast, the consecrated Host had been made one of the most powerful symbols in the church. The genius of the feast is that it magnified the symbolic power of the Sacrament to such a degree that its meaning radiated into the farthest boundaries of Christian history. The Sacrament had thus become a kind of monad of the theological imagination: a symbol which unified the history of Christian salvation into a single cosmic vision. Selecting from sacred history figures and analogues which led to or from this central mystery of the faith, the Corpus Christi feast offered a view of the historical manifestations of Christ's divine power more concentrated and contained than that found in Scripture itself.

Each of these three ceremonies offered an aesthetic as well as a spiritual appeal. As the most ancient rite of the church, the Mass evoked a subtle ebb and flow of emotions within a structure which had a clear beginning, middle, and end. The beauty of the Mass was experienced through all five senses and was projected by a variety of vehicles: words, cadences, colors, incense, music, movement, and the eucharistic bread and wine. The procession, one guesses, expressed the devotion Juliana of Liége felt before the Host, and seems unwittingly to have honored her vision by symbolically uniting the community, as the universal church, with its mystical analogue, the Body of Christ. Its beauty was of a more popular nature, coming from the formal attire and ordered ranks which marked all medieval processions, both sacred and secular. The Feast of Corpus Christi added an intellectual and metaphysical beauty to the otherwise indirectly articulated ideas of the day. By invoking the acts of Scripture which derived their typological reality from the Eucharist, the readings of the feast demonstrated the perfection and economy of the history of Christian salvation.

The Corpus Christi play—like the Mass, the feast, and the procession—was a type of sacred action performed in order to evoke, express, and sustain the community's faith in the ultimate meaning of Christ's presence in their lives. Like the ceremonies to which it was added, the play projected (through an active, melodic, and verbal medium) the central religious beliefs of its society. It shared the movability and some of the costumes of the procession, derived some of its language and music from the liturgy, proffered evidence in its annual performance of the sacramental identity of Christ's Body, and dramatized many of those acts selected by the feast from the cycle of history which the liturgy takes a year to commemorate.

Because the themes, techniques, or forms of some of these activities are similar, liturgists and literary historians have sometimes attempted to prove the existence of certain causal connections between them. For instances, Peter Browe suggested that the Corpus Christi feast resulted from the elevation of the Host.[13] O.B. Hardison has argued that medieval religious drama originated in the Mass: "The Mass is the general case—for Christian culture the archetype. Individual dramas are shaped in its mold."[14] V.A. Kolve has maintained that the Corpus Christi feast caused the Corpus Christi play to be written.[15] And numerous critics maintain that the Corpus Christi play developed out of the Corpus Christi procession.[16]

These hypotheses of historical causation are suggestive, but in order to be proved or discredited each would demand very close scrutiny of the cultural records of as many medieval communities as possible. Such is not the purpose nor within the scope of this chapter. However, as an analysis of what may be called the ritual-poetics of certain creative minds in the Middle Ages, each hypothesis is extremely limiting, for it is more likely that these individual activities were prompted by a complex aggregate of religious expectations and were influenced in their inception by a host of prior traditions. If one considers the range of imaginative responses to the Sacrament in the late Middle Ages, it is in fact quite possible to believe that the activities under consideration could have been initiated during these centuries without the prior promptings of the Host's elevation, the Mass's artistic form, the feast's vision of Christian history, or the procession's popular appeal. At the very least it must be recognized that other religious aesthetic structures,[17] other expressions of eucharistic veneration,[18] other ceremonial processions,[19] and other visions of the shape of Christian history[20] existed from which these activities might have developed or, more properly, toward which their creators might have turned for further inspiration and design. Thus it seems best to leave to others the search for single genetic sources, and to turn to an examination of how these sacred actions gratified in different ways what I believe is a cluster of similar religious and psychological needs.

II

The elevation of the Host, the allegorization of the Mass, the Corpus Christi feast, the Corpus Christi procession, the Corpus Christi play: each of these, I suggest, was a sacred action demonstrating the community's sense of its corporate identity with, and understanding of, Christ's real presence in time.[21] Each gratified the community's need to become at one with Christ by offering visible proof of Christ's physical presence: the proof offered was itself metaphoric, symbolic, or sacramental, but it became empirical and real through the transforming powers of the community's religious faith and historicizing imagination. The blessing of Corpus Christi (and a partial explanation of the feast's popularity) was its thorough indulgence of a late medieval popular faith grounded in the empiricizing imagination, an imagination calling for sacred spectacle which it could revisualize as both sacred history and theophanic reality.[22] On Corpus Christi day the proffering of visual evidence was therefore of preeminent importance: blessed were those who might first see, and then again believe.

The nature of faith evoked by Corpus Christi must be distinguished from a similar yet simpler level of belief which needs little in the way of external action to unite time past with time present. This stage of devotion has been described by J.K. Campbell in his study of the Sarakatsan tribes of modern Greece, a people normally quite pragmatic and offhand in their daily religious attitudes, whose sense of the sacred shifts radically at the beginning of Holy Week:

> There is an air both of anxiety and anticipation. The historical events which the liturgy commemorates on the different days of the week are not treated as such. They are re-lived, people participate in them. They know what will happen, He will rise again; yet they are anxious. The women discuss the events in the present or perfect tense as they would the local gossip at other times. As the drama proceeds the women in chorus make their simple and troubled comments, "They have seized Him," "He is being judged," "Now they are crucifying Him"; and finally, at

14

the critical moment of the service on Easter Day, "Christ is risen"....

On Good Friday the intensity of emotional feeling is scarcely bearable. The effigy of Christ is taken from the cross and placed in the representation of the tomb which is carried round the village and returned to the Church as to the sepulchre. During this service the atmosphere is heavy with grief; tears stream down the faces of the women. Before 1950 the Sarakatsan women used to make their own representations of the tomb and the body of Christ which three of them guarded throughout the day, their black scarves low over their faces, silently weeping, while one of them intoned monotonously the dirge of the Mother of God for her only Son. Finally, the service which begins after midnight on the Saturday is a transformation of joy and exaltation. Christ who was crucified is risen again.[23]

Although the reenacted vigil at the sepulcher has now died out as a practice among the Sarakatsani, one can easily imagine how this expression of unselfconscious faith could have developed over time into more complex ritual and then into drama. The activities I have been discussing, however, were in my judgment not instituted in response to the medieval counterpart of the Sarakatsani's level of religious faith: this stage of devotion had surfaced much earlier in the Middle Ages and had been given full and adequate expression by the enacted tropes and simple paraliturgical rites of the ninth and tenth centuries.[24] Rather, the Corpus Christi activities touched upon that core of faith as they attempted to gratify two major psychological and cultural needs which had intensified rapidly in the thirteenth century: a need to fill the vacuum of spiritual understanding left by the centripetal movement of the Mass, and an even greater need created by the increasingly more allegorical and, paradoxically, more literal level of popular religious intelligence.

As anthropological studies of various cultures have shown, whenever a traditional symbol or rite tends to grow darker, denser, and seemingly richer in significance, there is a growing danger of its being misunderstood by the community of the faithful. When, or before, that significance appears finally to be enveloped in mystery, a shift often occurs in its interpretation, as symbols and symbolic actions are allegorized, and as the mythic elements implicit in ritual

15

are made explicit. In the Corpus Christi activities I have been discussing there can be seen expressed a common desire to make the implicit explicit by literalizing the symbolic and by actualizing sacred metaphor: in the elevation of the Host proof is offered to believers that the Sacrament is not a symbol, but Christ's living body; in the feast the readings contain an exegetical explication of the Sacrament's typological history; in the dramatic interpretation of the Mass, the rite is made concrete for the imagination in terms of reenacted history; in the procession, the traditional metaphor (celebrated in the feast) that the church is the Body of Christ is literalized in the unified body of his followers; and, in the play, the events of sacred history are more than commemorated—they are re-presented before the viewing community as proof of the reality of the deeds they perform.

Each of these celebrations of Corpus Christi employed a mode of thinking that can be seen as having been allegorical in nature. Generated by a process of mind unsatisfied by sacramental density, each activity strove to clarify the symbolically opaque not by metaphysical abstraction but by historical literalization. The mysterious is clarified, the mystical is made historical, so that the sacred reality celebrated in the rite and contained by the sacrament may be more immediately apprehended. Although obviously a major departure from traditional exegetical practices, the interpretive mode of Corpus Christi is basically an allegorical one: that is, it offers a reductive translation of symbols and sacraments, sometimes "upward" into the realm of abstract ideas, but normally "downward" into the world of historical signs and empirical things.[25]

The major energies of these Corpus Christi activities were thus both empirical and centrifugal, moving from the cryptic center of ritual action outward toward the historicizing imagination and sense experiences of the laity. Each activity helped make more accessible and immediate for the community a sacred reality that otherwise, despite its magic and power, remained obscured either in time or in the understanding. Unlike earlier medieval forms of sacred action manifesting a simpler and perhaps "purer" level of faith, these activities were fashioned in response to a popular piety that insisted upon sensory proof, or at least evidence, of Christ's divine presence. Divorced almost totally from a direct understanding of the Latin rites, the laity were specially dependent upon the evocative power of visual spectacle, either liturgical or extraliturgical. Beholding sacred objects and sacred gestures, the late medieval imagination was prepared to conjure up a mythic reality which could immediately be equated with, and "seen" as, the objects and actions presented to the immediate vision. Thus the major mode of communication in these celebrations of Corpus Christi was ocular: the spectators viewed the Mass, beheld the elevation of the Host, saw the procession, and watched the play. And each of these visual spectacles was intended to prompt a subjective meditation upon the reality and significance of Christ's presence in time.

In their exploitation of ocular experience, the celebrations of Corpus Christi epitomized a late medieval need to see those realities upon which Christian faith is based.[26] Although of primary importance, however, the sense of sight was often deemed insufficient, and wherever possible the sacred objects of rite and art were so quickened by the religious imagination that almost all the senses were brought into touch with the living reality they represented. For instance, medieval viewers were often convinced that before their devoted gaze sacred icons came alive to perform anew their wondrous deeds. This psychological phenomenon, often known as "affective piety," has been documented in numerous records from the late Middle Ages, and in the ritual world is typified by the hundreds of wonders performed by the Sacrament: congregants believed that they had tasted the Host upon seeing it, that they had seen Christ superimposed upon the Sacrament, that they had heard Christ cry out when the celebrant broke the eucharistic wafer, or that they had tasted his blood in the bread when they communed.[27]

The feast and the play, as the two more self-analytic celebrations of Corpus Christi, honored in different ways this psychological phenomenon. Conservatively, the feast recognized the power of devotion and sensation to interpenetrate, as when at Communion belief transforms experience, and the senses both test and sustain belief:

> All that the senses can reach in this Sacrament, (look, taste, feel, smell, and the like, all these) abide of bread and wine, but the Thing is not bread and wine. And thus room is left for faith; Christ Who hath a Form That can be seen, is here taken and received not only unseen, but seeming to be bread and wine, and

the senses, which judge by the wonted look, are warranted against error.[28]

Much less conservative than the feast in these matters, the Corpus Christi play exploits its power as dramatic spectacle by offering its own performance as visible evidence of the reality of the sacred events it imitates. Within its realm of dramatic illusion the play occasionally does even more, by summoning up the experience of nearly every physical faculty to verify the truth which it presents. In the Chester cycle, for instance, after Christ's Ascension, his disciples summarize all the physical sensations and experiences which collectively have proved the reality of Christ's physical presence among them:

> Nowe mon we leeve yt no leasinge,
> for both by syght and handlinge,
> speakinge, eatinge and drinkinge
> hee prooves his deitee.[29]

The Corpus Christi exploitation of physical sensation as a means of reifying the spiritual is one indication of the fourteenth and fifteenth centuries' growing commitment to the literal as a radical level of sacred truth.[30] The objects and actions of the sacred past, as well as the things of the present, were more and more understood to contain within themselves their own spiritual significance. As several studies of the late medieval religious temperament have shown, the nominalism of schoolmen,[31] the everyday *exempla* used by preachers,[32] the numerous handbooks for the laity,[33] and the growing naturalism of the popular arts[34] all demonstrate a new commitment to the *historia* and *littera* of Scripture and a new interest in educating the laity in the significance of their faith, its sacred metaphors, and its rites. The procession and play of Corpus Christi are an apt expression of this religious sensibility, and served as a natural extension of the feast by adapting to the secular world two modes of "actualization" which the laity could participate in and directly apprehend.

Since the late medieval interest in the literal as a radical level of spiritual truth was expressed in numerous media—such as the sermon, the narrative poem, the graphic arts, and even the mystical tract—the strategies of reification common to Corpus Christi do not sufficiently explain the attachment of the procession and the play to the feast, but they do suggest that the clustering of these various activities was

far from fortuitous.[35] Numerous other elements, both substantial
and accidental, surely contributed to the choice of Corpus Christi as
the original occasion for the play's presentation. Common sense suggests the following: the feast's novelty; its separation in time and
sacred significance from the busy affairs of Holy Week; its unique
celebration of the history of Christ's church through a unifying sacrament; and its calendar position near midsummer—for with the assistance of heartfelt prayer, the English skies at such a time might be
clear.

III

The selection of Corpus Christi as the festal occasion for the play's
original performance is a cultural phenomenon rich in implication
concerning the nature of the Corpus Christi play as a form of sacred
drama. The play obviously constituted a major departure from medieval dramatic tradition, a departure as radical as the feast's departure from the antecedent Latin liturgy. However, despite the play's
dramatic innovations, it remained akin in a number of ways both to
the liturgy and to liturgical drama. In order to examine the designs
of one dramatic cycle, it is helpful first to consider the Corpus Christi
play's basic characteristics, those which were innovative as well as
those which it shared with liturgical rite and liturgical drama. One
way of illuminating these characteristics is by asking questions that
may help define those features distinguishing sacred drama from sacred rite: What forms of reality do they embody, what visions of time
do they embrace, and what techniques do they employ to achieve
their desired therapeutic effects?

These questions are not easily answered, especially when one considers the empiricizing spirit of Corpus Christi and its ardent cross-
pollination of faith and imagination. In the course of celebrating the
Sacrament's synapsis of logical opposites, the activities of Corpus
Christi willingly extended that union into less orthodox realms—
blurring if not obliterating the categorical distinctions between substance and accident, faith and imagination, metaphor and reality,
ritual and drama. The readiness of the Corpus Christi spectators to
see one form of sacred action in terms of another was most thor-
oughly exploited by the Corpus Christi play, which by a number of

strategies attempted an artistic closure with ritual: implying that analogy is equal to identity, the play subtly pretends that it enjoys the magic power of ritual to transubstantiate the past into the present.

Whether we must accept the play's pretended power to actualize sacred realities depends upon our understanding of the play's representational techniques and the kind of belief those techniques were intended to evoke. Some are obviously so central to the spirit and form of the play that they need little amplification here. The play's use of dramatic anachronism is one such technique, whereby scriptural figures appear and act as contemporary English people.[36] A Corpus Christi playwright apparently had to force himself out of a natural propensity if he wished to present a scriptural character as a person whose thoughts and actions were defined primarily by his having lived in the distant past. A second technique is potential to all iconic drama, and was fully developed by the play of Corpus Christi—its power to perform in time actions deceptively close to the audience's "memory" of those events. In the Middle Ages this collective memory was defined not only by Scripture and the liturgy, but by all the "true" apocrypha recorded in legend and promulgated in the arts and popular sermons.[37] But the Corpus Christi play required more of its audience than a gratified recognition of the contemporary verisimilitude of its sacred actions. Unlike secular drama which asks of its audience a willing suspension of disbelief, the Corpus Christi play demanded more—a willing assertion of belief not only in its dramatic credibility but in its historical veracity. This veracity, the play then audaciously insists, should be seen as a sacred verity, as though the history of Christian salvation were being relived before the credulous gaze of its viewers.

The play's seeming equation of dramatic representation with ritual magic is bolstered by the attitudes of some of its characters. An expositor appears on stage to exhort the audience to accept the truthfulness of the episode just enacted. Characters sometimes turn sideways to their mimetic world to remark on the absolute truth of the deeds they have just witnessed or performed. Others address the spectators directly to insist that they believe what they behold: Thomas proffers his bloody hand to the audience as proof of Christ's physical reality,[38] and Christ, appearing at his Resurrection and at the Last Judgment, appeals to his viewers' faith in his real presence by displaying his body before them as living proof of their sacramental belief in his person.

To define the kind of belief these dramatic techniques were meant to evoke, one must first decide whether the world of the play was ever accepted as a world of illusion. Some critics have insisted that because of the technical limitations of their craft, the Corpus Christi playwrights were unable, even unwilling, to create dramatic illusions: the play was performed out-of-doors, was acted by local people, and was staged with the use of symbolic, rather than realistic, properties and sets.[39] V.A. Kolve argues in addition that the Corpus Christi viewers would never want to suspend their disbelief "because they know that the actors are engaged in a mimetic game, and that the purpose of the game is to reveal, not to deceive (even temporarily or in part) through illusion."[40] In my judgment, both the notion that the achievement of dramatic illusion postdates the Middle Ages, and the quasi-Brechtian notion that the Corpus Christi play strove to be nonillusionary, are mistaken. The play's recurring demand that its audience believe in the veracity or verity of its actions is strong evidence that the playwright expected his audience to see the play as much more than a nonillusionistic game. Second, the widely documented power of late medieval affective piety imaginatively to transform into living history the static images of the graphic arts suggests that the same sensibility was inclined to perceive the serious actions of the Corpus Christi play as akin to sacred icons living in time.[41] Finally, our twentieth-century appreciation of the power of modern, symbolic, and ritualistic drama to create a world of artistic illusion serves as corollary evidence of the power of medieval vernacular drama to effect in its audience a similar suspension of disbelief. Judged by the dramatic standards of nineteenth-century naturalism, the speeches, gestures, and staging devices of the Corpus Christi play are of course stylized and symbolic; a character's directly addressing his audience would be considered by those standards an unconscionable rent in the veil of dramatic illusion. But in the fifteenth century such practices were part of dramatic tradition and popular expectation. Most, but not all, of the play's techniques therefore in no way impeded, but rather heightened, the realistic illusion of its actions.

A more fruitful debate is whether that world of dramatic illusion was ever understood to have been an actual recreation of sacred

21

realities. Despite our own sense of the generic distinctions between ritual and drama, should we not allow ourselves to be swayed by the Corpus Christi conflation of categories, and accept the play as a form of ritual action? Anne Righter is one who apparently thinks we should: in the opening chapter of *Shakespeare and the Idea of the Play,* she argues that the Corpus Christi play achieved for its audience a "communion with sacred history," for "While the performance lasted, audience and actors shared the same ritual world, a world more real than the one which existed outside its frame."[42] Righter's brief analysis is an appealing one, unfortunately weakened by her loose use of "communion" and "ritual" as critical terms. If by ritual she means a communal form of canonized magic, or (in the terms of Mircea Eliade) the destruction of temporal duration by the actual recreation of mythic time, then the play of Corpus Christi is hardly ritual.[43] I suspect that Righter would admit that her critical terms are only metaphorically accurate. The Corpus Christi play is not actually ritual; it is a serious form of play made even more serious by its deliberate imitation of certain ritual techniques. The play sometimes *pretends* to share ritual's power to reactualize sacred realities, and this pretence to ritual magic is heightened by the illusionistic techniques I have been discussing. But it is all ultimately illusion, achieved by the temporary fusion of artistic deception and suspended disbelief, whereas the reality created by ritual is Reality itself— orthodox and true. Medieval viewers, I believe, knew the difference between ritual action and dramatic fiction, and would have dismissed as a credulous simpleton anyone maintaining at the play's end that Christ's impersonator had been his person.

The Corpus Christi play is illusionistic drama, a series of words and mimetic actions, spoken and performed by impersonating actors —often spectacularly staged, often accompanied by music and song. Just as the Mass remained ritual despite the histrionics attending its medieval mode of celebration, so the Corpus Christi play remained drama despite its imitations of ritual techniques. The Corpus Christi playwrights, I am convinced, were fully aware of the limits of their medium, and employed their imitations of ritual not because they thought that the play was a form of ritual but because they sensed that as a form of play it was in danger of being taken less seriously than its content merited.[44] It should be noted as well that the play-

wrights countered their several ritualistic techniques by other strategies which were meant to remind the audience of the fictiveness of
the play's actions. Nevertheless, it is worth emphasizing here that as
realistic iconic drama, the Corpus Christi play during its performance
was often on the verge of being seen as embodying the reality it imitated.[45] The way in which a Corpus Christi playwright exploited and
controlled his art as metaphoric ritual thus constitutes a major concern in a detailed study of his craft.

We can more readily agree that the play in a general way is ritualistic if by ritual we mean what Adolph E. Jensen means by "cult"—
the demonstration (sometimes dramatic) of an ideal social order expressing the community's sense of its ideal place in that order.[46] In
this definition, Christian ritual is a commemoration, rather than an
actualization, of mythic realities, performed on sacred occasions for
its healthful social effects.[47] The Corpus Christi play is designed to
accomplish this kind of cultic therapy: the community of believers
is imaginatively transported into an ideal world of sacred power, is
unified and purified, and is then returned with more steadfast faith
to daily life. This spiritual transportation is accomplished (as Northrop Frye and others have noted) by the dramatic projection of the
eucharistic rite:[48] the audience is called upon to perform an imagined
role as communicants in a sacred act, and to feel after participating
in that act that their souls have been cleansed, their sins, to a degree
at least, forgiven.[49]

Although the Corpus Christi play proffers this kind of spiritual
therapy, what distinguishes it (in these terms) from most Christian
ritual is the way it sometimes makes that sense of communal grace so
difficult to attain. Normally the play is generous and compassionate, as
it honors its audience, compliments their intelligence, and praises
their faith; occasionally, however, the play treats its viewers as if they
were a host of unbelievers, doubting Thomases who had eyes yet
refused to see. At these moments the play seems deliberately to profane its sacred actions, it parodies the cherished beliefs of its community, and it assails their sense of Christian worth. Somewhat comparable is the homeopathic rhetoric employed in the liturgy (consider the *improperia* of Lent), but it is in the Corpus Christi play that
one finds the full artistic development of such strategies of profanation. The way a Corpus Christi playwright employs these psychologi-

23

cal strategies constitutes another major concern in a detailed study of his craft.

The "profanation" of the sacred is a dramatic phenomenon culturally linked to the extreme pathetic naturalism of the other late medieval religious arts.[50] As formal constituents of the play, however, these psychological strategies are directly related to the vision of time which subsists in the play's dramatic structure. Liturgical drama shared the liturgy's vision of time as eternal recurrence: since the past is ever in the process of being recreated by ritual action, time is a cycle of constant renewal.[51] The viewers of liturgical drama are thus brought into a world of sacred atemporality, as they share the recreation or commemoration of part of that eternal return. But the Corpus Christi play, unattached to the continuum of the liturgical year, did not celebrate a single segment of that continuum; rather, it attempted to embrace all of Christian time. As it selected events epitomizing the story of Christian salvation from the Alpha to the Omega, the Corpus Christi play was obligated to project a new dramatic conception of time as history, as some sort of evolution from the past to the present and into the future.[52] As they incorporated this sense of historical development into their conception of the play, the Corpus Christi dramatists succeeded in fashioning a number of dramatic stratagems by which they could subtly modulate the tense of an action to accord with the nature of its significance. Their most frequently chosen option was to counterpoint historical time with anachronistic time, so that dramatic characters manage to be contemporary both with their historical actions and with their audience. Some actions, however, are considered of such archetypal significance that they are cast as timeless and universal; other actions are conceived as being performed exclusively in the past—usually they are exemplary deeds to be imitated, or Old Law customs now replaced by their typological fulfillments; still others are rendered so "modern" that their primary significance is as timely, often satiric, commentaries upon present-day life. His manipulation of dramatic tense and historical time thus constitutes a third major area in the study of the craft of a Corpus Christi playwright.

This new dramatic sense of time created a new awareness of the audience's role as participants in the illusion of the play. In liturgical drama, time and the experience of time were cyclical; in the Corpus

24

Christi play, however, time and the experience of time were once-and-for-all. This vision of time as linear history, as a unique sequence of ages, brought with it a traditional understanding that present-day humankind was living at the close of history's final age.[53] Within and without the illusion of the play, the audience's opportunity to synthesize and apply the import of Christian history was thus rapidly reaching an end. It is no wonder that the Corpus Christi play developed its strategies of compassionate abuse, as it attempted to cajole and threaten its audience into a state of spiritual self-discovery. In their unique experience of the totality of Christian history, the viewers were expected to make a unique attempt to re-edify their faith. In this attempt they were assisted by the play's several techniques of self-interpretation. One example is the way the followers of Christ within the play projected for the followers of Christ who constituted the viewing audience a rediscovering of the major tenets of Christian faith. With God as the protagonist, and personified powers of evil as the collective antagonist, the nexus of the play's action may thus be seen to reside in those characters who manage to recognize the significance of events propaedeutic to the Last Judgment. Addressed to a community living at history's penultimate moment, the Corpus Christi play naturally developed a tone of rhetorical urgency, an urgency heightened by a concerned understanding that each spectator's responses to the play were telling indications of the place of his soul on Judgment Day. The ideal audience was therefore required to perform a responsible role as imaginative participants in the play's mimesis of history. The substance and design of their role constitute another major area of concern in the study of the art of the Corpus Christi dramatist.

In several ways, this new dramatic structure embracing the nethermost reaches of time generated a new kind of dramatic self-awareness. Because the liturgical plays could rely upon the occasion of their performance and the surrounding readings of the liturgy to explicate their import for the community, liturgical drama, even in its most developed form, remained essentially direct, presentational, and nondiscursive.[54] The Corpus Christi play, however, could not similarly rely upon the texts of the feast (which were read in the church services), but had to incorporate into its own dramatic structure ways of interpreting the significance of its dramatic actions. The

ironic result of the antisymbolic literalizations of Corpus Christi is
that the Corpus Christi play, in turning to the historical realities of
Scripture, was turning to a complex of words, gestures, and things
as rich in potential symbolic significance as any rites of the church.
To achieve dramatic coherence, some interpretation of these symbolic actions was absolutely necessary. The original dramatists con-
templating the idea of a Corpus Christi play therefore found themselves facing the inevitable problem of scriptural analysis: how does
the corpus of sacred history radiate eternal truth? Although their
concerns may have been essentially pragmatic, these playwrights
must have asked themselves questions similar to those which biblical
scholars had been mulling over for centuries. Were the *res, verba,* and
gesta of Scripture to be understood in and of themselves in a "spiritually literal" sense, or need they be interpreted? If interpreted,
which were to be seen as signs, which sacraments, which metaphors,
which *figurae?* Which do tradition, popular expectation, right reason, and the imperatives of dramatic form require: that the main
interpretive principle of a certain event be ethical, or typological,
or allegorical, or mystical, or what?[55] Thus the problems of scriptural interpretation which exegetes since Paul had been attempting
to solve according to their individual hermeneutics were confronted
again by playwrights working in a medium whose possibilities of
self-exposition had been only fitfully explored. How the cycles interpreted the meaning of the actions they dramatized is thus a fifth
major element in the art of the cycle.

The five major matters I have noted here are of course not the
only critical areas important to the study of the craft of a Corpus
Christi playwright. Nor are these five mutually exclusive. Rather,
each is complexly integrated with the rest. Therefore, to analyze the
dramatic hermeneutics of a cycle (its modes of self-exposition) is
one way of approaching the cycle's structuring and interpretation
of Christian history. The play's vision of Christian history, in turn,
partially determines the role of the viewing audience and the audience's place within the historical and spiritual frame of the play.
Similarly, the audience's role as vicarious participants in the dramatic action is obviously defined in no small part by the cycle's
rhetorical strategies. Finally, the cycle's manipulations of the audience's beliefs and doubts are very much bound up with the cycle's

understanding of its own form and powers as they relate to the form
and powers of ritual celebration.

IV

In these remarks on the sacred actions of Corpus Christi, I have in-
tentionally disregarded or relegated to the level of notes a host of
historical particulars, and have sustained for the sake of formal clarity a quite useful hypothesis—that the shape and content of these
several activities remained absolutely uniform throughout medieval
England. Except as applied to the Feast itself, this generalization is
historically inaccurate. In parts of England, the celebration of the
Mass differed slightly.[56] The procession varied considerably, and in
fact occasionally split into two processions, one civic, one ecclesiastic.[57] The generic idea of a single English play of Corpus Christi is
obviously a fabrication made out of several cycles, each of which
enjoyed its own very distinctive characteristics. Clearly, each of these
phenomena can be examined to advantage as a single genre: the Mass
has so been studied, as well as the play of Corpus Christi.[58] But the
scholarly appreciation of the dramatic art of the Corpus Christi plays
is now best served by the careful study of individual cycles—not in
terms of the degree to which they conform, or fail to conform, to a
generic ideal, but in terms of their own dramatic structure, artistic
principles, and imaginative integrity.

Of the dozen or more cycles which were performed in medieval
England, only four have survived in manuscripts that are nearly complete: York, Wakefield (Towneley), N-Town (*Ludus Coventriae*), and
Chester.[59] I have chosen to examine the Chester play of Corpus
Christi for a number of reasons, all of which should become evident
in the chapters that follow. Of the four extant English cycles, Chester, it is generally agreed, is the most conservative, the least realistic,
the most reminiscent of Latin liturgical drama. Its diction is generally direct and simple, its metrics quite regular and strongly reliant
upon those of the lyric, its verse-form best adapted to simple emotion and economy of thought, its stage actions often spare and formal. Because of its minimal dramatic embellishment and its relatively
austere fidelity to Scripture, Chester has often been considered, or
dismissed, as a crude and simplistic prototype of the three other,

27

more elaborate, cycles. For example, Rosemary Woolf has concluded her full and sensitive study of the Corpus Christi plays with the judgment that Chester's "simplicity of method is reflected in the thinness of [its] imaginative texture."[60] Since for a number of years I have been impressed by Chester's dramatic intelligence and artistic integrity, the following chapters are written in part as an implicit response to the sparse critical acclaim Chester has been accorded in the past few decades.

To arrive at an understanding of the dramatic integrity of a single cycle, it is not enough to examine it as if it were a literary text unattached to historical circumstance and a distinctive cultural milieu. Part of this cultural milieu was general and all-embracing. Thus I have opened with a brief study of the idea of Corpus Christi, the medieval activities expressing that idea, and some of the major elements defining the English Corpus Christi play as a distinctive form of dramatic action. But other, very local circumstances clearly influenced these plays, such as those realities which affected the plays' size, frequency of performance, staging techniques, number of actors, division into parts, growth and decline. These realities must be considered when one examines the cycle's formal dramatic principles. Another important cluster of influences comprises those artistic works—graphic, musical, literary, sermonic—which were incorporated in part or in toto, directly or indirectly, into the original construction, or the reconstructions, of the individual play. These artistic influences vary greatly from cycle to cycle. It is evident, then, that an individual cycle must be studied not only in terms of its own formal principles but in terms of those specific historical pressures and artistic works which contributed so much to the shape, and changing shape, of its dramatic form.

In the next chapter, therefore, I will turn to the question of Chester's development—to an examination of the cycle's inception as a play first performed on Corpus Christi day, its dramatic configurations during the fifteenth century, its major renovation as it was shifted to a three-day performance on Whitsuntide, and its final years under the Protestant Reformation. Although the Chester cycle of the surviving manuscripts is clearly a type of Corpus Christi play (properly studied in light of the five major elements I have outlined), it is nevertheless a distinctively individual cycle the designs of which are very much its own playwrights' creation. Likewise, although the Chester cycle was first conceived and last performed around the same times as the other extant English cycles, its various stages of growth and the various shapes it assumed over time constitute a story that must be analyzed in its own right. This analysis, historical in its perspective, will raise issues closely related to those discussed in my opening formal study of the Corpus Christi play as a type of sacred action. In turn, the issues raised in both Chapters 1 and 2 will serve as the definitive theoretical and historical matrix for the six remaining chapters, where the cycle as a whole is analyzed pageant-group by pageant-group.

2

The Development
of the Chester Cycle:
A Historical Analysis

T he great Corpus Christi plays, one would like to think, are in many ways similar to the great English cathedrals. The cathedrals, like the cycles, are each the work of more than one master draftsman. The construction of each, we may assume, was originally undertaken in accordance with a fully developed plan of the whole; but because they were built up over several generations (at the least), each finished work is in fact a composite of various artistic precepts and techniques. Although as a consequence all are stylistically "impure," some or many of them may nevertheless have realized a final, unique, and "organic" perfection—a blend of styles and elements which no single draftsman (save the last) could ever have fully imagined. We admire a cathedral's achieved unity of form in part because we recognize that writ large in the work itself is the history of its construction. Presumably our admiration of a cycle's finished form would be similarly enhanced if we could discover its several layers of composition. But precisely how to identify those strata is a scholarly problem of no mean proportions. We know that certain laws apply quite strictly to a cathedral's building sequence: one is structural (the supporting piers of the nave, for example, must antedate the clerestory above); another is stylistic (because a certain cathedral's Lady chapel is Gothic, it must postdate the Romanesque chapel adjacent to it). But similar laws do not generally apply to a cycle's order of composition. Structurally, it does not appear imperative that a pageant on one subject be written earlier than a pageant on another. Stylistically, we can no longer assume that a cycle's so-called "Gothic" elements (realistic, humorous, sensational) are all later additions to a core of early "Romanesque" plays (sober, hieratic, didactic).[1] Indeed, the texts of the cycles as they stand before us now are as much akin to well-worn palimpsests as to cathedrals: one or two hands beneath the surface script may at times be visible—but in many cases one suspects that only very sophisticated techniques, comparable in their power and objectivity to ultraviolet light, could successfully discriminate all the underlayerings of a cycle's composition.

I
The Documents and Studies
Related to Chester's Development

Of the four English cycles, Chester is in fact the one which appears least receptive to any sort of "palimpsest" scrutiny. The text of the N-Town cycle, it has been shown, underwent at least five revisions in the course of its history.[2] Although critics still argue about the number of layers apparent in the texts of the York cycle and the Wakefield cycle, agreement is nearly unanimous in identifying the respective pageants which were the work of those two dramatic geniuses, the York Realist and the Wakefield Master. But in Chester no Master has left his distinctive stylistic signature, nor does the cycle as a whole contain any very obtrusive patches or seams indicative of piecemeal revision. Chester's apparent stylistic and thematic homogeneity could signify that the early cycle, once completed, was revised little, or that perhaps it was later revised once and completely; if either inference is true, there would be little profit now in looking internally for layers of compositional accretion. However, two matters militate against both of these suppositions. The first is that Chester, despite its impressive interior consistencies, is clearly a composite of pageants constructed in quite different ways: some have an Expositor figure, for example; some juxtapose two "plays" to form one pageant; some are written predominantly in cross-rhyme, rather than tail-rhyme, stanzas; some are obviously influenced by *A Stanzaic Life of Christ*; others are influenced by Peter Comestor's *Historia Scholastica*; some are highly indebted to the Gospel of Saint John; some include French; others use live animals; one is influenced by a York pageant; another is influenced by a noncyclical play; and so on. It is possible that one playwright or one reviser was responsible for all of these variant dramatic constructions. But considering how much the three other cycles were fitfully revised over the course of their two-hundred-year histories, it would not appear very likely that Chester's twenty-four extant pageants were all the creation of one playwright or all the recreation of one reviser. The second matter is that because there are a number of surviving dramatic records, we need not restrict ourselves entirely to an "interior" study of the literary texts themselves. Among the surviving cycles, Chester is in fact second only to York in its wealth of civic and guild records relating to the production of the plays. To learn if and how the Chester cycle changed over time, therefore, it will be useful first simply to gather for perusal all the records and documents that could assist in such a venture.

The Chester cycle survives in not one but five manuscripts (with a sixth manuscript for two of its pageants and a part of a third).[3] Attached to three of the full-cycle manuscripts are the Chester Late Banns: composed and revised between 1548 and 1572, these post-Reformation banns describe in some detail the cycle's twenty-four pageants and ascribe them to their proper guild or guilds.[4] Copies of the Late Banns are also included in two versions of Archdeacon Robert Rogers' Breviary: this Breviary, a personal collection of antiquarian documents, includes a number of unique references to the Chester plays, among them a possible eyewitness account of how the pageants were performed processionally through the city streets over Whitsuntide.[5] The cycle's Early Banns also have survived, although in only one copy: revised at least once between 1521 and 1532 (and later partially excised), these banns may perhaps still contain evidence of the cycle's earlier, fifteenth-century, configurations.[6] Revised at about the same time as the Early Banns (and later partially excised) is William Newhall's Proclamation—an announcement of the plays which claims to identify, as do the Late Banns, the cycle's original playwright and time of first performance.[7] The earliest unretouched document to indicate the number, order, and identity of the cycle's pageants, however, is a single-leaf list of dramatic guilds (Harley 2104) dated by calligraphic tests to circa 1500.[8] Finally, there is the Harley 2150 List of Companies,[9] composed after 1548, and the invaluable "dramatic" civic and guild records of the city of Chester, recently edited by Lawrence Clopper for *Records of Early English Drama*.

One striking characteristic of these documents is that they are almost all very late. The earliest version of the Rogers' Breviary is dated 1609/10—that is, about thirty-five years after the cycle's final performance. The five cycle manuscripts, transcribed between 1591 and 1607, postdate the plays' last production—and thus their last acting texts—by about a generation. The three individual pageant manuscripts, the Early and the Late Banns, the Newhall Proclamation, the Harley Guild List and the Harley List of Companies are all sixteenth-century documents. And of the hundreds of civic and guild records that pertain directly to the production of the Chester cycle, no more than twenty can confidently be dated prior to 1500. Thus it would seem, at least at first glance, that only the last seventy-five years of the cycle's history could be described with any amount of accuracy. A second significant characteristic of the extant Chester documents is that few have survived unchanged. The Proclamation and the Early Banns were both revised and excised—apparently because the cycle was changed and because the Reformation effected a change in the official attitude toward the plays. The Late, post-Reformation, Banns were amended at least twice, and were perhaps revised somewhat to accord with later revisions in the cycle. The revisions most easily documented are those of the Rogers' Breviary, which was composed and then three times recomposed (by Rogers' son David) over a span of fourteen years. The result is that four different and somewhat contradictory versions survive: for example, we are given four different dates for the cycle's first performance—1329, 1332, 1339, and 1328. Thus these dramatic documents are sometimes like palimpsests themselves: their own layers of composition demand scrutiny before the evidence they contain may be used to assist in discovering the cycle's layers of compositional growth. Finally, matters are made even slightly more complicated by the emotional allegiances evident in some of these late documents—namely, a civic pride which may have exaggerated the antiquity of "these anchante playes," and a post-Reformation prejudice against the plays' so-called "Clowde of Ignorance" which may have clouded commentary on more empirical matters as well. Although late,

33

Chester's "empirical" documents are plentiful and useful; but they often are as rife with "textual" problems as are the dramatic texts themselves.

Among the scholars who have attempted to discover evidence of Chester's dramatic development, only a few have relied exclusively on internal data. These studies, each concentrating on a single pageant, have employed metrical, linguistic, and stylistic criteria for the bases of analysis (supported then by "literary" evaluation) to prize apart strata of composition. Oscar Brownstein, for example, has determined that eight or ten stanzas near the center of the "Noah" pageant constitute a late addition to an earlier and more unified play;[10] Bernice Coffee, after examining the two different but closely related Chester Balaam pageants, concludes that the H MS play is the earlier and "better" version;[11] and Hans-Jürgen Diller has managed to descry three layers of composition in the Shepherds pageant, the earliest constituting a "nuclear core" which contains a mixture of both comic and sacred elements.[12] Neither these nor any other similar study,[13] however, attempts to date the original composition or the time of its revision; none claims that the selected pageant's recomposition is in any way paradigmatic of the entire cycle's; nor does any such study even ask why the pageant, or the cycle, was ever revised. Perhaps the resolution of such problems requires first a complete textual, stylistic, linguistic, and metrical analysis of the entire cycle. But this sort of major "palimpsest" study of Chester is probably more than a single scholar could or should undertake, and would require among other things the full resources of a computer as well as an unusually rich and sensitive computer program.[14]

The majority of critical inquiries concerning the development of the Chester cycle have been based upon external documents and upon the question of their proper interpretation. Among the many significant contributions in this area, the most reliable work has been that of Lawrence Clopper, whose recently published "The History and Development of the Chester Cycle" will certainly remain definitive for decades to come.[15] What neither Clopper nor any other recent critic has attempted, however, is an alignment of Chester's external and internal evidences to see whether they complement each other in ways whereby the overall pattern of Chester's compositions may be discerned. Such a venture was undertaken once, by

F.M. Salter in his 1939-40 monograph "The Banns of the Chester Plays."[16] Salter's study, concluding with a chart of the probable entry date of Chester's twenty-five pageants into the cycle and the probable development of each thereafter, is an important work of critical synthesis and conjecture; unfortunately, as Salter himself later admits, he manipulated some of his material in order to sustain his supposition of the cycle's great antiquity.[17] When one considers the range of editorial, historical, and critical contributions to the field of Chester studies since the time of Salter's article, it would seem appropriate to attempt again in an unbiased way the kind of integration Salter had sought to achieve.

For several reasons, such an undertaking is in my judgment an appropriate beginning to the study of the Chester cycle itself. The question of Chester's dramatic development incorporates a number of important related problems—its authorship, the mode of its inception, its subsequent sources and influences, its manner of production, its means of support, and the relationships among its manuscripts. For the past generation (at least) these problems and scholars' attempts to resolve them have never been considered in one place. To review these issues here should be a service in itself, and will grant me the opportunity to offer my own judgments concerning several of them. My undertaking this historical and textual review at this point will clear the way for an uninterrupted formal analysis in my remaining chapters, as I examine the dramatic designs of the cycle, pageant-group by pageant-group. Since I keep much of the in-house critical debate to the level of notes, this survey (and it is meant in part to be just that) will acquaint the general reader not only with Chester's dramatic history but also with several of the more important studies of the cycle made during the "classical" period of medieval drama scholarship (that period, covering approximately the first half of this century, when anything but the cycle's dramatic excellence was normally considered fit material for examination). My attempt to uncover the cycle's earlier form will raise questions concerning the principles by which the cycle has been variously unified over time. That is, one may ask whether the designs employed by an early playwright were the same as those used by a later reviser, and whether the last reviser of the cycle must necessarily be accepted as the best. Indeed, it logically follows from these questions to ask whether those "deep structures" an ingenious critic is wont to discover within a cycle's final form could in fact ever have been intended by any one of its revisers. My primary intent here is to review Chester's dramatic history and to offer a new thesis concerning its development. In addition, however, this chapter is meant as a specific historical foundation and a theoretical corrective to all the formal arguments which follow.

Because of the several purposes of this chapter, I have chosen to focus upon three critical phases in Chester's dramatic history, each raising a different set of interpretive problems. The cycle's beginnings are the major concerns of part II; since no contemporary documentation of the cycle's origin has survived, what this means is a cautious review of the Chester "legends." These "legends" (which need by no means be all untrue) are of two sorts: those propounded in the sixteenth century by Chester citizens and those propounded in the twentieth century by critical conjecture. To balance my own rather tentative suggestions concerning the cycle's early design, I will offer in part III a fairly bold hypothesis concerning the expansion of that design circa 1519, as the cycle was shifted from its one-day performance on Corpus Christi to its three-day performance during Whitsuntide. Here I will argue that the careful alignment of internal and external evidence may reveal in considerable detail the elements of the earlier, fifteenth-century Corpus Christi play, as well as some of the principles which were employed to give unity to the newly expanded Whitsun cycle. In part IV, finally, as I trace the last years of the cycle's production history, I will attempt to determine from among the five surviving cycle manuscripts those variants which belong, and those which clearly do not belong, to the cycle's finished form. In doing so, I will once again raise the question of dramatic unity, a question leading (because it will be answered only in part) directly into the subsequent chapters, which are concerned entirely with the dramatic designs of the Chester cycle.

II
The Inception and Early Form
of the Chester Cycle

Newhall's Proclamation, the Early Banns, the Late Banns, and two of the five versions of the Rogers' Breviary agree that "Sur Iohn Aneway was maire of this Citie/ when these playes were begon truly." However, there is little agreement among these documents concerning the play's authorship. The Proclamation asserts that it was Sir Henry Francis, "monk of this...monesty" (Saint Werburg's Abbey), who wrote the plays and gained from Pope Clement and the bishop of Chester numerous days' pardon for those who resorted peaceably to the plays. The Late Banns, however, state that the Chester plays were "the deuise of one Rondoll Moncke of Chester Abbaye," as do in fact all versions of the Breviary except the Lysons copy, which contends: "These playes weare the worke of one Rondoll higden a monke in Chester Abaye." All versions of the Breviary agree, however, that the plays were first performed circa 1330: either 1329, 1332, 1339, or 1328. If any sense is to be made out of these various statements of putative fact, it appears that four matters must be settled in conjunction: whether or not the plays were first performed during the mayoralty of John Aneway (Arneway), Chester's most famous mayor; whether or not they were first performed circa 1330; whether or not the plays' author was Henry Francis, monk Rondoll, or Chester's most famous man of letters, Randle (Ranulph) Higden; and whether or not at the time of the plays' composition there was a Pope Clement in Rome. There are several problems here. John Arneway (who was erroneously believed to have been Chester's first mayor) died in 1278, and thus could not have been the plays' champion circa 1330. There were three Pope Clements in the fourteenth century: Pope Clement V (1305-14), Pope Clement VI (1342-52), and Antipope Clement VII (1378-94). Obviously none could have granted pardons to Chester playgoers circa 1330, although Clement VI could have a decade or two later. Ranulph Higden, author of the *Polychronicon*, died in 1364 and thus could have composed the plays in the 1340s; however, it is quite likely that Higden knew no English. Finally, Henry Francis, who was abbot of Saint Werburg's in the 1370s and 1380s, could have been the plays' author; but it is unthinkable that he would have sought indulgences from an antipope at Avignon.

Several scholars have tried to make sense out of this welter of contradictory materials. In *The Mediaeval Stage* (1903), E.K. Chambers suggests that Higden was the plays' author, and that the appropriate mayor was Richard Herneys—a man "bearing a name very similar to Arneway's"—who held office from 1327 to 1329; "About

1328 is just the sort of date to which one would look for the formation of a craft-cycle."[18] However, in 1945 Chambers concedes that
the notion of Higden's authorship is "not very plausible."[19] In
Mediaeval Drama in Chester (1955), F.M. Salter opts for Henry
Francis as the plays' begetter, suggesting that the pope in question
may have been Urban VI, and dismissing the Arneway and Higden
attributions as propaganda for the plays' antiquity and excellence.[20]
In *English Religious Drama* (1955), Hardin Craig restores Higden to
authority as the man who translated the plays (from the French)
around 1328; he suggests that it was probably Henry Francis who
later went to Rome (apparently to Clement VI) to seek papal indulgence.[21] In his recent study of the Rogers' Breviary, Lawrence
Clopper dismisses—as did Salter—the Arneway and Higden material
as local fiction; he passes no judgment on the Proclamation's assertions concerning Henry Francis and Pope Clement; and he concludes
that we are unlikely ever to discover the plays' authorship, although
"it is conceivable that a man named Rondoll did write most of them
and that, as time passed, this monk was identified with Chester's
well-known historian."[22]

My own position is that in these documents no assertion concerning the cycle's inception is likely to be trustworthy, and that scholarly
attempts to identify Chester's authorship and birth date have often
in the past been unduly influenced by prior assumptions about when
it should have been conceived. Chester has traditionally been held up
as the oldest of the English cycles, but in plain fact the first firm
evidence of the cycle's existence is a guild record dating from 1422.
If one were to accept the only assertion in these documents about
which there is no disagreement—that Arneway was mayor when the
plays began—then the Chester cycle, established before 1278, would
antedate by at least fifty years the introduction of the Corpus Christi
feast and by at least a hundred years the first solid evidence of the
existence of any other English cycle. This is highly unlikely. I would
prefer to appreciate the Arneway, Higden, Francis, and Pope Clement
stories as all similar phenomena: late legendary constructions answering the need to have the plays' origins explained in ways which made
them central to the city's cultural history. Quite a different phenomenon, however, is the David Rogers 1329/-32/-39/-28 syndrome:
here we see an antiquarian's vexed attempts to make historical sense

out of a host of unreliable records. All that is left, then, is monk Rondoll: it is possible that he is the cycle's original author, and his belonging to a cloistered order (rather than a secular or mendicant one) could shed some light on the plays' original "spirit." However, I think it best to leave the Chester plays anonymous, to suggest in passing that the Chester cycle may very well not be the oldest English cycle, and then to turn to related matters where conjecture is perhaps more likely to shed some light on the plays' original form and purpose.

Scholars in the past have not been reluctant to describe in some detail the manner of the cycles' creation, their original elements, and the place and day of their first performance. In the case of the Chester cycle, Glynne Wickham's scenario has been the fullest and most imaginative. Wickham suggests in volume 1 of *Early English Stages* (1959) that Chester existed first as a Latin play similar in shape to the 1303 Italian Montecassino Passion: opening with the fall of man and closing with Antichrist and the Last Judgment, the rest of the play consisted of Christ's ministry, Passion, and Resurrection. Acted by clerics in the large area before the gates of Saint Werburg's Abbey, the plays were performed on Midsummer (the birthday of Saint John), known locally in Chester as Saint Werburg's Day. During Arneway's mayoralty, Wickham fancies, the play shifted from Midsummer to Whitsun; some time later (apparently after 1350) the play was changed from Latin into English—"closely modelled on the liturgical Latin drama but not a literal translation of it, and written by ubiquitous friars rather than by officiating priests."[23] Wickham's full-blown vision of Chester's early years at least has the advantage of covering almost every major problem one would like to see resolved. Like a number of other critics, Wickham is convinced that, since the cycles apparently could not have been created ex nihilo, they must have been fashioned out of older plays.[24] But there is absolutely no evidence that there existed in medieval England a Latin play of the length or the shape Wickham has imagined; in addition, most critics now agree that there can be recognized within the extant cycles very little evidence of the direct influence of liturgical drama.[25] A corollary theory espoused by several scholars is that the original Chester cycle was a translation of a long French play.[26] Despite the existence of certain similarities between some episodes in Chester and some episodes in certain medieval French plays, this theory, I believe, is equally untenable.[27] What is more nearly possible, however, is that Chester was somewhat influenced by the long (now lost) London history-of-the-world play, which in turn may have been influenced by French sources.[28] It is better, at any rate, to consider Chester not as a translation of any sort but as an original dramatic construction which drew upon a variety of sources the majority of which probably were nondramatic.

Wickham's hypothesis that the Chester plays were first produced for the Midsummer festivities is equally suspect, for all the empirical evidence we have indicates that the Chester Corpus Christi play was performed first on Corpus Christi day, and that it became known as the Whitsun plays when it was moved circa 1519 to the first three days of Whitweek. Nevertheless, Wickham's curiosities concerning the nearness in time (and spirit?) of the Whitsun, Corpus Christi, and Midsummer festivities deserve further rumination. We know that Chester's last performance (in 1575) was held on Midsummer rather than during Whitweek, and we know that at least toward the end of its history some of the cycle's most popular characters processed (and performed?) in the Midsummer Watch.[29] The dishonest alewife shaking her "cuppes & cannes," for example, who appears in the records of the Watch as well as in four of the five manuscripts of the "Harrowing of Hell" pageant, may possibly have been first fashioned not for the cycle but for the secular festivities of Midsummer.[30] Reputed to have been established in Chester in the eleventh century, containing festivities which some sixteenth-century reformers felt were "vnlawfull and not meete," the Midsummer holiday may have included as early as the thirteenth century (as it did elsewhere in England) dramatic productions of a popular nature. It is therefore worth wondering whether any dramatic or other activity from this secular holiday could have influenced the construction of the early Chester cycle.

To entertain the possibility of the initial influence of such secular activities may be at odds with the traditional assumption that the early cycles were perforce more somber, didactic, and spiritual than their later "Gothic" accretions. But it is worth noting that two scholars, Chambers and Salter, both apparently having started with this as one of their assumptions, conclude their search for the earliest form of the Chester cycle with a play that contains a full mixture of the popular and the pious, the "Gothic" and the "Romanesque." What is additionally striking about their attempts at rediscovering the early play is that they have envisaged a continuous drama performed stationarily (like popular folk-plays) rather than individual pageants produced in ambulatory processions. Here is Chambers' scholarly intuition:

> I have an impression that behind the Chester cycle, as it has come down to us, lies a play of a more primitive type, the themes of which have been rather clumsily incorporated, with the result that discrepancies have been left in the action, which the late transcribers of the text have variously attempted to remove. The influence of the old play is clearest in those scenes in which an *Expositor*, also called *Preco, Doctor, Nuntius,* or Messenger, comments to the 'Lordinges' of the audience on the significance of the topics represented. He calls himself Gobet on the Grene, and his demands for "room" to be made, with the fact that both he and later the character *Antichristus* come in riding, suggest a stationary performance on a green or other open space, rather than one on moving pageants.[31]

If Chambers is at all accurate in his reconstruction of a "primitive" play performed stationarily and dominated by the Expositor (Salter's reconstruction is in substantial agreement),[32] a few elements in that play as well as the work of a few more recent scholars suggest that at its inception it could have been influenced by the nearly contiguous activities, dramatic and nondramatic, of Midsummer. Not only has Diller found in his "palimpsest" study of the "Shepherds" pageant that the pageant's earliest layer includes the popular entertainment-form of the wrestling match, but Richard Axton has reconfirmed the surprisingly high incidence in Chester of theatrical techniques typical of secular drama. Axton concludes:

> If the Chester plays were originally thought of (as they undoubtedly were in the sixteenth century) as in some sense a rival or alternative attraction to the Midsummer show, taking advantage of an established summer occasion of outdoor revels and folk-plays, then the festive style of much of the playing is placed in a new perspective. The use of formulae of presentation, the "game" with the audience, the repeated cries of

"room!" are explicable as the inherited social framework of a popular drama, old secular bottles for new ecclesiastical wine.[33]

The creative genius responsible for this new dramatic vintage, for this unusual integration of didactics and theatrical fun, may be—in theory at least—not hard to identify. The yoking together of high and low, of sacred and secular, is a technique—as several recent studies have shown—distinctive of the popularizing aesthetics of the Franciscans and by no means at odds with the sacramental themes of Corpus Christi.[34] Where we are rapidly led, then, is back toward a reconsideration of Wickham's vision, parts of which are quite plausible. Perhaps in fact the Chester cycle in its original form was a stationary play rather than a processional production; perhaps it was a single long drama of a shape similar to the Montecassino Passion's; and perhaps its original authors (or at least a major influence at its inception) were, in Wickham's words, those "ubiquitous friars." All of the conjectures in the preceding sentence I confess I am quite partial to; but in arriving at these conjectural conclusions, I am obviously reasoning in a fairly subjective way from circumstantial evidence.

As an antidote to these conjectures, we should remind ourselves that the first evidence even of the existence of the Chester cycle is a 1422 record of a dispute between two parties, the Fletchers, Bowyers, Coopers, Stringers, and Turners on the one side and the Ironmongers on the other, concerning their respective obligations *in luso Corporis christi* for producing the "Flagellation" pageant and the "Crucifixion" pageant.[35] This single record itself indicates that the Chester play at this time was apparently a "cycle" of some sort; that it was apparently divided into individual pageants; and that each of these pageants was apparently the responsibility of a guild or group of guilds. Since these pageants were given on wagons, it would seem to appear a safe inference that they were performed—as in York and several other English cities—several times for different audiences along the Corpus Christi procession route. And, if we limit ourselves to those very few dramatic guild records which have survived from the fifteenth century, it would also appear a fairly safe inference that the early Chester play contained at least these scenes— if, that is, the guilds mentioned in these records were associated with the same plays then that they were in the sixteenth century: Creation (Drapers), Nativity (Wrights), Magi (Mercers), Last Supper (Bakers), Flagellation (Fletchers, etc.), Crucifixion (Ironmongers), Emmaus (Saddlers), Ascension (Tailors), Pentecost (Fishmongers), Prophets of Doomsday (Shermen), and Last Judgment (Weavers, Walkers, and Chaloners).[36]

But because the empirical evidence surviving from between 1422 to 1500 is so sparse and so often cryptic, it would appear that even the most cautious inferences must border on conjecture and that conjectures concocted with little regard for (or knowledge of) this meagre evidence could possibly at times be quite correct. In this chapter, however, I would not have given such attention to the hypothetical reconstructions of Chester's beginnings did I not believe there was some truth in some of them. Nor would I have done so were I not confident that the validity of some could be substantiated by using more reliable evidence and more objective methods of reasoning. The pertinent pieces of evidence come surprisingly late: there are certain dramatic documents surviving from the early sixteenth century which, when examined together, may possibly suggest a good deal about the cycle's earlier career. Working with these records, Lawrence Clopper has given his support to the recently unpopular notion of the original Corpus Christi play's having been stationarily produced: the play was given, he reasons, not processionally but at the end of the Corpus Christi procession (probably before Saint John's Church) on pageant-wagons forming place-and-scaffold stages.[37] Working with the same documents but also with the play texts themselves, I plan to identify most of the dramatic episodes which I believe have survived from the "old" play of Corpus Christi. I plan, in addition, to identify certain structural principles and stylistic features, first of the "old" Corpus Christi play and then of the "new" Whitsun cycle. And although I do not pretend to have rediscovered the Chester play at the moment of its conception, I claim that the configurations of the Chester cycle early in its career can now be seen with greater clarity than they have ever been seen before. To arrive at those configurations, and to evaluate with greater confidence all earlier conjectures, it is best therefore to turn to the cycle during those years, from 1505 to 1532, when it was revised, amplified, and shifted to a new time and a new mode of production.

III
The Whitsun Amplifications
of the Chester Cycle

With the possible exception of its last performance in 1575, the Chester cycle's configurations in all likelihood changed most dramatically in the years between 1505 and 1532. It was during this time that the Corpus Christi play came to be called first (in 1521) the Whitsun play and then (by 1532 and thereafter) the Whitsun plays. And it was during this time that it shifted from its one-day Corpus Christi (and presumably stationary) performance to a processional and three-day performance during Whitsuntide. Although the play's gradually increasing size may well have been one cause for the shift in time and venue, the technical modifications which accompanied this change probably also required that the cycle be further revised and amplified as it gradually adjusted to its new environment. If these dramatic renovations can be determined with any certitude, we should be able to assess with considerably greater precision than before those elements which belonged to the cycle when it was a fifteenth-century Corpus Christi play. In addition, we may be able to discover from these renovations certain underlying principles— stylistic and structural—which unified the earlier Corpus Christi play and which were then revised at least somewhat to make the longer Whitsun cycle an equally coherent drama. To reach a point where these internal modifications may be scanned, however, one must begin with the pertinent external documents, most notably the Harley Guild List, the guild records, and the Early Banns. The first and foremost problem—as one comes to expect—is that the various sets of information supplied or suggested by these documents often appear to be mutually contradictory.

One of the most significant of Chester's guild records is the agreement made in August of 1531 or 1532 between the Goldsmiths and the Masons to share the pageant-wagon owned by the Vintners and the Dyers.[38] As Salter first pointed out, this arrangement was eminently feasible (if the cycle's pageants fell into their normal Whitsuntide divisions): the Vintners' "Magi" was the penultimate play performed on Monday, the Goldsmiths' "Herod" opened the Tuesday sequence, and the Dyers' "Antichrist" was the penultimate play for

Wednesday.[39] As Clopper sensibly argues, this arrangement was agreed upon only at this time (rather than much earlier in Chester's history) because the cycle had just recently shifted to a three-day and processional performance—making it necessary that each play performed on a single day have its own wagon.[40] It is likely that previous to this time, as both Salter and Clopper suggest, the Vintners shared with the Mercers a single "Magi" play, which may in fact also have been combined with the Goldsmiths' "Herod";[41] then, some time between 1521 and 1532, this dramatic material was divided and amplified to make up Paginae VIII, IX, and X. Our primary concern here is that the Early Banns, revised at least once between 1521 and 1532 in order to keep abreast of changes in the cycle, apparently retained in the varying number of lines describing the pageants indications of some of these changes. That is, all but six of the pageants are described in four-line half-stanzas; described by full stanzas or longer (and thus stanzas apparently revised) are the three pageants mentioned above (VIII, IX, and X), and also the Tanners' pageant (I), the Wrights' (VI), and the Shermen's (XXII). It has therefore appeared to follow that the pageants accorded anomalous stanza descriptions underwent revision, or were added to the cycle, after the original composition of the Early Banns but before their revision.[42] This one quirky indicator is not likely to have registered all changes, but it should serve as an important criterion as we attempt to reconstruct the cycle's transformations during these years.

Another important document for the reconstruction of Chester's shift to Whitsuntide is the Harley 2104 Guild List: this, in Clopper's judgment, was a list of those guilds which marched in the Corpus Christi procession before the Corpus Christi play.[43] What is perhaps most notable about the list, estimated by Greg to have been written "somewhere about 1500,"[44] is the absence of three guilds that by the time of the Early Banns were responsible for three pageants in the cycle: the Tanners ("Fall of Lucifer"), the Cappers ("Balaam and Balaak"), and the Painters ("Shepherds"). Because the Early Banns describe the Tanners' play in an eight-line stanza, we may assume that it entered the cycle after the Early Banns' composition but before their revision; because the Cappers' and Painters' pageants are each accorded four-line half-stanzas, we may assume they entered the cycle before (perhaps only shortly before) the Early Banns' composition. We know that the play of the Shepherds was in existence in 1515/16, for it was then performed together with the "Assumption of the Virgin" in Saint John's churchyard.[45] From another record we know that the Cappers had been granted special privileges by mayor Thomas Smyth so that they might "brynge forthe A playe concernynge the store of kynge balak & Balam the proffet"; Thomas Smyth was mayor of Chester in 1504-5, 1511-12, 1515-16, 1520-21, and 1521-22.[46] From these bits of information we can conclude: that the Cappers' play entered the cycle no earlier than 1505 but no later than 1522; that the Early Banns were composed within this same period of time but after the Cappers' play entered the cycle; and that the Painters' pageant in all likelihood was brought into the cycle at approximately the same time. Since the Early Banns appeared to have been originally composed for the play performed on Corpus Christi, and since the play came to be called the Whitsun play in 1521, the probability is high that the Whitsuntide shift occurred near the end of the second decade. Perhaps Alan Nelson's suggestion that 1519 was the crucial year is correct: because the Corpus Christi feast coincided with the Midsummer Watch in 1519, the imminent conflict of activities may have been anticipated and resolved by advancing the plays to the previous, Whitsun, week.[47] Between this time and 1531/32, when the Newhall Proclamation announced a three-day performance, a number of further and important changes were made in the cycle, and the Early Banns were consequently revised.[48]

Since they entered the cycle within such a short time of each other, it is natural to wonder whether the Tanners', the Cappers', and the Painters' pageants could have been composed by the same playwright—and if so, whether this playwright's dramatic "signature" may then be discovered elsewhere in the cycle. But the only obvious stylistic idiosyncrasy (shared by just two of the three pageants) is a distinctive rhyme scheme: whereas the dominant rhyme scheme of the Chester cycle is tail rhyme (rime couée),[49] the Tanners' play and a significant proportion of the Painters' play are written in cross rhyme. It is possible that the Tanners' playwright wrote or revised the Painters' pageant, and was responsible also for the occasional cross-rhyme passages that appear in the rest of the cycle—specifically, in Paginae III, V, VIII, X, XI, XVII, XVIII, and

XXIII. This at least is the position taken by Salter, who talks confidently of the work of Chester's "cross-rhyme redactor."[50] But the dangers of assuming that any variation in stanzaic form is immediate evidence of a different authorial hand are self-evident. There is no prima facie evidence that a single dramatist could not have employed two or more rhyme schemes, nor is there any reason why two or more dramatists could not have employed the same rhyme scheme. If the "cross-rhyme redactor" added his pieces to the cycle for the Whitsun shift, it would seem to follow that the rest of the cycle, written primarily in tail-rhyme stanzas, constitutes the Corpus Christi play in its original form (the only major exception would have to be the two rather long rhyme-royal passages, in Paginae VIII and XIII, which presumably were added to the cycle very late in its history): this, in a general way, has been the assumption of a number of critics in the past.[51] Salter's position, however, diverges from this assumption (as well as from the logic of his other contentions) in one regard: "The fact that the bulk of the Chester Plays come to us in a single stanza form," he writes, "is presumptive evidence of a very thorough revision *in toto* at some period."[52] It would therefore seem best in such matters to proceed with considerable caution. We have determined that the two pageants with the highest proportion of cross rhyme in the cycle entered the cycle at approximately the same time; but the significance of this fact can be measured only after it has been integrated with the other forms of evidence we have been given.

Another possible indicator of the stages of Chester's development is the figure of the Expositor. Chambers and Salter, as we have seen, both work from the assumption that this didactic explicator must have been part of the original play; therefore elements of the pageants in which he now appears (Paginae IV, V, VI, XII, and XXII) constituted a major portion of the cycle's first level of composition. But one of these pageants, the Cappers' play (V), we now know is a late addition, having entered the cycle early in the sixteenth century. If the Expositor is likely to have been the creation of only one playwright, or if he is the kind of paradramatic didactic figure which—as Chambers and Salter assume—would have been created at only one time in the cycle's history, it must follow that the five pageants listed above were devised or revised around the time of the Whitsun

47

shift. This would of course effectively reverse certain standard assumptions about how the aesthetics of the cycles developed: rather than progressing from the "stolid" and "didactic" to the "playful" and "realistic," Chester may have developed a "naive" and "presentational" dramatic form in its early years, which in later years became more "self-conscious" and "self-interpretive." But surely the Expositor's appearing in a single late pageant does not preclude his having been invented or used by earlier Chester dramatists. It is possible, of course, that the Expositor and the episodes in which he appears are all the work of one sixteenth-century playwright; but, as with the matter of the cycle's variant rhyme schemes, the validity of the Expositor figure as a register of the cycle's development must be determined in conjunction with the other kinds of information supplied.

A final important register is one that, in all likelihood, had to be the work of a single playwright: the incorporation into the cycle of passages adapted from *A Stanzaic Life of Christ*. Written in Chester itself, the *Stanzaic Life* is a verse narrative (intercalated with numerous glosses) compiled from two famous Latin works, Ranulph Higden's *Polychronicon* and Jacobus de Voragine's *Legenda Aurea*. In the judgment of Frances Foster, editor of the EETS (1926) edition, the *Stanzaic Life* had to have been composed in the fourteenth century, although the manuscripts are all from the fifteenth century.[53] This judgment she bases upon the fact that all the passages in the Chester cycle influenced by the *Stanzaic Life* are written in tail rhyme: and tail rhyme, she assumes, was the stanza form used exclusively by the cycle's original, fourteenth-century, playwright. But, as Robert Wilson has shown in his 1931 study, if the passages obviously influenced by the *Stanzaic Life* are removed, there remains in most cases a fairly complete play;[54] presumably, this play is the pageant in an earlier, if not its earliest, form. Thus it would seem apparent that the *Stanzaic Life* indeed was composed in the fifteenth century, as the manuscripts attest; and it would appear that the *Stanzaic Life* material was incorporated into the cycle not at its beginning but by a later reviser. However, it has never been determined when these amplifications were made.

In my judgment it is absolutely certain that the *Stanzaic Life* episodes were added to the cycle for the cycle's shift to Whitsuntide, and that the nature of these amplifications can in most cases determine or confirm the reliability of the criteria mentioned earlier (Expositor, rhyme schemes, etc.) as further registers of the Corpus Christi play's transformation into the Whitsun plays. Table 2.1 aligns the pertinent information for measuring this dramatic change. Listed first is the number of each pageant, the guild(s) responsible for it in the sixteenth-century records, the date (if any) of a guild-record entry indicating the pageant's existence in the fifteenth century,[55] and the pageant's title. Next is the number of lines (Lumiansky-Mills edition), the Harley 2104 Guild List indications, and each pageant's dominant (and subdominant) rhyme scheme. The last three columns record the appearances of the Expositor, the influence of the *Stanzaic Life*, and the number of lines in the Early Banns describing each pageant.

The influence of the *Stanzaic Life* is quite easily measured in the case of six of Chester's pageants; in the case of a seventh, however, it is difficult to determine what, if anything, happened. As Utesch recognized in 1909, the Cooks' "Harrowing of Hell" pageant in the Chester cycle conforms in its details and their sequence much more closely to the *Legenda Aurea* than to the traditional *Gospel of Nicodemus* account.[56] But since the *Stanzaic Life's* source for its Harrowing of Hell account is also the *Legenda Aurea*, it appears impossible to determine which work served as the source for the Cooks' pageant (or if both did).[57] My suspicion is that the Chester "Harrowing of Hell" was untouched by the *Stanzaic Life* reviser, and that its single source was the *Legenda*.[58] This judgment I arrived at, however, only after examining the principles of expansion evident in those six pageants which obviously have been influenced by the *Stanzaic Life*. While examining these expansions, I will also consider the most distinctive dramatic techniques employed within them.

The most complicated expansion was probably that of Pagina VI, the Wrights' "Nativity." The "old play" appears to have contained the following episodes: the Annunciation, Mary's visit to Elizabeth, Joseph's troubles, and Octavian's ordering the poll tax (ll. 1-296); the meeting between Joseph and Octavian's messenger (ll. 373-428); the journey to Bethlehem (ll. 453-68); and finally the Nativity itself (ll. 469-524). Intercalated into this nearly perfect "old play" (presumably very little has been discarded) are four dramatic sequences

49

Table 2.1 Possible Indicators of the Whitsun Expansions of the Chester Cycle,

Pageant Number	Guild(s)	Pageant Title	No. of Lines in Pageant
Whitmonday			
I	Tanners	Fall of Lucifer	301
II	Drapers (1467/68)	Adam & Eve; Cain & Abel	704
III	Waterleaders and Drawers of Dee	Noah's Flood	328
IV	Barbers	Abraham, Lot, and Melchisedec; Abraham and Isaac	491
V	Cappers	Moses and the Law; Balaack and Balaam	455 (H MS:448)
VI	Wrights (1422)	The Nativity	722
VII	Painters	The Shepherds	696
VIII	Vintners	The Magi	421
IX	Mercers (1437/38)	The Offerings of the Three Kings	263
Whittuesday			
X	Goldsmiths	The Slaughter of the Innocents	498
XI	Blacksmiths	The Purification; Christ and the Doctors	334
XII	Butchers	The Temptation: the Adulteress	312

1505–32

Harley 2104 Guild List	Rhyme Schemes: CR=Cross Rhyme TR=Tail Rhyme RR=Rhyme Royal	Expositor Figure	*Stanzaic Life* Influence	Early Banns: No. of Lines
No	CR			8
Yes	TR			4
Yes	TR (CR, 8 lines)			4
Yes	TR	Expositor		4
No	TR (CR, 4 lines in Group MSS)	Expositor		4
Yes	TR	Expositor	*Stanzaic Life*	8
No	CR, about 2/3 of play (TR, about 1/3)			4
Yes	TR (RR, 77 lines; CR, 8 lines in Group MSS)		*Stanzaic Life*	8
Yes	TR		*Stanzaic Life*	8
Yes	TR (CR, 18 lines)			11
Yes	TR (Purification); CR (Christ and the Doctors)		*Stanzaic Life*	4
Yes	TR	Expositor	*Stanzaic Life*	4

51

Table 2.1 Possible Indicators of the Whitsun Expansions of the Chester Cycle,

Pageant Number	Guild(s)	Pageant Title	No. of Lines in Pageant
XIII	Glovers	The Blind Man; Lazarus	485
XIV	Corvisors	Christ at Simon's; Money Lenders; Judas's Plot	432
XV	Bakers (1462)	Last Supper and Betrayal	366
XVI	Fletchers, Bowyers, Coopers, & Stringers (1422)	The Trial and Flagellation	394
XVI, A	Ironmongers (1422)	The Passion	479
XVII	Cooks	The Harrowing of Hell	336
XVIII	Skinners	The Resurrection	432
Whitwednesday			
XIX	Saddlers (1472)	Emmaus; Doubting Thomas	275
XX	Tailors (1439/40)	The Ascension	192
XXI	Fishmongers (1438/39)	Pentecost	390
~~U~~	Wives (1487/88)	The Assumption of the Virgin	––
XXII	Shermen	The Prophets of Antichrist	340
XXIII	Dyers	Antichrist	723
XXIV	Websters	The Last Judgment	708

1505–32

Harley 2104 Guild List	Rhyme Schemes: CR=Cross Rhyme TR=Tail Rhyme RR=Rhyme Royal	Expositor Figure	*Stanzaic Life* Influence	Early Banns: No. of Lines
Yes	TR (RR, 35 lines)			4
Yes	TR			4
Yes	TR			4
Yes	TR			4
Yes	TR			4
Yes	TR (CR, 4 lines)		*Stanzaic Life* (?)	4
Yes	TR (CR, 48 lines)			4
Yes	TR			4
Yes	TR		*Stanzaic Life*	4
Yes	TR			4
Yes	--	--	--	4
Yes	TR	Expositor		8
Yes	TR (CR, 24 lines)			4
Yes	TR			4

adapted from the *Stanzaic Life* (ll. 357–780): the senators' advising the emperor's self-deification, and Octavian's consultation with the Sybil concerning the promised birth of a child-king (ll. 297–372); Mary's vision of the mournful and the happy men, which is then explained by an angel (ll. 429–52); Salome's doubting Mary's virginity, her punishment, and her restoration of faith (ll. 525–63); and a rather long concluding narrative given by the Expositor, concerning the prodigies which occurred at Rome at Christ's birth—into which is inserted the dramatic episode of Octavian's conversion (ll. 564–722).

Most of the other dramatic adaptations of the *Stanzaic Life* material were less complicated than the "Nativity"'s. To create Paginae VIII and IX as they now exist, a single early "Herod and Magi" play was evidently divided, and each part then was amplified by the addition of an episode taken from the *Stanzaic Life*. The first 112 lines of the Vintners' "Magi" (VIII) constitute an episode on Mount Victorial, as the kings await the star and then set out to Bethlehem on their dromedaries: all the details from this unusual dramatic scene—including our being informed that a dromedary "will goe lightly on his way/ an hundreth myles upon a daye"—are derived from the *Stanzaic Life* (ll. 1729–84). Near the beginning of the Mercers' "Offerings" (IX), a passage has been inserted (ll. 33–123) where the kings offer an extended, three-level exposition of the meaning of their gifts: these allegorical glosses are taken, almost line for line, from the *Stanzaic Life* (ll. 2037–120). Two of the other pageants were no more complicated in their revisions. The Tailors' "Ascension" was simply split apart at the moment that Christ begins to ascend: added here is a powerful episode of ninety-nine lines adapted from the *Stanzaic Life* (ll. 8953–9064), dramatizing Christ's ascension as a prolonged rite of passage, with antiphons sung by Christ, by a chorus, and by angels who query his identity. The dramatic episode of Christ's temptation in the Butchers' pageant (XII) was apparently part of the early play of Corpus Christi; then, for the Whitsun shift, there was appended to that episode the Expositor's gloss—an interpretation of the significance of Christ's triumph over Satan taken from the *Stanzaic Life* (ll. 5241–332). However, when it was that the pageant's second dramatic episode (the woman taken in adultery) and its gloss (given by the Expositor) were added to the cycle is not at all clear: it is certain, though, that neither this episode nor its exposition was influenced by the *Stanzaic Life*.

The final pageant influenced by the *Stanzaic Life* is Pagina XI. Known throughout its history simply as the "Purification," the Blacksmiths' pageant comprises two major parts each of which reveals the influence of another work. The first part opens with Simeon's twice "correcting" the scriptural text prophesying the Virgin Birth, and an angel's twice restoring the original reading; this scene, climaxing with Simeon's acceptance of the miracle, is derived from the *Stanzaic Life* (ll. 2737–816). Then follows all that apparently remains of the earlier "Purification" play—Simeon's reception of the Holy Family in the temple. The pageant's second half is a cross-rhyme adaptation of York's "Christ among the Doctors." About half as long as the York play, Chester's version has translated about half its stanzas from the York pageant, successfully creating a new dramatic interpretation of Christ's youthful triumph in the temple. Because the relevant stanzas are scattered throughout both York and Chester, it is highly likely that no version of "Christ among the Doctors" existed in Chester before this adaptation.[59]

Setting aside the problematic "Harrowing of Hell" pageant, I think a number of remarks can be made concerning these dramatic amplifications. First, in most cases it is quite easy to rediscover the major outlines of the old play and to see how it was opened up to receive its new *Stanzaic Life* material. The "Nativity" was divided at four places; the "Magi" and the "Offerings" were each given a new episode near the beginning; the "Ascension" was cleanly opened at its center; and the "Temptation" drama, presumably unchanged from its earlier form, simply had added to it the Expositor's theological gloss. Only the reconstruction of the "Purification" seems complicated—and these complications may be the result of Protestant attempts in the late sixteenth century to alter and amend this "Marian" play. In the case of the other pageants, it appears that little, or nothing, was discarded from the earlier Corpus Christi play: new episodes were simply added. Second, it is quite evident that the dramatic interests and aesthetic principles of the *Stanzaic Life* reviser differed considerably from those of the earlier, Corpus Christi playwrights. Each addition from the *Stanzaic Life* offers an increased emphasis upon the marvelous—whether upon sensational dramatic spectacle, upon the wondrousness of an explicated theological system, or upon the magic of divinely wrought miracles. Thus in the "Nativity" we find added Mary's prophetic vision (interpreted by an angel), the midwife's sensational expression of doubt ("corrected" by an angel) and numerous Roman prodigies (reported by the Expositor). In the "Magi" we are awed by the exotic sight of three live "dromedaries"; in the "Offerings" we are impressed by the theological neatness of the kings' threefold explication of their gifts. In the "Purification" the miraculous restoration of scriptural prophecy (itself auguring a miracle) is performed by an angel before our eyes; and in the "Temptation" the typological perfections of Christ's triumphs over the devil are fully explained by the attentive Expositor. Finally, and most impressively, we are offered in the "Ascension" an extended rite of passage as Christ processes in graduated stages through the clouds toward heaven. It is obvious that the earlier versions of these plays were less theatrically ambitious: closer to Scripture and to orthodox tradition, the early Corpus Christi pageants were more conservatively concerned with presenting biblical events for their own sake, rather than for their "higher" meanings or histrionic brilliance. The aesthetic principles of these two layers are therefore quite distinct: a powerfully naive drama which interpreted little and relied heavily on the numinous significance of faithfully reenacted sacred events; and a layer of later accretion often spectacularly theatrical and sometimes hyperactively committed to sensational effects and "high sentence." As we shall see in the forthcoming chapters, however, one of the most impressive characteristics of the pageants influenced by the *Stanzaic Life* is how intelligently and carefully the two aesthetics have been combined: the result in each case is a quite new, and newly unified, play having been fashioned out of the old.

That the *Stanzaic Life* reviser did not redesign all six of these pageants at once is indicated by the Early Banns: whereas Paginae VI ("Nativity"), VIII ("Magi") and IX ("Offerings") are accorded full stanza descriptions, Paginae XI ("Purification"), XII ("Temptation"), and XX ("Ascension") are described in quatrains. Evidently, then, three were revised for (or before) the shift to Whitsuntide, whereas the other three (all performed on Whitmonday) were amplified for the three-day production. One reason for these amplifications may have been practical: in order to maintain a nearly continuous performance of the cycle at each station, it was necessary (as several time-studies have shown) to control quite carefully the lengths of individual pageants.[60]

Thus to this point we have determined that three pageants (I, V, and VII) were added to the cycle early in the sixteenth century and that six others were revised at the same time (VI, VIII, IX, XI, XII, and XX). Is it possible to discover any further additions or amplifications made during this shift to Whitsuntide? I think it is, although the reasoning from this point on will be based on less solid evidence. First to be determined is whether or not the Expositor's appearances throughout the cycle are a consistent register of the cycle's expansion. In the case of three pageants, "Balaam" (V), "Nativity" (VI), and "Temptation" (XII), we have determined that the Expositor and his glosses were added early in the sixteenth century. Does this hold as well for the two other pageants in which he appears, IV and XXII? Pagina IV, the Barbers' "Abraham, Lot, Melchysedeck and Isaac," clearly existed in some form in the fifteenth-century Corpus Christi play, because the Barbers appear in their proper place in the Harley 2104 Guild List. But one distinctive characteristic of this pageant is that its last part constitutes an adaptation and distillation of the Brome "Abraham and Isaac" play.[61] Because only one other pageant in Chester, Pagina XI, clearly contains an adaptation of a dramatic source ("Christ among the Doctors" from York); because Pagina XI was undoubtedly expanded during the Whitsun shift; and because in both of these dramatic adaptations ("Abraham and Isaac" and "Christ among the Doctors") the principles of compression are extremely similar, it is quite likely that both Paginae IV and XI are in their present form the work of the same redactor. In addition, it is worth noting that Pagina IV is constructed very similarly to Pagina V (which was added to the cycle between 1505 and 1522): each pageant is divided into three, discrete, "analogically related" units,[62] and each is fully explicated by an Expositor. Finally (as we shall see fully in the next chapter) the design of salvation history these six dramatic units and their expositions support is so carefully patterned that it is extremely unlikely that the two pageants (IV and MS H of V) as they now exist were not the construction of a single craftsman.[63]

There remains, therefore, only one other pageant in the cycle where the Expositor appears: the Shermen's "Prophets of Antichrist" (XXII), in which, as in Pagina V (H MS), the Expositor enters to interpret the augurings of each prophet. The similarity of construction between these prophecy/exposition episodes is itself suggestive; in addition, since we know (from the Harley 2104 Guild List) that Pagina XXII existed in the fifteenth century, whatever amplifications, if any, it may have been given would in all likelihood have involved not the prophecies themselves but their expositions. This inference is well-nigh confirmed when we turn again to the Early Banns: the one remaining pageant accorded an "abnormal" (full-stanza) description is, in fact, the Shermen's "Prophets of Antichrist." Thus these two registers are mutually supportive: the Expositor's appearances and the Early Banns' variant-stanza descriptions prove to be consistently valid signs of a pageant's having been constructed or revised for the Whitsun shift. Chambers and Salter were therefore correct in assuming that the Expositor is an accurate indication of one layer of composition, but this layer I have determined was not the cycle's earliest; rather, in the early sixteenth century it constituted part of what was a major transformation of a kind of Passion play into a full-scale history-of-the-world cycle.

Of the remaining possible registers of the Whitsun shift (see table 2.1), I think one is invalid and the other only sporadically meaningful. Salter assumed that the cycle's longest pageants were among the earliest, and that many of the shortest entered the cycle late.[64] But no correlation can now be seen to exist between a pageant's length and age: its length was surely determined in large part by the events it presented (and how they were dramatized), also quite possibly by a guild's forceful contention that it merited a "sizeable" play and, in some cases, by the pageant's place in the processional "queue." Rhyme scheme, on the other hand, appears occasionally to be a valid sign of authorship, or layer of composition. For instance, it is quite likely that one playwright (the "cross-rhyme redactor," if you will) was responsible for Pagina I ("Fall of Lucifer"), Pagina VII ("Shepherds"), and (in Pagina XI) "Christ among the Doctors." But I can discover no shared significance among the few remaining patches of cross rhyme. According to W.W. Greg, "wherever a change of stanza occurs without discoverable reason we are justified in supposing that we have not got the play in its original form."[65] But this rule of thumb simply does not work in Chester. We know that with the six *Stanzaic Life* pageants, although each is written throughout in tail rhyme, "we have not got the play in its original form"; conversely, in most of Chester's pageants where the rhyme scheme shifts "without discoverable reason," those shifts seem only an expression of poetic caprice. Thus, by itself, a pageant's changing rhyme schemes are usually too crude a register to serve as a measure of authorial signature.[66] The two long rhyme-royal passages appear, nevertheless, to be an exception to the rule, and have universally been accepted as late sixteenth-century additions to Paginae VIII and XIII.[67] However, because these two episodes have been so carefully integrated into their respective pageants, I suspect that they, too, were added to the cycle for the Whitsun shift.[68]

It would seem useful now to summarize what this chapter's explorations have, and have not, ascertained so far. Chester's original configuration, authorship, and time and manner of inception—despite all conjecture—appear to be permanently beyond our ken. Almost equally as obscure is the development of the play during the fifteenth century, although some sparse evidence has survived. In the section above, I have succeeded in clarifying certain particulars concerning the play's development in the early sixteenth century; but even here there have been numerous issues not raised, let alone resolved—such as how many playwrights were involved in the Whitsun shift, the sequence of their additions, their variant dramatic styles, and so forth. Even as a "palimpsest" study, this chapter has managed so far to descry only two layers—one of these a rough conglomerate of all earlier compositions, the other comprising the Whitsun additions (all of which we probably have not found). Nevertheless, I think we can now see the old Corpus Christi play, circa 1500, more clearly than it has ever been seen before. Centered in its Passion/Resurrection sequence (which was changed little, if at all, during the Whitsun shift), completed by a Doomsday epilogue (also changed only slightly), the play of Corpus Christi differed from the Whitsun cycle's configurations most strikingly in its Old Testament/ Nativity prologue. The only elements I am certain were contained in the Old Testament part of this prologue were the "Fall of Man" (first half of II), most of "Noah" (III), and some part of "Abraham"

(IV); the Nativity Group was also abbreviated, lacking the "Shep-herds" (VII), all the *Stanzaic Life* additions, and other episodes (such as the rhyme-royal sequence) as well. Even the Ministry offer-ings were more limited, and before the "Last Supper" (XV) they may have included only the "Temptation" (first part of XII), the "Lazarus" (last part of XIII), and selected episodes from XIV.[69]

Thus if the English Corpus Christi play as a dramatic genre is to be defined, typically, as a history-of-the-world cycle which reaches into eternity at both ends, the Chester play of Corpus Christi (circa 1500) clearly belonged to another order: Chester's special triptych design in 1500 would seem to have been a slightly modified version (as was the 1303 Montecassino Passion's) of what Rosemary Woolf has called the "Septuagesima cycle-form."[70] The implications of the structural and aesthetic differences which now can be discerned between the "old" Chester play and the "new" are therefore, I believe, extremely significant. First, any theory is quite suspect that would still maintain a direct and causal relationship between the Corpus Christi feast and a definitive, "proto-cyclic," and universally shared design for all the English Corpus Christi plays.[71] In Chester's case, as we have seen, the play in fact did not realize its "definitive" cyclic form until, ironically, it was moved to Whitsuntide. Second, the play's unique transformation during these years should help in this present study to define more clearly those structural principles which give the cycle its theological unity and historical shape. Spe-cifically, in Chapter 3 where I discuss Chester's unique dramatic design of Old Testament history, and in Chapter 7 where I argue for another unique dramatic design based upon the twelve articles of the Apostles' Creed, knowledge of how the cycle developed could sup-port, or could severely damage, my theses. Third, knowledge of how the play's dramatic techniques and rhetorical emphases shifted during its expansion will be of assistance in my detailed studies of the cycle's various dramatic strategies (in Chapters 4, 6, and 8). These strategies must now be understood in terms of sixteenth-century, as well as fifteenth-century, aesthetic principles. Finally, recognizing that the Chester cycle is in no small part a creation of the early sixteenth century will be important when I examine, in Chapter 5, Chester's late medieval theology and what I call the nominalist conservatism of its "neo-Romanesque" style.

One cannot assume, however, that the Chester cycle as it has survived to be printed in twentieth-century editions is in fact the play that was designed for that Whitsun shift; thus it is important to trace at least briefly the cycle's fate in its last years of production.

IV
The Cycle's Last Years;
Its Manuscript Difficulties;
Its Dramatic Unity

The Chester Whitsun plays were apparently produced in the same "stop-to-stop" processional fashion from the time that the revised Newhall Proclamation announced (in 1531/32) their three-day schedule, through what proved to be their penultimate performance in 1572: that is, each play, mounted upon its pageant-wagon, was wheeled through the streets to be performed first before the clergy at the abbey gates, next before the mayor and the city council at the Pentice at High Cross, and then two or three more times at other places in the city. As the Rogers' Breviary remarks, an uninterrupted performance of the cycle at each station was brought off with re-markable skill: "the[y] came from one streete to another. kepinge a directe order in euerye streete/for before thei firste Carige was gone from one place the seconde came. and so before the seconde was gone the thirde came. and so tell the laste was donne all in order withoute anye stayeinge in anye place."[72] But the Whitsun plays as a unified cycle did not proceed through the last decades of their career with comparable ease and fluidity. The cycle apparently was never mounted annually (perhaps because of its great expense), but rather was given at two- or three-year intervals.[73] In response to Reformation pressures, the play was reduced in size and deprived of some of its more "papist" elements; the Wives' "Assumption," for example, was allowed to disappear completely, the Bakers' "Last Supper" was left out of the cycle for at least a decade, and other pageants were examined and sometimes amended. These pressures became so concentrated that the plays almost did not "go" in 1572: a contemporary record mentions that "an Inhibition was sent from the Archbishop [of York] to stay them but it Came too late."[74] Not all the criticism of the plays (or of parts of them) was external, however, for another 1572 entry remarks, "In this yeare the whole Playes were playde thoughe manye of the Cittie were sore against the settinge forthe therof."[75] Even with the increasing criticism, however, there was in Chester such strong feeling not to discontinue this great dramatic tradition that it was decided to mount the plays again in 1575, when almost all other performances of the Corpus Christi cycles in England had been permanently halted.

Everything we know about the 1575 production of the Whitsun plays proves that it was unique. The City Assembly was cautious from the outset, determining that the plays "shalbe sett furth...with such correction and amendement as shalbe thaught Convenient by the said Maior."[76] Even after these amendments were apparently made, some of the pageants, "for the superstition that was in them,"[77] were not performed at all. Those that were performed were mounted on the secular holiday of Midsummer and performed over a four-day sequence, rather than the normal three. And (as it had been done more than a half-century earlier) the cycle was produced stationarily and "in on part of the Citty"—this "on" part perhaps being the first "civic" station, at the Pentice at High Cross.[78] Not only is this last performance of the cycle an interesting aberration in Chester's traditional production patterns of the sixteenth century, but its peculiarities raise a number of questions important to a formal analysis of the play. To what extent, in other words, do the five manuscripts, collectively or individually, represent the cycle—either as it was produced in 1575 (in partial and "corrected" form), or as it was produced in 1572 (as "the whole Playes"), or as it was produced earlier but under Protestant censorship, or as it was produced before any attempts were made to alter its shape and contents? This question surely will never be answered fully, but a brief inquiry into the cycle's reformation in its last years and into the relationship of its manuscripts at least should lead to a less than random—or editorially foreordained—definition of what the cycle is that we are to study.

In fact, little more than has already been mentioned about the cycle's changing configuration from mid-century onward appears to be forthcoming from the civic and guild records, despite their notable increase in number during this time. Earlier, in the latter part of the reign of Henry VIII (1508–47), the cycle appears to have thrived: having achieved its fullest size, remaining Catholic and "medieval" even though many of its parts were written for the Whitsun shift, the cycle's security and great popularity during these early Reformation years were by no means paradoxical.[79] Because the English Reformation, as Harold Gardiner has written, did not enter a phase of "doctrinal change" until after Henry VIII's death. "The beliefs and feelings of the people at large remained, until well beyond the middle of the sixteenth century, Catholic in all essential matters."[80] But immediately upon the accession of Edward VI (1547-53), Chester felt the doctrinal displeasures of London and York. The procession and the (lost) clergy's play of Corpus Christi were both suppressed in 1548. In 1550 the Bakers' "Last Supper" dropped away from the cycle, the vacuum left by it being partially filled by a slightly amplified Shoemakers' play; and at about the same time the cycle was deprived forever of its "Assumption." These cleansings of Chester, all obviously doctrinal, were similar to those expurgations of other Corpus Christi plays elsewhere in England: York, for instance, lost its "Assumption of the Virgin" play in 1548, and the Wakefield cycle at about the same time was excised of certain passages concerning the seven sacraments and transubstantiation. During Mary's reign (1553-58), certain older religious activities, such as the Corpus Christi procession, were briefly reinstituted; but it apparently was not until early in the reign of Elizabeth that Chester recouped one of its losses (the "Last Supper," presumably in its original form), and that the Shoemakers' play consequently returned pretty much to its earlier design. Only in the case of the Shoemakers' pageant, known as "Jerusalem Carriage," do the documents suggest something about internal modifications: whereas the pre-1550 pageant placed Christ's anointing by the Magdalene in her and Martha's house (following John 12:1-8), the post-1561 pageant places the episode in Simon the Leper's house (following Mark 14:3-9).[81]

The Late Banns, composed between 1548-61 and revised between 1561-72, should be expected to offer further information about the cycle's internal modifications during its last quarter-century. Like the Early Banns, the Late Banns are written in two stanza-lengths: the pageant descriptions written in quatrains would appear the original layer of composition, while those written in rhyme royal would appear to have been revised. The seven pageants described in rhyme-royal stanzas are the "Fall of Lucifer," "Nativity," "Shepherds,"

63

"Last Supper," "Passion," "Resurrection," "Antichrist," and "Last Judgment." But there is not much evidence in these pageants, insofar as I can determine, which might indicate late revision.[82] The Late Banns may be more helpful in the pageant descriptions themselves, for they mention (as does the 1548 List of Companies) certain characters and episodes not mentioned in the Early Banns: but none of these citations should, in my judgment, be accepted alone as proof of a pageant's revision or amplification.[83] Where the Late Banns are perhaps most helpful is in revealing the local, "orthodox" attitude taken toward the plays—an attitude which is at once apologetic, "jollified," and critical. The Banns scorn the stupidity of the plays' original audiences: "the fine witte at this daye aboundinge/ At yat daye & yat age, had uerye smale beinge."[84] However, the Banns see the plays' composition as having been proto-Protestant in spirit, for the monk who authored them, "nothinge affrayde/ With feare of burninge hangeinge or cuttinge of heade," heroically chose to make the Scriptures known to the people "In a common englishe tonge."[85] Disturbed nevertheless by the high incidence of nonscriptural events in the plays, the Late Banns advise that those "thinges not warranted by anye wrytte" were included in the plays "onely to make sporte."[86] Most obviously troublesome were those moments most closely identified with Catholic belief. The "Last Supper," rather than a sacramental celebration, was thus to be treated in performance as a happy "memorall," after which the Bakers from their wagon should "caste godes loues [loaves] abroade with accustomed cherefull harte."[87] Whether any aspects of this Protestant attitude seen in the Late Banns penetrated the surviving texts of the cycle itself, however, has yet to be determined.

Also as yet to be determined is the precise interrelationship of the four cycle-manuscripts known as the Group (HmARB), and the nature of their relationship—individually and collectively—to H, the last of the manuscripts transcribed, written out apparently as a presentation copy.[88] Although most of Chester's mechanical textual problems are best left to the ongoing labors of the EETS editors, in this study (which relies primarily on the Hm MS base-text used in volume I of the EETS edition) I will occasionally prefer a line or stanza from the H MS (and will always indicate when I do so): H's scribal-antiquarian emendations of "corrupt" passages often make better sense than the Group MSS. Why I raise the problem of manuscript relations here is that the Chester manuscripts (it has always been assumed) all derive from an archetype known throughout the cycle's history as the "Regenall." Recopied, and presumably somewhat changed, several times in the cycle's last years, the "Regenall" was a master-text containing all the plays: kept by the city, it was used when guilds wanted fresh copies of their plays, and may have served after mid-century as a way of controlling the doctrinal contents of the pageants performed. A fundamental question editors therefore must ask is, what pageant-versions in which manuscripts are closest to the "Regenall" when the "Regenall" existed in its least adulterate, most nearly pure, state? Or, since the "Regenall" itself has not survived, let the question be more hypothetical: what should an editor do if he were ever to discover five variant versions of the "Regenall"—say, from 1540 to 1575—and had to publish only the best, or the best synthesis of the five? Certain decisions he made would have to be based upon a sense of the cycle as a unified work of religious art, rather than upon his statistical tables of manuscript variants.[89] Similarly, I think it is incumbent upon any scholar studying the entire Chester cycle to make several preliminary judgments about the surviving texts. This I intend to do in a modest way, assisted by the guild records I have mentioned, by the apologetic prejudices of the Late Banns, and by the helpful notes of the recent EETS edition of the cycle.

Had only one manuscript of the Chester cycle survived and had we known nothing about Chester's dramatic history, it would perhaps have been advisable from the outset to share that common critical bias recently restated by Phillip McCaffrey:

> A modern student's only reasonable course seems to be to recognize the surviving form of the cycle as one of its many historical forms, and to analyze it as a single art work, judging its effectiveness as a unit in spite of its multiple authorship and irretrievably complicated history. Whatever virtue and whatever flaw is found in the work must simply be ascribed to the total, without hope of identifying individual contributors or nonliterary factors.[90]

But in Chester's case, "to recognize the surviving form of the cycle" is itself an act of creative scholarship. For all their objectivity, for example, the editors of the recent EETS volume chose to amend

Hm, their base-text, by adding to it a pageant it lacked entirely, the Tanners' "Fall of Lucifer." The common sense evidenced in that decision I think we can apply elsewhere to resolve most of the major differences among the manuscripts' offerings. The raven-and-dove episode is found only in the "Noah" of the H MS, but its exclusion from the play we wish to study would seem rather pointless. The H "Shepherds" lacks the Group's closing scene, where the shepherds' boys appear and offer their gifts: although this epilogue is not essential, to include it would seem only in keeping with the pageant's own generosity of spirit. The H "Passion" lacks Peter's denial of Christ, an episode not essential to the pageant itself; but it is quite acceptable as part of the cycle, for it anticipates Peter's remorse, dramatized later. The H and Group "Passions" also differ slightly in their closing episode; however, since the same characters say nearly the same things in the same order, only an editor might wish to quibble over the "better" choice. Nor would most wish to argue about the appropriate closure to the "Resurrection": HmAB stop abruptly as Magdalene approaches the angel, whereas HR finish this episode and conclude with Christ's forgiving Peter. For an editor these may all present major problems. But since there appear to be no reasons to exclude any of these passages—reasons arising either from historical evidence or from concerns about artistic integrity— these issues appear not to be matters demanding scholarly concern.[91]

However, there are three places (at least) where I think common sense and a generous spirit need critical assistance. The first is an old problem in Chester studies: of the H version and the Group version of the Cappers' play, which (if either) is older or is to be preferred? Of those scholars who have compared these two quite different "Balaam" plays, all but one have said either that the issue has yet to be resolved, or that the Group version is older (and, for some, better). Bernice Coffee's is the one dissenting voice, and it is her arguments I find convincing: the language in H is more often older, the meaning of its lines is more often more intelligent.[92] But why two versions, and why not now accept both—as we do with the two Wakefield "Shepherds" plays? There are two versions, I would argue, for the same reason that the Smiths in 1575 had to present two versions of their play "before the Aldermen to take the best."[93] In the case of the Cappers' play, we know which version was determined the best in 1575 because it is clear from its last stanza that the HmARB "Balaam" closed the first day's sequence of plays: "tomorrowe nexte yee shall have more." The reason the H version was rejected in 1575 I find equally apparent: the prophecies uttered in its *processus prophetarum* (which is not included at all in HmARB) are "Marian," and thus papist, in cast. And the reason I reject the Group play and accept the H version is that the latter is Roman Catholic, medieval, and (as we shall see in Chapter 3) absolutely essential to the cycle's historical scheme of Old Testament time.

My second and third pieces of editorial revising both involve some minor textual surgery. All manuscript versions of the "Noah" include those stanzas Brownstein has proved were an addition to an early, more unified, pageant: linguistically late and poetically crude, these stanzas break with the character consistencies of what Brownstein called the "Old Play."[94] But—after accepting without pause all the Whitsun additions—it would seem indefensible here were I to excise one episode, full (as it is) of delightful anachronisms (such as Mrs. Noah's swearing by "Sancte John") and thematically justifiable as a comic scene typologically mediating between Eve's disobedience and Mary's humility. But the "Old Play" version of "Noah" is the one I insist on in the cycle I am about to study: as Chapter 3 will prove, those added verbal anachronisms were (unwittingly) in violation of a carefully controlled dramatic tense, and of a historical vision of "pre-Christian" time, both central to the design of Chester's Old Testament Group. I suggest that this farcical patch was added late, and would agree with Axton—if we are to look for its source— that it is "possible that Mrs. Noah's *maistrie* is a state of topsy-turvy licensed by traditional practice on St. John's Day, Midsummer Day."[95] The other episode I intend to excise is one that we know was licensed by the topsy-turvy practices of Midsummer: the alewife epilogue, added (in the Group manuscripts) to the "Harrowing of Hell" pageant. Salter has hypothesized that this episode is a fragment surviving from an old "Tapsters' Play" (the existence of which has yet to be documented);[96] equally unconvincing is Lumiansky's attempt to prove that this satiric farce offers an appropriate artistic and thematic closure to the "Harrowing."[97] From the Late Banns we can see that the Catholic version of what Christ did while in hell was not approved; but since there was no official Protestant version, the alewife scene was apparently tacked on to leaven the seriousness and the importance of the entire pageant. This pageant's only proper version is that retained in H: it concludes with the "Te Deum laudamus," as Michael leads the saved toward heaven.

What remains after these minor operations, then, is the "preferred" cycle I am to study, although the exact text of this cycle is not to be found in any edition of the plays. All that I have done, however, has been to restore to the body of the text most of the episodes that the recent EETS edition relegates to the Appendices section, and to remove from that body an appendix or two it never in fact needed. These few editings may be self-serving, but they are in line with certain historical implications as well as with my own aesthetic judgments. Alan H. Nelson has surmised that "characters from the Whitsun plays were introduced into the Midsummer Show in 1554."[98] Relying upon the same "doubtful evidence" as he did, I would surmise that a mutual interchange of characters and playlets between these two festivities was begun soon after 1548, and as a consequence of this exchange as well as of Reformation emendations the cycle as we have it now is somewhat corrupt. That none of the English cycles died a natural death has been well documented, but we should remind ourselves that in their later years most were in partial decline: not only were parts excised and patches added on, but certain sacred scenes were not treated seriously, and others may have been mocked.[99] Because this mockery of the plays themselves is so foreign to the comic joy of the pre-Reformation dramatic productions, I think it appropriate (when possible) to recover the plays' designs before their decline: in Chester's case this means before the influence of the Midsummer frolics and of Protestant reprobation. My "preferred" text does not represent the Chester cycle quite at its height (that is, during the second quarter of the sixteenth century), but with the exception of the lost "Assumption" it would seem reasonably close enough so that we may consider it a full and unified cycle. From this point onward, I will accept the Chester cycle as the work of a single playwright—of one who successfully brought to completion the complete works of a number of playwrights before him. However, as the limitations of this chapter's reliance on historical reconstruction and commonsense editing have shown, the overall unity of Chester's dramatic design, although it can be appreciated from the outside, will never be adequately understood until it is analyzed extensively and formally from within.

In conclusion, then, it would seem appropriate to return to the analogy with which I opened this chapter's discussion of Chester's construction. Since I have been considering a single cycle, let me counterpose a single work of religious architecture. Romsey Abbey, admired as one of the finest English examples of the Romanesque, is in fact—like Chester—a composite of various styles and stages of construction. The choir, transepts, and four bays of the nave are late Romanesque; the three other bays of the nave and the west front are Early Gothic; added later, in the Decorated style, are the two east windows; and the style of the north aisle, because it was widened in the fifteenth century, is Perpendicular. Yet the achieved effect of these different stages of construction and of these various styles is one of nearly perfect harmony. The Abbey is handsome, balanced, strong and (perhaps surprisingly) "Romanesque"; so, too, is the Chester cycle. But neither work is perfect. In Romsey's south transept there is a fifteenth-century ogee canopy: cutting off sight of the window behind it, crudely plastered onto the wall, this canopy is a grotesque mistake—to accept it as part of the whole is to embrace all taste and to exercise none. In Chester, as well, we have found that a few of the cycle's accretions had to be removed, not as a desecration of any of its integral parts but as an act of reverence for the unity of the whole. And although I have hardly managed to discover in Chester as many layers of composition as can easily be seen in Romsey Abbey, I hope that our imperfect education in the cycle's plans of construction will lead in the direction of a deeper understanding of its finished form.[100] I have been examining that form, for the most part, only from the outside. It is time, then, to enter the interior and to undertake a careful study, part by part, of the group of plays known as the Chester Whitsun, alias Corpus Christi, cycle.

3

The Dramatic Hermeneutics of Old Testament Time: Paginae I-V

The Chester Play of Corpus Christi begins with the glorious figure of God, who in the opening twenty-five lines of Pagina I describes with solemn magniloquence the immutable essence of his own being. As "greate God gracious," he is a "pearles patron," an omnipotent pattern in which all things "bouth viscible and inviscible" reside. He emphasizes his triune nature ("three tryalls [excellences] in a throne/ and true Trenitie/ be grounded in my godhead"), notes his royal preeminence as "Prince principall," and cites the superlative attributes of his being: "will," "sapience," "meirth," "potentia," "might," "prudence" (H), and "southnes" are all "dissolved under a deadem/ by my devyne experience." Then with one turn of his "comelye compasse" God makes his potential "patron" actual, creating the "biglie blesse" of heaven and nine orders of angels "to walke aboute the Trenitie." The moral implications of heavenly creation are instantly made evident. Directing the angels' gaze to a "dungion of darkenes," an eternal world "bouth voyde and vayne" just formed, Deus Pater warns:

> loke you fall not in noe dispaier.
> Touche not my throne by non assente.
> All your beautie I shall appaier,
> and pride fall oughte in your intente.

With the assurances of the nine angelic orders, led by Lucifer, that they will honor his "covenante," Deus Pater departs to "see this blesse in every tower," promising "To be revisible in shorte space."

Immediately upon God's departure, however, Lucifer begins to exult in his own glory, his earlier praise of his Creator proving to have been mere flattery. Dazzled by his own brilliant beauty, Lucifer wonders aloud whether the other angels would worship him if he were to sit in God's throne. Warned at length by the host of good angels yet coaxed on by his loyal lieutenant Lightebourne, Lucifer after considerable hesitation finally assumes God's throne and demands of the astonished angels that they worship him—"pearlesse and prince of pride,/ for God hymselfe shines not so sheene." Deus Pater returns immediately, rhetorically asks of Lucifer and Lightebourne "Who is your prince and principall?" and casts them for their "fowle pride" into "the deepe pitt of hell ever to bee." In the distress and discord of hell, the two fallen angels revile each other, rue their lost brilliance and "forfayted" grace, and enviously begin their plot to "destroye" mankind. In heaven, distressed yet not despairing, Deus Pater resolves to continue his divine plan, forecasting his creation of man:

> ... that I first thought, yet soe will I.
> I and two persons be at one assente
> a sollempne matter for to trye.
> A full fayer image we have imente,
> that the same stydd shall multiplye.

Pagina I ends with Deus Pater's command, "Lightenes and darkenes, I byde you twene," as he blesses all that had been wrought on this first day of creation.

In dramatizing the character of God and eternity, God's creation of heaven and the angels, and the rebellion of Lucifer, the Corpus Christi playwrights translated into dramatic action various exegetical and iconographic traditions to make visible and memorable for their audiences the perfections of heavenly existence.[1] Chester Pagina I, the longest opening pageant of the English cycles, relies heavily upon the effects of symbolic spectacle, ritual gesture, and liturgical music to figure forth the harmony of heavenly creation and the hierarchy of eternal life. In Chester, as in *The Holkham Bible Picture Book* (a fourteenth-century pictorial world history which may have influ-

71

enced, or have been influenced by, contemporary English dramatic practices), God the divine architect creates heaven by circumscribing space with a golden compass.[2] The harmony of that creation is personified by the nine orders of angels: accorded separate speeches, probably dressed in distinctly different costumes,[3] and assigned individual "seates," the angelic orders project heaven's multiplicity as well as its unity. The eternity of heaven is suggested by the angels' circular procession about their Creator,[4] its regality by a multitowered stage set,[5] and its solemn joy, its "meirth," by the three hymns which the angels (undoubtedly professional choristers) sing in God's honor.[6] The recurring visual emphasis in Chester is upon the spectacular beauty of heaven, its Creator, and his creatures. God is a figure of light: apparently wearing a sun-disc mask,[7] he calls attention to the "beames" of his own "brighte face." The brightly clad angels time and again praise the light emanating from their Creator, and before their fall Lucifer and Lightebourne revel in the golden beauty which their own bodies have received from God. At the play's end the brilliance of heaven is once again emphasized, this time by the contrasting darkness of the fallen angels, who react with horrified disgust to each other's "stinckinge face." Symbolizing the "patrons" of eternity by costume, staging, formal gesture, and ritual music, Pagina I in its spectacular effects is a kind of ceremonial masque representing those qualities of perfection which God defines at the play's beginning as the essence of his being.

The major dramatic conflict in Pagina I is of course that between divine light and diabolical darkness, a conflict whose genesis constitutes a primary cause of the uneven course of subsequent human history. In dramatizing the self-creation of evil and Lucifer's prototypical rebellion, the Chester playwright adheres carefully to certain narrative and exegetical traditions interpreting the events of Genesis 1. He is careful, for instance, that God appear not to have been the author of darkness (i.e., evil); rather, Deus Pater at the end of the first day simply "twenes" light from darkness as he had divided the tarnished angels from those who remained steadfast.[8] Similarly, as in the Anglo-Saxon *Genesis B* narrative, Satan after his fall is bound in chains; but lest the devil's future appearance in paradise to tempt man seem inconsistent with Satan's chaining, Chester, like *Genesis B*, has Satan send off his emissary, one "Ruffyn," or "ruffian" [H], to "keepe mankinde from blesse."[9] Finally, those two prevailing vices which Saint Thomas[10] and others found to be the source of Satan's evil are explicitly defined in Chester: it is pride, God explains, which has brought Lucifer to sin, and it is envy, Satan admits, which motivates his plot to tempt mankind from bliss.

The feature which distinguishes Pagina I most notably from the opening pageants of the other cycles is its careful exploration of the character of good and evil and of the nature and significance of free moral choice. Whereas God in the N-Town and Wakefield cycles never warns the angels against proud ambition, and in York merely suggests in one line that they be "stabill in thoghte," Deus Pater in Chester harps at length on the necessity of angelic obedience to his will. Singling out Lucifer and Lightebourne from the rest, he shows them the pit of hell which will be the punishment of pride, deceit, and disobedience, and then places them immediately next to his throne, which he commands them not to touch. Unlike in N-Town and York, where God apparently never leaves the stage, Deus Pater in Chester conspicuously departs, promising as he does so to return, his clear intention being to test by his absence his angels' obedience and love. In contrast to York and Wakefield, where Lucifer simply and suddenly falls, in Chester Lucifer and Lightebourne are questioned and reprimanded by their Maker for almost twenty lines before they are catapulted into hell. In fact at one moment before judging his errant vicegerent, God descends from his august diction and displays a quite human sense of hurt and disappointment:

> Lucifer, who set thee here when I was goe?
> What have I offended unto thee?
> I made thee my frende; thou arte my foe.
> Why haste thou tresspassed thus to me?

God's careful warning of the angels, his deliberately absenting himself from their company, his thorough analysis of the willful pride of the disobedient angels upon his return, and his personal response to their rebellion, all dramatize God's just yet loving character and underscore the freedom of choice all the angels shared equally before the fall of Lucifer.

The characters of both the good and the bad angels are also fully portrayed. Each of the nine orders is accorded a speech immediately revealing his nature, either in praising God's love or in censuring the proud acts of his sinning fellows. The willful turning of the deceitful angels from love of God to self-love, however, reveals itself more slowly. Lucifer's praise of his Creator at first appears genuine, although an accomplished actor might have emphasized the slightly saccharine tone of Lucifer's first words and their undue emphasis upon his own glory as "bearer of lighte." Lucifer's false show of humility is blatantly mimicked by Lightebourne (a character unique to Chester, his name a travesty of his master's):[11] even before God's departure Lightebourne obviously revels more in his nearness to Lucifer than in his nearness to God. After God departs, the sinbound angels appear in their full deceit. Lucifer, assuming God's throne, gloats in his own beauty, and Lightebourne, sidling up to his newly acclaimed master, exudes a sycophant's love of reflected glory:

> And I ame nexte of the same degree,
> repleth by all experience.
> Methinkes yf I might sit him bye
> all heaven shoulde doe us reverence.

In the judgment of Rosemary Woolf, Pagina I's analysis of free will and its relationship to the character of good and evil is an unfortunate piece of dramatic ingenuity: the Chester playwright, she believes, "raises in his diffuse play a moral and psychological problem [Satan's *gradual* change of heart] that it was well beyond his capacity and intention to answer."[12] But as we have noted, Satan's gradual shift toward evil is an important part of the play's exploration of the phenomenon of free choice. And as the foregoing critical notes have implied, Pagina I should not be understood merely as a self-enclosed play, for it is in part a dramatic overture to history, serving as a gloss to human deeds that will be accomplished in time, perhaps the most important being the first: the temptation and fall of man. As in Anselm's *De Libertate Arbitrii*, which argues that both "the apostate angel and the first man sinned by their own [free] choice,"[13] so in Pagina I the analysis of Satan's free will projects itself forward as a commentary upon the choice of man in paradise and upon subsequent human decisions made either in obedience or in disobedience to God's will.[14] Pagina I is thus an accomplished opening pageant: it figures forth the perfections of God and heavenly life; it establishes the genesis and universal character of good and evil; and it analyzes the freedom of choice by which humankind in time can accomplish good or evil.

For all its sophistication, Pagina I is a pageant fairly easily interpreted because the foundation of its dramatic hermeneutics is essentially nontemporal. That is, the play represents self-defining universal verities—the absolute perfections of God and eternity, and the unchanging essences of good and evil. However, once the mimetic action of the cycle has fallen into time, a more complex hermeneutics in all likelihood will obtain—will obtain, that is, if the Corpus Christi playwright wishes to project in his cycle a coherent vision of the underlying patterns of salvation history. Major elements of that vision would perforce be evidenced in the historical pageants of his Old Testament Group, for in these few plays—by their selection, integration, and individual development—the playwright had to figure forth his understanding of the relationship of the Old Testament to the New, of ante-Atonement time to a time initiated by Christ's Nativity yet embracing the present lives of the cycle's audience. Several historical models were available to any playwright with a modicum of exegetical training, but the interpretive principles and temporal designs of these models, once selected, had then to be translated into dramatic form and adapted to adhere to the peculiar powers and restraints of continuous mimetic action. In the following pages I shall argue that of all the English cycles only Chester has adapted systematically into its Old Testament plays a coherent and identifiable scheme of salvation history. Certain precepts of this scheme serve as the shaping principles of Paginae II and III (representing Adam's fall, Abel's death, and Noah's flood); the remaining precepts account for Chester's unique mixture of historical events and exegetical interpretations in the pageants which conclude its Old Testament Group (Paginae IV and V). But before I turn to a close study of these plays, I must consider in a general way some of the historical models and dramatic options available to the Corpus Christi playwrights. Even if these models and options were used only sporadically, the very fact that they required artistic consideration is itself testimony to the new imperatives of the Corpus Christi dramatic form. These imperatives—artistic and historio-theological—differed radically from those of liturgical drama.

Chapter Three

I

In my judgment there are three major historiological models that are central to understanding the individual designs of the English Corpus Christi cycles. First, a Corpus Christi cycle may offer a model of salvation history—of history seen as the progress of gradual spiritual enlightenment. To this historical model, and to later variants of it, German Protestant theologians eventually gave the name *Heilsgeschichte.* Working within the restraints of this first model, a dramatist had to establish his cycle's vision of the shape of salvation history, a shape which then presumably dictated the structure and tone of each pageant. Whether a pageant was tragic, comic, "mixed," or otherwise in its form, whether its main principle of development was typological, tropological, historical, or whatever, and whether it was integrated causally or connected some other way with other pageants, all depended upon its place within the cycle's overall historical design. Second, a Corpus Christi cycle may be seen as a modest *summa* of the primary tenets of Christian belief. According to this second model, the major aim of a cycle was "to exhort the myndes of the comen peple to gud deuocion and holsom doctryne ther of."[15] The tenets of that wholesome doctrine could presumably accord with the personal convictions of the playwright, or they could be determined by a more formal set of *credenda,* such as the twelve articles of the Apostles' Creed.[16] Third, a Corpus Christi cycle may be understood as an evolutionary sequence of tests and recognitions subtly analogous to the education of the Christian spirit, to the maturation of Christian Everyman from his creation to his day of judgment. According to this third model (which obviously is related in its dynamics to the English morality plays), the cycles project obliquely a spiritual biography of their own audience. Because that biography is far from ideal, one nexus of the cycle's historical design would reside in the dramatic characters who either recognize, or fail to recognize, the significance of scriptural events propaedeutic to the Last Judgment. The implications of these three models as they apply to the cycles' Old Testament plays are many. One of the most immediate issues, however, is the problem of how these historical designs could be fully integrated into a form of "realistic" drama that normally presents its actions and characters as, seemingly, absolutely contemporaneous with its audience.

76

In shaping and interpreting their Old Testament plays, the Corpus Christi dramatists were free to build upon that bond of kinship their audience felt with proto-Christians living before Christ, and to emphasize to a degree the contemporary realism of Old Testament characters. Encouraged by the historical shape of the liturgical year, medieval Christians were expected to identify at least in part with the *antiqui iusti* of the Old Testament: during Advent Christians anticipated Christ's second coming as they commemorated the historical prelude to his first coming, and during Lent they chastened their souls by retracing the trials and wanderings of the Jewish nation. Although the Old Testament *antiqui iusti* were known to have lived in a crepuscular world deprived of the direct light of truth emanating from Christ's Incarnation, the world of the Corpus Christi viewers was in many ways similar. They too were living in a time of semidarkness, patterning their lives postfigurally (rather than prefigurally) after the paradigm of Christ's historical ministry.[17] To paraphrase Origen: "We still walk among shadows and figures, but at least we know now that we walk in the shadow of Christ."[18]

The major characteristic traditionally distinguishing Christ's followers from his precursors, as Origen implied, was not their faith in God and their hope for salvation, but their full knowledge of those truths revealed by the deeds of his Son. Lest the two Testaments appear to be not only one, but equal, exegetes sensitive to the historicity of Scripture and artists committed to a certain kind or degree of realism had to achieve in their interpretations of Old Testament time a blend of lights and shadows: the higher or future truths mirrored in Old Testament history may be made visible to the reader or viewer, but they should be understood not at all, or only in part, by the Old Testament characters themselves.[19] The graphic arts, in portraying individual scenes, could often easily honor this double commitment to past ignorance and present understanding: in *The Holkham Bible Picture Book,* for example, a pelican nesting in the Tree of Life feeds her brood blood from her own breast, while Adam and Eve—standing below and praising their Creator—appear unaware of this self-sacrifice and of its future significance.[20] In historical *summae,* the precise degree to which the corpus of Old Testament history knowingly embraced the spirit of its Christian meaning was a thorny exegetical problem: there were a few, wrote Augustine, who in the Old Testament preceded their spiritual Head, as did the hand which emerged first from Tamar's womb; but by and large, the church fathers agreed, the mysteries which Christ revealed to the saints had remained hidden from prior generations.[21] In biblical commentaries, it is of course the exegete himself who discovered prefigurations of Christian mysteries, hidden from the understanding of those in the Old Testament by the veil of allegory, and in the graphic arts iconographic signs could communicate the hidden mysteries to the viewers. But in a realistic play representing characters acting and speaking in time, only an accomplished playwright could consistently reveal through his characters higher Christian truths beyond the ken of the Old Testament figures themselves.

It is important to recognize at this point that, in most Middle English Old Testament plays, this tension between historical and contemporary realism, between Old Testament ignorance and present understanding, was treated as a quite minor problem. In these plays anachronistic foreknowledge is common: Old Testament characters sometimes call upon Christ, swear by the names of his saints, and even, occasionally, explain the figural significance of their own actions, momentarily transforming themselves from unknowing types to informed prophets. The one dramatic exception to this casual Christianizing of Old Testament knowledge is the Chester cycle: very rarely, and then only for clearly accountable reasons, do Old Testament characters in Chester allude to Christ or reveal any understanding of future events.

The care with which Chester has limited the Christian intelligence of Old Testament time is clearly indicative of its playwright's exegetical training, but it may also be a small but significant factor contributing to the cycle's overall scheme of salvation history. To determine the nature of this scheme, it will be necessary to consider out of chronological order the two pageants with which Chester's Old Testament Group concludes. Paginae IV and V are crucial in at least two ways. First, Pagina IV tests the validity of a certain exegetical method many critics have seen as an organizing principle operative in all the cycles' Old Testament pageants. Second, the two pageants considered together suggest a more satisfactory (albeit more complex) program of interpretation. The method that has attracted so much attention is the typological form of scriptural exposition: a selected Old Testament event seen as a prefiguration of a selected New Testament event, the second paralleling the action and fulfilling the implicit spiritual import of the first. Typology—Hurrell, Kolve, Meyers, Gardner, and others have argued—is a basic hermeneutical technique controlling the entire structure of the cycles, both in their Old Testament pageants as *figurae* and in their New Testament pageants as fulfillments.[22] Because of this figural construction, it would appear to follow that the cycles' vision of history is founded upon "a particular theory of time arising from the typological method of exegesis."[23] But by studying Pagina IV (the one pageant in Chester which is clearly typological in design) we shall discover that even in this kind of pageant typology must be subordinated to a more complex view of Christian history. Then, with the assistance of Pagina V, we will discover that Chester in fact does entertain a more complex vision of history. This vision, unique in its dramatic use to Chester, is translated into dramatic form by the use of an unusual variety of interpretive techniques.

II

Entitled "de Abrahamo et Melchisedech et Loth" (H), Pagina IV is introduced by a "Preco" who reports that the "Noah" play is over, and Abraham's about to begin, "in worshippe of the Trynitie." Episode One opens with Abraham explaining that he has just won a battle by which he had been able to restore his "brother" Lot to safety. Thanking God for their victory, he and Lot plan to offer God their "teath" through the medium of God's priest, Melchisedec. When Melchisedec hears of Abraham's victory, he prepares to offer Abraham "bread and wyne,/ for grace of God is him within." In a brief exchange, Melchisedec gives the two kinsmen wine and bread; Abraham presents the priest the "teathe" of his booty, and Lot offers a "royall cuppe." At the close of this brief episode, an Expositor enters *equitando* and explains to the audience the significance of the actors, the exchange, and the gifts: the "teath" is the tithe all men then gave and must now give to the church; in offering bread and wine Melchisedec prefigures the celebrant of the Eucharist, and Abraham is therefore the "Father of heaven." The central part of the Expositor's exegesis makes clear both the historicity of these events and the fulfillment of these Old Testament sacraments and obligations in New Testament practice:

> This present, I saye veramente,
> signifieth the newe testamente
> that nowe is used with good intente
> throughout all Christianitye.
>
> In the owld lawe, without leasinge,
> when these too good men were livinge,
> of beastes were there offeringe
> and eke there sacramente.
> But synce Christe dyed one roode-tree,
> in bred and wyne his death remenber wee;
> and at his laste supper our mandee
> was his commandemente.

Episode Two is very brief. God appears and tells Abraham that his race shall prosper, he shall have "kinges" from his seed, and "one chylde of greate degree/ all mankynde shall forbye." He then orders that "eyche man-chylde" be circumcised on the eighth day, and departs. After Abraham's prayerful agreement, the Expositor comes forward again. He informs the audience that the "one seede mankinde for to bye" was "Christe Jesus," and explains that although circumcision was "an sacrament/ in the ould lawe truely tane," when "Christe dyed away hit went,/ and then beganne baptysme."

Neither one of these short episodes is very complicated. Each represents one or more historical events in the life of Abraham, and these events illustrate certain customs and sacraments Old Testament patriarchs were obliged to practice according to the Old Law. But hidden within these obligations are future customs and sacraments which those living in New Testament time are now obliged to practice. Thus an extradramatic figure, the Expositor, serves as the New Testament exegete explaining the figural significance of these events to the audience. Their tropological import is clear: one should pay one's tithes, communicate, and baptize one's children. In addition, the episodes conveniently demonstrate the restraints typology normally places upon drama. Figural correspondences are revealed most easily in stasis, as in the graphic arts or in biblical commentary. In drama, the form best suited to typological demonstration is normally an emblematic vignette (as here), or a tableau vivant momentarily frozen within the ongoing mimetic action.

But the exception to this general rule is found in the sustained Abraham and Isaac drama which completes Pagina IV. Chester's version of this popular Middle English play opens with God's ordering Abraham to sacrifice his son on the mount. Abraham assents to God's harsh command immediately, and he and Isaac set out "to an hyll here besyde," the boy carrying wood, the father "sworde and fyer." Soon, however, Isaac perceives his father's distress, and asks imploringly if it is he who will be sacrificed. Abraham assures him that "our lorde will sende of his godheade/ some manner beast into this stydd" (H), but shortly thereafter he breaks down and confesses, "Ah, Isaack, Isaack, I muste thee kyll." Isaac is confused, fearing he may somehow have incurred his father's wrath, but when he understands his death is God's wish, the boy poignantly and simply accepts his fate, and in fact helps his trembling father to bind and blindfold him. At the last moment tragedy is averted, as two angels appear to stay Abraham's raised sword. A wether tied among the briars is placed as substitute sacrifice, and the drama concludes happily as God commends Abraham for his obedience and promises him that his race shall prosper.

What is perhaps most impressive about the Chester Abraham and Isaac episode is its subtle harmonizing of literal history and figural significance, of the Old Testament event with its New Testament referent. Christ's Passion is alluded to consistently without depriving the pre-Christian drama of its naturalistic integrity. Although the typology of Isaac's sacrifice was probably "part of the small stock of knowledge which the common people might be expected to have received,"[24] Chester leaves little in doubt. Four times in less than 160 lines Abraham alludes to the triune Divinity of which he is the *figura* by exclaiming that his "harte will breake in three." Loathe to shed the blood of his son's "body soe free," Abraham prays, "The blessinge of the Trynitye,/ my deare sonne, one thee light." Isaac also assists in emphasizing the play's figural meaning, although the dramatic irony of his lines only the audience could understand. He calls upon "Marye" twice, after he exclaims:

Would God my mother were here with mee!
Shee would kneele downe upon her knee,
prayeinge you, father, if yt might bee,
for you to save my liefe.

Here, assisted by Isaac's grieving imagination, the viewers are expected to conflate in their own imaginations two scenes of sorrow:
Sarah and the Virgin complaining to the father that their son be saved
from reasonless death. The remembrance of future suffering is emphasized subtly throughout the drama, but at certain moments the
double reference works perfectly, as when father and son address
each other immediately before the sacrifice:

Abraham
My sonne, my harte will breake in three
to here thee speake such wordes to mee.
Jesu, one mee thow have pyttye,
that I have moste of mynde.

Isaack
Nowe, father, I see that I shall dye.
Almighty God in majestie,
my soule I offer unto thee.
Lorde, to yt bee kynde.

The equation of Abraham and Isaac with the divine Father and
Son is at this moment well-nigh complete, and which historical narrative dominated the perceptions of the audience, that of the Old or
of the New Testament, probably depended in part upon the gestures
of the actors. The balance between figure and fulfillment is completed in Chester despite the deux ex machina salvation of Isaac: a
lamb is found in the briars, its sacrifice prefiguring the human death
which the Old Testament drama has narrowly averted.[25] If any
doubts remain about the drama's figural level of significance, the
Expositor concludes the play with a most specific explication:

This deede yee seene done here in this place,
in example of Jesus done yt was,
that for to wynne mankinde grace
was sacrifyced one the roode.

By Abraham I may understand
the Father of heaven that cann fonde
with his Sonnes blood to breake that bonde
that the dyvell had brought us to.
By Isaack understande I maye
Jesus that was obedyent aye,
his Fathers will to worke alwaye
and death for to confounde.

Pagina IV is an example of typological drama at its best, but simply to admire the success with which the dramatist has harmonized
typology and "realistic" mimetic action does not, I think, do justice
to the entire play. Two of the episodes in Pagina IV are unique in
Middle English drama, as is their juxtaposition with the Abraham
and Isaac episode. One must ask why these episodes were selected,
and then not only why but *how* they were figurally interpreted.[26]
For, as A.J. Maas reminds us, there are several forms of literal cor-
respondence and several levels of figural significance which typology
can employ.[27] A type, he argues, may be "personal" (Melchisedec
seen as a type of Christ), "real" (where events or objects in the Old
Testament prefigure events or objects in the New), or "legal" (where
sacraments of the Mosaic Law are seen as *figurae* of the New Law);
the antitype fulfilling the type may be interpreted "allegorically"
(a truth to be believed), "anagogically" (a boon to be hoped for, a
judgment to be feared), or "tropologically" (a virtue to be practiced).
Thus in a pageant with three distinct episodes which appear to be
related some way other than causally, both on their literal and figural levels, there must be some higher design than typology which
has determined both their principles of selection and their principles
of interpretation.

Ever since E.K. Chambers first remarked that Chester was "much
concerned with the exposition of religious formularies, such as the Ten
Commandments, and of Jewish and Christian ritual observances,"[28]
Pagina IV's unusual interest in the customs, obligations, rituals, and
sacraments of the Old Testament Jews has been the cause of minor
critical bewilderment. Why—in a popular dramatic form which normally cleanses Old Testament history almost entirely of its Jewish
"taint"—does the Chester dramatist emphasize the pre-Christian past-

ness and the cultural differences of the Old Testament patriarchs? Why is the obligation of tithing sacralized here, in this pageant, when all the other English cycles explicitly place the ritual much earlier, in the offerings of Cain and Abel?[29] Why is circumcision mentioned at all, when the New Testament sacrament replacing it, baptism, could easily have been dramatized in the cycle's Ministry Group? And why prefigure the Corpus Christi sacrament, which is instituted later in the cycle by Christ at the Last Supper? Although each of these questions automatically prompts certain kinds of critical responses, such responses are likely to be as loosely related as the episodes appear to be in the pageant itself. Similarly, past attempts at accounting for the curious divergence among the English cycles in the historical events they dramatize after Noah's Flood have succeeded only in inspiring further controversy. In the particular case of Chester Pagina IV, I think the questions posed above cannot be answered by analyzing the pageant in isolation. At the very least, it is necessary to consider it along with the pageant that closes out Chester's Old Testament Group, for this pageant shares a number of the same kinds of idiosyncrasies as Pagina IV. These two plays, in turn, differ radically in their dramatic structure and means of self-interpretation from the two Old Testament pageants which precede them. Thus only after examining Pagina V, I believe, can one arrive at a set of historical-dramatic principles which explain the peculiarities of both plays. This set of principles, in turn, will assist us in understanding the interpretive principles of the other two historical pageants in Chester's Old Testament Group.

The Cappers' Play, Pagina V (H MS version),[30] employs the same principles of dramatic structure as Pagina IV: distinct and causally unrelated actions juxtaposed and individually explicated by an Expositor. The pageant's first episode is a brief scene dramatizing a major moment in the education of the Jewish people. God addresses Moses and "all the people that be here," recites in slightly amplified form the ten precepts of the Decalogue, and charges his people to obey them. Speaking *quasi pro populo*, a character named Princeps Sinagogae expresses his dread of God "so grym," and thanks Moses for serving as intercessor. The Expositor then explains to the audience that the precepts of the Ten Commandments are still to be believed by Christians:

> Lordinges, this comaundment
> was of the old testamente,
> and yet is used with good entent
> with all that good bene.

Entering *equitando,* Balaak opens the pageant's second action: he is "so wroth" with the victories of the Jewish people that he sends a soldier to fetch Balaam to "curse the people here." When the soldier reaches Balaam, God appears *in supremo loco;* He commands Balaam not to curse His people, and then allows him "thydder to goe." Balaam submits to God's will, but as he rides his ass toward Balaak's mountain he changes his mind, deciding to curse the Jewish nation instead. An angel appears before the travelers *cum gladio extracto in manu;* the ass sees the angel and stops, Balaam whips his beast, who understandably complains of his unjust punishment. Balaam then sees the angel, kneels, and at the angel's urging reverts to his former intention to bless God's Chosen People. This he does, much to Balaak's increasing rage, as he blesses the Jews from three sides of the mountain; finally, casting his eyes *ad caelum respiciens prophetando,* Balaam utters the prophecy which made him famous: *Orientur stella ex Jacob.* Immediately upon this prophecy, Isaiah appears, utters his own prophecy, and is then followed in succession by six other prophets—Ezechiel, Jeremiah, Jonah, David, Joel, and Micah—each of whose prophecies is interpreted in turn by the Expositor. Pagina V closes with Balaak recognizing his ignorance—"For God of Jewes is crop and roote,/ and lord of heaven and hell"—and with the Expositor's promise that in the next play three kings will appear at Christ's Nativity.

Although all the English cycles include a recitation of the Ten Commandments[31] and a *processus prophetarum,*[32] Pagina V is nevertheless unique in several respects: in its incorporation of these two quasi-dramatic actions into one pageant, in their being interpreted by an Expositor, and in the *processus prophetarum's* springing directly out of the Balaam episode—an episode found in none of the other English cycles. The pageant is a curious mixture of tropology and prophecy, of unchanging and of revealed truth. Even the precepts of the Ten Commandments are received by revelation, passed from the awesome figure of God "so grym," to the powerfully impressive "horned" Moses, then to Princeps Sinagogae, and thus to the audience—"all the people that be here." The viewers witnessing the power of Christian illumination to penetrate into the Old Testament world are themselves given a role in the pageant's action: represented by Princepes Sinagogae in the first episode, in the pageant's final episode the audience becomes the Jewish *populus* cursed by Balaak and blessed by Balaam. One intention of this and the previous pageant clearly was to prove to the viewers (who alone are graced with the Christian edifications of the Expositor) that the foundations of their Christian customs, precepts, and sacraments rest in the Old Testament as well as in the New.

Several distinct episodes juxtaposed; an Expositor glossing each episode; an unusual interest in Old Testament customs and beliefs; an audience taught that it shares both the Old and the New; a curious mixture of tropology, typology, and prophecy—this congeries of dramatic peculiarities distinguishes Paginae IV and V not only from the corresponding pageants of the other cycles but from the preceding pageants in Chester as well. To explain these two pageants, it is insufficient to rely upon past interpretive schemes, such as a general "prophetic principle" dominating the entire Old Testament Group,[33] or the group's being divided according to a historical plan conflating typology and the Ages of Man,[34] or the simple need to dramatize the major scriptural events up through Genesis 22, because "the effects of the Fall have by then been fully displayed and the Redemption has been fully foreshadowed."[35] Rather, I believe we should return to the three historical models I outlined earlier, and primarily to the scheme which interpreted the entire cycle as a dramatic *Heilsgeschichte* retracing for the audience the major events of Christian history.

I wish to propose now that the four historical pageants of Chester's Old Testament Group were organized and interpreted according to a vision of salvation history which divided Old Testament time into two ages: the age of natural law and the age of written law. This division of Old Testament time was hardly novel with the Chester dramatist: it is at least as old as Bede, and is casually alluded to by several English writers contemporary with Chester.[36] Of all the exegetical studies of this historical scheme, however, Hugh of Saint-Victor's *De Sacramentis* remained the most definitive, and will serve as primary source here. I use it not because it was also Chester's primary source (which is unlikely) but because, like Chester, it exhibits a sensitive awareness of the principles of gradual change operative in what it defines as the three ages of Christian history. According to this vision, the two ages of Old Testament time were early yet distinctly different stages in the advancing education of the human spirit. The age of natural law was a time of near darkness, of *umbrae veritatis,* truth's shadows. Primitive man in this age had little sense of the human community, knew nothing of the future coming of Christ, and was able to express his devotion to God only through the few natural sacraments and precepts he understood according to his natural reason. The age of the written law was a time of increasing light, of *imagines veritatis,* truth's images. During this age God's people advanced dramatically in their sense of community, their education, customs, precepts, and sacraments. The light emanating from history's third age, the *corpus veritatis* of the New Testament, was brighter now, although the refractions of that truth were still oblique, reflected in signs and images. The age of the written law made advances in three things, according to Hugh: *sacramenta, precepta,* and *promissa.*[37]

Of history's three periods (that of the shadow, that of the image, and that of the body of truth), Paginae IV and V clearly represent the second—the age of the written law. The *sacramenta* of that age (represented by tithing and circumcision) are dramatized in Pagina IV. The *precepta* of the age (the Decalogue) are duly revealed and explained in Pagina V. The pageants' remaining episodes account for the *promissa* of redemption: Christ's Passion is figured forth typologically in Isaac's sacrifice, and his entire career—from the Nativity to the Last Judgment—is accounted for prophetically by Balaam and by the prophets who follow. But because (as Hugh insists) the Old Testament characters themselves understood the lasting significance of only a few of their customs and deeds, a post-Atonement intelligence is necessary to uncover the Christian significance of these *acta* and *imagines.* Thus in Chester the Expositor enters after each episode to explain its present meaning. Tithing and the Ten Commandments are moral obligations still to be honored. However, baptism has now replaced the sacrament of circumcision, Melchisedec's offering foreshadows the Eucharist, and Isaac's narrowly averted death prefigures

87

the Crucifixion. Closest in time to the New Testament, the prophets are closest to revealed truth; but the vision of each is incomplete, and thus must be decoded and amplified by the ever-attentive Expositor. Behind these pageants' apparently haphazard mixture of various historical episodes, exegetical commentaries, and dramatic techniques, I assert, there can be discovered a unified vision of historical change, as human civilization advances from the dispirited ignorance of the past and prepares itself, with the help of God's revelations, for a new age with a New Law. Thus the historical model most important in explaining these two pageants is that which interprets the cycle as a *Heilsgeschichte* dramatizing the integrated process of historical and spiritual evolution. In support of this model's organization of these two pageants are the other two historical models I have described—Christian history as an education of the race, Christian history as a *summa* of the faith. In a brief study entitled "Chester's Sermon for Catechumens," Joseph Bryant has revealed that the typological exposition of Abraham's three "blessings" found in Pagina IV was common teaching for those seeking confirmation, and part of a catechetical tradition which can be traced back at least to Saint Ambrose's fourth-century tract *De Abraham*.[38] The preliminary Christian learning taught in Pagina IV thus integrates early into the Chester cycle that dramatic model which interprets history as an oblique projection of the religious education of Christian Everyman. As one of the Old Testament *antiqui iusti*, Abraham cannot understand fully the significance of his blessings, but the audience, reminded of the blessings' future fulfillment and Christian meanings, is asked to reconsider their import by retracing the early stages of its own Christian education.

That education continues to mature as the cycle progresses, but it is only toward the end of New Testament time that the *credenda* of Christian belief are fully formalized and that Chester's third historio-dramatic model becomes clearly evident. As a dramatic *summa* of the central tenets of Christian faith, the Chester cycle—I shall argue in Chapter 7—is uniquely designed to verify the twelve articles of the Apostles' Creed. Although Chester's choice of prophets in Pagina V may possibly have been influenced by the cycle's credal design,[39] it is not until late in Chester's mimesis of history that the audience is offered the chance to understand fully this third dramatic model, when at Pentecost the apostles recite the twelve articles of their creed.

At the stage of time represented by Paginae IV and V, Chester's dramatic strategies have drawn the audience toward an identification with the Old Testament, and have implied that history's second age is comparable to a critical stage in the individual's spiritual development. Human nature in these two Old Testament pageants has moved from the shadowy ignorance of early adolescence into an age of greater maturity and of refracted illumination, where customs are understood, moral rules are codified, rituals are more intelligible, and the promises of salvation are more directly revealed. But the viewers of the cycle have arrived at this plateau of learning only after first suffering through the dramatic traumas of human nature living in a younger age. To this earlier stage of historical development, to the age of natural law as it is dramatized in Paginae II and III, I shall now turn.

III

Whereas the cycle's first pageant, written in cross-rhyme stanzas, offers a single dramatic action integrating numerous iconographical and exegetical traditions, the characteristics of the Drapers' pageant are noticeably different: written in tail-rhyme stanzas, Pagina II embraces two complete actions (the Fall of man and Abel's slaughter) and relies upon Scripture and apparently only one exegetical commentary for its sources. In the pageant's first ten stanzas God creates the universe from the first to the fifth day. Then fashioning man in His own image—"man and woman I will there bee"—God blows into man the "goste of lief," leads him to paradise, warns him not to eat of the tree, and puts him into an ecstatic sleep. From Adam's side God draws a "feere," whom Adam, then awakened, calls "viragoo," explaining that "out of man taken shee is" and inferring from her name the sacramental union of marriage:

> Therfore man kyndely shall forsake
> father and mother, and to wife take;
> too in one fleshe, as thou can make,
> eyther other for to glad.

At this moment of blissful harmony "Demon" makes his entrance and explains to the audience his envious plot against mankind: to "make him by some gynne/ from that place for to twyne / and trespasse as did I." Assuming the guise of a winged adder with a "maydens face," the devil as "Serpens" approaches Eve—"for wemen they be full licourouse"—and advises her that if she wishes to be as wise as God she should eat of the "good meate": "And but thou finde yt to thy paye,/ say that I am false." Eve eats of "the fruite sweete" and carries it to her husband; Adam takes "one morsell," immediately to discover their nakedness and to recognize their broken "commandemente." As "minstrelles playe," God appears; Adam blames Eve and Eve the serpent for their sin. In judgment, God condemns the serpent to crawl on the earth, commits woman to painful childbirth and submission to man, and damns both man and woman to a life of sorrow and hard labor, ending in death. Clothing the sinners in "Dead beaste skynes," God reveals the ironic fitness of their curse: they had desired to know good and evil, "both weelle and woe," and "nowe is it fallen to thee soe." The first complete action of Pagina II thus concludes, in less than 400 lines, with the expulsion of Adam and Eve from the garden and the appearance of four angels with flaming swords, so that neither by "crafte or countyce" might man regain his lost paradise.

The most impressive characteristic of Chester's version of the Fall, as the above summary suggests, is its fidelity to Scripture and the simplicity and austerity with which it has translated into dramatic action the Genesis narrative. Chester in no way attempts to particularize personality or emotion, nor does it strive for that kind of "contemporary realism" which Auerbach found so appealing in the Anglo-Norman *Jeu d'Adam.*[40] Rather, Chester emphasizes the scriptural authenticity of its dramatic representation, the universality of the characters of Adam and Eve, and the archetypal nature of their sin. Chester's major dramatic contribution to the original Genesis narrative resides in the severity of its judgments. Most of these judgments (many of them antifeminist) have been derived from Peter Comestor's *Historia Scholastica.*[41] Demon reasons that because a woman will do anything she has been forbidden, he will approach Eve first, and cunningly assumes the female guise of the serpentine temptress as described by Comestor: *Supremus volucris, penna serpens, pede forma, forma puella.* As in the Vulgate, Adam calls woman "viragoo"; but after the Fall he rails against all womankind, calling them twins of the devil, and converts the name of "womman" into "woe-man" (and perhaps *virago* into *vir-agon*):

> Yea, sooth sayde I in prophecye
> when thou was taken of my bodye—
> mans woe thou would bee witterlye;
> therfore thou was soe named.[42]

It is in the emotional tone attending the expulsion, however, that Chester most manifestly reveals its unmitigatingly harsh judgment of both authors of original sin, a judgment which contrasts sharply with the other Fall pageants, each of which attempts to cast some light of hope into the tragic circumstances of the outcast pair. In York, at the end of her bitter railings with Adam, Eve fully confesses her guilt. In N-Town, Eve asks Adam to kill her, but Adam emphasizes their mutual guilt and their need for mutual love, and the two are consoled further at the pageant's end by an angel prophesying Christ's redemption of man. Norwich Pageant B is the most optimistic. Immediately after their expulsion Adam and Eve first meet with the two allegorical figures "Dolor" and "Myserye"; but they are then consoled by the Holy Ghost, and the play ends with their singing a hymn of thanksgiving for their fortunate fall: "With hart and voyce/ Let us reioyce/ And prayse the Lord alwaye/ For this our joyfull daye."[43] But in Chester there is no suggestion that, driven from the garden, Adam and Eve find in their mutual sin a common bond to unite them in their woe. On the contrary, the sin of each has bitterly estranged them: Eve's last words blame the serpent for her sin, Adam's last words continue reviling his wife. As in Comestor's *Historia,* God has clothed them in the skins of dead beasts, not as a comfort but to remind them that "death noe way may you flee." Driving the pair from the garden, God pitilessly underlines the ironic fruition of their wish to know "both weelle and woe": sorrow, hard labor, and death, he explains, will be their lot. The four angels at the garden's gate serve as a final menacing chorus of doom, repeating three times (in the H MS) the bitter phrase: "gright [begrudged] they bene that grace."

The angels also serve to span the "xxx yeare" which Adam, in the opening speech of the pageant's second half, explains to his children have passed since he and their mother were expelled from the garden.

Thanking "Hight God and highest kynge" for the blessing of their two sons, Adam and Eve relate their former sins to their offspring, and then explain that as a family they must work to gain their sustenance—Adam with spade, Eve by spinning, Cain as husbandman, and Abel as shepherd. In response to his parents' sermon on obedience and hard work, Cain volunteers a sacrifice to God, and Abel follows suit, offering the "beste beaste" of his flock. But selecting "earles corne," which he had judged was "good inough for him," Cain sees his own sacrifice, but not his brother's, rejected by God. In response to Cain's anger, God asks:

> Cayne, why arte thou wroth? Why?
> Thy semblant changes wonderously.
> If thou doe well and truely,
> thou may have meede of mee.

Despite this gentle warning, Cain invites his brother into a field on an "errande," and there he slays him. In restrained rage, God calls out and curses Cain and his offspring to the seventh generation, and the elder son of man, deeming himself "dampned without grace," goes to his "Dam and syre" to relate his crime, and then departs to wander in the outer darkness until his death.

By joining the dramatization of Cain's crime to that of Adam's original sin, Chester efficiently underscores the parallel elements between the disobedient acts of father and son and emphasizes the continuing descent of mankind into sin. This descent, in its human psychology and moral options, iterates some of the patterns of Lucifer's paradigmatic revolt dramatized in Pagina I. Therefore Augustine's psycho-tropological analysis of the angels' revolt sheds light as well on the nature of the sins committed by the Adamic family:

> That the contrary propensities in good and bad angels have arisen, not from a difference in their nature and origin, since God, the good Author and Creator of all essences, created them both, but from a difference in their wills and desires, it is impossible to doubt. While some stedfastly continued in that which was the common good of all, namely, in God Himself, and in His eternity, truth, and love; others, being enamoured rather of their own power, as if they could be their own good, lapsed to this private good of their own, from that higher and beatific good which was common to all, and, bartering the lofty dignity of eternity for the

inflation of pride, the most assured verity for the slyness of vanity, uniting love for factious partisanship, they become proud, deceived, envious. The cause, therefore, of the blessedness of the good is adherence to God. And so the cause of the others' misery will be found in the contrary, that is, in their not adhering to God.[44]

The "contrary propensities" of good and evil, first manifested by the angels, are redefined in the first family and their acts. The love of God, personified by the steadfast angels, and by Adam and Eve before they are consumed by pride, assumes its first unwavering human form in Abel, whose soft-spoken obedience to God, his parents, and his elder brother epitomizes the perfect human devotion to "the common good." Bartering the love of God for "the inflation of pride," Lucifer, Adam, and Cain each fly in the face of God's commandments in willful response to their own private desires.

Despite its fidelity to Scripture, Chester adds a number of significant touches of its own. As they are dramatized in Pagina II, Cain's character and sin are noticeably closer to Lucifer's than to Adam's. Although, like Cain, Adam committed his heinous sin despite God's warning, his better judgment was partially lulled by the devil's deception and his wife's pleadings. Adam was once the paragon of innocence, and, thirty years after his fall, it is obvious he has labored in humble penance before the "Hight God" whom he had offended. Cain's character, on the other hand, is presented as darker than ever was his father's, and intimations of evil are evident in his first words, his obedience to his parents as suspect as Lucifer's initial praise of God. Although it is Cain who suggests making sacrifice, his motives undercut the meaning of the gesture: he has "great plentee," but hopes God will send him more. His oblation is not an act of thanksgiving but, in Augustine's terms, an attempt to increase a private good. Then, despite his great plenty, Cain selects sheaves from which the fruit has fallen and offers seedless corn to his Maker. The fatalistic ambivalence of his response to God's reprimand, "A, well, well, then it is soe" (H), disguises a decision put into action by his ominous words, "Come forth brother with me to goe" (H). Like Lucifer, Cain is thus a "congeon," a subtle deceiver whose evil desires, although slowly revealed, are in retrospect seen to have been operative in his first words. Again, like Lucifer, Cain shows no signs of guilt: he allows that he is a "losell," and pities himself for the pain of his future sufferings, but, feeling himself beyond the recall of grace, he seeks no forgiveness.

Pagina II's patternings of action obviously derive in large part from Genesis itself, but through his dramatic amplifications of the scriptural narratives, the Chester playwright has emphasized on a number of levels history's early motif of "twyninge," or what Gower called its "divisioun":[45] the divisions of light and darkness, fertility and sterility, obedience and disobedience, love and self-love, harmony and discord. Many of these symbolic patterns were first initiated in Pagina I, although Pagina II, the first historical pageant, offers at least one new motif—the decline of nature as man's nature declines. Thus the cycle's opening two pageants trace a sequence of freely committed yet interdependent deeds, each of which casts its perpetrator from a state of harmony into a barren and bleak world: the sin of Lucifer, Satan explains, deprived him of the "Gostlye paradice" which was once his to enjoy; in like manner, he wishes man deprived of his "earthely paradice" (H). Because of his disobedience, Adam is "wayved" from paradise to earth, where God warns him that "thornes and bryers" (H) shall be the fruit of his labors; and Cain, damned to wander endlessly over the face of the earth, shall, God promises him, find the earth so "warryed" that all shall become barren in his path.

The graphic imagery of light and darkness—made visible to the audience by God's brilliance, the blackness of the demons, the tree of knowledge "fayre and bryght," the angels' flaming swords as they guard paradise, and the fire of Abel's sacrifice—is intertwined with a series of verbal and dramatic images which contrast unity with division and fruition with death. The perfect unity, in heaven and among men, is naturally conceived in images of social harmony, and the discord created by "factious partisanship" is accomplished in each pageant by an act of "twyninge." Emphasizing his own triune nature, God warns the angels in Pagina I not to fall into "dispaier," a state soon realized by the sinful angels' rebellion and subsequent bickering among themselves in hell. Having "twynned" light from darkness at the angels' fall, God creates man in his own likeness, "too in one fleshe." Yet through the inflation of pride, Adam and Eve "twyn" themselves from God's will and are "wayved" from paradise, divided bitterly from each other. Then, after Adam and Eve are reunited and are at one with their family, Cain violates his filial and fraternal trust,

94

"twyninge" himself from good the very moment that Abel is destroyed.

Each of these divisive acts involves a violation of light and a descent into darkness. The ultimate source of light is of course the "beames" of God's "brighte face." When Lucifer violates the throne God has commanded him not to touch, he feels that his own "brightnes" surpasses God's, but as part of his punishment he is changed into a blackened demon in the darkness of hell. Similarly, having violated the tree both "fayre and bryght" they were commanded not to touch, man and woman leave the spiritual harmony of the garden, pass beyond the flaming swords of the angels, and find themselves in the skins of dead beasts; reduced to the animal component of their nature, they are forced to reproduce their species, since they must die. In the hope that they may sometime regain their lost immortality, they must fertilize the earth out of which man was made and offer to God from nature the best results of their regenerative labors.

In dramatizing the mythic power of these variegated patterns, Chester remains close to the universal symbolism of Scripture and far from any temptation to make contemporary, comic, or satirical the deeds of the first family. Characterizing the early adolescence of salvation history, the Adamic family in Chester are cast as ancient and august children of God: powerful, tragic, and ignorant. The deep psychology of their actions reveals the passionate depth, moral center, and spiritual potential of human nature unavailed of New Testament belief. The lack of dramatic *figurae* and the absence of an Expositor in Pagina II are both appropriate, for the New Testament light cast into the age of shadows is, at best, faint and inconstant. And although the viewers of the play are certainly free to discover for themselves momentary figural reminders of the New Testament, their main charge is to rediscover their own primitive natures dramatized within the context of history's first age.

Although Chester's vision of early Old Testament history is noticeably more tragic than either Hugh's or those of the other English cycles, like the other cycles Chester alleviates to some degree the ever-increasing darkness represented by Cain's crime. In Wakefield and York, the somber aura of Abel's death is moderated by the roughneck antics of Cain and his servant. In both plays, Cain is portrayed as a coarsely vigorous and ill-tempered medieval farmer, his saucy servant ("Pik-harnes" in Wakefield, "Brew-barret" in York) serving as a loutish butt to his spleen. The N-Town pageant, on the other hand, keeps its level of action serious, yet offers a ray of hope by Abel's exposition of the typological fulfillment of his sacrifice in Christ:

> throwh thi gret mercy
> which in a lombys lyknes
> thou xalt for mannys wyckydnes
> Onys ben offeryd in peynfulnes
> and deyn ful dolfoly.

Chester also includes a note of prophetic solace, but in doing so carefully explains how that foreknowledge was gained—in order to avoid the kind of anachronism found in Abel's figural exegesis in N-Town. In the first part of Pagina II, as Adam rises from his sleep, he mentions a wonderful dream:

> A, lorde, where have I longe bine?
> For sythence I slepte much have I seene—
> wonder that withouten weene
> hereafter shalbe wiste.

Thirty years later, in his homily to his sons, Adam finally tells how his "gost to heaven banished was" and there beheld "thinges that shall befall." Relating this prophetic vision (which the Chester dramatist has lifted in its entirety from the *Historia Scholastica*),[46] Adam reveals that God will come in human form "to overcome the devill soe slee":

> and my blood that hee will wyne
> that I soe lost for my synne;
> a new lawe then shall begine
> and soe men shall yt finde. [H]

Beyond that, a cataclysm of "Water or fyer also witterlye/ all this world shall distroye"; and, finally, "God will come the laste daye" to transport the good to heaven and allow the evil to fall into the eternal fires of hell.

Although vague both in chronology and detail, Adam's vision at least gives promise of man's potential salvation and offers a ray of hope in the dark postlapsarian world he and his family inhabit. But the dream is itself darkened by its inclusion of two universal destructions; these cosmic judgments, made necessary because "men shall synne soe horryblye," convert the vision into a homily directed against mankind's disobedience, backslidings, and blind lusts. Addressed to those who may "escape that noy" (H), Adam's prophecy places his sons in a historical perspective as men who ultimately may be saved if they faithfully attend to their religious obligations and adhere to their communal precepts. Had Adam recited his dream at the moment of his awakening, its import could have applied only to himself, and had he mentioned it only after Cain's crime, the tragedy of that crime would dramatically have been less powerful. Placed as it is as a warning to Cain and Abel—men who must suffer hardship because of their parents' original sin, yet who can freely determine the moral tenor of their lives—the vision serves as a warning to all men at all times that good deeds are a requisite foundation for salvation. Cain's murderous act is thus made all the more tragic by his awareness of his own possible salvation. The audience, cognizant of the historical realities of the Atonement, could freely interpret Cain's sin as a half-witting crime against Christ himself, and would therefore feel all the more deeply the intensity of their original parents' grief when Cain returns to them to report his crime:

> Adam
> Alas, alas, is Abell deade?
> Alas, rufull is my reade!
> Noe more joye to me is leade,
> save only Eve my wyfe.

> Eva
> Alas, nowe is my sonne slayne!
> Alas, marred is all my mayne!
> Alas, muste I never be fayne,
> but in woe and morninge?

I have offered this extended analysis of the patterned actions, themes, and images of Chester's second pageant to show how it is controlled not by a single hermeneutical principle (such as typology or allegory), nor even by an obvious collection of several such principles. Rather, the way Pagina II's meaning is projected would have to be defined in modern aesthetic terms as "symbolic," "polysemous," "mythic," or "archetypal."[47] In medieval aesthetic terms, because of Chester's considerable emphasis upon the sacramental nature of the nuclear family, the play's major rhetorical thrust was probably perceived as tropological. Of all the English cycles, only Chester, curiously, includes Genesis' sacralization of the marriage bond; only in Chester does Adam lecture to his family on the necessity of harmonious labor; only Chester emphasizes the tragic destruction of familial unity by having Cain return to his parents to report his crime. But the pageant's concerns are more than ethical: they are psychological, historical, and spiritual as well. Hugh of Saint Victor defined the moral precept of the age of natural law as "Do unto others as you would have them do unto you"; Chester Pagina II twice dramatizes this moral precept and the effects of its violation. In addition, however, Chester like Hugh is concerned with offering a historical vision of man's radical nature unavailed of the direct light of grace. The Genesis family are prototypes of human nature, Christians only *in potentia:* deprived of future knowledge, expressing their love of God only through the simple oblations they understand, culpable in a world of falling nature, they must rely strongly upon each other to achieve a human community. They thus represent the potential of *Humanum Genus*—as an emotional, rational, spiritual and social being—early in his life and at the outset of his education. This education will not be completed until the end of time.

IV

Because the Chester dramatist has offered such a dark vision of early man and his interrelated crimes, the artistic task posed by the pageant closing out the age of natural law was a difficult one. This pageant, comic rather than tragic in structure, abruptly shifts from the despair of the preceding events to a sense of hope and human accomplishment dramatized in the salvation of Noah and his family from the Flood. Put on by the "Waterleaders and Drawers of Dee," Pagina III was an ambitious piece of theatrics and probably a very impressive spectacle. Stage directions and spoken lines call for God's appearing in the clouds *si fieri poterat* (H), a mock-construction of the ark, the procession into the ark of a multitude of animals, a possible attempt at simulating the Flood, the flight of raven and dove, and the appearance of an unusual-looking rainbow as the waters recede. A considerable amount of playing time may have been occupied by the procession of animals alone: fifty different kinds are counted off, and the stage directions demand that for each name called a pair of animals *depicta in cartis* (H) be boarded onto the ark. Yet despite its obvious spectacular appeal of props and special effects, Pagina III dramatizes a serious event in biblical history, God's saving Noah and his kin while the world is cleansed of the lost and damned. In the Chester cycle as a whole, Noah's salvation counterbalances the sins committed before his time, exemplifies man's evolution in his relationship to God, his community and nature, and looks forward to the two remaining Old Testament pageants, which dramatize further advances in human culture and foreshadow the coming of Christ.

The difficulties faced by the Chester dramatist as he attempted to shape and interpret the events of the Flood existed on several levels. First, the Genesis account of the Flood does not contain the kinds of tension that translate easily into dramatic action; rather than personal conflict, there is only God's hatred for a vast, anonymous populace, leading to a cosmic destruction impossible to stage realistically. Second, the ark and the Flood were both favorite topics of typological and anagogical commentaries, and Noah himself was often seen as a *figura* of Christ.[48] Writing of the Wakefield Noah play, Alan H. Nelson has asserted that "Noah is a medieval man acting out the story of the Flood without discarding everything he knows from having lived after the Flood. He does not dissociate himself from his knowledge of Christ and His fulfillment of the prophesies."[49] But if Chester is to maintain its vision of the historical limitations controlling the Christian understanding of Old Testament characters, neither Noah nor his family could explicate any future, Christian significance of themselves or their actions. Finally, Pagina III must serve as the dramatic completion of history's first age and perhaps offer an implicit transition into the second age as well. Since exegetes even as sensitive as Hugh was to the interaction and progress of scriptural events rarely, if ever, contemplated how one age ended and meshed with the next, the historiological problems posed by Pagina III demanded a carefully imagined dramatic resolution.

The way the Chester dramatist solved these problems and interpreted the Noah story to conform to the historical designs of his cycle is proof of both his artistic ingenuity and his theological sophistication. The pageant as we now have it is not precisely the play he conceived, I contend, for in ten stanzas near the play's center—dramatizing the trials of marital discord and including a song of Mrs. Noah's gossips—there is a sudden break in character consistency and in Chester's "historical realism": Uxor Noe briefly turns shrewish, and she and Noah twice call out to "Christe" and "sayncte John" as they scuffle on the ship's ramp. However, as Oscar Brownstein has proved in a helpful metrical and linguistic analysis of the pageant, these few stanzas constitute a later addition to an earlier and more unified drama.[50] It is this earlier play I wish to analyze, for in certain scenes and signs which distinguish Chester's version of the Flood narrative from those of the other cycles, we may see very clearly Chester's historical hermeneutics at work.

In Chester, Noah and his family are perfect. After God mentions briefly the sins of men and the reasons they must be destroyed, Noah, responding to God's command to build the ark, immediately sets to work, without any of the grumbling he indulges in momentarily in the other cycles. Whereas Wakefield, York, and N-Town ask Noah to build the ark alone, Chester gives him the assistance of his entire family. Shem takes an axe, Ham a hatchet, and Japhet makes a "pynne" with which to bind the hull; Noah's wife brings timber, Shem's wife produces a "hackestocke," Ham's wife finds some "slytche" for caulking, and Japhet's wife gathers "chippes" with which to make the fire for dinner. Whereas Wakefield and York suggest Augustine's "factious partisanship" by Mrs. Noah's wranglings, and N-Town symbolizes the extermination of the "city of men" in an interlude dramatizing Cain's accidental slaughter, Chester's early version sustains its vision of social harmony from beginning to end. Like living didactic icons, Noah's family, tools in hand, realize the hardworking social ideal which Adam's family had hoped to achieve. Their immediate and uninterrupted willingness to buckle down and assist their patriarch—paralleled on the natural level by the animals who obediently process two-by-two into the ark—is thus a tropological *exemplum* sustained throughout the play, at the end of which the embryonic human community is granted the salvation their perfect moral behavior has merited.

The precise nature of that salvation, however, and its place within the cycle's construct of salvation history, was more than a minor problem, at least for a dramatist sensitive to the analogies between the Genesis protomyth of history and the total Christian vision of human time. Although the typological exposition of these analogies was immediately available, Noah in Chester is not interpreted as a *figura* of Christ, nor has the ark been projected as Christ's church.[51] Nevertheless, because of the nearly perfect harmony of its salvific conclusion, the Flood narrative (somewhat like the chaining of Satan and quite similar to the Harrowing of Hell) remains one of those moments in salvation history whose mythic closures appear nearly identical to eschatological completion.[52] In part because Christ himself had emphasized the similarities between the world's first and second endings (Luke 17:26, 27), the typological referent of the Flood which exegetes most often pointed to was the Last Judgment. Indeed, Chester for a moment honors this tradition, asking the audience to see in Noah's forestalled completion of the ark a subtle (and imperfect) analogue to Christ's extension of the age of mercy:

> An hundreth winters and twentye
> this shippe-makinge tarryed have I,
> if throughe amendemente thy mercye
> would fall to mankynde.

But a dramatist wishing to determine precisely the place of this triumphant protosalvation in the history of Christian salvation would have to close his Noah pageant carefully. This the Chester playwright does. First, although Noah and his family are saved and their sacrifice is accepted, God explains to them that mankind has grown physically weaker and must now be allowed to eat the flesh of clean beasts, rather than the trees and roots "yee have eaten before." Scriptural man learns at this time that, despite his moral fortitude, his powers of natural sustenance have diminished. Then, as a "verey tokeninge that you may see/ that such vengeance shall cease," God places his *arcus in nubibus*, his bow in the clouds, a "forwarde" with man which God himself interprets:

> Where clowdes in the welkyn bynne,
> that ylke bowe shalbe seene,
> in tokeninge that my wrath and teene
> shall never thus wroken bee.

The stringe is torned towardes you
and towardes me is bente the bowe,
that such wedder shall never showe;
and this behett I thee.

If God's description is accurate, the stage property used to depict
the bow in the clouds was a powerfully emblematic and strikingly
unusual configuration: rather than a covenant of concord and harmony, it is an image of savage destruction—an archer's bow aimed at
God himself, its string within man's reach. Having appeared in the
pageant's first episode "in the clowdes," God in the pageant's final
episode places in the clouds an iconic prefiguration of the Crucifixion.
God has just brought death to sinful man; but the bow in the clouds
is a prophetic reminder (for the audience) that in the future, man—
again sinful—will bring death to his own divine Redeemer.

In his commentary upon the individual plates of *The Holkham
Bible Picture Book,* W.O. Hassall has perceived in the destructive
bow of Lamech, in the tree bowing down to Noah as he constructs
the ark, and in the rainbow in the sky three arcs or arches that together "are like a window which allows rays of light to illumine [the
bending rood-tree] which they forefigure."[53] Within the limits of
my knowledge there is no definitive medieval document illustrating
the survival of the archer's bow as an image of the Crucifixion in
England (Hassall's interpretation is modern, and the significance of
the archer's bow of the Ruthwell *Dream of the Rood* Cross is debated).[54] However, on the Continent this emblem had a brief and
minor career. In an extremely useful chapter, F.P. Pickering has traced
the replacement of the harp by the bow and then by the crossbow as
late medieval images of the Crucifixion.[55] The Continental example
most closely related to Chester's use of the image is found in the
works of Gotfrid of Admont (d. 1169):

A bow consists of a piece of wood or horn, and a string, which
is a worthy representation of our Lord and Redeemer. This string
may be taken to mean his most holy body which in the various
dire tribulations (of His Passion) was wondrously spanned and
stretched. By the wood or the horn his invincible divinity is meant
which in a manner of speaking remained rigid and unbending for
the bearing of the sum of human miseries. Until the noble bow-
string, his holy body, began to be drawn in mockery, spanned

with insults and stretched to the *affixiones* (notches of the bow, nails of the Cross) for our salvation. This is the bow which the Father promised when he said: I do set my bow in the cloud.[56]

Although the image of the cruciform bow is employed in the French Angers Passion play,[57] it may in Pagina III simply be an example of Chester's theological ingenuity, a recreated rather than a received tradition. But as we shall see in forthcoming chapters, the Chester dramatist's erudition was considerable. (I should also note in passing that the Wakefield Master was apparently influenced in his Crucifixion pageant by an equally minor Continental tradition, where the cross was seen as a five-directed cross with a unicorn seat.)[58] Whether or not Chester's stage icon was a subtle or obvious sign, a longbow or a crossbow, one cannot tell. My major point, of course, is that the Chester playwright felt it necessary to place this image of the Crucifixion at this moment in Old Testament time. First, it is an image whose future and Christian significance is understood fully only by the audience; Noah's unexpressed comprehension is partial at best. Second, the bow in the clouds is an *imago veritatis* interpreted by God as Expositor and serving as a graphic transition in Old Testament history from the age of shadows to the age of images. Finally, this prefiguration of the Crucifixion emphasizes the historical, Old Testament setting of Noah's imperfect salvation. The Flood is not the Eschaton, and their good deeds alone cannot bring the *antiqui iusti* to salvation, for, as the stage icon of the *arcus in nubibus* subtly predicts, history has yet to suffer through the necessary, future sacrifice of Christ. If future persons (such as the audience) believe and understand the truths embodied in that sacrifice, then, and then only by adding to those beliefs the works of corporal mercy, may they humbly hope for true salvation at the end of Christian time.

V

"The problem of time and place in the Corpus Christi drama," Kolve has written, "is not a wholly consistent one, to which one consistent answer may be found."[59] With this general caveat I totally agree. Not only do the historical emphases vary from cycle to cycle, but within each cycle the temporal dynamics often change considerably from one group of pageants to the next. What I have been responding to in this chapter's discussion of the dramatic hermeneutics of Old Testament time has been, in part, the frequent acceptance of both the "verticality" of Christian time and the "contemporary realism" of the cycles as absolute principles.[60] Any form of absolute contemporary realism—wherein the knowledge and beliefs of Old Testament characters are conceived as equal to the knowledge and beliefs of their Christian audience—would move a cycle's implicit theology dangerously close to heterodoxy and would undermine any dramatic attempt to interpret history's horizontal patterns of spiritual development.

I have also been responding in this chapter to a widespread acceptance of typology's hermeneutical techniques and temporal patterns as principles preeminently operative in all the cycles' Old Testament plays. Typology often employs a rather mechanical interpretive system based upon a time-plan too simplistic to explain adequately the dynamics of any cycle's Old Testament pageants. Not only are the static symmetries of figural parallelism normally inimical to the continuities of dramatic action (in the Old Testament pageants only half of the parallel is of course enacted), but typology's binary vision of history is dramatically and theologically too restrictive. By positing and paralleling two moments in time which represent the Old and the New, figuration as an exegetical method is an inadequate basis for *any* artistic scheme attempting to dramatize the gradual spiritual change from the Old Testament into the Gospels and beyond. As Henri de Lubac reminds us, "typology by itself says nothing about the dialectical opposition of the two Testaments nor about the conditions of their union. It does not explain the unique passage from prophecy to Gospel."[61] In addition, typology as an exegetical technique cannot by itself determine the selection of the New Testament fulfillment, or the hermeneutical level on which that fulfillment is to be interpreted; nor, in fact, do the basic tenets of typology explain how that New Testament figural fulfillment may itself at times become a new type to be fulfilled later in salvation history.[62]

Thus I have attempted to define a set of historical principles and a complex of general hermeneutical techniques available to all the Corpus Christi playwrights. Working within these received traditions, the Chester dramatist—by emphasizing certain temporal values, by interrelating selected historical events, and by adding to Scripture certain motifs, signs, and exegetical commentaries—has succeeded in dramatizing in his Old Testament pageants an individual vision of history's principles of gradual change. That vision is prefaced by Pagina I's expression of eternity, its ceremonial representations of beatific grace, and its absolute division of good and evil; in this pageant, we have seen, the dramatic hermeneutics are "atemporal" and quite easily apprehended. But as soon as man falls in Pagina II from the perfections of paradise, Chester's mode of self-interpretation becomes "shadowy" and symbolic; the universal implications of natural man subsist holistically in his character, and the "spiritually literal" meanings of his deeds are not overlaid with any typological allusions or with allegorical glosses added by an Expositor. The exemplary qualities of history's first age are most clearly represented in the religious comedy of the "Noah" pageant, yet the pageant also makes clear to the audience that the moral grounds for Noah's "salvation" are insufficient grounds for their own. The delineations of Chester's *Heilsgeschichte* design are made most apparent in Paginae IV and V, as the interpretive code for each episode hovers close to the dramatic surface. With the assistance of the Expositor's glosses, the audience is educated straightforwardly in the cultural advances made by the age of images: its prophecies of Christ, its moral precepts, and its typological prefigurations. In contrast to the earlier historical pageants, the complex of episodes here requires a more cognitive, and less psychological, exegesis, as the meaning of history's second age is examined from the perspective of both the past and the Christian present. Thus the dramatic hermeneutics of Chester's Old Testament pageants change, shifting gradually from symbolism to signification as the shadows of early history give way to the images of Christian revelation.

Obviously the development of sacred history and the education of Christian Everyman are not completed at the initiation of the New Testament, although the light attending Christ's Nativity fulfills many Old Testament prophecies and dispels many shadows of incomprehension. Just as Christ reveals gradually in his ministry that he had come into time not to reject but to fulfill the Old Law, so the signs and shadows of history's first two ages are sustained symbolically in the incomplete faith and imperfect understanding of certain New Testament figures. The vestigial qualities of Everyman's Old Testament self are cast off slowly, and it is not until the Last Supper (dramatized in Pagina XV) that Christ can triumphantly proclaim:

> For knowe you nowe, the tyme is come
> that sygnes and shadowes be all donne.
> Therfore, make haste, that we maye soone
> all figures cleane rejecte.
>
> For nowe a newe lawe I will beginne
> to helpe mankynd owt of his sinne
> soe that hee may heaven wynne,
> the which for synne hee loste.

This proclamation suggests that the objective patterns of spiritual enlightenment have been fulfilled in history's first eucharistic feast, and that the fullness of time has come. But it is not until Pentecost that Christ's apostles are purged entirely of their natural doubts; and it is not until the abolition of time, in the Doomsday pageant, that the still imperfect Christian race completes the history of its own education and arrives at the trial of its final judgment.

Chester's vision of the patterns of salvation history and its self-interpretation as a dramatic *summa* of the central tenets of Christian faith are both dramatically integrated with its iterated insistence that the viewer rediscover his own place and progress within historical time. Thus of the three dramatic models I have been discussing, most important is that which the viewers would most easily have discerned or felt: world history seen as an oblique and corrective projection of the course of their own spiritual lives. By beginning with eternity and falling into the genesis of time, the Corpus Christi plays drew their viewers back to an examination of postlapsarian man in a fallen natural world. Chester's Old Testament interpretation of man's natural self can be compared to those English morality plays which emphasize the Adamic quality of *Humanum Genus,* the barrenness of his natural environment, his freedom of choice, and his need to cultivate his inner and outer spiritual promptings. Like the proleptic world of Chester's Old Testament plays, where God's grace gradually enlightens man's natural darkness, so the opening ambience of several of the morality plays is suggestively ante-Christian; guided by grace and prompted by a rediscovery of his fallen condition, Mankind must educate himself in the primary precepts of his faith before he can move into a New Testament world of more nearly deserved salvation.[63]

For a variety of reasons, then, I think the "Jewishness" of Chester's Old Testament patriarchs and the historicity of their actions are significant elements in the cycle's dramatic strategies.[64] Because they live in a world of Christian adumbrations, the well-intentioned Old Testament characters are treated compassionately by the cycle as projections of the human spirit in an early stage of its development. But as that development progresses beyond the threshold of the New Testament, stronger medicines and less benevolent strategies soon will obtain, and those characters who fail to cast off their "Jewish" doubts despite the revelations surrounding them will be judged with severity. As he watches the progress of world history, the viewer of the Chester cycle eventually discovers that the severer standards of New Testament judgment apply to him as well: intermittently, yet often at the cycle's most serious moments, the cycle's strategies caricature the viewer as a Christian heretic wilfully uninstructed by history's patterns of enlightenment. Although for Hugh of Saint-Victor "The ascent of individual men to God is an exact replica of the ascent of the human race throughout history,"[65] for Chester the progress of Christian history, especially in its later stages, is painfully tortuous. History's wished-for ascent to perfection, compromised repeatedly by the backslidings of human nature, is rendered so uneven that the play's thoughtful viewer may discover that the form of his own spiritual life—reflected in this world history—approximates at best "a tragedy of narrowly averted disaster."[66]

4

The Comic Structures
of Communal Celebration:
Paginae VI-XI

That some forms of dramatic activity are related to forms of ritual celebration is a critical assertion of long standing. Many years ago Gilbert Murray suggested that Greek tragedy derived much of its power from its ability to objectify the myth implicit in Dionysian rite, although in the process of this dramatic translation the tragedy was "weakened" by having lost, or severely limited, the direct, corporate participation of its cultic audience.[1] More recently and with a greater amount of supporting evidence, C. Clifford Flanigan has argued that the earliest Christian liturgical drama, while explicating the myth implicit in the Easter ceremonies, nevertheless remained ritual in both form and effect: neither purposefully representational, entertaining, or instructive, the *Visitatio Sepulchri* sought actively to involve the congregation in the event of the first Easter, an event magically transported into the present by its own imitative form.[2] The six pageants of Chester's Nativity Group are obviously further removed than is early church drama from the mysteries of ritual actualization. These pageants are clearly a kind of "realistic" drama: they are entertaining, representational, and (to a degree) instructive; they are performed in the vernacular and in a secular environment. Nonetheless, I think Chester's Nativity pageants are best understood as a group of plays that are designed at times to be similar to ritual in both form and effect. Like the liturgical celebrations of the Christmas season, these plays seek to achieve a unification of the cultic community with the incarnated presence of the newborn Christ child.

It is hardly surprising that a number of elements found in Chester's Nativity plays are elements found in the Advent/Christmas/Epiphany liturgy, as well as in the early Latin church dramas performed during this season. The Wrights' Nativity play (Pagina VI) shares some of the emotions of the Ember Days' Feast of the Annunciation and represents several of the scriptural episodes reenacted in the Christmas liturgical plays. The Painters' Shepherds' play (Pagina VII) shares a number of elements found in both simple and more complex versions of the *Officium Pastorum*, traditionally performed on Christmas Day. The Vintners' and Mercers' Magi plays (Paginae VIII and IX) include the motif of hopeful expectation iterated throughout Advent, and represent the manifestation of Christ to the Magi performed in the *Officium Stellae* on Epiphany. And the Goldsmiths' Herod play (Pagina X) focuses upon the death of the first Christian martyrs celebrated by the *Ordo Rachelis* during the Feast of the Holy Innocents.[3] Only the Blacksmiths' play (Pagina XI), entitled "De Purificatione Beatae Virginis," would appear to find its liturgical counterpart outside the general Christmas season.[4] The pageant concludes, however, with the episode of Christ among the doctors, the Gospel account of which served as a reading for the Sunday within the Epiphany octave. Thus, as Paul E. Kretzmann has noted, the drama of Christ's first entrance into the temple "served to round out the nativity series in the cycle plays, just as it practically closes the Christmas festival in the liturgy."[5]

Not only does the overall design of Chester's Nativity Group conform generally to the shape of the Christmastide liturgical celebrations, but certain ritual elements of that liturgy were obviously transported unchanged into these vernacular plays. Most notable are the many Christmas hymns sung to express the wonder of Christ's Incarnation. The harmonies of liturgical song—rarely heard in the Chester cycle after the fall of the angels from heaven and of man from paradise—constitute a recurring motif in the plays' celebrations of the *adventus dei*.[6] It could be argued that other ritualistic elements in Chester derive ultimately, if obliquely, from the Christmas liturgy. For instance, the recurring emphasis in the Christmas antiphons upon *hodie* (the repetitions of which epitomize the season's insistence that Christ is reborn in the very present for the salvation of all mankind) could be seen as a verbal, liturgical emphasis transformed by the plays into an ocular, dramatic insistence that they themselves, as affective spectacle, prove the reality of Christ's present Incarnation. But in my judgment such arguments of artistic dependence upon the Christmas rites reach a point of diminishing credibility not because they are wrong entirely, but because they depend upon a too limited field of reference and upon a rather narrow appreciation of the playwright's powers of innovation.[7] Most of the "ritual" designs employed in the Chester Nativity plays, I suggest, were novel artistic inventions conceived within a late medieval religious and aesthetic context which relates only incidentally to the rites of the Christmas liturgy.

This context may be briefly described as the "sacramental psychology of comic salvation." The most articulate expression of this late medieval psychology is the writing of Saint Bonaventure, which argues the necessity of appealing first (often by the use of affective images) to man's physical sensations and "natural" emotions in order to lead him gradually toward a more spiritual apprehension of God's divine nature.[8] The sacramental component of this affective psychology is epitomized (as we have seen in Chapter 1) by the Corpus Christi feast, which celebrates the joyful unification—effected in and by the Host—of nature and grace, the physical and the spiritual, the human and the divine. The redemptive optimism of this psychology is related, in turn, to the liberal indulgence of the senses granted by the rich music and lavish spectacle of the Nativity pageants themselves. If an iconoclast were ever to challenge the orthodoxy of these sensuous indulgences, a medieval apologist could turn to the Incarnation itself as an implicit defense. Since God had happily assumed the form of a human child, he could hardly criticize the childlike emotions of wonder and delight evoked by these comic celebrations of his birth. The Chester Nativity pageants, in other words, are a dramatic celebration of the Incarnation whose designs derive from several different imaginative contexts. They are plays unified into a group by their individual and overall comic structure, by the various "ritual" strategies they share, and by their benign vision of man's potential for salvation.

The image of the innocent, whimsical child is central to the spirit and form of Chester's comic dramatization of the Nativity. These pageants play freely with the dramatic variants of youthful pleasure—

110

high humor, vicarious delight, broad irony, and melodramatic farce— as they celebrate the triumph of innocence, energy, natural feeling, and social inferiority over their worldly, cranky, and devious opposites. Relying at times on broad character types and a humorous purgation of the old order, the pageants are even capable (like the Christmastide Boy-Bishop festivities) of playfully profaning the sacred as a way of purifying it. But their major dramatic emphasis is upon the emergence of a new social order, a *communitas* of moral equals which graciously embraces all within the drama and within the audience who willingly assent to the comedy's spiritual norms. As Northrop Frye has noted, such acts of "communion" between audience and dramatic action are typical of dramatic comedy, both religious and secular: "The resolution of comedy comes, so to speak, from the audience's side of the stage; in tragedy it comes from some mysterious world on the opposite side."[9] What distinguishes the Chester Nativity Group as a religious comedy is the ritual-like repetition of these communal resolutions and the sacramental motifs contained within them.

The image of the innocent child in these plays is consistently conflated with the image of the Blessed Sacrament, just as the pageants' various comic designs are given deeper resonance by gestures and movements reminiscent of that archetypal Christian ritual, the Mass itself. The several means by which such subtleties are accomplished, as these realistic comic plays seek a "ritual" purification of their viewing audience, will be a major concern in the following pages. Yet the fundamental purpose of the Nativity plays' sacramental motifs and ritual designs is obvious: to charge the youthful delight evoked by the plays with an underlying sense of serious purpose. Delight, pleasure, entertainment and merriment are clearly meant to dominate in these dramatic celebrations and are central to the pageants' comic designs and ritual strategies. The general benevolence of these strategies is perfectly appropriate as well, for in contrast to the mature Easter *agon*, Christ's painless Nativity suggests almost free access to salvation: medieval celebrations of the Incarnation typically crossed that *limen* dividing the old from the new, the flesh from the spirit, with a minimum of anxiety and guilt. Chester's sacramental metaphors and ritualistic elements therefore serve simply as subliminal reminders that Christ's Incarnation should be an occasion for

111

religious introspection as well as carefree merriment: that easy redemption promised so freely by the plays' comic designs may, they imply, be granted only to those who are willing to move through physical sensation to an active participation in the communal life of the spirit.

I

Pagina VI is made up of so many episodes that it has appeared to lack any sense of dramatic unity. The first episode presents the Annunciation, the second Mary's visit to Elizabeth, the third Joseph's complaint. In the fourth Octavian orders a poll tax, in the fifth Joseph is informed of the tax, and in the sixth the Holy Family travels to Bethlehem. The seventh episode presents the Nativity itself, and the last episode splices the Expositor's narrative of the miracles which occurred in Rome during the sacred birth with the dramatic interlude of Octavian's conversion. In a pageant of so many discrete episodes, some ordering principle was obviously necessary to give to these various events an observable dramatic unity. This principle is suggested by the repetition of "tokeninge," a word found here and there in *A Stanzaic Life of Christ* and in the other cycles, but developed by the Chester dramatist as a technique central to the dynamics of his Nativity Group and of preeminent importance in Pagina VI. A tokening, as defined by its uses in these episodes, is similar in meaning to the Middle English word "sonde": a preternatural event or sacred sign revealing a truth normally beyond man's ken. At times in Chester the tokening's significance is explained by an angel, at times it is directly understood by the observer, and at times it is conveyed directly by an angel without the assistance of a symbolic vehicle. At the center of six of the pageant's eight episodes, a major character is arrested in a moment of bewilderment or unenlightened ignorance by a sign or visitation from heaven. As a result of this tokening, he experiences a spiritual illumination which brings to him a fuller understanding of God's love for mankind.

This pattern of repeated illuminations through a series of divine signs is sustained throughout the pageant, both in the episodes constituting part of the pageant's earlier form as well as in those adapted later from *A Stanzaic Life of Christ*.[10] In the first episode, Mary is

112

informed by Gabriel that the fruit of her womb shall bear "endlesse liffe...renowne and ryaltye." Puzzled, she asks, "How may this bee...?" but assured by the angel that "The Holye Ghoste shall in thee light," she accepts the miracle of Christ's conception and rejoices, "Loe, Godes chosen meekelye here." Elizabeth's illumination in the second episode is immediate. At Mary's salutation, Elizabeth's child quickens in her womb, a sign convincing her of the miracle Mary bears in hers; she praises the Virgin, "Godes mother free," and Mary in turn praises God, singing the *Magnificat*. The third episode presents Joseph's befuddled inability to understand Mary's pregnancy until in a dream an angel reveals the truth, and Joseph rejoices: "A, nowe I wott, lord, yt is soe,/...Nowe Christe is in our kynde light,/ as the prophetes before hight./ Lord God, most of might,/ with weale I worshipp thee." On the journey to Bethlehem in the sixth episode, Mary has a vision of "Some men...glad and merye/ and some syghinge and sorye." The vision troubles her, and she prays, "A, lord, what may this signifye?" An angel explains that it is a "tokeninge" of the future: the weeping men are "Jewes that shalbe put behinde," the happy men "The commen people" who shall recognize Christ's divinity. The seventh episode presents the boldest expression of incomprehension, as Salome, the second midwife, *tantabit tangere Mariam in sexu secreto* to test her virginity. God's reproach is swift—her hand withers—yet mercifully brief. Directed by an angel, Salome asks forgiveness of the Christ child; she is healed immediately, and believes: "Nowe leeve I well and sickerlye/ that God is commen, man to forbye./ And thou, lord, thou art hee." Thus, in these simple domestic scenes, four characters—Mary, Elizabeth, Joseph, and Salome—accept the mystery of God's Incarnation and adore the wonder of his birth once the reality of that event is certified by divine agency or preternatural sign. Their conversion is one not so much from disbelief to belief, but from ignorance to understanding; the miracle of Christ's Nativity once recognized, they respond with joy, praise, and thanksgiving. Impressed that God should choose such "symple," "meeke," and "commen" people to witness his birth, they feel profoundly and personally blessed.

The pattern of illuminations experienced by those attending the Christ child is amplified by the episodes in which Octavian, the Roman emperor, appears. In the judgment of Robert Wilson and

Samuel Hemingway, Octavian in Chester is in his first appearance a typical Herodian figure—bombastic, angry, and ridiculous.[11] Yet a number of qualities distinguish the two earthly rulers, Herod and Octavian, even in the bravura of their opening soliloquies. Whereas Herod's estimation of the extent of his power in Chester Pagina X is totally false, Octavian's boast is quite accurate: "For wholey all this world, iwys,/ is readye at my owne will." Herod's reign brings death, but Octavian's, to his own satisfaction, has brought harmony: "Syth I was soverayne, warre cleare can cease,/ and through this world now is peace." Most significant, however, is Octavian's recognition of his human limitations. When his senators ask that he make himself a god, Octavian refuses, "For of all flesh, blood, and bonne/ made I am, borne of a womane." In words adumbrating Christ's birth, Octavian defines the power exclusive to divinity:

> And godhead askes in all thinge
> tyme that hath noe begininge
> ne never shall have endinge;
> and none of this have I.

Thus, although of high station and extensive worldly might, Octavian is a figure who in spirit differs little from the humble people near to the Christ-child. Octavian's conversion is also effected by a "tokeninge": having been told by the Tiburtine Sybil that a god is to be born among men, he asks her for a sign to "certyfye/ what tyme that lord soe royallye/ to raigne hee shal beginne." In the pageant's final episode, numerous prodigies bespeak Christ's birth— the central being the "wondrouse sight" of "a mayden bright,/ a yonge chylde in her armes clight,/ a bright crosse in his head," and an angel singing "*Haec est ara Dei caeli*."[12] With the sybil's interpretation of the Christian significance of these signs, Octavian recognizes that "this childe is prince of postye/ and I his subject," and orders "everychone" in his entire empire to worship the newborn King as his savior.

Octavian is the only worldly regal figure in any of the English cycles to be treated sympathetically. Upon hearing of Christ's birth, Caesar Augustus in Wakefield and Herod in the other cycles immediately plot to kill him. But in Chester Octavian's character and his illumination through the certification of preternatural tokenings are

114

in keeping with the dramatic pattern established in the pageant's other episodes. As Higden's *Polychronicon* reports, Octavian was a good ruler with some failings;[13] in Chester, these failings make him more human but not more sinful. Although far removed from the Nativity stable, Octavian shares with the characters attending the Christ child a longing to understand and honor this manifestation of God's love for mankind. Thus the general image of mankind in the Chester "Nativity" is remarkably egalitarian and catholic: carpenter and emperor, midwife and sybil, virgin mother and devoted friend all share equally in the light of Redemption.

The central illumination in the Chester Nativity pageant, however, is Joseph's, and it is he with whom the audience may most easily identify. Although quite "human," Mary and Elizabeth are in such close kinship with Christ that they approximate divinity and are incapable of any real doubt. Salome's expression of incomprehension, on the other hand, is too shocking to summon much fellow feeling. But, cast slightly "beneath" the audience, Joseph encourages both sympathy and a certain amount of respect. As Hardin Craig notes, Chester's depiction of Joseph is "almost serious,"[14] remaining faithful to the account of Joseph's patient and just nature as presented in Scripture. When compared to his wild raging in Wakefield and York (where he is convinced that "som man in aungellis liknesse" had beguiled Mary), and his intention to have Mary stoned in N-Town, Joseph's doubts in Chester are very mild. Chester's treatment of Joseph's conversion also differs from those of the other cycles: whereas in them Joseph repents and asks forgiveness either of God or Mary, in Chester he does neither. His response to the angel's message is a simple resolution to attend to his wife, "while I may on yearth goe," and to worship God.

The simplicity of Joseph's illumination in Chester, his "undeveloped" anger, and the lack of any conflict between him and Mary are in Eleanor Prosser's judgment all dramatic weaknesses:

> The scene is a brief insertion (fifty-three lines) in the *Nativity* and has the sole purpose of presenting facts. There is no dialogue at all between Mary and Joseph. His lament is directed to the audience, and the scene closes with his praise of God. That is, there is no meeting of the two characters, no conflict, and no reconciliation. The little scene is independent, having no struc-

115

tural link with what precedes or follows, but it can scarcely be called drama. It is a brief interlude, really a "dramatic monologue."[15]

Prosser is obviously judging Pagina VI according to a definition of dramatic form uncongenial to the pageant, although quite suitable to a play of conflict and repentance, such as the N-Town "Nativity." The Joseph "interlude," as we have seen, is structurally connected with the other episodes, although it is clear that the pageant itself is unified by an underlying dramatic principle which is not primarily didactic, or based upon causal interdependence, or concerned with the development of conflict. As Elder Olson remarks in *Tragedy and the Theory of Drama*, a plot need not have intrigue or conflict to be a plot. There are, he writes, "at least four different kinds of unifying principle in plots: the consequential, the descriptive, the pattern, and the didactic."[16] The Chester Nativity pageant, in Olson's terms, is a "pattern play," having a plot which finds its unity in the repetition of modes of behavior by a number of different characters. Each in turn experiences an illumination, a lightening of the heart, as the miracle of Christ's birth is recognized. In most episodes, this recognition is brought about by a symbolic "tokeninge," a certification of God's love through a preternatural sign. Prosser is perfectly correct in her charge that the pageant lacks conflict, for this is precisely its intent; unlike the tragic rite of passage projected in the Chester "Passion," for example, the ceremonial transitions of the "Nativity" are achieved with a minimum of anxiety and an absence of guilt.

Therefore the pageant's structural unity, its patterning of various discrete illuminations, serves as the foundation for its major strategic design—to effect in the audience a renewed recognition that Christ is born for the salvation of all. Just as each character in the play experiences a revelation and a lightening of the heart, so the play's viewers are expected to partake communally in the elation and understanding attending each recognition. Not only Joseph's lament (vide Prosser) but the entire pageant, I suggest, is "directed to the audience"; in their concelebration of this joyful occasion, the viewers are symbolically confirming that Christ's historical Incarnation reoccurs not only every year (at Christmas) but every day (as in the Mass) for the consecration of all who are received as part of his mystical body. As in the calendric rites of many cultures that celebrate the salvific advent of life, Pagina VI both commemorates and effects a "comic" transition, as the old joyfully gives way to the new. In his studies of such rituals, Victor Turner has characterized the "old" as symbolic of "structured society"—"society as a structure of jural, political, and economic positions, offices, statuses, and roles, in which the individual is only ambiguously grasped behind the social persona."[17] This everyday order of society, which we may call *societas*, is represented by the Chester dramatist in episodes four and five—the two episodes, incidentally, which fail to conform to the tokening-patterns of the rest of the play. Here, the jural, political, and economic powers of the world are symbolized (nonsatirically) by Octavian's court, by his senators, and by his taxes. The rest of the pageant's episodes and characters represent the emergence of what Turner calls *communitas*—"society as an undifferentiated, homogeneous whole," made up of "concrete idiosyncratic individuals, who, though differing in physical and mental endowment, are nevertheless regarded as equal in terms of shared humanity."[18] In celebrating the transition from *societas* to *communitas*, the Chester "Nativity" avoids any confrontation between the two orders, with the single exception of its structural keystone, episode five, in which Joseph meets Octavian's messenger "Preco." Joseph is at first intimidated by this messenger from Rome and by the impossible levy of a tenpence tax; he feels awkward about his poverty, admits he is but a "symple carpenter," and confesses he is of "greate age and noe powere." But as he recalls the angel's prophecy that Christ "should man owt of bale bringe," Joseph discovers that his remembrance of his special dream "makes me more bowld."

Joseph's emboldened spirit epitomizes the renewal of energy and hope shared by characters and viewers alike, as they shift their sense of identity from the subordinations of the past toward an image of an ideal community of spirit in a new order of time. Because the lasting realization of this new order depends upon the viewers' steadfastness of conviction, Pagina VI does not claim that the transformation is presently complete: "Nowe mans joy *beginns* to newe," exclaims Joseph, "and noye to passe awaye." Yet within the play, the ancient world is reportedly transformed: not only does Octavian order the conversion of the entire Roman Empire, but he appears to recognize even before his own conversion that because Judea is "in the middest of the world," it is the *axis mundi* of the human spirit.[19] This phrase, "in the middest of the world," repeated twice again in the same speech, serves as a geographical metaphor for the pageant's primary concern with recentering the audience's spiritual orientation upon the *axis mundi* of Christ's Incarnation. Therefore, although Pagina VI has been condemned as a pageant "singularly crowded and diffuse in its effect,"[20] we can see that the play's generosity of scope is a symbolic means of embracing all of humankind, and that its major dramatic strategy concentrates upon a single desired effect: the "sacramental" unification of the viewers with their newborn King. This unification accomplished, the pageant has succeeded in its strategic purpose: it has become a symbolic "tokeninge" itself, certifying the salvific effects of God's Incarnation and the omnipresence of his love.

Whereas Pagina VI dramatizes a series of isolated illuminations as a number of historical characters at different moments in time and different places in the ancient world recognize the tokenings of Christ's advent, Chester's next pageant, the well-known "De Pastoribus," focuses upon the process of a single illumination shared communally by its four central, "contemporary" characters. Like Pagina VI, Pagina VII is constructed as a comic celebration of the transformation of *societas* into *communitas*; but unlike the "Nativity," Chester's Shepherds' play fully examines the psychology of that transformation and explores in detail the spiritual state of its characters before, during, and after their conversion. Brilliantly comic in its characterization, naturalistic and contemporary in its representation of the shepherds' Old Testament *ethos* before it joyfully embraces the New, the pageant in its overall design is a dramatic projection of a universal rite, celebrating the wondrous transubstantiation of the flesh into the spirit. Through the use of displaced metaphors and symbolic gestures the ultimate referents of which are sacramental and ritualistic, the "De Pastoribus" objectifies the psychological process of spiritual enlightenment experienced by all faithful Christians who are summoned into communion with the Real Presence of their Savior.

There is no question that the Old Testament lives and the preliminal values of Chester's shepherds appear to be far removed from a world of sacramental identity and ritual praise. The pageant is opened by Primus Pastor, Hankin, who boasts of his diligent care of his sheep and displays the medicinal herbs with which he treats their illnesses: "henbane and horehounde,/ tybbe, radishe, and egermonde"—cures so powerful that they "woulde a whole man bringe to grownde." The second shepherd, Harvey, appears, followed by Tud, the third, who displays his sheep-salves and complains briefly about his fearsome wife. Harvey asks, "will we shape us to some solace?," and the shepherds in turn produce from under their clothing an extraordinary array of foodstuffs: bread, onions, garlic, leeks, green cheese, pudding, a "jannock," a sheep's head, a "grayne," sour milk, a pig's foot, a "panchcloute" (H), a "womb-clout" (H), liver (H), chitterlings (H), another pig's foot, "gambonns," another pudding, ox tongue (H), and ale. They consume this prodigious meal in an instant, pass the bottle round, and then blow their horn for Trowle, their apprentice tending their sheep. He appears and displays his own sheep-cures; but refusing to eat the remainder of their meal (covered, he says, with "dyrte" and "grubbes"), he suddenly challenges his masters to a wrestling match. Hankin finally accepts the challenge, only to be thrown on his back; shepherds two and three are treated to the same "solace," and Tud, dumped on the ground, complains:

> Though wee bine werye noe wonder,
> what betweene wrastlinge and wakinge.
> Ofte wee may bee in thought wee be now under.
> God amend hit with his makinge.

In response to this prayerful complaint, there suddenly appears in the heavens the star which will amend their lives completely.

Almost every critic who has examined the "De Pastoribus" has felt that some kind of symbolism has been disguised in the exhibitionist antics and pastoral pratfalls of these opening episodes.[21] The shepherds' activities and their range of values can be understood in part simply as a successful translation into dramatic form of a number of serious images and themes traditionally employed to describe the state of the world before Christ's advent. The *Legenda Aurea*, for example, offers a standard medieval definition of the plight of the Old World and its need for a Savior:

With regard to the advent in the flesh, three things should be considered: its timeliness, its necessity, and its usefulness. Its timeliness is due first to the fact that man, condemned by his nature to an imperfect knowledge of God, had fallen into the worst errors of idolatry, and was forced to cry out, "Enlighten my eyes." Secondly, the Lord came in the "fulness of time," as Saint Paul says in the Epistle to the Galatians. Thirdly, He came at a time when the whole world was ailing, as Saint Augustine says: "The great physician came at a moment when the entire world lay like a great invalid.''...

As to the usefulness of Christ's coming, different authorities define it differently. Our Lord Himself, in the Gospel of Saint Luke, tells us that He came for seven reasons: to console the poor, to heal the afflicted, to free the captives, to enlighten the ignorant, to pardon sinners, to redeem the human race, and to reward everyone according to his merits. And Saint Bernard says "We suffer from a three-fold sickness: we are easily misled, weak in action, and feeble in resistance. Consequently the coming of the Lord is necessary, first to enlighten our blindness, second to succour our weakness, and third to shield our fragility."[22]

Much of this passage can be applied to Chester, but only if one takes into account the dramatist's sustained use of comic displacement to alleviate any sternness of judgment. The Old Testament world as it is depicted in the pageant does not lie "like a great invalid"; those social and political ills so cleverly satirized in the two Wakefield shepherds' plays are scarcely alluded to; the Chester shepherds are hardly cast as a set of religious idolators. Yet the dark images of the *Legenda*—the sickness, benightedness, poverty, blindness, and spiritual fragility—are nevertheless obliquely evidenced in Chester as well. The shepherds' consuming concerns with sheep-illnesses appear like unwitting, iterated expressions of their own, spiritual dis-ease. Despite the extravagance of their (mock?) feast, they complain of their poverty; their impressive physical energy (like their gargantuan meal) may give hyperbolic, physical expression to an inner appetite which is weak and undernourished. Their occasional pieties and moderately good intentions cannot disguise their "imperfect knowledge of God." And the moral ambivalence which Rosemary Woolf has discerned in their attitudes toward their vocation[23] confirms that, although attractive in their creatural humanity, the shepherds are similar to those described in the *Legenda*: "easily misled, weak in action, and feeble in resistance." As such, the shepherds are slightly more "fallen" projections of those natural attributes the viewers all share as sons of Adam, and the shepherds' exhibitionist displays are thus only half-parodic projections of their own interior selves. In medieval iconographic tradition, saints typically held before their viewers attributes symbolic of their spiritual lives. Clowning before the audience, the shepherds unwittingly do the same for theirs: the medicines they flaunt are potentially toxic rather than restorative; their food, although prodigious in its physical bulk, is covered with "dyrte" and "grubbes"; their wrestling skills (or lack of them) succeed only in upsetting regular social order. Yet because of the comic disproportions of their physical existence and the congenial laughter they evoke, the shepherds can hardly be judge judged (cf. the *Legenda*) as "sinners": rustic clowns rather than religious scapegoats, they are destined to become, as the audience knows, apprentices to the true shepherd, who is Christ. The amused affection their childlike innocence evokes is thus heightened by the recognition that in the shepherds' self-identification with things natural subsists a rough-hewn potential for things of the spirit.

This spiritual potential is also indirectly symbolized by the shepherds' "attributes": their medicines, their mock-feast, and their wrestling-match. The innovation of these fascinating dramatic tropes can best be understood, I believe, if they are seen as displaced metaphors or physical profanations of qualities traditionally associated with the eucharistic Host. As several recent studies have shown, Christ's Nativity was understood in the late Middle Ages to be that historical event with which the worship of the Blessed Sacrament was most closely conjoined.[24] Just as the eucharistic wafer contained within it the Christ-child, so the historical adoration of Christ's Nativity represented in disguised form the ongoing communal celebration of his mystical body. The displacement of the Bethlehem manger by an altarlike structure in medieval art,[25] the identification of communicants in various liturgical practices with those who adored Christ's historical birth,[26] and the imposition of the *praesepe* on the church altar in Latin Christmas drama,[27] all confirm the dominance of this cross-identification. One exegetical example, taken from a twelfth-century Christmas sermon by Saint Aelred, should serve to epitomize this cast of mind, whereby the communal adoration of Christ at the moment of his birth is identified with the communal celebration of his mystical presence in the Mass:

> Bethlehem, the *house of bread*, is the Holy Church, in which is offered the body of Christ, that is, true bread. The manger in Bethlehem is the altar of the church. There feed the animals of Christ....In this manger is Jesus wrapped in swaddling clothes. The wrapping with swaddling clothes is the veiling of the sacrament. In this manger, under the species of bread and wine, are the true body and blood of Christ. There, we believe, is Christ, but wrapped in swaddling clothes, that is, invisible in the Sacrament. We have no greater and more evident sign of the birth of Christ than when we daily consume His body and blood at the holy altar; and when we daily see sacrificed Him who once was born for us of a virgin. Therefore, brothers, let us hasten to the manger of God; but as much as we can, let us prepare ourselves beforehand through His grace, so that united with the angels, *with pure hearts, a clear conscience, and true faith* (I Tim. v) we may sing unto the Lord in all our life and conversation: *Glory to God in the highest, and on earth peace, good will toward men.* (Luke ii 14)[28]

Of course the exegetical mode by which Aelred discovers the eucharistic bread (*panis*) represented in Christ's swaddling clothes (*pannus*) is fundamentally different from the artistic mode by which the Chester dramatist disguises the eucharistic feast in the shepherds' gross banquet. Whereas in the first instance two sacred realities are conflated by religious faith, in the second a future reality is artistically adumbrated by its profane and "fictional" inversion. Elsewhere in the Chester cycle Christ's identity as a spiritual feast is much more openly expressed. At the moment of his Resurrection, Christ steps over the bodies of the dazed soldiers and directly addresses the audience:

> I am verey bread of liffe.
> From heaven I light and am send.
> Whoe eateth that bread, man or wiffe,
> shall lyve with me withowt end....
>
> And whosoever eateth that bread
> in synne and wicked liffe,

122

> he receaveth his owne death—
> I warne both man and wiffe.

Addressing the audience at this moment of ocular communion, a moment when, according to J.W. Robinson, "the dramatic experience is...temporarily transformed into what is really a religious rite,"[29] Christ demonstrates for the faithful the self-evident identity of his body as the "verey bread of liffe." But the shepherds' prodigious feast is hardly identical with that spiritual bread which will nourish the multitude throughout Christian time; rather, it is a disguised and deformed "Old Testament" adumbration of the Nativity *epiphania*, the feast for the eyes with which the pageant concludes.

Christ's Resurrection Testament can also assist in our discovering the likely genesis of the shepherds' medicaments for their flock. Like the moral ambivalence of the shepherds themselves, their cures are also apparently ambiguous—both tonic and toxic in their effect. So too is the salvific Bread of Life. Glossing 1 Corinthians 11:28-29, Christ in his Resurrection "Appeal to Man" explains that although the sacrament of his Body may bring eternal life, it will bring eternal death to "whosoever eateth that bread/ in synne and wicked liffe." The most disguised dramatic trope is probably the wrestling match, yet this, too, can be seen as a translation into physical, parodic form of another power accorded the eucharistic Host. As evidenced in all the English cycles, Christ's charismatic presence has the power—normally held in reserve—to put down the mighty: the soldiers in N-Town arresting Christ are suddenly felled to the ground by an invisible force; without ever being touched by his divine adversary, Satan in the Harrowing of Hell pageants topples back in defeat as Christ enters; in the Resurrection plays the soldiers who swear "Yf that he ryse, wee shall found/ to beate him adowne" are themselves prostrated and immobilized by his resurrected Presence. The Corpus Christi wafer shares the same spiritual strength. In the Chester Antichrist pageant, for example, the two men resurrected from death by Antichrist appear to offer irrefutable proof of their master's powers until the sacramental bread is brought before them: blinded and stunned, they fall back in confusion, as the fraud of Christ's archparodist is triumphantly exposed.

Once these three dramatic tropes—the feast, the medicines, and the wrestling match—are seen as foreshadowings of the Host's powers to nourish, to save, and to "defeat," then it is essential that the degree and the mode of Chester's metaphoric displacements be immediately underscored. Whatever parallels do exist between the physical burlesque and the Reality itself are carefully integrated into the comic naturalism of the shepherds' activities. Erwin Panofsky, while studying the growing realism of medieval Netherlandish painting, has traced the gradual disappearance of once obvious Christian symbols into an increasingly naturalistic landscape, so that finally, to the untrained viewer, symbols become so "hidden" that they appear indistinguishable from everyday things.[30] Chester's dramatic tropes are obviously near the end of this artistic spectrum: hovering in their meaning between ante-type and anti-type, Chester's symbols blend perfectly with their Old Testament environment. The probability that a majority of the play's viewers would fail to perceive these things as disguised eucharistic types does not appear to have troubled the Chester dramatist at all, presumably because the dramatic environment in which they appear is comic, rather than satirically didactic, in design. In the *Digby Mary Magdalene*, by way of contrast, it is essential that the prodigious feasts of the secular potentates be seen as sacrilegious indulgences antithetical to the "repast contemplatiff" of Christ, who as the eucharistic "oble" sustains the Magdalene for years in the wilderness.[31] In the "De Pastoribus," however, it is sufficient simply to enjoy the "solace" of the shepherds' buffooneries as farcical play-and-game, and then to discover the higher "solace" of the pageant's concluding episodes, as the shepherds' fleshly existence is transformed into one of spiritual vocation. In the playful festivities of these opening episodes we find a concrete illustration of Kolve's (overly general) thesis that the cycles are deliberately antiillusionistic,[32] for I am convinced that the fun of these scenes was heightened by the use of special theatrical effects: by ludicrous, antinaturalistic stage properties for all the medicinal wares and foodstuffs, and by highly exaggerated histrionics in the staged wrestling match.[33] Yet even the pageant's self-conscious finger-pointing at its own illusionistic form may be part of its dramatic manipulation of eucharistic metaphors. That the palpable, natural bread—once consecrated—contained hidden within it a physical Presence which the senses would determine an illusion but faith renders real was a mystery evoking the wonder of all medieval believers, both high and low. Saint Thomas, as we have seen in Chapter 1, expresses this wonder in his Corpus Christi *lectio*, and Saint Aelred, in his Christmas sermon, shares the same fascination with the "swaddling-clothes" of the Host's natural appearance. By unveiling in its early, "Old Testament," episodes the illusionistic tricks of its mimetic form, the Chester Shepherds' pageant prepares the way for a dramatic pilgrimage from things natural and deceptive to things spiritual and real.

This transition, comic in its urgencies and exciting in its discoveries, constitutes the pageant's pivotal scenes, for the enlightenment experienced by the shepherds as they cross the threshold of the two testaments projects a universal enlightenment shared by all who discover Christ's Real Presence in their lives. When the star suddenly appears in the heavens, the shepherds are amazed by its brilliance ("now is it nigh daye"), confused, and frightened. Trowle prays:

> Lord, of this light
> send us some sight
> why that it is sent.
> Before this night
> was I never soe afright
> of the firmament.

In answer to his prayer, an angel appears, singing the famous hymn (the first response at Matins on Christmas Day): *Gloria in excelsis Deo et in terra pax hominibus bonae voluntatis.* Although the shepherds fail to see the angel, they are determined to decipher his words—"Expounded shall yt bee"—and set about like "an idiot critical-panel" (Kolve's perfect phrase) to gloss the import of the heavenly song. Tud thinks "hit was 'grorus glorus' with a 'glee'," Hankin is certain "yt was 'glorus glarus' with a 'glo'." Tud suspects "hee was some spye,/ our sheepe for to steale"; Trowle is convinced "On tyme hee touched on 'tarre'"—therefore he came at night "our tuppes with tarre to teale." Despite their small Latin and limited hermeneutical training, they slowly begin to piece the song together: Tud remembers "celsis," Hankin "pax," and Harvey "hominibus." They get excited, nearing the end, as all the pieces begin to fit:

> Tertius Pastor
> Yett, yett, hee sange more than all this,

125

for some word is worthye a forder.
For hee sange "bonae voluntatis";
that is a cropp that passeth all other.

Garcius

Yett and yett he sange more to;
from my mynde yt shall not starte.
Hee sange alsoe of a "Deo";
me thought that heled my harte.

And that word "terra" hee tamed—
therto I toke good intent.
And "pax" alsoe may not be blamed;
for that to this songe I assent.

Overjoyed by their success in expounding such a difficult text, the shepherds sing "a mery songe us to solace," as they walk, then run, toward Bethlehem to honor Christ. On their way, the star leading them suddenly stops, the shepherds stumble to a halt, thinking "our Savyour is found" (H), but the angel appears again and redirects them to Bethlehem. Welcomed by Mary and Joseph, the shepherds have trouble deciding who should adore the Child first, finally accord the honor to the eldest, and each in turn offers the infant his gifts.

In the shepherds' maladroit exposition of the angel's song, in their growing excitement as they turn from things earthly to things heavenly, and in their Alphonse-and-Gaston procession to Bethlehem there is a joyful and comic demonstration of the spiritualizing effects of Christ's Incarnation. "The entire theme of the Incarnation," according to the twentieth-century theologian Alan W. Watts, "is the transformation of manhood into God—the birth or awakening of the divine and eternal nature in man as his true Self."[34] The sixteenth-century Chester shepherds, as they slowly begin to understand that a man-God has been born for their salvation, experience an awakening of the divine in themselves, as their natural desires are transformed into a spiritual yearning to see their Savior. The psychological process of the shepherds' transformation also conforms perfectly with the tenets of Bonaventuran epistemology. For Bonaventure, the journey of man's knowledge to God perforce begins with the delights and the desires of the senses, not only because of the limitations of human cognition (the shepherds fully illustrate such limits), but because complementing the physical senses are the five inner, spiritual senses—extensions of the first which have the power of restoring them to their proper place:

> Indeed every sense seeks its proper sense object with longing, finds it with delight, and never wearied, seeks it again and again, because "the eye is not filled with seeing, neither is the ear filled with hearing." In the same way, our spiritual senses must seek with longing, find with joy, and time and again experience the beautiful, the harmonious, the fragrant, the sweet, or the delightful to the touch. Behold how the Divine Wisdom lies hidden in sense perception and how wonderful is the contemplation of the five spiritual senses in the light of their conformity to the senses of the body.[35]

As the opening episodes of the pageant amply demonstrate, the shepherds' preliminal lives are founded upon the delights of the physical senses—touch, smell, and taste especially. But as the shepherds react to the inexpressible brilliance of the star and the divine melody of the angel's song, sight and hearing transformed into spiritual senses are now for the first time in their lives brought into play. The shepherds are hardly in immediate control of this new level of spiritual sensation: they are nearly blinded by the star; they fail entirely to see the angel; and although they hear the angel's song, they have trouble recollecting what they had heard. Yet in the course of their journey, even in its early stages, they make heroic progress, especially in their ability to hear spiritually: the joys of spiritual sight, which for Bonaventure was the most magical of senses,[36] are reserved for their arrival at Bethlehem. Thus it is the shepherds' ardent desire to hear and to follow the angel's song which represents most directly the spiritual transformation they undergo. To be "united with the angels," Aelred beseeches his brethren to sing the *Gloria* as they hasten to the manger. The shepherds, as they stumble toward Bethlehem, are understandably more humble: they do not try to reproduce the *Gloria*, but simply sing a "merey song us to solace." Nevertheless, they are men made in God's image, for as any medieval theory of music will assert, in the fit proportions of such earthly melodies subsist harmonies symbolic of heavenly grace.[37]

The shepherds' spiritual procession, progressing from a world of deformed adumbration and parodic illusion to a world of self-defining Reality and "spiritual" seeing, objectifies an inner process of growth.[38] As in Bonaventure's analysis of the stages of this growth, so in the shepherds' pilgrimage, we see how "Sense perception begins in delight and ends in transcendent delight, as language and desire retranslate, in tangible expression, the metaphor of the body."[39] Within the comic designs of the pageant, the age-old dualities of body and spirit vanish: rejecting its unnatural deformities, nature is fulfilled in grace; the physical senses learn to apprehend the spiritual; humanity is divinized, yet remains wonderfully human. Finally seeing the marvel of God Incarnate before them, the shepherds respond spontaneously and with touching simplicity. Kneeling before the child, each offers him a gift as a token of his esteem: the first shepherd presents him with a bell, the second a "flackett" and "spoone," the third a cap, and Trowle his "wyves ould hose," a gift he recognizes is meagre, so he offers his "good harte" and his "prayers tyll death doth mee call." In all the Group MSS, the shepherds are attended by boys who proffer gifts as well: a bottle, a hood, a whistle, a nut-hook. Unlike the gifts in the Wakefield *Secunda Pastorum*,[40] these gifts carry no disguised allegorical significance, apparently because the world of figures has given way to their Reality; as in the popular medieval Marian legends, the only import the givers' gifts need bear is the loving adoration with which they are offered.

Had the "De Pastoribus" ended with the shepherds' adoration, its design as a religious comedy would have been roughly similar in structure to the two Wakefield shepherds' pageants, but Chester adds another stage in the spiritual process, one which adds balance to the pageant's form, gives further weight to its serious conclusion, and emphasizes the sacralizing effect the sight of Christ has upon Christians. Since I have been emphasizing the pageant's sacramental metaphors and processional shape, a passage from the *De Imitatione Christi* which summarizes the ideal effects of Communion should serve as an appropriate gloss for the play's conclusion:

> For thys hyghe worthye sacrament ys the helthe of soule/ and body. It is the medycyne of all spyrytuall sekenes, in the whyche my synnes be heyleed, passyons be refrayned, temptacions be ouercome/ and mynysshed, more great graces be gyuen, the

vertue begonne increased/ faythe ys enestablysshed/ hope ys
made stronge and fortyfyed/ charyte is brannynge & spred
abrode.[41]

In Chester the ideal therapeutic effect of the vision of Christ is
dramatized by a radical conversion in the lives of all four shepherds,
as each undergoes a complete change of vocation: the first decides
henceforth he will be a "hermitte...to walke by stye and by streytt,/
in wildernes to walke for aye"; the second will return homeward to
preach God's work "Singinge alway" (H); the third will preach "Over
the sea"; and Trowle intends to become "an anker herby" and "in
my prayers wach and wake." Having changed from shepherds of
sheep to shepherds of men, these perfect believers dramatize what it
now means to live a life *in imitatione Christi*: "vertue" is increased,
"faythe ys enestablysshed," "hope ys made stronge," and "charyte
is brannynge & spred abrode."

Because of the disguised eucharistic symbolism employed early in
the pageant, the procession motif at its center, and the communal
sharing of the sight of Christ near the end, the "De Pastoribus" en-
tertains some distant analogies with the rite of the Mass. This association is perhaps long-standing, for many of the early paraliturgical
dialogues between the celebrant and the *pastores* took place either
immediately before the Introit of the first Mass of Christmas, or at
its very close, in place of the *Ite, missa est*.[42] Chester's ritual design
becomes most visible at its conclusion. The four shepherds first
exchange the *osculum pacis*: "In youth/ we have bine fellowes,
iwys," says the first shepherd, "Therefore lend me your mouth,/ and
frendly let us kysse." After this ceremonial display of their ideal
sense of human community, the third shepherd, in the Group MSS,
asks them all to sing "Amen." Since it is the group MSS which
include the four shepherd-boys, it is likely, as Nan Cooke Carpenter
has suggested, that they were four choirboys who first sang Gabriel's
Gloria and now sing "an effective, melismatic *Amen*."[43] After this
ceremonial closure, the shepherds go their separate ways, as if the
final words of the Mass had been proclaimed: *Ite, missa est*.

Pagina VII thus dramatizes the slow learning of the mystery of
Christ's Nativity and the significance it holds for all men of good
will. As in the *Officium Pastorum*, where the climax of dramatic
action is the shepherds' exulting *Iam vere scimus*,[44] the pivotal scene

in the Chester "De Pastoribus" is the deciphering of the angel's message, a moment of "seeing" which leads naturally to the sight of the Child and the spiritual conversion his Real Presence effects. Assisting in the audience's understanding of the nature of this spiritual conversion are the symbols of light and music—symbols central to the liturgical celebrations of Christmas vespers and Corpus Christi[45]— but translated here into dramatic "realities" which objectify the sense transformations of enlightenment.

As in the pageant preceding it, a major motif is the ease with which Christ's presence can effect the transformation of *societas* into *communitas*, of painless *tristia* into shared *gaudium*. But in the "De Pastoribus," much more dramatic focus is given to the characters' state of spiritual confusion before their illumination, to the process of discovery and recognition itself, and to the therapeutic effects that recognition has upon the order of their lives. Unlike the "Nativity," this play is a comedy in the more popular sense as well, for its early episodes are full of humor, pratfalls, and theatrical burlesque; but the accomplished form of the "De Pastoribus" is that of a festive religious celebration, where the "darker" elements of the community are treated benevolently, rather than satirically. If the consecrated Host unites flesh with spirit, the play's highest aim is to do the same in its viewers who, like the shepherds, have come "before" Christ to honor Him.[46] Thus the Chester dramatist refuses to censure those characters who are destined to enter the city of God, in part because their innocence will contrast sharply with the cunning wickedness of those who do not rejoice in Christ's birth, and in part because the audience's early laughter at the shepherds is ideally converted by the pageant's comic strategies into a joy shared with them, and then into an admiration for them, as the perfect effect of the sight of Christ is displayed by their exemplary responses.

II

Chester Paginae VIII and IX, "De Tribus Regibus Orientalibus" (H) and "De Oblatione Trium Regum," were originally (possibly along with Pagina X as well) part of a single pageant later divided and amplified to provide dramatic material for two new guilds.[47] Influenced in a number of passages by *A Stanzaic Life of Christ*, they dramatize the Magi's pilgrimage to the Christ-child and the beginnings of a counterplot, Herod's attempted vengeance. Unlike the Nativity Group's first two pageants, which focus upon the patterns of spiritual transformation, these two, briefer, plays concentrate on the qualities of unmediated spiritual opposites. In addition, they are concerned with offering a theological understanding of Christ's Nativity, one which interprets the Incarnation as the central event of scriptural time. To this point Chester's Nativity plays have been slightly out of the ordinary in the sense that religious intellection, in every episode, has been subordinated totally to the evocation of religious feeling. The York Nativity Group, by contrast, is opened with 144 lines delivered by "Prologue" explaining the meaning of Christ's birth; Wakefield weaves into its Nativity pageants a clever interpretation of Christ as the beguiler deceiving the arch-beguiler, Satan; N-Town, the most patently "intellectual" of the cycles, opens its Nativity sequence with a theological debate between the four daughters of God. Yet, as the Sarum Christmastide liturgy insists, knowledge must complement faith;[48] in Chester, this knowledge is supplied in Paginae VIII and IX by the recitation of numerous prophecies—Old Testament prophecies which Christ's birth has fulfilled, and New Testament prophecies auguring the works of his ministry and the saving grace of his Passion. Undoubtedly influenced by the prophetic motifs of the Advent and Christmas liturgies, the recitation of prophecy in Chester is hardly a high form of religious intellection, but for an audience whose majority was illiterate, "scholarly" readings from Scripture were surely impressive validations of Christ's historical reality. In these two pageants dramatizing the dynamics of spiritual opposition, the prophecies recited within them successfully demonstrate that Christ is the embodiment of spiritual unity and the perfect conjunction of the Old Testament and the New.

An extended interpretation of Christ's birth as the fulfillment of various Old Testament prophecies is offered by a scholar attached to Herod's court. Vexed by the Magi's news of a newborn king, Herod calls upon his "Doctor" to read from the prophets to determine the validity of the wise men's quest. The scribe, much to Herod's displeasure, reads at length from the prophecies of Jacob, Daniel, Michah, Isaiah, and David, and certifies that indeed the coming of the King of kings had been foretold. In seven rhyme-royal stanzas, interrupted regularly by Herod's ragings, the Doctor builds up an edifice of historical proof so incontrovertible that he is forced to conclude: "My lord, by prophecie is proved you beforne/ that in Bethlem should be borne/ a child to save that was forlorne/ and rule all Israell." Although Hardin Craig characterizes the scribe's extended scriptural citations as so much "padding,"[49] these verifications from the past of Christ's present advent as the promised Redeemer are, I believe, central to the pageants' comic design. Learnedness, often the butt of satiric humor, can, in the form of sacred and even arcane learning, serve as a weapon of gleeful triumph and comic justice, whereby the high and pompous are hilariously discomfited. In the Benediktbeuren Christmas play, for example, there is a protracted "learned" debate between Augustine and the prophets on one side and Archisynagogus and his followers on the other. Although Archisynagogus's opening rebuttals have the appearance of logic, it is obvious he is not winning the contest; he thus gets increasingly more sarcastic and illogical until he is consumed finally in a manic fit, *movendo corpus et caput, et direndo praedicta* (agitating his body and head, and deriding the prophecies).[50] Similar in its dynamics, Chester's combat between scriptural learning and heretical antagonism is even more comically lopsided (Herod goes into a rage immediately) and delightfully ironic: it is through the agency of his own scribe, merely obeying his master's orders, that Herod's sensitive spleen is aggravated.

Complementing the Doctor's exposition of past prophecy is the Magi's exposition of the meaning of their gifts in Pagina IX. In a series of glosses taken almost directly from the *Stanzaic Life*, the Magi interpret the symbolism of their gifts on a number of exegetical levels.[51] The first is pragmatic: gold will assist Mary in her poverty, incense will cleanse the "stynke of the stable," and myrrh will be used to anoint "the childes members—head and knee." The kings then interpret their gifts symbolically: gold "should be given him dewlye/ because of temporalitye," incense is given "in name of sacrifice," and myrrh is to "balme him" since he will "dye on roode-tree." The kings interpret their gifts once again, each glossing all three oblations. According to the first king, gold represents kingly power, incense godhead, and myrrh bodily death. For the second king, gold symbolizes love, incense prayers, and myrrh death; for the last, gold is godhead, incense "a roote of great devotyon," and myrrh "cleane flesh both quicke and dead."

These two episodes fully compensate for the absence of overt theology in the two preceding pageants: the recitation of Herod's scribe emphasizes the fulfillment of prophecies in Christ's birth; the Magi's allegorical interpretations of their gifts predict the triumphant consummation of Christ's future ministry in his death. The "intellectual" unity these prophecies give to salvation history is thus a theological foil to Herod's absurd opposition to both the Magi's faith and God's divine plan. According to the *Stanzaic Life*, it was necessary that the Magi see the "signe" of the star, for "signes verrayly shewede bene/ to sich as knowen not God expresse,/ that they moun leue thyng that thai sene."[52] But in Chester the Magi's faith is perfect; they need not move, like the shepherds, from partial ignorance to "expresse" knowledge, for they are of the few who believe before they see. In their prophetic pronouncements that articulate what Marius Sepet has called "la voix de l'Eglise,"[53] the Magi represent an exemplary ideal against which Herod's vain stupidity and hateful wrath can easily be measured.

Herod was undoubtedly intended in the English cycles to evoke laughter: ranting and strutting before the audience, frantically drinking wine, brandishing his sword, swearing by Mahound, and waxing "nere wood," he is a grotesque tyrant and a parody of kingship. Like the character called "Strength" in the *Pride of Life*, who flaunts his powers, flytes with all adversaries, and flourishes his sword continually,[54] Herod is a theatrical personage conceived in secular, as well as religious, dramatic traditions. In part because of his affinity with these secular dramatic traditions, where "Playing is pure entertainment, diversion, patently worldly and ultimately unreal,"[55] Herod can be seen as performing the role of diversionary scapegoat to the audience's inventive jibes. Yet in the context of the Corpus Christi cycles, as Murray Roston has noted, Herod is far from being a totally comic figure.[56] In Chester, particularly, his blasphemies are more shocking than they are laughable because the power he claims to possess are both parodic of Christ's future powers and hyperbolic expressions of an earthly might which he will shortly wield with devastating effect:

> I kinge of kinges, non soe keene;
> I soveraigne syre, as well is seene;
> I tyrant that maye both take and teene
> castell, towre, and towne!

> I weld this world withouten weene;
> I beate all those unbuxone binne;
> I drive the devills all bydeene
> deepe in hell adowne.

> For I am kinge of all mankynde;
> I byd, I beate, I loose, I bynde;
> I maister the moone. Take this in mynd—
> that I am most of might.

Herod is the first figure in the New Testament pageants to represent the active forces of evil opposing God's will and determined to confound the happiness of the children of light. A few "dark" moments preceding Herod's appearance can be isolated in the Chester Nativity Group: Salome's testing of Mary's virginity, for instance, and Trowle's unwitting parody, in physical combat, of the spiritual powers of Christ's Blessed Body; but Salome repents immediately, and Trowle is converted to a life of preaching. Herod, in contrast, responds in an opposite way to the "tokeninges" presented to him of Christ's divinity: finally convinced of the validity of the prophecies, he only hardens in his antagonism. Herod's soul is obviously cast beyond the pale of repentance the moment he appears on stage, and his evil is only moderately mitigated by the ludicrous excesses of his wrath. Although these excesses may be curiously comic in themselves, the fact that Herod is indeed king "most of might" adds edge to his threats and terror to his machinations.

The result of these machinations is dramatized in Pagina X, "De Occisione Innocensium ex Heredis Tirannica Persuasione," where the spiritual opposition established in the Magi pageants climaxes in violent conflict and painful suffering. The pathos evoked by the slaughter of the innocents is obviously a threat to the comic spirit which so far has controlled Chester's communal celebrations of Christ's advent. Although the liturgy for Holy Innocents' Day is notable for the emphasis it places upon the eschatological symbolism of the slaughter, its responses to the children's death are in the main joyful, for these innocents are the first to be led into heaven as triumphant Christian martyrs.[57] Similarly, in the Fleury play *Ad Interfectionem Puerorum* the death of the children (represented by choirboys) is far from tragic, for they immediately rise again, as an angel summons them to heaven, and enter the choir rejoicing and praising Christ.[58] But such happy resurrections and liturgical rejoicing in a Corpus Christi cycle would clash violently with the naturalism of its more realistic mode. To sustain the comic designs of its Nativity Group, the Chester Herod pageant somehow had to embrace the tragedy of undeserved suffering within a larger and comic dramatization of transcendent joy and divine justice.

The pageant opens with Herod's ordering his soldiers to "mar that mysbegotten marmosett/ that thinkes to marre mee" (H). His knights, Sirs Grymball and Lancherdeepe, are at first disappointed their adversaries are to be so young, "all knave-children within two yeere/ and on daye ould." Grymball complains, "A villanye yt weare, iwys,/ for my fellowe and mee/ to sley a shitten-arsed shrowe," but Herod cheers up his soldiers, "you shall sley...a thousand and yett moo," and the knights begin to boast of their prowess in the coming battle, imagining that Sampson himself might be among their foes. The knights' delusions of grandeur, and the dramatic assurance offered in the next episode that the Holy Family will safely escape Herod's wrath, mitigate some fears of the encroaching slaughter. But the killing of the children is a chilling event, made even more gruesome by the pleasure the knights take in their work. In the scene of battle, represented on stage by the two knights fighting two "Mulieres" trying to protect their sons, Lancherdeepe jests with "Secunda Mulier" (H) about her son's imminent death:

> Dame, thy sonne, in good faye,
> hee must of me learne a playe:
> hee must hopp, or I goe awaye,
> upon my speare ende.

Although the wives are finally overpowered by the soldiers, they succeed in out-flyting their adversaries and achieve a verbal triumph in the face of physical defeat. "Secunda Mulier," hammering on

Lancherdeepe's armor, abuses him with words as she encourages her ally to press on into battle:

> Saye, rotten hunter with thy gode,
> stytton stallon, styck-tode.
> I reade that thou no wronge us bode
> lest thou beaton bee.
> Wherto should we longer fode?
> Laye we on them large lode.
> There bassnetts be bygge and broade;
> beates on now, letts see.

Despite the fierce resistance of the women, the children are killed, and the stark reality of their deaths is inescapably unjust. Their mothers are offered no heavenly consolation, as is, for example, Rachel by "Consolatrix" in the Laon *Ordo Stellae*: "*Namque tui nati uiuunt super astra beati*" (Now your blessed infants live above the stars).[59] For the audience, however, the innocents' death is not completely tragic. Although unsuccessful in their attempts to save the children, the women succeed in partially converting the slaughter into a moral victory of the righteous. That emboldened energy and spiritual strength felt by Joseph and by the shepherds when they see the truth is personified here in the women, whose valiant courage offsets the cowardly depravity of Herod's men. This exposure of the moral absurdity of evil is, as Ernst Curtius notes, typical of medieval martyrologies: "The pagans, the devils, the men of evil may behave as savagely as they will—they are the fools, and the saint reduces them *ad absurdum*, unmasks them, dupes them."[60]

Thus the comic elements of the battle mitigate some of the fearful elements of the tragedy, for the dramatic focus is not upon the Christ-child, nor upon the speechless innocents, nor upon Herod, but rather upon the attenuated variants of pious awe and impious rebellion—the feisty wives and the cowardly knights. Had Chester's Herod play concluded with the innocents' death, however, as do the York and Wakefield versions, its primary consolation would be limited to the catharsis of martyrdom. Chester concludes with a deeper sense of justice. Herod dies, and his death is caused not by divine retribution alone, as in N-Town and the Digby "The Killing of the Children,"[61] but as a result of his own wrathful acts as well. Toward the end of the slaughter, Secunda Mulier reveals that the boy under her protection "was not myne, as you shall see;/ hee was the kinges sonne." Told of his son's death, Herod waxes wroth one last time, and this time his anger progresses into an intimation of justice, for his son, the future king, has been killed by his own father's attempt to manipulate the future. "Yt is vengeance, as drinke I wyne,/ and that is now well seene," Herod exclaims, and that vengeance takes the remainder of its toll as he suddenly shrivels up and dies on stage, legs and arms rotting:

> Alas, my dayes binne now donne!
> I wott I must dye soone.
> Booteles is me to make mone,
> for dampned I must bee.
> My legges roten and my armes;
> that nowe I see of feindes swarmes—
> I have donne so many harmes—
> from hell comminge after mee.
>
> I have donne so much woo
> and never good syth I might goo;
> therfore I se nowe comminge my foe
> to fetch me to hell.
> I bequeath here in this place
> my soule to be with Sathanas.
> I dye now; alas, alas!
> I may no longer dwell.

Although Herod's machinations had threatened to convert the Nativity Group's communal celebration into an anxious rite of passage, the pathos of the stage death of the one child not Herod's is triumphantly replaced by the audience's gleeful delight in Herod's ludicrous and just death. The pageant's melodramatic scales of justice were obviously already tipped in the audience's favor by the tyrant's recognizing his responsibility for his own ruin: having but taught bloody instruction, he lives only long enough to see that instruction return as a literal plague to its inventor. Then, as the ultimate deflation of evil, Herod is granted a stage exit as ignominious as his dying: a demon from hell, after exchanging taunts with the audience, indecorously lugs off Herod's corpse, "in woe ever to dwell."

The last episode of the pageant complements the solace of Herod's death with the dramatic reassurance that Christ has escaped unscathed. An angel comes to the Holy Family, assures them "dead is now your enimye," and leads them back to Judea. As they proceed, the angel gives final emphasis to the prophetic fulfillments of Paginae VIII and IX, singing: "a worde was sayd in prophecye/ a thousands yeares agoe:/ *Ex Egipto vocavi Filium meum, ut salvum faciet populum meum.*" Thus Pagina X, concluding on a double note of triumph, succeeds in converting the potentially tragic threat of Herod into a comic demonstration of divine justice. In their dramatic structure the three Magi/Herod plays differ from the earlier Nativity pageants: rather than celebrating the illuminations of God's chosen people, they melodramatically oppose innocence and evil, truth and falsehood. But in their further fulfillments of prophecy, in the dramatic death of disbelief, and in the salvation of the Christ-child, these three pageants are shaped as a religious comedy, befitting the patterning of joyful celebration which controls the Nativity Group as a whole.

III

The concluding pageant of the Nativity Group, although entitled "De Purificatione Beatae Virginis," is actually a series of three discrete scenes, each occurring in the temple: its first two episodes, Simeon's accepting the miracle of the virgin birth and the Virgin's presentation at the temple, have been influenced by the *Stanzaic Life*;[62] the third was derived in large part from York XX, "Christ with the Doctors in the Temple."[63] Although slightly confused in its adaptation of the York pageant, Pagina XI celebrates—as do the preceding Nativity pageants—the "tokeninges" which attest to Christ's divinity, the triumph of sacred truth over doubt, and the joyful emergence of the new order out of the old. The first episode opens with the old order, as Simeon, the ancient "preist in Jerusalem," reads in Isaiah that a virgin shall conceive and bear "Emanuell." Although he has waited faithfully throughout his life for the Savior's advent, Simeon is convinced of a scribal error, erases "a virgin," and writes in "a good woman." While he converses with Anna, the priestess of the temple, an angel corrects the text in red letters. Returning, Simeon is astonished by the change, but corrects the passage again; the angel reappears, rewrites "a virgin," this time in gold letters, and Simeon is finally convinced of the validity of the scriptural prophecy. In response to Simeon's prayer, "Lett me never death tast, lord full of grace,/ tyll I have seene thy childes face," the angel appears before the priest promising, "death shall thou never see/ tyll thou have seene Christe verey."

The pageant's second episode opens with Joseph and Mary appearing before Simeon in the temple, offering doves and "virgin waxe" as a token of Mary's purity. Immediately recognizing their son as the Messiah, Simeon welcomes Christ fervently and embraces the child in his arms:

> Welcome, Christ my saviour!
> Welcome, mankyndes conqueroure!
> Welcome, of all fruites the flowre,
> welcome with all my harte!...
>
> Though I bere thee nowe, sweete wight,
> thou rulest mee as yt is right;
> for through thee I have mayne and myght
> more then through waye of kynde.

After singing the *Nunc dimittis*, Simeon prophesies the triumphs and sufferings of Christ's adult ministry, and the episode concludes with Anna's further adoration of the child:

> that thou art commen, Christ verey;
> this wott I well by many a way.
> Therfore I honour thee now and aye,
> my Christ, my creatour.

In the pageant's final episode Christ appears before the three priests in the temple as a young boy claiming, "The kingdome of heaven is in me light." The three doctors patronize the unknown upstart, but after Christ recites and explicates the Decalogue, they concede that he indeed is divinely guided. The most skeptical of the priests, Tertius Doctor, is the first to recognize Christ's divinity: "I hould him sent from the high justice/ to wynne agayne our heritage." Mary and Joseph then retrieve their "lost" son, and an angel closes out the pageant, summarizing for the viewers the import of the events they have just seen.

It could be argued that Pagina XI, when compared to the anagogical richness of its liturgical counterparts, demonstrates how vernacular drama often lost more than it gained by explicating the mythic narratives implicit in the liturgical rites: it was obviously beyond the powers of the pageant's mimetic form to interpret, for instance, Mary's and Christ's entrances into the temple as the preparation for and consummation of the mystical marriage between the Bride (the church) and her Bridegroom (Christ).[64] Yet in many ways Pagina XI offers an appropriate dramatic closure to the comic designs, religious celebrations, and sacramental motifs of Chester's Nativity Group. Simeon's mild consternation before he understands the angel's "trick" and Christ's precocity as he flabbergasts the sages call once again for bemused merriment as the old order awkwardly confronts the new. Like the other father-types (Herod excluded) in the Nativity pageants, Simeon and the doctors are not the butts of satire but only slightly wayward old men whose good intentions are revealed the instant that they recognize Christ's divinity.

Of equal importance is the conclusion Pagina XI gives to the Nativity Group's sustained plot—a variant of the archetypal "cosmic return" of the hero. The hero has appeared within his cult (Pagina VI); his unification with his followers has been celebrated (Pagina VII); and the significance of his theophany has been articulated and debated (Paginae VIII and IX). Then, during the dark interregnum of his adversary, he disappears into a foreign realm as the cult's faith is tested and matured (Pagina X). Now, having matured in the process of his own passage, Christ returns in triumph, his adversary defeated. In the preceding pageants the *praesepe* had served as the spectacular cynosure of dramatic faith, but now Christ rewards this faith by appearing before his community in the flesh—young and winsome, wise and articulate beyond his natural years. Thus of the three episodes in Pagina XI, the most affecting was probably its central one, where Simeon recognizes, embraces, and adores the Child. Although the ecclesiastical stage setting helps sacralize this scene, its potential sacramental significance is not wrenched into the foreground, as in N-Town, where Mary places Christ upon the altar. Rather, as in the other Chester Nativity pageants, the dramatic image of the innocent Child is allowed to dominate and contain the sacramental image implicit in it. Simeon's loving embrace of Christ is thus sufficient unto itself—a nonverbal gesture of exquisite human tenderness.

This physical embrace consummates the strategic attempts of the preceding pageants to unify the community with the newborn Savior. As with most liturgical drama, the Chester Nativity pageants are rarely didactic and rarely proffer intellectual self-explications of their own actions; rather, they rely primarily upon the power of the enacted events to evoke those joyful emotions which for centuries had been associated with their celebration. In the final speech of the Nativity Group, an angel steps forward to explain the import of the preceding episodes. In fact all he does is remind the viewers of what they have seen and must believe: "Christ is commen through his grace/... Leeve you well this, lordes of might." Therefore the essential "meaning" of these Nativity plays resides in their dramatic surface—in their power as realistic spectacle to authenticate the scriptural narratives they represent, and in their power as comic celebrations to unite the viewers' spiritual identity with those realities. Yet, as E. Catherine Dunn has suggested, the cycles' "manner of expression, though apparently a surface phenomenon, is [nevertheless] the product of deeply-rooted tendencies, and is essentially a way of grasping the liturgical meaning and shaping it into beautiful form."[65] While studying Chester's Nativity pageants, we have seen that suffused in their surface phenomena there are gestures, images, and rhythms which indeed attempt a nearly perfect return to the sacred centers of ritual celebration. Because they offer artistic images rather than sacramental realities, the pageants must rely finally upon their viewers to realize those realities in their own spiritual lives. Yet in their brilliant integration of ritual technique and comic design, these pageants succeed in demonstrating how the Savior's birth can be celebrated in a variety of dramatic forms which any child, human or divine, would love.

5

Christ's Neo-Romanesque Ministry: Paginae XII-XV

In contrast to the narrative breadth and multitude of events accorded Christ's public life in each of the Gospels, the English Corpus Christi cycles are relatively chary of episodes representing Christ's ministry, preferring to dramatize more fully the events clustering about the two most sacred moments of Christ's earthly career—his birth and death. Yet the historical structure, thematic motifs, and rhetorical concerns of each cycle made necessary a selective representation of the public ministry: to give proof through Christ's adult deeds and words that he is in truth the Son of God (as the Nativity pageants had proclaimed), to interpret the responses of true believers to Christ's miracles, and to depict the nature and motives of his detractors—thereby establishing fully a counterplot which will lead with dramatic probability into the betrayal and Crucifixion.[1] In satisfying these various dramatic requirements the four English cycles vary considerably in their selection, number, and sequencing of ministry episodes. Wakefield presents only the Baptism and the raising of Lazarus; Chester, although overall the shortest of the cycles, offers the greatest number of ministry episodes (eight); York and N-Town share with each other or with one or both of the other cycles certain episodes in common; yet only the resurrection of Lazarus appears in all four Ministry Groups, and its dramatic interpretations differ remarkably from one cycle to the next.

The cycle authors apparently enjoyed this freedom of selection and interpretation because of the great number of ministry events afforded by any Gospel harmony and because of the great variation among the four canonical Gospels in their narrative interpretations of Christ's public life. It would of course be desirable in every instance to determine precisely why a certain playwright selected one ministry episode—and then often only one Gospel's recounting of that episode—rather than another. But of more pressing importance in this chapter is to determine why one English Corpus Christi playwright, the Chester dramatist, remains strikingly dependent in his Ministry pageants upon his selected scriptural sources, while the other playwrights amplify and invent freely. A standard explanation of such matters has been that all the more conservative, less "inventive" plays were closer in their mode and in their time of conception to twelfth-century liturgical drama, whereas the more "imaginative" plays were, for the most part, fifteenth-century creations, influenced by the nominalist particularity and affective piety of the very late Middle Ages.[2] In the following pages, however, I would prefer to suggest that the scriptural allegiance and conservative aesthetics of Chester's Ministry pageants disprove the universal applicability of this standard explanation: Chester's dramatic restraint is not proof of its early development, but rather one manifestation of its playwright's deliberate returning to "ancient authorities"—artistic, scriptural, and theological.

Chester's eight ministry episodes are presented in three pageants: the Butchers' play (Pagina XII) offers the temptation in the wilderness and Christ's judgment of the adulteress; the Glovers' play (Pagina XIII) follows Christ's healing the blind beggar with his raising of Lazarus; and the Corvisors' play (Pagina XIV) conjoins four episodes near the ministry's end—the anointing at Bethany, the entry into Jerusalem, the scourging of the temple, and Judas's joining the conspiracy. These pageants, Hardin Craig has noticed, have an "episodic or consecutive quality" reminiscent of liturgical drama: "They are relatively bare in their manner of treatment and have the characteristic of introducing scene after scene in sequence without much provision for interrelations."[3] Craig's slightly negative evaluation of Chester's spare style deserves positive amplification, for despite their local application the salient features of Chester's Ministry pageants typify the cycle's overall dramatic reserve: preferring balance to synthesis, distillation to elaboration, iconic gestures to realistic action, and low- rather than high-relief secondary characters, these plays are all starkly Christocentric in their focus. The Ministry pageants of the other English cycles are less so: in the York Baptism, for example, John appears to be the dominant character, speaking fifteen stanzas to Christ's six; N-Town's "The Woman Taken in Adultery" develops an elaborate plot out of the adulteress's private life and callow lover; Wakefield gives over half its Lazarus play to Lazarus's chilling report on the horrors of the underworld. In the Chester Ministry Group, on the other hand, every character and every action gain definition exclusively through their subordinate relationship to Christ.

As a few scholars have noted, each of the four English cycles, not only in its parts but in its entirety, enjoys a dramatic style uniquely its own and very easily distinguished from the rest, despite the fact that each cycle was built up gradually over time. In one of the most sensitive appreciations of these aesthetic differences (although limited exclusively to a discussion of the Passion sequences) Waldo McNeir has compared the cycles' individual styles to individual stages in the development of medieval art and architecture. The lavish detail of York, he suggests, gives dramatic form to the Perpendicular Gothic; Wakefield typifies the unresolved tensions of the late Gothic; N-Town's high emotionalism corresponds to the pathetic naturalism of the fifteenth-century plastic arts. Chester's style, however, may appear extraordinary and even inexplicable, if simply because its architectural analogue comes so early: according to McNeir, Chester's "restraint and . . . conventionalization of figures so as to adapt them to the places they occupy show a feeling for organic structure that recalls the sturdy solidity of Romanesque building."[4] I think McNeir's analogy is apt, but it raises at least one major critical problem: why should Chester, the last cycle to have attained its full shape (in the early sixteenth century), be defined in aesthetic terms appropriate to the twelfth century? The resolution of this problem involves so many elements and stages of argument that it is best to begin cautiously—by recognizing that in its Ministry Group Chester's "Romanesque" restraint and its interrelation of "conventional figures" with the "places they occupy" is, at the least, a quite appropriate way of giving dramatic expression to a theological program consistently conservative and, if you will, "Romanesque" in its perspective.

This theological program would appear to derive essentially from the Ministry Group's primary scriptural source. Whereas the other cycles range freely through all four Gospels, Chester avoids the three Synoptic Gospels on most possible occasions. Whether it was a playwright or scribe who added in MS H the marginal notations to Paginae XII–XIV, the fact that seventeen of these nineteen scriptural citations refer to John underscores the sustained and controlling influence the Johannine narrative had upon the formation of Chester's Ministry plays.[5] Both in their literal lines of narrative or dramatic action and in their theological perspectives, the Gospel of John and the ministry episodes in Chester have much in common. To be more precise, the interpretive emphases normally seen as unique to John among the Gospels are unique among the English cycles to Chester. These basic emphases—as defined by *The Interpreter's Bible*—are an "explicative" emphasis revealing directly the meaning of Christ's deeds, a "mandatory" emphasis giving prominence to Christ's titles, and an "anticipatory" emphasis whereby "what is represented in the earlier [Synoptic] Gospels as a gradual revelation is boldly announced."[6] These three emphases are granted most direct expression in Chester in a rhyme-royal macaronic speech given by Christ when he addresses his disciples at the opening of Pagina XIII. In an amalgamation of John 8:12, 32, 10:11, 16 and 30, Christ defines the essence of his being (as did his Father at the cycle's very beginning) and the purpose of his ministry. "Ego sum lux mundi," he begins; "Qui sequitur me non ambulat in tenebris sed habebit lumen vitae." He is "Filius Dei," who had promised the "patriarches and prophets" "before the world beganne/ to paye there ransome and to become man." "Ego et Pater unum sumus," he declares, his Father having sent him "from the throne sempiternall/to preach and declare his will unto man." He is the "good sheppard," whose "mynd and will" it is to go among his flock "my Fathers hestes and commandmentes to fulfill." Assembling his disciples, Christ determines to go forth "while the day is light" to "heale the sicke and restore the blynd to sight," declaring in conclusion: "Si vos manseritis in sermone meo, veri discipuli mei eritis, et cognoscetis veritatem, et veritas liberabit vos." In John, so in Chester, Christ emphasizes his titles, announces his future deeds, and explains their spiritual significance. As the Light, the Life, and the Truth, Christ clearly conceives of his ministry as a victorious reign on earth wherein he will fulfill his Father's will: he will contend with darkness, conquer death, and set free all who believe in Him. And indeed in Chester's ministry episodes Christ substantiates each of these self-conceptions and proves valid each of his claims in the miracles he performs.

Because of Chester's allegiance to John and because of their mutual emphasis upon Christ's kingly nature and divine powers, it could be assumed that the Chester playwright merely rendered into mimetic action episodes from his chosen Gospel without much sense of dramatic design or any theological vision of his own. The second part of this contention can I think be immediately discredited, for it is clear that Chester successfully sustains its distinctive Christological perspective—which we may provisionally call "Johannine"—even in episodes which are not derived from John. Chester's theological independence from its scriptural sources (as well as its great divergence from the other cycles) may be illustrated best by contrasting briefly the four cycles' handling of one episode. This episode, the Agony in the Garden, in Chester could be understood as the triumphant conclusion of Christ's "private" ministry; but in the three other cycles it must be understood as a "pathetic" prologue to his Passion because of its revelations of Christ's human frailties and doubts.

In the Wakefield Agony episode, Christ prays three times, complaining that his soul is "heuy agans the deth," his flesh "seke for fere"; asking that "this passyon thou put fro me away," he begs his Father to "comforte me that am drery," until "Trinitas" appears finally to solace him. Similarly, in York Christ utters three long prayers, lamenting "My flessh is full dredand for drede, . . . I swete now both watir and bloode"; the sight of his sleeping disciples only increases his pain, until in response to his cry for "Some comforte" an angel appears to console him. N-Town, typically, is most extreme in its rendering of Christ's physical agony and most obvious in its incorporation of images adapted from the Passion:

> The Water and blood owth of my face
> Dystyllyth for peynes that I xal take
> My flesche qwakyth in ferful case
> As thow the joyntys A-sondre xuld schake.

Pathetically beseeching his Father "Thou wotyst I dede nevyr dede but good," Christ remains unconsoled until an angel descends and offers him the ultimate balm: "A chalys with An host ther in." Chester's theological emphases could scarcely be further removed

146

from these. whereas Wakefield, York and N-Town have all relied
heavily upon the account (in Luke 22.43, 44) of the angel's descending to an agonized Christ sweating "drops of blood," Chester
insists on a "Johannine" interpretation of these moments—even
though the events in the garden are not included at all in the Johannine narrative. The first prayer Christ utters in the Chester dramatization is in fact not from any of the Synoptic Gospels, but rather
from John 17:1-26. This, a distillation of the so-called Sacerdotal
Prayer, is a "prayer" of praise, thanksgiving, and fulfillment. Christ
asks God to glorify him so that he may glorify God; having used
God's "postie" on earth, Christ reports that he has "donne with
harte free" God's work "and brought yt to an ende"; he then prays,
not for himself, but for the salvation of his disciples, since "nowe
they knowe verelye/that from the Father sent am I." These are
scarcely the words of a man troubled by his own human frailty or
doubting the justice of his earthly career. Christ's second (and concluding) prayer in Chester is a brief conflation of those three Synoptic prayers so fulsomely rendered in the other cycles:

> My hart is in great mislikinge
> for death that is to me commynge.
> Father, if I dare aske this thinge,
> put it awaye froe mee.
>
> All thinge to thee possible is;
> neverthelesse, nowe in this
> at your will I am, iwys.
> As thou wilt, lett yt bee. [H]

It may be possible to detect a moment of human uncertainty here,
but it should be noted that Christ appears in absolute control: it is
he who determines his own dislike of death; it is he who courteously
beseeches his Father; it is he who is absolutely certain of God's omnipotence; and it is he who then concludes that his will is in the service of his Father's. Just as Christ in Chester is confident that all
things are possible to God (cf. Matthew 26:39, "Father, *if* it be
possible . . .), so should the Chester audience be confident of Christ's
own divine powers. Thus no angelic messenger is necessary in Chester to bridge the chasm between Christ and his Father because no

147

such chasm exists: Christ does not suffer, or doubt, because his will and God's are one. Although the result may here be an iconic and seemingly static form of drama, it should be evident that Chester's New Testament episodes are controlled by a consistent and fully defined Christology. This conservative Christology, although firmly based in the Gospel of John, appears to have been consciously developed and does not derive from Scripture alone.

When we remind ourselves of the time of the cycle's composition, however, Chester's strangely conservative aesthetics and its "Johannine" Christology present a greater problem than normally has been recognized: not only was the Chester cycle obviously composed centuries after the culmination of the Romanesque traditions in the twelfth century, but (as we have seen in Chapter 2) several episodes in the Ministry Group were written into the cycle quite late in its career—for the Whitsun shift early in the sixteenth century. These late additions seem to include Pagina XII's The Adulteress episode, that episode's gloss, and the gloss to The Temptation episode; Pagina XIII's five-stanza rhyme-royal opening, and its Blind Man episode; and possibly parts of Pagina XIV as well. Therefore, unless we are willing to believe, as Hardin Craig does, that the Chester cycle is "an accident of English provincial conservatism"[7] and thus, apparently, a freak of cultural history totally out of touch with the aesthetic tastes and theological perspectives of the fifteenth and early sixteenth centuries, Chester's seemingly archaic dramatic style and its unusual emphasis upon Christ's divinity (rather than his humanity) are phenomena for which late medieval analogues and influences must be found.

Although there has yet to be written a full survey or interpretation of the revival of Romanesque motifs and themes in fifteenth-century art and architecture, a few art historians have noted, in passing, the strange return in the fifteenth century to forms definitive of the twelfth. One of the fuller analyses of this phenomenon appears as a single paragraph in Erwin Panofsky's *Gothic Architecture and Scholasticism:*

> The *Summa* was again displaced by less systematic and ambitious types of presentation. Pre-Scholastic Augustinianism (asserting, among other things, the independence of the will from the intellect) was vigorously revived in opposition to Thomas, and Thomas's anti-Augustinian tenets were solemnly condemned three years

148

after his death. Similarly, the "classic" cathedral type was abandoned in favor of other, less perfectly systematized and often somewhat archaic solutions; and in the plastic arts we can observe the revival of a pre-Gothic tendency toward the abstract and the linear.[8]

As Panofsky quite rightly implies, the development in the late Middle Ages of what we may perhaps call a "revisionist" or "neo-Romanesque" style was an integral part of a general cultural reaction against what were discerned as having been the indefensible excesses of the high Gothic. In the Chester cycle and especially in its ministry plays, I think we can also find a deliberate "revival of a pre-Gothic tendency toward the abstract and the linear": Chester's chaste dramaturgic style, in my judgment, represents among other things a conscious rejection of everything that the Gothic was believed to have symbolized. To appreciate in a general way what the Gothic, on the one hand, and the neo-Romanesque, on the other, could symbolize in the fifteenth century, it is best to consider first a closely related phenomenon—the late medieval philosophic rejection of Thomistic Scholasticism.

Although the tortuous course of the nominalist *via moderna* is often hard to follow, it is clear that the primary intuitions expressed in Bishop Tempier's 1277 condemnations of the excesses of "Scholasticism" remained basic to the spirit of retrenchment felt throughout late medieval thought. Tempier's main target, we know, was in fact Siger of Brabant and Averroistic Aristotelianism. But at the time and in succeeding centuries, many felt the culprit was the Scholastic manner of thinking generally, a manner epitomized best by Saint Thomas himself. "Viewed with a minimum of bias," writes Josef Pieper, this is what the "heresies" of so-called Thomistic Scholasticism boiled down to:

> that felicity is to be sought in this, not another, life; that the Christian religion hinders learning; that the soul of man is inseparably bound to the body; that creation out of nothing is impossible; that the practice of theology in no way enlarges one's knowledge; that there is no state finer than devotion to philosophy.[9]

What else, Pieper concludes, could the official church have done but to "declare authoritatively: These propositions are in opposition to Christian doctrine"? In the fourteenth and fifteenth centuries, the nominalists accepted as one of their major tasks the "theological" destruction of the "philosophical" arrogance of the Scholastics; these Scholastics—it was held—had presumed that God's nature could be logically circumscribed, that his will and his actions were controlled (even determined) by analyzable laws, that human *ratio* was not only compatible with *fides* but sometimes superior to it, and that all seeming contraries were ultimately reconcilable. In reaction, the nominalists emphasized the paradoxicalness of God's nature, the inscrutability of his ways, and the great distance between the divine and the human spheres.[10] Rather than dissect God into parts and then determine the significance of each through *pro-et-contra* dialectic, the nominalists chose often simply to praise his virtues (such as his omniscience, freedom, will, and justice) by subsuming them all under God's greatest quality, his power. To emphasize the incomprehensible range of that divine power, Ockham (and theologians after him) tended to emphasize the traditional differences perceived to exist between God's *potentia ordinata* (with which he freely had created the world and now sustains it) and his *potentia absoluta* (which operates outside of space and time). Since this second and more important operation of divine power was totally beyond man's ken, nominalists sometimes tried to imagine how paradoxical the registered effect of his will could be: Robert Holcot (to take a fairly extreme example) suggested that God's ways are so indeterminate and arbitrary that he could cheat and lie, he could damn a good man and save a sinner. While agreeing upon certain basic tenets such as God's absolute transcendence over our logical categories and the heinous *hubris* of Scholastic speculations, the nominalists nevertheless were wont to disagree violently among themselves; the result was that various "schools" may be identified (Oberman finds four),[11] ranging all the way from an uncompromisingly skeptical empiricism to a form of affective spiritualism close to mysticism. Despite their differences, nominalists often sought comfort and wisdom (as well as rhetorical leverage) through reading and identifying with certain pre-Scholastic spiritual thinkers—especially, that is, with men of the twelfth century, such as Bernard of Clairvaux, William of Saint Thierry, and the Victorines.[12] And in ways they obviously never could have foreseen, the nominalists in their attacks on the intellectual hierarchisms of Scholastic thought anticipated certain positions later to be taken up by the Reformers of the sixteenth century.[13]

What I have suggested so far is that Chester's heavy reliance upon the Gospel of John, its development of an unusually conservative dramatic style, and its allegiance to a theological position emphasizing Christ's divinity rather than his humanity, are all interdependent phenomena carefully designed and integrated by the Chester playwright himself. These phenomena, I have also meant to imply, may be related to certain cultural movements (such as the progress of nominalism) in the fourteenth, fifteenth, and even sixteenth centuries. With this much as an introduction, I intend now to examine Chester's Ministry Group in such a way that each of the phenomena will be seen as a force helping to shape each of the Ministry pageants. My first concern, then, is to account for, as well as describe, Chester's allegiance to John. Rosemary Woolf has remarked that in his Ministry plays "the Chester author is especially timid in his moulding of the gospel text into dramatic form";[14] I intend to prove that his reliance upon Scripture is as bold an artistic decision as is his rare departure from it. Second, I intend to reveal within these pageants the influence of certain basic nominalist ideas which helped to shape the selection and design of each episode. To set these ideas into sharp relief, I may at times flatten out an episode in order to define with greater precision each of Chester's nominalist precepts and to determine where as a philosophic "cluster" they fall among the various schools of fifteenth-century thought. My final concern is a fuller appreciation of Chester's conservative dramatic style. Although as I examine the pageants individually this will perforce remain a tertiary consideration, in my conclusion I will evaluate that style and then try to place it within certain artistic movements of the fifteenth and early sixteenth centuries. Any of Chester's New Testament plays could have served as the object of these enquiries, but the Ministry pageants seem the most fitting. Placed between the shared joy of the Nativity and the shared terror of the Passion, the events of Christ's public ministry, with their even balance of light and darkness, figure forth in unusually clear demarcation a number of qualities characteristic of the entire Chester cycle.

I

It is rather appropriate that Chester's first Ministry play, Pagina XII, dramatizes two incidents in Christ's early ministry where "intellectual" adversaries attempt to comprehend his nature and to discover his identity through the use of logical distinctions. The first episode opens in hell as Satan, in an extended speculative soliloquy, determines to find out whether this "doseberd" Christ is God or man. "What maister mon ever be this," he poses as his *quaestio:* his father is unknown and his mother, although "a deadlych woman," is one who "did never amisse." Christ himself appears a "man from foot to crowne," but unlike the other sons of Adam he is "blotles eke of blood and bonne," "wiser then ever man was," and free of the deadly sins Adam brought into the world. These contradictions and alternatives, set out, it has been noted, with "syllogistic precision,"[15] test the elasticity of Satan's philosophic powers. Concluding, however, that a god cannot be hungry and a hungry man cannot refuse bread, he puts his plan into action: "if that hee be God verey/honger should greeve him by no waye;/ that weare agaynst reasoun." In the three consecutive temptations in Chester, it is clear that Christ is never tempted: he sees through Satan's stratagems from the beginning and accedes to these crude tests only because he wills to, and because through them he may reveal his own "postee" and "Goddes will omnypotent." After being foiled in his third unsuccessful ploy, Satan finally gives up—"all my cunninge is sett at nought"—and retires dolefully to hell, "a court ful diligent" to convene.

Chester's dramatization of this episode has a number of features in common with the other two cycle versions, all of which are based on Matthew 4:1-11 (John does not include the Temptation). Where the three versions differ, however, is in their Christological emphases and in their applications of the temptations to the viewing audience. The N-Town pageant closes with Christ's address to "All mankende":

> all this I suffyr ffor mannys sake
> to teche the how thou xalt rewle the
> Whan the devylle dothe the Assayle
> loke thou concente nevyr to synne.

The York version concludes on a similar homiletic note; Christ explains to two angels that just as the Holy Ghost led him through temptation, so he shall guide all men in similar moments of trial:

> For whan the fende schall folke see,
> and salus tham in sere degre,
> Thare myrroure may thei make of me,
> for to stande still.

In N-Town and York, it is clear that Christ suffered the fleshly enticements of sin to serve as a human *exemplum,* a paradigmatic "myrroure" of moral steadfastness upon which the potential sinner should reflect in times of temptation. In Chester, on the other hand, Christ, the Son of God, is seen as all that weak humanity, that is, Adam, is not; Satan, in his turn, is not an archetype of sin and temptation so much as he is an arrogant philosopher testing his powers against Christ's. And the Expositor's "application" of the temptation concludes not with a *moralitas,* but with a further, discursive reverence of Christ's Godhead and a recognition of Satan's own deception:

> Thus overcome Christ in this case
> the devill, as playd was in this place,
> with those three sinnes that Adam was
> of wayle into woe waved.
> But Adam fell through his trespas,
> and Jhesu withstoode him through his grace;
> for of his godhead Sathanas
> that tyme was cleane disceived. [H]

In his study of the Temptation as dramatized in the English cycles, Alan H. Nelson has argued that Christ here reverses roles with Satan, beguiling the arch-beguiler as he successfully disguises his own true nature.[16] Although a branch of nominalist thought would allow God the right to deceive, Chester's implicit theological position is, I believe, considerably less "skeptical": it is not Christ's deceptions which have been dramatized in Chester but rather Satan's misconceptions, for his *pro-et-contra* ratiocinating allows no room for divine revelation or a higher order of faith. If such a higher order of truth existed, the Scholastic presumably believed it could be apprehended by reason, but the nominalist was insistent that such truths were trans-rational and paradoxical. Employing their so-called "three-value logic," nominalists were wont to argue, for example, that a proposition regarding future contingencies may be true, or not true, or simultaneously true and not true.[17] Similarly, in Chester Satan reasons in an old-fashioned, Scholastic way that Christ must be either God or man, but it never enters his rational head that he may simultaneously and paradoxically be both. Thus what Christ reveals of his own nature in Chester and what is assented to by the audience's faith is a truth which Satan's philosophic training can never comprehend; no wiser than before, Satan returns truculently to his diabolical court and to its maze of endless dialectical thought.

The dramatic structure and theological perspective of Pagina XII's second episode—a twelve-stanza representation of Christ and the adulteress—obviously complement those of the Temptation episode. Primus and Secundus Judeus (H) open the scene as they plot to trap Christ with the moral conundrum posed by adultery: either Christ must violate the Mosaic law that adultery be punished by death, they reason, or he must violate his own new law of mercy. Yet after confronting the prophet with the adulteress, the Jews watch in confusion as Christ writes on the ground and bids whoever is without sin to cast the first stone. Each Jew reads the inscription and flees, leaving the sinful woman to Christ. Asked where her accusers are, she replies, "Lord, to dampne mee there is non," and Christ charges, "Nowe I dampne thee not woman./ Goe forth and synne noe more." The woman kneels to worship Christ, assuring him that she will amend her life, and the pageant closes with the Expositor's summarizing the episode and explaining that it was his sins which each Jew saw written on the ground.

It is especially important in this episode that Chester's dramatic and theological conservatism be understood in its own terms rather than in terms derived from the other cycles or from other works. In her evaluation of the cycles' renderings of this narrative, Eleanor Prosser judges N-Town's the most successful—for its imaginative plot, its full characterization, and its thorough exploitation of the three stages of Christian repentance.[18] Although she recognizes the dramatic unity of Chester's brief version, the episode in her judgment is unsuccessful as a call to repentance despite the contrition-speech the playwright adds to his source, John 8:3–11 (where the woman remained silent):

A, lord, blessed muste thou be,
that of mischeiffe hasse holpen mee.
From hence forth synne I will flee
and serve thee in good faye.
For godhead fully in thee I see
that knoweth all workes that done be.
I honour thee lord, kneelinge one my knee,
and so I will doe aye. [H]

Prosser's assessment of the contents of this speech is fairly accurate: "There is no contrition, no confession—merely a brief statement of purpose to amend."[19] What she fails to see, however, is that the episode's dramatic and rhetorical focus is upon Christ throughout, rather than upon the woman. In fact, the adulteress's conversion appears in Chester to have been effected primarily not by her recognizing her own sin but by her recognizing Christ's "godhead." Christ's supernatural ability to read the hearts of the Jews, she properly believes, is an act of grace revealing his divine omniscience: he "knoweth all workes that done be." The ideal response to Christ's superhuman knowledge is therefore represented by the woman's kneeling—an iconic attitude of spiritual reverence iterated by other exemplary characters throughout Chester's Ministry Group.

The two parts of Pagina XII, congruent in formal structure and theological emphasis, thus complement each other to form a thematic and artistic unity. Each opens with an attempt by a supercilious force to trap Christ through logical opposites, and in each case the stratagem fails: recognizing his own inability to apprehend Christ's nature, Satan scurries back to hell; recognizing his own sin, each of the Jews runs off in shame. Opposed to the mean-spirited syllogisms of Christ's adversaries is the adulteress's immediate perception of Christ's revealed Godhead: it is her reverence of the Son of God's omniscience that the audience is expected to emulate in both episodes. Christ's divine powers are therefore proved not by his discomfiting his foes but by his absolute transcendence of their philosophic categories. In the Temptation episode, Christ does not deceive Satan; rather, he merely refuses to conform to Satan's Scholastic *distinctiones.* Similarly, in the adulteress episode, Christ does not obey either the Old Law or the New, at least as they are understood by the Jews: he neither condemns nor forgives the Jews but mercifully reveals their sins—not in public, as they had done with the woman, but privately to each sinner.[20] Pagina XII is therefore better understood to be not a "morality play" underscoring the need of mankind to avoid sin and forgive sinners but rather a "miracle play" revealing through Christ's suprahuman accomplishments his transcendent divinity. Solid, unadorned, and evenly balanced, Pagina XII, through the selection and slight alteration of its scriptural sources, succeeds in dramatizing two complementary episodes from Christ's early ministry which prove the validity of certain basic nominalist beliefs: the divine Godhead is rationally inscrutable, his powers of omniscience are absolute, and the nature of his being can be seen only in the authority of Scripture and through his own self-revelations in time.

The second pageant of Chester's Ministry Group, Pagina XIII, juxtaposes two miracles Christ performs later in his ministry: his healing the blind beggar and his resurrecting Lazarus from death. In both episodes the Chester playwright remains close to his scriptural source, the Gospel of John, yet in both he reshapes events and words slightly in order to give dramatic expression to a contemporary theological precept. Whereas the basic precept of the preceding pageant was God's omniscience, in Pagina XIII it is God's omnipotence, or what the nominalists called the *potentia absoluta* of the Godhead. This fundamental article of the nominalist canon is verified by both episodes in the pageant: each proves that divine power—as revealed through God's Son—is beyond the limits of human understanding and above all laws of nature. It is absolute, perfect, complete, and free.

After Christ's self-defining speech (which we examined at the beginning of this chapter) the blind beggar Chelidonius enters, led by a boy. In response to his disciples' queries, Christ explains that the man's blindness was not the result of any personal or original sin,

> but for this cause spetiallye:
> to sett forth Goddes great glorye,
> his power to shewe manifestlye,
> this mans sight to reforme.

In a gesture reminiscent of God's creative act in Genesis 2:6,7, Christ makes a paste of dust and spittle, anoints the man's eyes, and orders him to wash them in "the water of Siloe." Chelidonius does so and returns miraculously healed: "Praysed be God omnipotent," he exclaims, "which nowe to me my sight hath sent." Two neighbors, however, at first unconvinced that the miracle has occurred, then distressed that it has been performed on the Sabbath, drag Chelidonius and his parents to the Pharisees for extended interrogation. His parents testify to their son's former blindness, while Chelidonius refuses to assert that the restoration of his sight was a sinful act. As the irate Pharisees are about to "curse [Chelidonius] owt of this place," Christ suddenly speaks, asking the former blind man, "Beleeves thou in Godes Sonne trulye?" (H). In response to Chelidonius's answer, "Yea, gratious lord. Whoe is hee?" Christ reveals himself— "Thou hast him seene with thy eyee./ Hee is the same that talketh with thee"—and Chelidonius immediately kneels and worships him: "Then I here, I honour him with hart free,/ and ever shall serve him untill I dye." The Pharisees, however, refusing to believe that Christ's words and works bear witness of his divinity, suddenly prepare to stone him; Christ just as suddenly disappears, and the confused Jews run off to report his heresies to "syr Cayphas."

In both word and action this episode (which of the four cycles only Chester dramatizes) is derived almost entirely from John 8:12–10:40; but as the summary above is meant to suggest, the scriptural source has been shaped dramatically to emphasize certain themes and images. By excluding Christ's two sheepfold parables recorded in John 10:1–18, and by conflating the two separate events of Christ's healing the blind man and his dispute in the temple with the Pharisees (John 9:1–41 and 10:19–40), Chester creates a continuing line of action wherein the Jews' decision to stone Christ appears as a nearly direct result of his miraculous healing. This dramatic compression heightens the contrasting images and themes extant in John: illuminated sight as a symbol of revelation, spiritual blindness as an image of benighted ignorance. To render these themes more immediate and explicit, Chester occasionally changes the Johannine account. As the blind beggar kneels to worship Christ in John, he says simply, "Credo, Domine." In Chester, however, Chelidonius worships Christ "with hart free," underscoring Christ's earlier proclamation,

"veritas liberabit vos." John describes Christ's escape from the Pharisees as a prudent retreat: "exivit de manibus eorum" (he escaped
out of their hands). In Chester, however, Christ's escape is a magic
trick of the first order, as the stage directions make clear: *statim
evanescit* (he instantly disappears). This fabulous disappearance,
as spectacular as Christ's later vanishing from the company of Luke
and Cleophas, totally astonishes the Jews, who cry, "Owt, owt, alas
where is our fonne?" The dramatic disappearance was obviously
meant to astonish the audience as well, for even a close reading of
Scripture would have failed in preparation for this miraculous con-
travention of the laws of nature. The point of Christ's sudden vanishing, dramatically much more impressive than his restoration of
the blind man's sight, is, I believe, precisely the point nominalists
made time and again about God's absolute power: his omnipotence
is infinite and indeterminable, his will so free that it at times appears
arbitrary, and his ways—if they may be comprehended at all—characterized best by what Scotus called their "radical spontaneity."[21]
Thus for the audience, as for nominalists in general, there was very
little "rational" sense to be made of such divine acts: one could only
respect the incomprehensible range of God's will and discuss in vague
ways "the sheer unrestricted limits of His omnipotence."[22]

Before proceeding to the raising of Lazarus episode, I should
emphasize that Chester's general theological position is much more
conservative than the positions assumed by many of the more influential philosophers of the fourteenth and fifteenth centuries. As has
often been recognized, there was a tendency among some nominalists
to elevate things divine so far above human powers of discrimination
that for Ockham, for example, God's "attributes melted in the blaze
of His omnipotence, leaving no certainty."[23] And because the supernatural realm was believed only very rarely to penetrate the natural,
a form of skeptical humanism developed, emphasizing the autonomy
and absolute freedom of man and threatening to eclipse the traditional roles of faith, Scripture, revelation, and dogma as ways of
governing and judging human action. Insofar as it can be defined,
Chester's theology has nothing in common with these philosophic
extremes: Chester's position, satiric of Scholastic attempts rationally to circumscribe God, is equally disapproving of any attempts
to remove the divine from direct human experience.

Chester's very conservative nominalist theology, emphasizing much more than did the major philosophers the reactionary elements implicit in their anti-Scholastic positions, could be simply the product of an artistic imagination aware of the central theological topics of its time but most attracted by the twelfth-century spiritual pieties with which they were distantly related. But in fact it should be noted that among the English nominalist parties there was one "school" the basic tenets of which conform with many of Chester's. Led by the "reactionary theologian" Archbishop Thomas Bradwardine, this school attacked the rest of the nominalists as "neo-Pelagian" heretics. it reasserted the primacy of faith over reason, argued that all truth was in fact revealed truth, and demanded a complete return to the absolute authorities of Scripture and dogma. Once this return to faith and Scripture was effected, most of the arcane philosophic problems of the time were "solved" or proved meaningless. Since, as Leff writes, for Bradwardine God was omnipotent and had all the attributes enumerated in dogma,

> all discussion became merely the enunciation of first principles:
> in the case of the creation of the world in time, for example,
> there was no need for hesitation over its probability; it sufficed
> that God, as creator of all things, must also have created time.
> Similarly, with grace, merit, free will, future contingents, these
> problems allowed of equally definitive answers. Because God
> must be involved in all that His creatures did, His grace must
> come before a meritorious act of free will; the future was not
> only known to God but willed by Him: hence contingency far
> from being outside His knowledge was the product of His willing.
> By these means Bradwardine was able to regard the whole of
> creation as the extension of God's will; given His nature as re-
> vealed in Scripture, everything else followed.[24]

Similarly, in Chester, the primary concern of the Ministry plays is with what could be called the dramatic enunciation of first principles as revealed in Scripture. Because the Gospel according to John is equally concerned with the enunciation of first principles—with the revelation of the divine Logos through the words and deeds of the Son—it is not surprising that Chester only very rarely feels the need to change its scriptural source. Occasionally, as in the first episode of Pagina XIII, Chester amends the Johannine account in a

159

rather major way (Christ's vanishing) in order further to heighten Christ's authority; but normally, as in the pageant's second episode (Lazarus's resurrection) John's narrative designs conform almost perfectly with Chester's theological themes. In this episode dramatizing the greatest miracle of Christ's ministry, Chester's fidelity to John is exceptional. For example, following John 11:4, Christ explains to Mary the purpose of her brother's mortal illness:

> Yea, woman, I tell thee wytterlye,
> that sickenes is not deadly
> but Godes Sonne to glorifie.
> Loe, I am him, as may be seene.

Following John 11:25, Christ utters his great climactic "I am" revelation as he stands before Lazarus's tomb:

> I am risynge and life verey;
> which liffe shall last for aye
> and never shall ended be.

And following John 11:42, Christ explains, after Lazarus's resurrection, why he thanked his father openly:

> But for this people that stande hereby
> speake I the more openlye,
> that they may leeve steedfastly
> from thee that I was sent.

When Chester does amend the Johannine account slightly, it is typically in order to delete any possible ambiguity about Christ's divinity and his absolute power as the Lord of light and life (although the scriptural narrative hardly leaves much in doubt). For example, in response to Christ's asking if she believes that whoever believes in him shall never die, Martha in John 11:27 tactfully avoids a direct answer by simply avowing her personal trust in Christ as the Messiah: "Utique, Domine, ego credidi, quia tu es Christus filius Dei vivi, qui in hunc mundum venisti" (Yea, Lord, I have believed that thou art Christ, the Son of the living God, who art come into this world). In Chester, however, she answers Christ's question, "Leeves thou, woman, that this maye be?" (H) with an unqualified, "Lord, I leeve"; she then asserts, as in John, her belief in Christ as God's Son and man's savior. Chester's scriptural fidelity is evidenced, finally, in its dramatic

160

structure, which adheres closely to the narrative design of the Johannine account. Whereas N-Town gives considerable stage-time to the
sorrow of Lazarus's slow dying, and Wakefield—through Lazarus's
extended report—emphasizes the horrors of death and the need of
mankind to repent, Chester's dramatic focus is upon Christ throughout, testing his followers' faith as he strides forward to perform the
great miracle. In all four cycles, the dramatic import of the resurrection is defined by Lazarus himself, who speaks (he does not do so in
Scripture) on his return to life. Since the York and Chester dramatizations of the Lazarus story are very similar, the divergences between
their two resurrection addresses should define for us quite clearly
Chester's major dramatic interest and central theological concern:

York	Chester
A! pereles prince, full of pitee!	A, lord, blessed most thou be
Worshipped be thou in worlde alway,	which from death to life hast
That thus hast schewed thi myght	raysed mee
in me,	through thy micle might.
Both dede and doluen, this is the	Lord, when I hard the voyce
fourthe day.	of thee,
By certayne singnes here may	all hell fayled of there postie,
men see	so fast from them my soule
How that thou art goddis sone verray.	can flee;
All thou that trulye trastis in the	all divells were afrayd.
Schall neuere dye, this dare I saye.	
Therfore ye folke in fere,	
Menske hym with mayne and myght,	
His lawes luke that ye lere,	
Than will he lede you to his light.	

Both addresses open similarly: Lazarus reveres Christ, praising his
great power as revealed in the resurrection (although Chester quite
typically does not characterize Christ as "full of pitee"). Then in
York Lazarus mediates between the audience and Christ, beseeching
the viewers to believe in Christ as the Son of God, to worship him,
and to learn his laws. Chester, however, is little concerned here with
the homiletic interpretation of "certayne singnes." Rather, Lazarus
in Chester continues addressing Christ exclusively, heightening his
praise of Christ's power with the revelation of ultimate proof: that
is, at the very sound of Christ's voice all hell failed of its power.
What Chester has done here is to amplify the significance of Christ's

returning Lazarus to life by casting the return as a cosmic triumph. Just as Satan's defeat in the Chester Temptation assumed characteristics of his prototypical fall ("endles payne must I have unsought," he cries), so Lazarus's resurrection is conceived in terms of its grandest archetype—Christ's triumphant harrowing of hell. For most playwrights, Christ's salvation of one man from death would serve as a sufficiently impressive demonstration of his divine power; but for the Chester playwright that divine power could be accorded adequate dramatic interpretation only if all hell was rendered impotent by that single act.

Thus, like John, Chester's preeminent concerns are theological rather than ethical, and this theology—so often consonant with John's emphasis upon Christ as the eternal Logos—underscores even more than its scriptural source the significance of Christ's act as revelations of his divine powers. "Ego et Pater unum sumus," Christ had proclaimed at the pageant's beginning; at its conclusion, Christ has revealed that his powers, coequal with his Father's, are apparently unlimited by any known laws either natural or divine. In human guise and during his earthly ministry Christ may freely have chosen to conceal his omnipotence from the eyes of some, but before others he has sufficiently exercised that power so that the revealed truth may set them free. Christ's resurrection of Lazarus is indeed a spectacular liberation, but this triumph over the forces of hell is only one of several, past and future, the last of which Christ will perform on the day of doom. Chester's sustained emphasis upon Christ as victorious *actor* is thus one characteristic out of many which distinguish him from his counterparts in the other cycles: as Alexandra Johnston has noted in her comparison of the Ministry Groups, "In York he teaches; in Chester he acts; in Towneley he suffers; in N-Town he forgives."[25] Equally as important, however, is the overpowering impression given by Christ in Chester that he always acts, as it were, from above: he is *Christus rex*—aloof, commanding, and perhaps severe—who dispenses grace upon his subjects in order to liberate them from his only adversary, the corporate powers of hell. At such moments of spiritual liberation, one senses as well an unlimited power held in reserve, for by the utterance of a single command Christ may again and at any time reduce hell to impotent disarray.

With the two supreme attributes of Christ's divine kingship—his omniscience and his omnipotence—having been given full dramatic expression in Paginae XII and XIII, Chester's last Ministry play, the Corvisors' pageant, is able to emphasize certain of his other suprahuman qualities. Assisted by its four-episode structure, Pagina XIV succeeds also in bringing to rapid culmination the two basic historical *mythoi* initiated earlier: that is, the "Plot of Light" climaxes with Christ's triumphal entry in the second episode, while the "Plot of Darkness" congeals in the last episode as Judas, Annas, Caiaphas, and the Pharisees seal their conspiracy to take Christ. Whereas the two preceding Ministry pageants had each defined one divine attribute in an almost ahistorical dramatic frame, Pagina XIV emphasizes much more than they the forward thrust of events, moving from the "house" of Simon the Leper, to "Jerusalem," to the "temple," and then to "Syr Cayphas and his companye." Because of "the Chester's author's unwillingness [sic] to select or rearrange"[26] these four episodes, it has often been assumed that "he did not have a clear purpose in mind."[27] I suggest that he had several purposes in mind: as well as deliberately following a "scriptural" sequence of events, he was committed to giving dramatic definition to certain other theological precepts central to his nominalist program. Of primary importance is the pageant's demonstration of two more of Christ's suprahuman powers: his divine mercy and his divine justice. In addition, albeit obliquely, the pageant is concerned with that traditional philosophic problem of the nature and the degree of human freedom in relationship to God's will. Although the direct influence of a single nominalist's work can hardly be proved here, it is nevertheless impressive that Pagina XIV's thematic emphases complement, amplify, and define more fully the conservative nominalist theological position projected in Chester's preceding Ministry plays.

The quality of Christ's mercy is figured forth in the pageant's first episode, where Christ forgives the penitent Magdalene. Opening with a round of "Welcome" lyrics spoken by Simon, Lazarus, Martha, and Mary, closing with Mary's impassioned reverence of her lord ("My Christ, my comfort and my kinge,/ I worshippe thee in all thinge"), this episode contains elements of powerfully affective drama. However, spliced into the center of that drama (which is otherwise a harmony of Mark 14:3-9 and John 12:1-11) is Christ's parable of the forgiving creditor and its "application" (both taken from Luke 7:41-50). In Prosser's judgment this "didactic interlude" is an unfortunate "mechanical" contrivance which "destroys the emotional progression" of the "play."[28] Indeed, this homiletic passage does succeed in arresting the action's forward progress at the moment that the penitent sinner kneels before her Savior. The intended effect of this freeze-framing seems to be twofold: the iconic scene itself is given added emphasis as well as the "text" delivered "over" it. That is, Simon and Judas had both expressed their distress immediately before this scene, while the Magdalene was anointing Christ's body: Simon had been upset that a "verey prophet" should allow a shameful woman to touch him, Judas that the precious oil was being wasted. Christ then reprimands them both: he cites to Simon the "example" of the two debtors, one owing fifty pence and the other five hundred, each forgiven by the "userer," and then chastises Judas by pointedly reminding him of the precious short time he, Christ, will remain among them—"poore men you have with you aye,/ and me yee may not have, in faye,/ but a little space." In relying in this iconic scene upon Luke (the Gospel which in the Ministry plays he most often avoids), the Chester playwright must have been satisfied that the imagery and themes of the passage were both congenial to his dramatic purpose. The monetary image used here (and sustained then throughout the pageant) suggests that there are two emotional "currencies" by which one can express one's response to Christ: the first, epitomized by Mary, gives all that it has—both spiritual and material— in reverence of the Redeemer; the second measures and calculates things of the spirit, setting a price on that which is priceless. This simonist mentality, as epitomized in Judas, is clearly similar to that of Christ's earlier detractors, who had attempted by rational integers to tabulate his nature. Likewise, the homiletic theme of this passage from Luke also appears to be consonant with Chester's earlier precepts. Christ's forgiving a great "detter" as freely as he forgives a lesser one may—to a "moral rationalist" such as Simon—seem inconsistent and illogical, but perhaps that is just the point. We have seen in earlier episodes that it has not been simply Christ's knowledge or power which has been emphasized, but rather the greatness of each of these divine attributes; similarly, here it is not Christ's mercy which is praised so much as its infinite and perhaps even paradoxical nature. "Amend me through they great mercy" (H) Mary had cried out to Christ at the episode's beginning: it is indeed the greatness of that mercy which has been given dramatic expression in this iconic scene.

It was not, however, God's immeasurable mercy which attracted the nominalists so much as the grandeur of his justice. Here was an attribute more congenial as well to Chester's dramatic emphasis upon Christ's divine kingship. As the Chester playwright was undoubtedly aware, *Christus miserator*, especially if his human sympathies were fully characterized, was in danger sometimes of descending into *Christus miserabilis*, as one worthy of pity himself. But in Christ's triumphal entry, which in Chester immediately follows his forgiving the Magdalene, we are presented with the awesome image of *Christus rex* in his most glorious hour of his ministry. York's dramatization of this procession is admittedly the more spectacular: opened by a host of citizens who cite the many prophecies Christ had fulfilled, carried forward by Christ himself who heals the lame and blind as he enters the city, and climaxing with the communal chanting of forty-eight lines of verse each introduced with "Hayll!" the York pageant (545 lines long) is an encomiastic celebration of the triumphal conclusion of Christ's earthly ministry. Although much briefer (88 lines) Chester's Triumphal Entry episode is also quite powerful and may like York have been unusually impressive, for the Corvisors' pageant was regularly referred to in Chester's dramatic records simply as the "Jerusalem Carriage." Although Christ in Chester performs no miracles and speaks not a word, his is a royal procession of great dignity: palms and garments are thrown in his path, the citizens testify seriatim that "hee is verey Goddes Sonne," and the procession reaches it celebratory climax as the citizens of the city chant the antiphon: "Hosanna, filio David! Benedictus qui venit in nomine domini! Hosanna in excelsis!" But the triumphal entry in Chester does not conclude at this moment of apparent universal joy. Christ speaks, and his first words assume the shape of a curse. Looking out over Jerusalem, he predicts that this "holye cittie" shall soon be

> destroyed, dilfullye dryven downe.
> Noe stone with other in all this towne
> shall stand, for that they be unlevon
> to keepe Christes commen
> and Goddes owne visitation,
> donne for mankyndes salvation;
> for the have no devotyon,
> ne dreiden not his dome.

Hardly (as in York) a "comic" celebration of the unification of the Redeemer and the redeemed within the heavenly Jerusalem, Chester's more austere version of the triumphal entry at this point turns potentially "tragic," as Christ suddenly reveals that he has come neither to bless nor to forgive, but to judge and to judge severely. Christ's eschatological prophecy of the city's damnation is so formidable that the citizens kneeling in the streets before him may well—as his procession continues—genuflect in terror as well as awe. To intensify the dramatic image of Christ as the just judge and to render even more immediate the imminent damnation of those who shall be "dilfullye dryven downe," Chester concludes Christ's triumphal entry with an episode not found in any of the other cycles. This episode is Christ's scourging of the temple. Christ enters Jerusalem, descends from his ass, and then advances into the temple, whip in hand. As Christ lashes back and forth, upsetting the tables and cursing those who would profane his Father's house, the moneylenders retreat, hurling imprecations which emphasize the regality and power of Christ's wrath: "Nowe yt seemes well that hee/ would attayne royaltee," cries the first "Mercator," the second adding, "Hit seemes well he would be kinge/ that casteth downe thus our thinges." Indeed, Christ concludes his earthly ministry as an angry God coming to judge and punish with regal indignation those who had sought to violate his command. If with his lashing whip *Christus rex* now appears indistinguishable from *Christus victor,* if his administration of justice seems an awesome display of divine wrath, and if the violent purgation of evil with which his ministry concludes anticipates the merciless judgments to be made at the *Dies Irae,* all this is clearly in keeping with Chester's developing Christology: coequal with his Father, Christ radiates on earth as well as in heaven the glory, severity, power, and mystery of the Divine King.

We have seen, then, in the events of Christ's ministry as selected and interpreted by the Chester dramatist, that a number of basic nominalist precepts have been given dramatic definition: these precepts are, quite simply, God's great knowledge and great power, his great mercy and great justice. In addition, because of its theological allegiance to "first principles," its dramatic fidelity to Scripture, its apparent distrust of religious intellectualism, and its emphasis upon revealed truth, Chester's "conservatism" shares a number of characteristics with Bradwardine's "reactionary" school of theological thought. But Chester's theological perspective—having gained full definition only after the Whitsun shift in the early sixteenth century—may have been influenced as well by certain more moderate ideas expressed during or after the time of Bradwardine. Gabriel Biel, for example, whose late fifteenth-century works constitute in many respects a synthesis of late medieval nominalism, took issue with Bradwardine on several counts. Bradwardine was an uncompromising apologist of the *sola scriptura* thesis—arguing that, concerning matters of doctrinal truth, Scripture must serve as exclusive and absolute authority; Biel's position, however, would seem closer to Chester's practice—emphasizing the primary importance of scriptural authority but allowing that certain truths are extrascriptural or derive not from Scripture alone.[29] Bradwardine (anticipating the Reformation again) had seen man as a predetermined instrument of God's will; Biel (as did the majority of nominalists) insisted on the autonomy of the Christian *viator*.[30] Such a basic idea as human freedom could hardly be allowed as a controlling dramatic precept in Chester were it not for its Ministry plays' insistent iteration of the *veritas-libertas* tropes found in the Gospel of John. Furthermore, those characters who discover their true freedom typically express their perfect love of God (which Biel called *amor dei super omnia propter deum*) by an act of "fredom," or unconditional giving: in Pagina XIV this is exemplified by Mary's lavish use of the oil and then by the Janitor's free gift of the ass and foal. The obverse of this "free" love of God is that possessive love which Biel called *amor concupiscentia;* it is with the perfect expression of this false love (Judas's covenant with his conspirators) that Chester's Ministry Group concludes.

Other corollaries between Biel and Chester may be discovered. Biel's careful exposition of the simultaneous expressions of human penitence and divine grace could serve as a fitting gloss to Chester's Magdalene episode; likewise, his analysis of the necessary interdependence of God's *misericordia* and *iusticia* stands as a philosophic complement to Pagina XIV's dramatic counterweighting of Christ's divine mercy and justice.[31] But perhaps most appropriate to Chester's entire Ministry Group is Biel's general definition of the nature of Christ's person and of his significance as *Christus victor*. While Biel cleverly "resolved" the conundrum of the hypostatic union by establishing the relationship of Christ's two natures as that of substance to accident, "the heart of the mystery of the Incarnation" (writes Oberman) remained for Biel the divinity of Christ rather than his humanity—"the fact that the immutable God became man without diminution or loss as regards any of his attributes."[32] In Chester's Ministry pageants we have seen that the preeminent precept in each is that Christ on earth enjoyed without diminution or loss the immutable attributes of his Father. Biel also chose to emphasize in his writings the primacy of Christ's *obedientia activa* over his *obedientia passiva.* That is, whereas Anselm had felt that the most significant moment of Christ's life was the expiatory death he had "passively" suffered for the sins of mankind, Biel argued that more important were the many deeds performed by Christ as divine actor: "sent "active" fulfillments of God's law. In Chester we have seen a similar emphasis during the Ministry plays upon Christ as divine actor: "sent from the throne sempiternall" his "Fathers hestes and commandmentes to fulfill," Christ emphasized in his own words the importance of his deeds as proof of his divinity and as realizations of his Father's will. In Chester of course the "passive" moments of the Passion will be fully dramatized, as will Christ's Agony in the Garden. But these moments contain a philosophic significance very close to that which Biel attributed to them: Christ's death thus becomes "only the culmination of a whole life dedicated to obedience and fulfillment of the law."[33]

In discovering these similarities between Biel's overt and Chester's implicit theologies, I have not meant to imply, any more than I have in my allusions to Scotus, Ockham, and Bradwardine, that the Chester dramatist was an ardent member of a single school of nominalist thought, or that he was self-consciously mediating his allegiance between two or more philosophic camps. Rather, I have been insisting simply that the Chester cycle, if it is to be understood theologically, must be examined first in terms of a general point of view which is nominalist. "Nominalism," Oberman has written, "is not a doctrinal unity, but a common attitude, on some points at least, of remarkably different strands."[34] The way in which Chester shares this common attitude is I believe illustrated best in its Ministry plays, but many of the different strands of Chester's nominalist program are to be discovered elsewhere in the cycle as well. The theme of divine power, for example, is not reserved exclusively to Pagina XIII. As Kathleen Ashley has shown, this theme is given linguistic and dramatic emphasis at all of Chester's "theological high points."[35] Likewise, the playwright's artistic commitment to scriptural fidelity as a theological principle could be illustrated easily with other pageants serving as evidence; this principle is reinforced even after the cycle's "mimetic" conclusion, when the four evangelists appear before the audience to verify the authenticity of the preceding dramatized events. Not all the techniques used in the Ministry Group to emphasize a nominalist precept, however, are to be found at work throughout the cycle. The salvific power of faith, for instance, is consistently opposed throughout the cycle to the limits and dangers of reason; but the playwright hardly insists that this dramatic dialectic is part of an ongoing nominalist-Scholastic debate, or that Christ's detractors are all doubting Thomists in disguise. Yet it should be noted that that epitome of Christian belief which nominalists so often held up as the proper replacement of the Scholastic *summa* is elevated as well in Chester to a position of unique importance: the Apostles' Creed, that is, serves not only as the spiritual resolution of the Resurrection Group but also, as we shall see, as a structural foundation of the entire cycle.

II

Thus it is evident that the Chester dramatist, an intellectual playwright committed to a kind of drama that on one level at least is antiintellectual, shaped his plays to accord philosophically with a limited set of basic nominalist ideas. These ideas are so few and so fundamental, however, that they scarcely form a cluster distinctive enough to identify Chester's perspective with that of any single fifteenth-century philosopher: Chester's implicit position can be defined only as a kind of conservative nominalism, perhaps a modified form of neo-Bradwardinism. It is important nevertheless that Chester's nominalism be carefully disaffiliated from the more liberal reaches of fifteenth-century thought, especially those which could have influenced the development of the three other English cycles. It may for instance be argued that the "Franciscan" left wing of nominalism, with its highly refined phenomenology of particulars, its emphasis upon Christ's human nature, and its "liberal" defense of the imagination, contributed to the distinctive styles of York, Wakefield, and N-Town—to their fascination with realistic detail, their emphasis upon Christ as a man of sorrows, and their exploitation of religious emotion through sensational pictorialism.[36] The Chester dramatist, on the other hand, appears deliberately to have composed his plays as an antidote to these liberal extremes. It is not the audience's love and pity for Christ which are evoked but its reverence and awe. It is not the realistic particulars of Christ's human gestures but the universal significance of his hierophantic acts that Chester seeks to define. And it is not Christ's human proximity to his followers that matters so much as his distance as a divinity from them. In his Ministry Group the Chester dramatist accentuates this distance between the human sphere and the divine by emphasizing a single attitude of human adoration. Assumed by the adulteress, the blind man, Martha, and then Mary—who all kneel before their Lord—this attitude is iterated by individuals until finally, in the triumphal entry, "all the world" (as Annas later complains) "honored him upon there knee/ as God had comon that daye." By so insistently elevating Christ above the world of his kneeling followers, Chester gives spatial expression and "iconic" definition to tenets basic to its conservative, nominalist, and "Johannine" Christology.

In addition, Chester attempts to evoke an ideal contemplative response to the various acts of Christ's ministry by its manipulation of certain other "conservative" dramatic strategies. That is, whereas the other cycles emphasize the emotional immediacy of events, Chester often holds them at a meditative distance in order that each may be contemplated and recalled in terms of its interpretive text. In Pagina XII the Expositor retraces within his homiletic gloss the graphic outline of each preceding episode: the intended effect is that both the scene and its significance etch deeply into the audience's memory. Pagina XIII employs a somewhat similar exegetical device, this time glossing events in anticipation of their accomplishment: Christ opens the pageant by interpreting his future deeds, the significance of which is then reinforced by their subsequent performance. Pagina XIV uses a technique differing from these only in that it simultaneously presents both tableau and text: the scene and its gloss are offered in conjunction so that each may complement and edify the other. Thus, rather than exploit high emotion through a moving sequence of intensely "dramatic" scenes, Chester appeals to the meditative faculties by lifting a scene from, or freezing it within, its temporal medium so that as a kind of unmoving icon it may unite with its spiritual significance. One major purpose of these techniques is mnemonic. "Printe these sayinges in your mynd and harte," Christ had charged his disciples at the opening of Pagina XIII; "recorde them and keepe them in memorye." So could Christ have said as well of the iconic deeds of his ministry. An equally important purpose is that these techniques appeal specifically to the viewers' spiritual understanding. Rather than developing a highly affective dramatic style, Chester is thus concerned primarily with achieving a dramatic form which is iconic, meditative, and didactically self-interpretive.

It is now sufficiently clear that Chester's dramatic style, homiletic strategies, and conservative theology are not only all interdependent phenomena but are all part of a deliberate "archaizing" spirit which informs the entire cycle. It is apparent as well that this "archaizing" spirit was fashioned quite late in Chester's history, achieving its full realization only in the early sixteenth century—when those additions to the cycle of episodes and glosses for the Whitsun shift were complete.

Although strikingly different from the theological allegiances of the other cycles, Chester's "archaic" theology, we have seen, was hardly a unique cultural phenomenon: many branches of fifteenth-century theological thought shared such conservative propensities, and many nominalists were accustomed to turn back on occasion to the "ancient" authorities of the pre-Scholastic eleventh and twelfth centuries for guidance and inspiration. Chester's implicit theology is in fact not all that similar to anyone's in the twelfth century. And because of Chester's strong reactions against the Franciscan humanizings of Christ, its divinizing, "Johannine" Christology is (ironically) rather close to Aquinas's. But these are retrospective observations which by no means invalidate what was clearly perceived at the time to be a consistent artistic statement defining a return to the ways and values of the ancient authorities. Chester's conservative dramatic style, I have concluded, was also a deliberate, rather than accidental, achievement: it was consciously designed to figure forth its Christology and to evoke a meditative response to the reenacted events of Scripture. Although Chester's conservative theology is not defined fully enough to be identified with any single philosophic party of the fifteenth or sixteenth centuries, its tendencies toward a kind of Augustinian fideism links it tonally with a variety of anti-Scholastic positions held in the very late Middle Ages.

Were it not for a recent examination of a very rarely studied artistic phenomenon, I would not have been fully convinced that Chester's archaic dramatic style must be understood (like its theology) as part of a larger cultural movement of its time. In an address given in 1976 entitled "The Neo-Romanesque," Robert C. McGrath has shown that in fifteenth-century English, Flemish, and Burgundian art there was a concerted revival of certain Romanesque motifs and *topoi,* where the Romanesque, both as an idea and as a congeries of images, served artists as "a source of formal and stylistic inspiration, as well as a direct source of symbolic and iconographic enrichment."[37] Three of McGrath's major findings are especially pertinent to my understanding of Chester's style and of its place within this "neo-Romanesque" artistic tradition. The first is the commitment in fifteenth-century art to recapturing the "mural presence" so distinctive of the Romanesque: cathedral statuary, for instance, was often "left unfinished behind," so that a "dynamic interaction between statue and niche" was again effected. It could similarly be said of Chester's dramatic characters that they too had been deliberately "left unfinished behind" so that they might interact more organically with the theological frame that defined their meaning. Second, McGrath's documentation of the return in the fifteenth century of the end-of-the-world fantasies and eschatological horrors so distinctive of the twelfth is also partially relevant to an appreciation of Chester's dramatic uniqueness (although Chester hardly shares a Romanesque fascination with the weird and grotesque): not only is Chester the only cycle to include a signs-of-doomsday and Antichrist sequence, it is unique as well in the apocalyptic tenor it accords the ending of Christ's public ministry.

Finally, McGrath in his address examined how the Romanesque was used by several fifteenth-century painters to symbolize a spiritual norm "ancient" in its reference but contemporary in its significance: for Van Eyck the Romanesque represented the Heavenly Jerusalem, for Campin it represented the era *ante legem,* for Hugo van der Goes it represented the old world yet-to-be-redeemed, and for Bosch it represented hell or the present wicked world. The symbolism of the Romanesque in Chester surely differs from the significance it is given by any of these painters; nevertheless, it is clear that as an "ancient authority" the Romanesque was as important symbolically to the Chester dramatist as it was to these fifteenth-century painters for whom, McGrath concludes, it offered "a set of forms that articulate a culture both near and remote." In Chester's iconic definition of human action, its careful balancing of weighty and unadorned scenes, and its reliance upon a programmatic frame that gives to individual gestures a universal significance, we can sense an artist's attempts to revive the dignity and authority of a "classical" and long-ago tradition. It is hardly surprising that Chester's dramatic style will never be mistaken for the style of a twelfth-century liturgical play: classical revivals always constitute a new form of art. What *is* surprising, perhaps, is the artistic confidence and success with which this "old style" has been given dramatic definition during what proved to be the last decades of the English Middle Ages. Chester's neo-Romanesque style, one may therefore conclude, stands itself as a symbolic statement: it argues that in their spiritual humility the ancient authorities were wisest, that God's nature is understood best in unquestioning reverence and quiet meditation, and that God's powers—if they are to be expressed at all in art—are revealed best through the unchanging and iconic forms of the classical authorities of the "ancient" past.

6

The Ritual Aesthetics
of the Passion:
Paginae XV-XVI

I wanted to be actually there with Mary Magdalene and the others who loved him," Juliana of Norwich wrote at the end of the fourteenth century, "and with my own eyes to see and know more of the physical suffering of our Saviour, and the compassion of our Lady and of those who there and then were loving him truly and watching his pains. I would be one of them and suffer with him."[1] Juliana's longing "to be actually there" on the hill of Calvary and to share Christ's physical suffering was a personal longing which articulated both a belief and a need cherished generally by the late medieval religious imagination: that is, not only was Christ's Passion (rather than his Resurrection) now considered the center of Christian history and thus central to the meditative lives of all Christians, but its significance was assumed to be understood best by a direct experiencing of all the sensational realities of the original events themselves. Juliana's prayer was answered—as seen in her *Revelations of Divine Love*—by that unique vision of the historical and crucified Christ which served thereafter as the determining force of her spiritual life. The common run of late medieval believers, however, were rarely graced by such visionary or mystical revelations. Their longings to "see" the historical Christ could be gratified in part by their own attempts at reimagining

---

Part of this chapter is reprinted with slight changes from my "The Dramatic Strategies of Chester's Passion Pagina," *Comparative Drama* 8 (1974):275-89, by permission of the editors.

Christ's dying, death, and Resurrection whenever they observed the Mass; and of course they annually recollected the story of Christ's final days in the course of their ritual celebrations of Holy Week. But more and more in the late Middle Ages it became the religious arts— the sermons, lyrics, narrative poems, wall-paintings, statuary, wood- cuts and plays—which for the lay imagination captured the details of Christ's last hours, evoked the pathos of his sufferings, and held in focus for contemplation each of those memorable scenes, from the arrest through the Crucifixion to the burial.

Of all the religious arts, drama clearly enjoyed special powers in its reproduction of these highly charged events. Since it alone oper- ates in a moving and mimetic medium, drama was able (both its critics and apologists agreed) to quicken the scenes of sacred history with an impressive and sometimes even frightening verisimilitude. In addition, as it realistically reenacted these sacred events of the past, drama perforce had to give special consideration to the rhythms of its own temporal designs in the present. That is, just as the speeches of individual characters needed to be measured against each other (in terms of tempo, length, pitch, stress, etc.), so the continuum of the entire dramatized sequence had to be modulated carefully and intelli- gently: ground rhythms established, rhetorical patterns shaped, emotive fields counterpointed, and gestures choreographed so the achieved dramatic effect would offer a coherent vision and compre- hensive experience of Christ's Passion. As can be seen in the individual Passion sequences of the four English cycles, each playwright was fully aware of the fundamental contribution of such rhythms to his overall dramatic design. Of the many kinds of rhythm he could employ, two would appear to have been basic: those rhythms sug- gestive or reminiscent of ritual action (either sacred or profane) and those rhythms suggestive of the cadences of "real life."

That Chester was particularly interested in developing the rhythms of ritual action is evident in its dramatic treatment of the Last Supper. Wakefield and York clearly found the Last Supper, itself obviously a ritual celebration, rather slow-moving and undramatic. Each therefore attempted to improve upon the scriptural account: Wakefield by building up suspense at dinner as eight disciples, one after the other, anxiously ask "Is it oght I?" until Christ identifies Judas as his betrayer; York by Christ's introducing a child "Both meke and mylde" to his disciples as an *exemplum* of the humility they are to emulate. N-Town's Last Supper sequence enhances the scriptural narrative by a brilliant piece of double-staging: the ceremonial meal is fully represented (the sacraments instituted and allegorized by Christ) while "outside" and in between these episodes the conspiracy intermittently advances until it is finally consolidated by Judas, who serves as an interloper between the two dramatic worlds, sacred and profane. Chester's interpretation of the Last Supper, in contrast to these three, is a very simple affair, offering a faithful and uninterrupted reenactment of the ritual, each gesture of which (the stage directions make clear) is reproduced with loving exactitude. After the disciples seat themselves at table, for example, Christ joins them and *Johannis in gremio dormit*. A stanza later Christ *accipiet panem, frangit, et discipulis suis dat*. A stanza later Christ ceremonially *accipit calicem manibus* and then prays to his Father, *oculis elevatis*. A stanza later all twelve disciples commune, as Christ *edit et bibit cum discipulis*. Whereas York and Wakefield fail even to include the blessing and sharing of the Eucharist,[2] and whereas N-Town on the other hand elaborates at length upon the typological interconnections between the lamb, the "oble," and Christ, Chester is content to reproduce the ceremony itself with little elaboration and no diversion. The Last Supper for Chester was clearly an inviolate ritual whose profound significance was best expressed by a literal representation of each of its scripturally authorized elements.

The precision and care with which each moment of Chester's eucharistic supper is acted out are qualities found again in the accompanying ritual of the washing of the feet. Whereas the three other cycles cut the full ceremony short, apparently because it held up dramatic progress, Chester finds its drama in the prolonged and repeated rite itself. Christ first washes Peter's feet; he then *lavabit pedes omnium singulatim et abstergit lintheo*. Having washed and dried the feet of all the disciples present, Christ then charges them "doe eychon to other in fere / as I have done before," and the ceremony is duly repeated by each of the eleven disciples, as the stage directions require: *Tunc invicem omnes aliorum pedes lavant*. In its careful reproduction of every ritual gesture—both in the supper and the washing of the feet—it can be seen that Chester's dramatic interest resides here in developing a rhythm which is neither suspenseful, "individual," or forward-moving, but rather commemorative, communal, and circular. Although Christ had begun by charging, "make haste, that we maye soone / all figures cleane rejecte," both ceremonies are fully acted out, slowly and lovingly, so that the disciples' celebration of their sacramental unity and fraternal order may be perfectly expressed.

Whereas the rhythms of Chester's Last Supper are simple and "benevolent," the rhythms of the Passion sequences of the four cycles are quite different. In its own way, each Passion sequence is a tense, complex, and "malevolent" emotional drama. The dramatic realism of Christ's agony and slow death as represented in these sequences need not of course deprive them of elements reminiscent of ritual, but such ritual elements are likely to resemble those appropriate to a painful rite of passage. In contrast to the "comic" transitions of the Nativity plays where the community of spectators is allowed to move easily from sorrow to joy, Christ's Passion is interpreted by each of the Corpus Christi playwrights as an extended *agon*, difficult for the audience to behold and potentially tragic in its implications. And even if the pain were on occasion deliberately palliated (as in the Ukrainian Holy Week ritual of flagellating with pussy-willow branches), the mixture of suffering and solace in the Corpus Christi Passions tended to be a bitter one, and whatever emotional catharsis the spectators achieved at the end of their long and sad passage was well-earned. It has become a staple judgment of medieval drama criticism that the extended brutalities of Christ's humiliations and tortures dramatized in the Passion sequences of the English cycles were intended to evoke from the community of spectators a complex cluster of emotions—a powerful mix of pity, piety, grief, horror, guilt, and awe. The ways in which the cycles controlled the evocation of these emotions and made the viewing of Christ's protracted sufferings an aesthetically satisfying, or at least tolerable, experience have therefore been preeminent concerns in evaluating the craft of the Corpus Christi playwrights. The progress of that evaluation, however, has been compromised by an assumption that the analysis of certain techniques employed by most of the cycles will reveal the strategies used in all the cycles to control the emotions and sway the beliefs of their viewers.

Two influential studies approach the dynamics of the Passions in this way. Waldo McNeir selects from the four Passion sequences three dramatic devices which he believes offered in the midst of Christ's tortures a "sort of dramatic relief": an occasional inclusion of comedy, a close-up dramatic focus upon the means of torture, and a melodramatic "heightening of situation," which "may have the effect of anesthetizing the feelings and inducing a half-hypnotized absorption in the circumstantial interest of intolerable occurrences."[3] V.A. Kolve isolates two further major dramatic devices which, he believes, served in all the cycles "to make the physical horror tolerable as an aesthetic experience."[4] By splicing into the central *mythos* of Christ's sufferings episodes which revealed the personal motives and private lives of Christ's judges and persecutors, Kolve argues, the cycles time and again distracted the audience and alleviated the emotional pressures of Christ's agonies. Second, by developing the metaphors of play into a major theme, as Christ's *tortores* transform his dying into a macabre game, "a kind of distancing is achieved which assists in controlling the audience's response to Christ's death.[5]

Although the observations of McNeir and Kolve are acute, the devices they mention do not appear in all the cycles; when they appear, they are often employed in different episodes, to varying degrees, and for various effects; and wherever employed, they are coordinated with other major dramatic devices which these critics have not discussed. Therefore, to understand fully the dramatic strategies of the Corpus Christi Passions, it seems imperative that each be studied fully, individually, and from beginning to end. My purpose in this chapter is to examine the major devices Chester employs in its presentation of the events of the Passion, to follow the emotional configuration the patterning of those techniques describes, and to argue that Chester's dramatic principles are controlled by a vision of Christ's mission clearly different from the visions of the other cycles. In establishing a basic dramatic rhythm reminiscent of ritual, in formalizing the characters of evil into a collective, impersonal force, in affording occasions for the expression and release of the most painful emotions evoked by Christ's tortures, and in insisting upon an intellectual apprehension of the significance of Christ's dying, Chester coordinates its strategies into a dramatic pattern which finally demonstrates the salvific power of Christian

belief. Chester's major rhetorical pressures therefore do not emphasize the theme of God's mercy, the shared guilt of the spectators
watching Christ's death, or the imperative need for charity in their
lives; rather, Chester requires of its audience a communal assertion
of awakened faith in the divinity of Christ's person and in the
sacred truth of those historical events reenacted upon the pageant
stage.

I

Three notable characteristics of Chester's dramatization of the
Passion stand out: its unification of all the events of the Passion into
one play,[6] the brevity of that play itself (873 lines),[7] and the deliberate speed with which it moves from one major event to the next.
The swift pacing of events is illustrated in the first six episodes: the
examination by Caiaphas takes place in eight stanzas; the buffeting
in six stanzas; the first trial before Pilate in six stanzas; the examination by Herod in six stanzas; the second trial before Pilate, the
longest episode, in twelve stanzas; the scourging in eight. Unlike the
other three cycles, Chester adds to these opening episodes no ancillary
characters, no "backstage" events to protract and complicate the
action or to divert the audience from the central spectacle of Christ's
humiliations. In Chester's presentation of the buffeting, examinations,
and scourging, Christ's exposure to vilification and his endurance of
physical punishment are the center of dramatic focus, and the horrors
of his torments are unalleviated by diversion into the private lives
and motives of his persecutors. But the pacing of these events is itself
an aesthetic device which may have offered some relief: by rapidly
passing Christ to and fro, from Caiaphas to the buffeters to Pilate to
Herod to Pilate again and then to the scourgers, Chester avoids
bearing down too painfully upon any one form of humiliation.

Within these events, and in contrast to the examination episodes
of the other cycles, Christ's persecutors are remarkable for their near
indistinguishability.. With the single notable exception of Pilate—
whose dramatic role I will discuss shortly—the characters of Christ's
examiners are as stylized as the speeches they utter. Speaking in
rhythmic, chanting sequence, a quatrain or stanza each, Annas,
Caiaphas and the two Jews form a unified malevolent chorus of re-

venge, reciting Christ's crimes, challenging his powers, and eventually demanding his death. The opening speeches of the play establish the heavy cadence of their queries and the closed unanimity of their minds:

Primus Judeus

Syr byshopps, here we have brought
a wretch that mych woe hase wrought
and would bringe our lawe to naught—
right soe hath hit spurned.

Secundus Judeus

Yea, wydewhere we have him sought,
and deare alsoe we have him brought,
for here manye mens thought
to him he hase turned.

Annas

A, janglinge Jesus, art thou nowe here?
Nowe thou may prove thy postie powere,
whether thy cause be cleane and cleare;
thy Christhood we must knowe.

Cayphas

Meethinke a maistrye that yt were
other for pennye or prayere
to shutt him of his dangere
and such sleight to shewe.

Their cross-examination proceeds in this heavily stylized manner: none of the questioners individualizes himself by revealing a private motive or assuming an individual approach to the prosecution. Rather, together, they rhythmically, almost ritualistically, question, challenge, and revile Christ, until *Omnes Simull* (H) they cry, "Wytnes of all this compenye / that falsely lyes hee," and then fervidly agree with Primus Judeus: "Buffetes him that makes this bere." The character of Herod, revealed separately in the fourth episode, is essentially the same as theirs. When Christ refuses to answer his cynical queries, Herod mocks Christ in the same manner as had the two Jews, Annas, and Caiaphas:

What! I weene that man is wood,
or elles dombe and can no good.

Such a scalward never before me stood,
so stowt and sterne is hee.

The sum effect of this general characterization of evil is to elim-
inate any potential interest in the personalities or private motives of
these men. No deep psychology of individual human nature is probed.
Rather, evil is cast as a generic force shared equally and indistinguish-
ably by Christ's detractors.

In the other cycles the portrayal of evil is clearly more personal—
in Herod's childish toyings with Christ in N-Town, for instance, and
in the devious hypocrisies of Pilate in Wakefield.[8] But it is York
which is most ample in its satirical individuation of sinister characters.
Annas and Caiaphas parody each other as each in turn wrathfully
lashes out against "this traitoure" Christ, and must be restrained by
the other. Pilate is consistent in the inconsistency of his motives;[9]
his wife is effetely enamored of court fashions; Herod out-herods
himself, shouting at Christ in strange tongues. All three cycles have
properly been praised for the relative realism of their characters and
the satire they generate, but in the dramatization of the secular
density and moral anarchy of the lives of Christ's judges lay a
danger that the spiritual significance of their victim might be up-
staged and forgotten. This danger was recognized by the York
Master, who added to the prolix noise and moral bedlam of the
examination episodes a character whose sane wisdom serves as a
norm by which Christ's secular judges may be judged. Yet in creating Pilate's Beadle as a "crypto-Christian," the York Master seems
implicitly to admit that Christ's presence and his few words of truth
were—in dramatic terms—not powerful enough to give the episodes
the moral control and emotional balance they needed.[10] Of the four
cycles, Chester is the only one which chooses not to exploit the
diversions of diversely evil characters. Evil in Chester, stylized in
character, generic in nature, derives its power from the speech-
rhythms of archetypalized spleen and hatred. Yet by presenting
Christ's detractors as a unified and self-defined vendetta of collective
wrath and vengeance, Chester sustains in its examination episodes an
easily apprehended division between good and evil, truth and falsehood.

Although the nature of the truth Christ represents is only implied
in the examination episodes by the cynical charges and reproaches of
Christ's detractors, the spiritual significance of his sufferings is articu-

lated clearly in his two trials before Pilate. In these episodes Pilate's role is unusual. In the first he appears briefly as a "good" Pilate, but in the second he is uniquely characterized as a Roman stoic curious about the philosophic ramifications of Christ's definition of truth. Influenced by the *Acta Pilati*,[11] the central dialogue of the episode defines Christ's kingship and answers Pilate's unanswered question in John, "Quid est veritas?"

Pilatus

Ergo, a kinge thou art, or was.

Jesus

That thou sayes, yt is no lesse.
But nowe I tell thee here expresse
that kinge I am and be maye.
In world I came to beare wytnes
of soothnes, and therfore borne I was,
and all that leeven soothnes
take heede to that I saye.

Pilatus

What is soothnes, tell thou mee?

Jesus

Soothnes came from Goddes see.

Pilatus

In yearth then hath trueth no postie
by thyne opinion?

Jesus

Howe should on yearth bee
while so deemed in yearth is hee
of them that have non authoritie
in yearth, agaynst reason?

Chester is the only cycle to include at this point such a disquisition upon the nature of supreme truth and divine kingship. The rapid rhythms of the highly alliterated stanzas of the examination episodes are exchanged here for a slower, more meditative tempo, as the traditional Chester stanza is broken down into a serial interchange of philosophic question and response. This sudden alteration in dramatic rhythm serves to emphasize Christ's claims to truth, and assists in forming a detached and transcendent perspective from which the proceedings of his trial may be judged. Christ's definition of truth as transcending all earthly power is a statement within the play meant to mitigate in part the painful reality of his sufferings, suggesting that the torments he endures in this world are in some manner a falsehood and fiction. Once Pilate has served his purpose, he degenerates quickly through the rest of the play: his Roman interest in truth bends to a Roman allegiance to civic duty, as he orders Christ's scourging, and then declines further into a self-centered interest in preserving his own office, as he orders the Crucifixion. But in his brief role as philosophic catalyst, Pilate grants Christ the occasion to assert a timeless vision of truth by which the rapidly moving and painful sequences of his trials and tortures may be judged.

Despite the partial consolation offered by Christ's words, the physical horrors of the episodes flanking his appearances before Pilate—the buffeting and scourging—are graphic and powerful. Chester therefore employs one further dramatic strategy in these most horrific episodes preceding Calvary: the heavy verbal cadences used earlier by Christ's examiners are reduced in the speeches of the *tortores* to the short, pulsating rhythms of a primitive chant. The more grotesque the actions of the *tortores* become, the more primitive is the cadence of their lines, as they grunt and shout in regular rounds, a quatrain each. The last round of the buffeting indicates the primal rhythms of their words and gestures:

Primus Judeus

Though he him beshitt,
a buffytt shall bytt;
maye no man me witt,
though I doe hym woo.

Secundus Judeus

He failes for to flyte
or ought to despytte.
For he hase to lite,
now must he hame moe.

Tercius Judeus

And moe if I maye.
I shall soone assaye

and haste thou large paye,
thou prince, one thy pate.

Quartus Judeus

Yf he saye naye,
I shall, in faye,
laye. I dare laye
yt is not to late. [H]

The strident cadence, the heavy alliteration, and the stinging rhymes of these dimeter lines reveal that the brutality of the *tortores* was probably highly stylized in its enactment. Stepping forward at every fourth quatrain, buffeting Christ at the end of each line, each torturer appears a humanoid brute playing by rote a role ordained by a power beyond his ken. Although the manner of acting employed can only be conjectured, the nonhumanity of the *tortores* and the high stylization of their words suggest that their actions were more ritualistic than mimetic, and that the ritualistic elements, despite the brutality of their effects, formalized and ordered the horrors performed. An obvious contrast is established between the barking imprecations and sadistic curses of Christ's persecutors and the silent dignity of his impassive endurance. In contrast to the other cycles, York and Wakefield especially, where Christ nearly breaks under the physical pains inflicted upon him, Christ in Chester apparently remains unmoved by the buffeting and scourging, and thereby offers further, physical proof that his truth is not of this world.

The dramatic strategies employed in these early episodes are therefore clearly coordinated for a major purpose. By keeping the focus of dramatic action upon Christ, by telescoping the personalities of the evil characters to a stylized ignorance and ill will, and by steadily moving from episode to episode, with the most brutal events ordered by stylized chants and ritualistic actions, Chester never diverts the audience's attention from Christ's fate nor does it strive to heighten suspense concerning the outcome of the examinations and trials. What Chester achieves through its relatively austere fidelity to the major events of Scripture is an overriding sense of their ineluctability, as episode follows episode with inexorable, steady pacing. But the apparent inevitability of Christ's doom is controlled by two major dramatic strategies, and these strategies moderate the horror of the events enacted. By formalizing to the point of ritual the words and actions of Christ's persecutors, Chester suggests that they are agents involved in a rite whose movements are ultimately controlled by a power beyond their comprehension. Then, by allowing Christ, through Pilate's questionings, to assert a definition of truth as divinely transcendent, Chester implies that the power ultimately controlling the *tortores* is divine, and that Christ's fleshly suffering is to some degree of his own creation and under his Father's control.

II

The tempo of Pagina XVI changes noticeably in its second half, moving from the general hubbub of the examinations, buffeting, and scourging to a quieter verbal and dramatic cadence which allows for a steady contemplation of Christ's last living moments. This shift in dramatic rhythm is anticipated by the procession to Calvary, which briefly includes Simon of Cyrene's carrying the cross, and by the last grisly work of the *tortores*. Chester's insertion of the dicing before the Crucifixion is uniquely strategic, for in momentarily distracting the audience from its heretofore uninterrupted contemplation of Christ's progress, the dicing episode briefly suspends the growing emotions of compassion and terror. Although Christ is present throughout the dicing, standing as a bloody spectacle before the audience, the shift in dramatic focus away from him to the *tortores'* myopic interest in the fall of dice makes the dramatic return to Christ's next torture all the more powerful. Called back to work by Caiaphas, the *tortores* set about their job, and with crude relish stretch Christ, nail him, and hoist the cross into place. Although the game the *tortores* make of stretching Christ on the cross is mercifully brief (unlike this action in the other cycles), the brutality of their actions and the pathetic sight of their victim were clearly intended to evoke a profoundly agonized response from the audience. Like the contemporary graphic Images of Pity and the popular meditational poems upon his wounds, the dramatic spectacle of Christ— buffeted, scourged, "tugget, lugget, and all totorne"—appealed to the deepest sensations of grief and guilt.[12] Yet to have protracted this dramatic spectacle without comment, to have allowed the *tortores* to proceed with some other brutal business, or to have given the disbelievers surrounding the cross this occasion further to revile Christ, would have broken the principles of aesthetic restraint Chester has nurtured so far in the play. Thus, with compassionate dramatic timing, Chester gives relief to the most profound emotions raised by the sight of Christ on the cross. The Virgin and then the three Marys enter and grieve. Their poignant laments express the feelings shared by the community of spectators. The Virgin cries:

> Alas, my love, my liffe, my leere!
> Alas, nowe mourninge, woe ys mee!
> Alas, sonne, my boote thou bee,
> thy mother that thee bare.

In her five-stanza lyrical lament (H MS), the Virgin expresses the wavering of her ability to comprehend the tragic paradox of the blissful Passion:

> Alas, the sorrow of this sight
> marrs my mynd, mayne and might,
> but aye my hart methink is light
> to looke on that I love.
> And when I looke anonright
> upon my child that thus is dight,
> would death deliver me in height,
> then were I all above.   [H]

The three Marys then amplify her emotions, as they beseech Christ to "break thy bandes," and to arrest the Crucifixion, "syth thou art God and man." The sixty-four lines of the *planctus Mariarum* thus form a single lyrical threnody expressing a human bewilderment in response to Christ's self-inflicted death. Yet through the expression of their emotional dilemma, and through the formal art of the lyric itself, that grief is ordered and partially purged. Here, at the most tragic point in the play, the Marys reassert their belief in Christ's divinity, despite their limited ability to rationalize his death. By raising these subliminal fears and then laying them to rest, Chester ameliorates the most potent doctrinal doubts which Christ's dying may evoke. As in the second trial before Pilate, where Christ defines the divinity of his truth, here, at the penultimate moment before his death, the Marys reassert the truth of his divinity.

In contrast to the other cycles, the sufferings of the Virgin in Chester are carefully controlled. She does not swoon (as she does twice in N-Town) and she is mercifully led away by John *before* her son's death, with John's consoling assurance that Christ shall rise victoriously in three days. Finally Chester allows Christ's detractors a brief expression of disbelief: Annas and Caiaphas challenge Christ to save himself, for only then, they say, will they believe "that Gods Sonne is he" (H). But their bitter reproaches have an elliptical dramatic effect, for the lament of the Marys has moderated the horror, expressed the sorrow, and reinforced the belief of the Passion's audience.

Christ's last words and death are thus in Chester not a bitter climax to an unmitigated, painful torture. Faithful to Scripture, Christ momentarily doubts. He cries, "My God, my God, I speak to thee!...Why hasse thou forsaken mee?" (H) and grieves, "My thyrst ys sore, my thyrst ys sore." But he dies quietly, almost peacefully, asserting once again that his will and God's are one:

> Almighty God in majestie,
> to worke thy wyll I will never wonde.
> My [spiritte] I betake to thee;
> receyve yt, lord, into thy hand. [H]

To this point I have examined the dramatic techniques Chester employs in the episodes proceeding through the Crucifixion which make Christ's dying a tolerable aesthetic experience. Although Christ's agonies on the cross are powerfully presented, the gruesome effects and pathetic appeals of Chester's Crucifixion are considerably less sensational than those of Wakefield, for instance, of which McNeir writes: "Nothing is omitted to make the scene graphic, but spirituality is lost in this insistence on the physical agonies of Calvary."[13] Chester's rendering of the Crucifixion plumbs the deeply ambivalent emotions evoked by Christ's death; but by strategically formalizing these emotions in speeches spoken by characters surrounding the cross, Chester tactfully expresses and reaffirms the most "positive" emotions, while attempting a catharsis of the "negative" ones.

Chester employs one further dramatic strategy in these episodes to emphasize the central spiritual significance of the Passion. Several secondary scriptural characters appear, and each in turn is "illuminated" by Christ. In dramatic valorization these characters approximate spiritual "neutrality"; but drawn into Christ's presence, they are drawn away from that neutrality as they recognize the divinity of his person. The first is Simon of Cyrene. In all the cycles, after first resisting their orders, Simon is forced by the soldiers to bear Christ's cross, but only in Chester is the reason for his reluctance a concern for Christ and not for himself. He identifies Christ as an innocent man and a prophet, "full of the Holy Ghoost," and beseeches God to bear witness that he acts against his will.

Dysmas is the next to recognize Christ's powers. His words are taken directly from Scripture. The first thief challenges Christ to descend from the cross, but Dysmas reprimands him, then beseeches Christ, "when thou art in they majestie, / then that thou wilt thinke on mee," and Christ promises him "in paradyce thou shalt be todaye." The last two illuminations are carefully introduced to mute the painfulness of Christ's death. Whereas Wakefield has the *tortores* immediately after Christ's death order Longinus to "pryk hym with a spere," and N-Town and York protract the anguish of Calvary through the extended laments of the Virgin, Chester immediately reasserts Christ's divinity through the character of the centurion, who at the moment of Christ's death suddenly proclaims:

> Lordings, I say you sickerly
> that we have wrought wilfully,
> for I know by the prophesy
> that Gods Sonne is he. [H]

The centurion's proclamation is followed immediately by the Longinus episode, where the blind soldier, directed by Caiaphas, wounds Christ's side. The N-Town treatment of this popular scene may be the most "dramatic," as Rose Peebles claims in her study of the Longinus legend, for upon gaining his sight and recognizing Christ, Longinus "ffallyth down on his knes" and cries for forgiveness: "Mercy mercy mercy I crye."[14] In Chester, however, the emphasis is typically not upon man's guilt and God's mercy, but upon the needful recognition of Christ's divinity. His sight restored, Longinus exclaims:

Thee will I serve and with thee be,
for well I leeue in days three
thou wilt ryse through thy posty
and save that on thee call. [H]

The recognitions and assertions of the centurion and Longinus, following immediately upon Christ's giving up the ghost, help to assuage the mortal terror of his death: he is, they believe, God's son, who will rise of his own power from the grave and offer salvation to all who believe in his divine person. The various illuminations of these "neutral" characters thus form a pattern of recognitions which emphasize Christ's divinity and alleviate part of the horror of his dying. As in its Ministry Group, which offers dramatic proof of Christ's omnipotence and omniscience, and in its Resurrection Group, which concludes with a recitation of the Apostles' Creed, Chester emphasizes in its Passion the significant power of belief, and it is the dramatically verified truth of that belief which modifies and interprets the tragic implications of Christ's death.

Although Chester is probably the cycle most committed to a spiritual interpretation of the Passion, there remains after its Crucifixion, as in the other cycles, an irrevocable sense of loss which no triumphant assertions of illuminated figures can abolish. After Christ's death, each of the cycles recognizes the need to turn from mourning toward a more tolerable emotional norm. Wakefield mercifully concludes its Passion in seventy-four lines after Christ's death; similarly, in York, Christ dies and is buried within 156 lines; N-Town interposes the triumphant harrowing of hell between Christ's death and deposition. Chester again does something unusual, as it concludes with one final dramatic innovation. Its deposition episode, the second longest in the play, "goes," according to Hardin Craig, "as far in the delineation of character and the expression of individual thought as perhaps anything in the whole cycle."[15] Yet the psychology of this long episode, where Joseph of Arimathea and Nicodemus converse, leave the hill of Calvary, go to Pilate, convince him to allow them to bury Christ's body, return, and take Christ from the cross, is a humanly simple one, projecting as it does a willful concentration upon practical matters after a deep personal loss. The mission of these two men thus fills an emotional void: as they proceed towards Pilate they distract the audience from the dead Christ and reestablish a dramatic rhythm closer to the rhythm of daily realities. Yet even as they go about their business, the two men steadfastly assert their belief in Christ's divinity, as "Gods Sonne almighty" (H). Kneeling before Christ on their return, they worship him and recite the many preternatural "signes" which occurred at his death. The play closes as they gently lift Christ's body from the cross and carry it towards the tomb, with spices "to balme his swete body, / in sepulchre for to lye" (H).

Thus the dramatic rhythms of the Chester Passion shift subtly according to the actions each episode presents and the place of each episode within the emotional contours the pageant describes. Chester's quasi-ritualistic elements and its more realistic techniques both assist in its intelligent control of emotion as it succeeds in making an unswerving observation of Christ's Passion a dramatic reality. Through the stylization of evil and evil action, through the expansion, contraction, and timely expression of emotion, Chester contains the horrors of the bloody Passion and controls the flow of emotions it raises. In Christ's definition of kingship and truth, in the developing pattern of characters who recognize his true divinity, Chester strategically enforces a spiritual understanding of the import of Christ's dying. The dramaturgy which supports this interpretation of the Passion may appear relatively simple, but we need to remind ourselves that the simple in art need be simplistic, and that elements of ritual are found in the most sophisticated drama.[16] What Chester achieves with these simple techniques is a stark representation of the Passion, made bearable by its benevolent emotional strategies, made intelligible by Christ's definition of transcendent truth, and made religiously edifying by its insistence that the audience reconfirm its own belief in Christ's divinity.

My emphasis upon Chester's ritualistic aesthetics does not mean that the other English cycles are devoid of actions and speeches so highly stylized that they verge on ritual. Two ritual-like moments in fact stand out in the other cycles, and both are additions to Scripture which heighten the pathos of the Crucifixion. The first is found only in N-Town: after nailing Christ to the cross, the *tortores* celebrate their success in a grotesque *danse macabre* as they "dawncyn a-bowte the cros shortly."[17] A second ritual-like moment in the

Passions, a dramatic lyric known as "Christ's Appeal to Man," is included in all the cycles but Chester. Directly addressing the audience from the cross, Christ interrupts the progress of his Crucifixion and forces the spectators to share the guilt of those who had allowed the horror to occur: "My folk," he asks in Wakefield, "what haue I done to the, / That thou all thus shall tormente me?" Like the *danse macabre* in N-Town, a major purpose of this extradramatic appeal is to heighten the guilt and anxiety of the spectators.[18]

In marked contrast to the strategies of the three other cycles, the Chester Passion is dominated by a ritual-aesthetic that brings order, solace, and understanding to the dramatic experience. In the formal gestures, collective complaints, and stylized recognitions of sacred characters, Chester has designed elements that are reminiscent of early liturgical drama. In the primal rhythms, collective brutality, and apersonal gestures of profane characters, Chester formalizes evil into an archetypal power whose movements may be seen to be controlled ultimately by God. Less realistic than the other Passion sequences in its mimesis of contemporary life, Chester succeeds in combining its two ritual elements—one sacred, the other profane—into a play that is evocative of a timeless and universal rite. Thus the legend of Pope Clement's having offered a thousand days' pardon to any who peaceably resorted to the Chester plays is a perfectly appropriate response to the Passion's design.[19] To be a viewer of the Chester Passion was to be a participant in a painful yet purgative celebration, as the Savior through the ritual strategies of the dramatic performance is reunited once again with the community of his faithful.

191

7

The Credal Design
of the Cycle:
Paginae XVII-XXI

I n Chapter 5 I noted briefly the various ways the Agony in the Garden episode might fit into the larger dramatic units of the cycles: that is, the Agony could be seen as a completion of the Ministry Group, as a prologue to the Passion Group, or as some kind of transition between the two. Even though the average viewer is rarely likely to concern himself with such finical discriminations, both the common critical practice of arranging the pageants into groups and the occasional inadequacies of these groupings help to illuminate the major principles upon which the cycles were constructed. As we shall see, these principles are in turn intimately bound up with the role the viewers are asked to play within the cycles' projections of Christian history. That each of the cycles contains a unit of pageants appropriately called the Resurrection Group has never been disputed. In Chester, four pageants obviously belong to this group: the Skinners' "Resurrection" (XVIII), the Saddlers' "Emmaus" (XIX), the Tailors' "Ascension" (XX) and the Fishmongers' "Pentecost" (XXI). But whether or not the pageant which immediately precedes these, the Cooks' "Harrowing of Hell" (XVII), belongs to the Resurrection Group, to the Passion sequence, to both, or to neither is, I think, an important critical question in a way that the Agony-in-the-Garden question probably is not.

Part of this chapter is reprinted with slight changes from my "The Credal Design of the Chester Cycle," *Modern Philology* 73 (1976):229–43, © 1976 by the University of Chicago, by permission of the editors.

The Harrowing is unique in several ways: of all the pageants it is the one which appears to have "progressed" the very least from its original source; of all the pageants it is the one which appears to vary the least from one cycle to the next; and of all the pageants it is the only one which occurs exclusively in hell. To this aggregate of unusual dramatic features must be added the fact that, while aware of the special importance of the Harrowing in the cycles' total design of salvation history, critics have been unable to reach a consensus concerning the Harrowing's place within that design. Peter Macaulay, for instance, believes that the Harrowing constitutes the climax of each cycle because it "resolves the epic conflict, and the Devil is defeated for all eternity";[1] Clifford Davidson, on the other hand, argues that the epic climax of the cycle is the Passion, and thus "All that remains in the harrowing episode is a mock battle and a ceremonious rescue of souls."[2] In short, for all its seeming "ritual simplicity" the Harrowing may have raised for the Corpus Christi playwrights as many dramatic issues as it raises critical issues for modern scholars. Coming at such a crucial historical juncture, the Harrowing perforce engages numerous matters—theological, rhetorical, and even psychological—all of major significance. Thus to open a chapter by simply asking which pageant-group Chester's Harrowing belongs to is tantamount to requesting a definition of the major dramatic designs of the entire cycle.

I

Chester's "Harrowing of Hell" is opened by Adam, who interprets the appearance of a bright light shining into hell as a "signe" of the fulfillment of God's promise to restore him "and all my kynd also." Patriarchs and prophets—Isaiah, Simeon, John the Baptist, Seth, and David—then kneel and in turn cite scriptural proof that Christ is indeed God's son and man's savior. In the second episode, Satan confidently argues with his demon underlings about the prudence of allowing Christ to enter hell; but as soon as Christ approaches hell's gate, Satan intuitively senses his own defeat, recognizing that Christ comes "to reave me of my power." The "battle" between Christ and Satan is cast as a ritual verbal confrontation. Christ demands, first in Latin and then in English, "Open up hell-gates anonne, / ye prynces of pyne everychon, / that Godes Sonne may in gonne, / and the kinge of blys"; Satan in turn queries, "What, what ys hee, that kinge of blys?"; Christ responds, "That lord the which almightie ys"; and even before Christ's entrance through the gates, the "combat" is complete—as Satan is hurled from his seat by his own demons. Then taking Adam's hand, Christ promises bliss to him and "eke to all thy osspringe / that ryghtwise were in yearth livinge," and orders Saint Michael to "lead these men singinge / to blys that lasteth ever." The pageant concludes with this procession toward heaven, as all solemnly sing the "Te Deum."[3]

The *mythos* of this brief pageant (276 lines) is in most respects identical to that of the other cycles (although N-Town's special staging allowed its Harrowing to be split into two parts): in each, Christ's coming is anticipated by the Old Testament *antiqui iusti* waiting in hell; in each, Satan is judged even by his own lackeys to be a foolish and doomed braggart; in each, Christ's triumph is posed from the outset as inevitable; in each (except for N-Town), the *salvati* celebrate their procession toward heaven with the communal singing of a Latin hymn. The minimal variation among the four pageants may perhaps be explained by the role the Harrowing must serve as the dramatic climax of Christ's career: since in at least three of the cycles Christ's Passion is conceived as more nearly a tragedy than a triumph, it is essential that his sufferings be followed immediately by his greatest victory. Thus if Christ is understood to be the hero of these plays, the Harrowing is not only the climax of his career but the climax of each cycle. The cycles' principal design would then conform rather neatly to an Aristotelian scheme, with the dramatic events which follow the Harrowing serving as a gradual denouement to this glorious *peripeteia* in which Christ finally defeats his arch-enemy and leads toward salvation those souls formerly held in the devil's dominion.

From the point of view of certain characters—the Old Testament patriarchs waiting in hell—this placement of the cycle's dramatic climax is quite correct: Christ's harrowing is proof that the promise of redemption is fulfilled, the fullness of time has come, the final reward of salvation is at hand. But from a second dramatic point of view—that of Christ's disciples—the spiritual climax of salvation history is not yet realized. Not having witnessed the harrowing of hell, they in the future will hear of Christ's Resurrection and only later will they arrive at an adequate understanding of the entirety of Christ's salvific career. Thus the disciples—as the potential collective hero of the Resurrection Group—will define their anagnorisis as that moment when they triumphantly come to believe in the Resurrection and then belatedly subordinate the histories of their own lives to the perfect paradigm of Christ's. In addition to these two dramatic climaxes there is potentially a third—one which must be discovered and defined by the viewers themselves. The viewers, unlike the disciples, are privileged observers of Christ's harrowing of hell; in the succeeding episodes they will observe, perhaps bemusedly, the disciples' early and awkward attempts to comprehend Christ's Resurrection; but by the end of the Resurrection Group they will witness the disciples' achieving a spiritual state far superior to their own. The viewers are free to interpret as they choose, and some may possibly accept the salvation of the Old Testament patriarchs as a guarantee of their own salvation; others may see the achieved perfection of the disciples as a reflection of their own state of grace. But as the potential collective hero of the entire cycle, most spectators are likely to discover (and only belatedly) that the climactic turning point of their own spiritual history is one nearly coincident with the end of history at the Last Judgment.

The Harrowing may thus be seen as one of several climaxes in the cycle, each defined by a different "hero" and controlled by a different rhetorical emphasis and dramatic design. Accordingly, it is quite legitimate to accept the Harrowing on one level as the triumphant climax of Christ's earthly career—its dramatic grandness perhaps somewhat qualified in Chester by the victorious aspects of the Passion itself. But I would prefer to emphasize the Chester Harrowing's importance as part of its Resurrection Group—not only as prelude to the disciples' pilgrimage toward complete belief but especially as one of a series of events challenging and defining the fundamental tenets of the viewers' faith. Yet even an appreciation of the Harrowing from these various perspectives will not adequately explain why in all the cycles the Harrowing has remained so close to its source, *The Gospel of Nicodemus*.[4] That is, in contrast to those quite varied and realistic pageants dramatizing Christ's Resurrection, why have the Harrowing pageants remained so ritual-like and so similar to each other?

The answer, I believe, is to be found in the Harrowing's theological proximity to (and historical distance from) the Last Judgment. In a perfect world the Harrowing would have been the conclusion rather than the climax of salvation history.[5] But because so much significant Christian history intervenes between the Harrowing and the Last Judgment, the Corpus Christi playwrights (for both dramatic and theological reasons) have had to discriminate as much as possible between these two "conclusive" salvations of mankind. The playwrights, that is, could underscore only to a minor degree the Harrowing's potential ethical implications: in York and Wakefield, for example, Christ finds himself momentarily agreeing with Satan that certain criminals such as Cain, Judas, and "tyrantis euerilkone" must remain in hell, "ellis were it wrang." But any more emphasis than this upon the juridical and moral aspects of the Harrowing might have diminished the power and preempted the significance of the Last Judgment. A corollary risk, I have noted, was that viewers would identify too fully with those whom Christ now saves from perdition. Each cycle mutes this possible inference by maintaining the historical individuality of each of the characters in hell: in contrast to the general types of the saved and damned souls in the Last Judgment pageants, the Adams, Seths and Davids of the Harrowing pageants are obviously specific individuals who (like the prophets in the *processus prophetarum*) name themselves first in a speech which then anticipates the Savior. Both of these features—the minimal juridical emphasis and the historical specificity of character—are features found in *The Gospel of Nicodemus* which help in the cycles to distinguish this salvation from that which will be effected at the end of time. All the cycles are willing to expand somewhat the comic elements of the original version, so that the confrontation between Christ and Satan takes on the qualities of high melodrama: Satan's impotence, farcical fits, and verbal bluster serve as a laughable contrast to Christ's charismatic powers. The result of this heightened comedy, I believe, is that the high seriousness of the entire salvation of the *antiqui iusti* is somewhat underplayed. Not that the Harrowing is an unimportant event in the cycles: as one of the twelve articles of the Apostles' Creed it would appear to have been absolutely essential. But the slight dramatic "distancing" of the Harrowing from the viewers was surely meant to contrast sharply with the solemn urgency and dire immediacy of the Last Judgment plays with which the cycles conclude.

Of the four cycles only Chester adds anything to the Harrowing which is dramatically unique: this is a brief scene at the pageant's end where the *salvati* on their way to paradise are met by Enoch and Elias, who tell of their ordained struggle with the Antichrist at the end of time. Like the other dramatic techniques I have noted, this allusion to a future combat serves to remind the viewers once again that the terms and the time of their own final judgment will both be distinct from those they have just seen enacted. The Corpus Christi playwrights evidently chose to remain extremely close to the original Harrowing because they sensed that any major dramatic renovation—in the direction of realistic contemporaneity, universal characterization, or greater length—would have exaggerated the significance of the Harrowing as merely one part of the entire history of salvation. It follows as a matter of course that the playwrights were also happy to retain the ritual characteristics of the original version because these, too, distanced events slightly and helped to prevent the viewers from indulging in a "narcissistic" interpretation of Christ's salvation of Old Testament man.

There is one other place within the Chester Resurrection Group where similar ritual techniques are deliberately employed to distance the viewers from a "narcissistic" involvement in the dramatized events. This is Christ's Ascension, which Chester alone casts as a form of high ritual. Why Chester developed the Ascension as ritual can best be understood by examining briefly the very different handling given it in Wakefield Pageant XXXIX. In Wakefield Christ appears to his disciples before his Ascension, bids them be of good cheer, and departs, promising that he will send the Holy Spirit to comfort them. Although the disciples recognize "that he must nedys fro vs twyn," they immediately mourn their Lord's departure, their grief growing so intense that Christ finally must return to them with words of stern reproach: "ye haue bene of mysbilefe / hard of harte and also of will." He tries to comfort them with a vision of their glorious apostolic mission, and then departs for a second time. But the disciples once again renew their clamorous lamentation, Christ returns and exhorts them once again to be steadfast in their trust in him, before he departs for a third time, and quickly ascends into heaven.

What the Wakefield Ascension illustrates is a major difficulty (beyond the obvious technical one) which all the cycles had to try to resolve. That is, in a drama which has emphasized Christ's earthly nature—his brotherly love and human nearness—his final leave-taking could easily be received as a cause of grief rather than joy. Recognizing this possibility, the Wakefield dramatist chose to exploit it by casting the Ascension as a kind of corollary to the Crucifixion: before ascending, for example, Christ once again places his mother in John's care. The Chester playwright, on the other hand, chose to circumvent this "tragic" interpretation by shifting the dramatic focus to Christ's act of ascending and by casting that Ascension as a protracted rite of passage. Deriving ultimately from the Ascension Day liturgy itself, the scene comprises a series of antiphonal chants exchanged between Christ and the angels guarding heaven. Christ begins his Ascension by announcing in song: "Ascendo ad Patrem meum et Patrem vestrum, Deum meum et Deum vestrum. Alleluya." As he sings this declaration, Christ ascends to a point *in medio quasi supra nubes*. He is then cross-examined in Latin by the angels; he responds to their queries; a chorus sings; he responds again. Then the entire exchange is repeated *in materna lingua*, as the first angel asks:

> Who ys this that cometh within
> the blysse of heaven that never shall blynne,
> bloodye, owt of the world of synne—
> and harrowed hell hath hee?

Christ identifies himself as "forbyer ... of all mankynd through grace," who brings with him into heaven "all that in hell were." Another angel asks, "Whye ys thy cloathinge nowe so reedd, / thy bodye bloodye and also head," and Christ, alluding first to his Crucifixion, explains the ultimate purpose of his wounds:

> These bloodye droppes that yee nowe see
> all the freshe shall reserved bee

tyll I come in my majestie
to deame the laste daye.

The angels all sing "Exaltaremus, domine, in virtute tua," as
Christ finally completes his Ascension into heaven, the ritual concluding with one more hymn, sung by angels who have descended
to earth: "Viri Gallilei, quid aspicitis in caelum?"

It can be seen that Chester's unique dramatic version of the
Ascension serves as both a formal and thematic complement to the
Harrowing of Hell. Both pageants celebrate the hero's passage from
a lesser world into one of greater spiritual power: Christ's ceremonial
procession through the gates of hell as he conquers his old enemy is
counterpointed by his gradual ascension past the angels guarding
heaven as he displays the talisman of his victory. The sublimity of
Christ's otherworldly triumphs is enhanced in both pageants by a
distinctive ritual ambience—regularly iterated rhythms, Latin proc-
lamations, and liturgical hymns. Christ's cosmic victories are surely
cause for exultation among his New Testament disciples and present-
day viewers; but the ritual "otherness" of Christ's world is also a
reminder to his followers that they remain on earth and must contend with the irregular rhythms of their own vernacular lives. In fact
it will not be until Pentecost that Christ's disciples in Chester manage
to order their faith sufficiently so that together they may ceremonially sing, in Latin and English, the articles of their newly
created Creed.

The implication of this opening discussion of the Harrowing and
the Ascension is that the major dramatic focus of Chester's Resurrection Group is to be found not in Christ's ritual triumphs but
rather in the realistic attempts made by Christ's followers to assimi-
late, understand, and believe the evidence and testimony which
collectively bespeak the truth of the Resurrection. The central
dynamics of the Resurrection Group are in certain respects notably
similar to those of the *Visitatio Sepulchri* plays of Holy Week: as
secondary and primary pieces of verbal and ocular evidence are
progressively offered, characters within the drama will on occasion
turn to the audience for corroboration of their state of belief.[6] But
the Resurrection pageants in the cycles obviously differ from the
Latin plays in a number of important ways. First, the pageants
involving the disciples' *agon* of doubt and belief obviously employ

199

an aesthetic of heightened realism: more than the liturgical plays ever needed to, they emphasize the physical reality and sensational immediacy of their enacted events. Rather like this study's frontispiece (from *The Holkham Bible Picture Book*) where the awestruck Marys are kneeling so close to the resurrected Christ that they almost kiss the wounds as they examine them, so these pageants attempt to draw the viewers' doubting senses deep inside the dramatic frame. Second, these pageants clearly differ from the liturgical plays in the complexity of their formal design. In contrast to the rather straightforward transformation of doubt into belief and of *tristia* into *gaudium* found in the *Visitatio* plays, the cycles had to design a complicated yet unified series of isolated, partial, communal, and then complete illuminations which progressed through many episodes and over several pageants extending from the Resurrection to Thomas's conversion. While enjoying its own dramatic integrity, in other words, each of these pageants had to function as part of a larger unit, the Resurrection Group, which in turn had to serve as an integral part of the entire cycle.

A third difference between the cycles' Resurrection Groups and the Latin plays is only a potential one. Whereas the typical *Visitatio* play culminates in the joyful recognition of Christ's Resurrection (usually symbolized by the communal singing of the "Te Deum"), a similar conclusion to the Resurrection Group would seem inadequate and limiting. For, as we have noted, in addition to Christ's triumphant Resurrection, two of his other great victories are presented as part of the Resurrection Group: Christ's Harrowing of Hell and his Ascension into heaven. Not to celebrate these as well at the culmination of the Resurrection Group would seem to deny their integral part within that group. In addition, since the disciples of Christ and the viewers of the cycle have witnessed many more triumphs of Christian history than these three, the denouement of the Resurrection Group could potentially incorporate most of the essential articles of Christian faith. I believe that of the English Corpus Christi dramatists, only the Chester playwright recognized this potential design and realized it within his cycle. How he managed to make actual this dramatic design, and how he integrated it with the complex structure, the "sensational realism," and the special role of the Resurrection pageants within the entire cycle, will be the major concern of the remainder of this chapter.

II

The recurring dramatic imperative of the English Corpus Christi plays—"Behold and believe!"—is most emphatically employed in the sequence of episodes that opens with Christ's Resurrection and climaxes at Thomas's conversion.[7] The paradigm of this sequence, which constitutes the "rising action" of each cycle's Resurrection Group, is an intense and prolonged trial of faith, wherein skepticism and middling conviction time and again confront accumulating evidence of the reality of Christ's Resurrection and of his physical return to the world of men. The conflict within this sequence is generated in the form of an *agon* of faith and disbelief, as Christ's followers debate the validity of proffered evidence, the credence of testimonies, and the seeming rationality of their own "fletchinge" doubts. The debate is sometimes acrimonious; the pattern of suspended disbelief and backsliding faith repeats itself; the pilgrimage toward truth is hesitant and awkward. But even for those of little faith, the sum of evidence—the empty tomb, the discarded graveclothes, Christ's appearances to the Marys, his breaking the sacramental bread at Emmaus,[8] his eating fish and honey, and finally his offering of his bloody side to touch—ultimately comes to constitute indubitable proof that Christ has risen as he had prophesied. As John says in the Chester Ascension:

> Nowe mon we leeve yt no leasinge,
> for both by syght and handlinge,
> speakinge, eatinge and drinkinge
> hee [Christ] prooves his deitee.

Beholding the disciples' tortuous pilgrimage toward belief, the Corpus Christi audiences would seem to be unusually privileged, for not only did they, as Christian believers, know those credenda of faith toward which the disciples were groping, but, within the affective illusion of the play, they alone among Christ's followers are honored as witnesses of his Resurrection and as auditors of the words he speaks directly from the edge of the tomb.[9] However, time and again in the cycles the viewers are treated as if they were men and women of little faith, doubting Thomases who have eyes yet will not see.

What was required of them, then, was they see fully and clearly that within the plays subsisted those mysteries upon which their faith should be founded, the very mysteries which Christ's disciples strive to discover, understand, and believe. Although the rhetorical demands upon the viewers are deeply embedded in the cycles' dramatic strategies, they occasionally are directly demonstrated, as when, in N-Town, Thomas turns to the audience and holds before them his bloody palm as proof of Christ's physical reality:

> The prechynge of petir myght not conuerte me
> tyll I felyd the wounde that the spere dyde cleve
> I trustyd nevyr he levyd that deed was on A tre
> tyll that his herte blood dede renne in my sleve
> Thus be my grett dowte · oure feyth may we preve
> be-hold my blody hand · to feyth that me Avexit
> be syght of this myrroure · ffrom feyth not remeve
> Quod mortuus et sepultus nunc resurrexit.

Thomas's speech indicates that a fairly complex reciprocity of spiritual illumination takes place between the audience and the play, for, despite the cycles' disclaimers that their enactment of history is a "myrroure" of truth, they present their mimesis of sacred events as a reification of those events themselves, as dramatized proof of the authority and truth upon which Christian belief is founded. Managing at times to be contemporary both with their historical actions and with their audience, the followers of Christ in the play thus project for the followers of Christ who constitute the viewing audience a rediscovering of the fundamental truths of Christian belief.

That some such affective and didactic design is operative in the cycles is a critical commonplace, easily substantiated by observing those characters who here and there turn sideways to the action to ask that the viewers believe what has been presented before their eyes. I intend to argue here, however, that the pattern of evidence in Chester determines a pattern of beliefs much more rigorous and formal than has yet been suggested. That pattern of beliefs is the Apostles' Creed, the basic statement of faith for every medieval Christian. The Chester audience, I assert, as it beheld the unfolding episodes of its cycle, was beholding (among other things) a dramatic "sacralization" of the twelve articles of the Apostles' Creed.

Since I suspect that the verification of the Creed's twelve articles was not part of Chester's fifteenth-century dramatic design but rather a didactic pattern completed only late in the cycle's history by means of a few subtle innovations, and since the credal design these innovations form may not have been discerned by many of Chester's contemporary viewers, I intend to proceed with critical caution: to entertain at first as hypothesis Chester's credal design, then to discuss supporting evidence—namely, medieval interpretations of the creed and modern speculations on the contents of the lost Creed play of York—and to return finally to Chester for confirmation of my thesis. With the assistance of further information concerning medieval interpretations of the Communion of Saints, I hope to prove that the Apostles' Creed determines the structure of certain of Chester's episodes, specifically those at the beginning and the end of its Resurrection Group, for it is here that several unusual features, unique within English dramatic tradition, indicate that the Chester cycle in its present form is credal, or, if you will, symbolical, in one of its rhetorical patterns.

Chester Pagina XVIII, "De Resurrectione Jesu Christi," shows all the signs of careful craftsmanship. The counterplot of Pilate and his miscreant soldiers is dealt with briskly, completed before the visits to the sepulcer begin. Christ's appearances to the Marys, to Magdalene, and to Peter are organized into a pattern of belief based upon varying degrees of faith and evidence. Characterization is consistent: none of the Marys believes until she meets Christ face to face; Peter believes without seeing but remains despondent until Christ forgives him for his sin. The concluding episode where Christ forgives Peter forms a fitting climax to the action. As Eleanor Prosser notes, by "carefully adapt[ing] the traditional actions to focus on the penitent Peter," the Chester Resurrection "shows how a series of loosely related events could be rehaped into good drama."[10]

Yet within this successful adaptation of certain "traditional actions" there are several unusual features. The first is the odd nature of Christ's lyrical address to man from the verge of the tomb. Although the lyric fits into the poetic genre known as Christ's Testament, Christ's Charter, or Christ's Appeal to Man, research has yet to discover for this dramatic poem a source or even a close analogue.[11] What is striking about the Chester Resurrection lyric (which later I shall quote in full) is Christ's emphasis upon his body as the bread of life, the Blessed Sacrament of the Eucharist. When so many traditional versions of this popular genre were close at hand, is it not worth asking why the Chester playwright apparently felt compelled to fashion a new, and perhaps unique, Resurrection lyric here?

A second oddity is Chester's giving to Peter the honor of being the first of Christ's followers to believe in his Resurrection. Although the choice of Peter as the first believer can be found in some Middle English narrative poems,[12] the choice is unique within Middle English drama: N-Town, in concert with its prevailing Marian interests, honors the Virgin as the first to believe; York and Wakefield honor Magdalene as the first, although in each her faith backslides and must be reconfirmed. Of all the cycles, then, why alone does Chester cast Peter as the only follower of Christ to believe in Christ's Resurrection before beholding his resurrected Lord?

A third oddity is Chester's dramatic focus upon Peter's repentance, for of the four cycles only Chester includes a scene where Christ appears before Peter to forgive him. Such an episode would be less exceptional in the other cycles, where dramatic calls to repentence are numerous, but Chester elsewhere consistently eschews the themes of penitence and divine mercy in favor of emphasizing the motif of divine recognition. If one agrees with Prosser that the Chester playwright was normally a methodical technician, one must again ask, to what purpose did he select and shape this episode?

There are thus three exceptional features in the Chester Resurrection play: the sacramentalism of Christ's Resurrection Testament, Peter's being honored as the first believer, and Christ's appearing before Peter to forgive him for his sins. It can be argued that each of these features was the result of extracyclical influence, such as the office of the Corpus Christi feast (where the meaning of the eucharist Host is fully analyzed),[13] Latin liturgical drama (the Fleury *Visitatio*, for instance, accords Peter the same honor),[14] and homiletic traditions (such as the doctrine of repentance) in English vernacular poems and sermons.[15] But the inclusion of these features, I suggest, is explained and justified elsewhere in the Chester cycle—most notably in the play that closes out the Chester Resurrection Group, the Pentecost pageant.

Although the *agon* of disbelief and faith climaxes in each cycle at the point of Thomas's illumination, each cycle in some way attempts

to extend and amplify the disciples' pilgrimage toward full and steadfast Christian belief in the remaining New Testament events it dramatizes. Of the four cycles, Chester's Resurrection Group is the most
careful in developing the final steps in this pilgrimage. Avoiding the
potential emotional vacuum left by Christ's ascending, Chester casts
the Ascension as a hieratic rite of passage. Chester then concludes
its Resurrection Group with a Pentecost play that figures forth the
spiritual integrity and achieved beliefs of those men who are to serve
as the apostles of Christ's church. Entitled "de Electione Mathie
et de Emissione Spiritus Sancti de symbolo apostolorum" (H),
Chester Pagina XXI dramatizes in three episodes the final perfection,
divinely wrought, of Christ's disciples. In the first episode, God
selects Matthias to fill out the ranks of Christ's disciples to numerical
perfection.[16] The second episode opens in heaven, as God and his Son
recount their providential plan of history. They then send the Holy
Ghost to the disciples, and the kneeling disciples, having received the
Spirit *in spetie ignis*, describe the perfect wisdom, love, and courage
with which they feel imbued. The final episode is unique within
Middle English dramatic traditions: a dramatized version of the
popular legend that on Pentecost the twelve apostles agreed upon
the twelve articles of their creed. In a quatrain each, each apostle
recites in slightly amplified form the article traditionally ascribed to
him. Dramatizing the social, personal, and spiritual perfection of
Christ's apostles, the Chester Pentecost play completes the *agon* of
faith and the pilgrimage toward belief which were initiated at the
opening of the Resurrection Group. Made steadfast in belief by the
trials they have undergone, purified of all "fletchinge" doubts by the
fires of the Holy Spirit, the apostles have arrived at a full understanding of the credenda of Christian faith and are ready now to preach
the articles of their creed.

As the expression of their discovered faith, the creed of the
apostles substantiates the truth of those marvelous events—dramatized by the cycle—upon which that faith is founded. At this dramatic
moment of spiritual illumination, it can be argued that the cycle
requires that its audience reciprocate in kind by recollecting those
dramatized events which correspond to the Creed's twelve articles of
faith. That such a rhetorical pressure exists in the Pentecost play is
suggested further by the unusual nature of the dialogue between
God and his Son before they send down the Holy Ghost. This dia-

logue (garbled as it is in the manuscripts) Rosemary Woolf finds artistically inept because it "too manifestly serves a narrative and didactic function in its resumé of the Fall and Redemption."[17] But the function she objects to may have been precisely that desired: as a brief historical resumé, the dialogue, sketching for the audience the cycle's narrative outline, underscores one of its several didactic functions—the authentication of the twelve articles of the Apostles' Creed. In order to achieve the purity of the apostles' belief, therefore, the audience is simply required to recall, and to reconfirm their belief in, the major events dramatized in the cycle.

This theory is unfortunately extremely vulnerable, despite the interesting account in *A Hundred Merry Tales* of the Warwickshire priest who advised his parishioners to go to the Coventry Corpus Christi play in order to see the articles of the creed performed.[18] Neither Chester nor any other extant English cycles includes within its historical frame twelve episodes which obviously demonstrate the Creed's twelve articles. The problem of discovering an episode for each article is illustrated in table 7.1, which includes the Latin *Credo* (the Latin article is quoted first by each apostle in Chester before he translates it); Chester's farsure, or verse expansion, of the Creed; and then a list of corresponding cyclical scenes.

What this table reveals is that most of the articles can easily be accounted for: articles 1, 3, 4, 5, 6, 7, and 8 constitute beliefs in historical events dramatized in all cycles, and articles 11 and 12 can be included in the final play, of Doomsday. But articles 2, 9, and 10 appear to have no corresponding episodes, in any cycle, that would authenticate their historical truth. Concerning the dramatic possibilities of these three articles, two critical studies concerning the lost Creed play of York have helped to illuminate Chester's dramatic options. In *Drama and Imagery in English Medieval Churches*, M.D. Anderson offers a scheme for the scenes of the York Creed play, based upon her study of the Arundel Psalter and the Creed Window of Great Malvern Church. Article 1 she suggests may have been represented by the scene of "God enthroned," 2 by "Christ enthroned," 3 by "Nativity," 4 by "Crucifixion," 5 by "Resurrection," 6 by "Ascension," 7 by "Second Coming," 8 by "Pentecost," 9 by "Three arches each containing a white robed figure, a symbol of the Holy Catholic Church," 10 by "Penance," 11 by "Resurrection of the Dead," and 12 by "Coronation of the Virgin." She then adds this pertinent note: "If the first two groups [representing the first two articles] were treated as an introductory scene in Heaven, either a Creation Play or a Parliament of Heaven scene, and numbers 9-11 were combined in some sort of morality play akin to *Everyman*, stressing the need for penance and the Sacraments of the Church before the Last Summons, *all other scenes of the Creed Play could have been adapted from existing mystery plays*" (emphasis added).[19]

For Anderson, all but three articles could have been dramatized by episodes taken from a cycle, and those three problematic articles, she suggests, might best have been represented by allegorical rather than historical scenes. In a study based upon much evidence heretofore unpublished, Alexandra Johnston argues that the York Creed play—which we know in 1535 was substituted in performance for the Corpus Christi play—was made up of twelve pageants, and that ten of the Creed play's pageants appropriated their wagons and properties from the cycle itself. Article 10, she believes, was performed using the properties and wagon for "The Woman Taken in Adultery," and article 11 with the properties and wagon for "The Harrowing of Hell." The remaining pageants, she believes, were essentially those suggested by Anderson's list of graphic scenes, with the exception of articles 2 and 9. Concerning the possible dramatic form given these two articles, Johnston's research has been most fruitful. Examining the accounts of the York Corpus Christi Guild (in whose care the performance of the Creed play was originally entrusted), she has found a list of dramatic properties which in all likelihood were used for the performance of the pageants representing articles 2 and 9. Among the properties listed are a diadem for Christ, a gilded mask, and two pieces of a painted tunic. Johnston conjectures that these properties (the same articles of costuming used by the Mercers for their "Christ in Judgment" play) were used for the performance of "Christ Enthroned"—the scene traditionally ascribed, as Anderson has noted, to article 2.[20] "Also among the properties held by the Guild," Johnston continues, "were one key for St. Peter, one pope's mitre, two bishops' mitres and one king's crown with sceptre and glove. These were clearly used in the representation of the Holy Catholic Church [article 9], probably indicating the supremacy of the church over all temporal

Table 7.1

Article	Latin Credo
1	*Credo in Deum patrem omnipotentem Creatorem Caeli et Terrae*
2	*Et in Iesum Christum filium eius unicum Dominum nostrum*
3	*Qui conceptus est de Spiritu Sancto, natus ex Maria Virgine*
4	*Passus sub Pontio Pilato, Crusifixus, mortuus, et sepultus*
5	*Descendit ad Inferna, tertia die resurrexit a mortuis*
6	*Ascendit ad Caelos, sedet ad dexteram Dei Patris Omnipotentis*
7	*Inde venturus est judicare vivos et mortuos*
8	*Credo in Spiritum Sanctum*

Chester Farsure	Corpus Christi Pageants
I beleeve in God omnipotent that made heaven and yearth and fyrmament with steadfast hart and true intent, and hee ys my comford.	Creation
And I beleeve, where I be lent, in Jesu, his Sonne, from heaven sent, verey Cryste, that us hath kent and ys our elders lord.	Creation?
I beleeve, without bost, in Jesus Christe of mightes most, conceyved through the Holy Ghooste and borne was of Marye.	Nativity
And I beleeve, as I can see, that under Pilate suffred hee, scourged and nayled one roode-tree; and buryed was his fayre bodye.	Passion and Crucifixion
And I beleeve, and sooth can tell, that hee ghoostly went to hell, delyvered his that there did dwell, and rose the third daye.	Harrowing of Hell and Resurrection
And I beleeve fully this, that he stayed up to heaven-blysse and on his Fathers right hand ys, to raygne for ever and aye.	Ascension
And I beleeve, with hart steadfast, that hee will come at the laste and deeme mankynd as he hath caste, both the quycke and the dead.	Last Judgment
And my beleeffe shall be moste in vertue of the Holye Ghooste; and through his helpe, without boste, my lyffe I thinke to lead.	Pentecost

Table 7.1

Article	Latin Credo
9	*Sanctam Ecclesiam Catholicam, Sanctorum Communionem*
10	*Remissionem Peccatorum*
11	*Carnis Resurrectionem*
12	*Et vitam aeternam.*

rulers."[21] The use of the few remaining dramatic properties is suggested by the records themselves: diadems and wigs were for Christ and his apostles (perhaps representing the Communion of Saints), and twelve scrolls for the apostles, each inscribed with an article, must have been used to introduce the twelve separate pageants.

Although she believes that the York Creed play appropriated only properties and wagons, and not dramatic scripts, from the York cycle, Johnston's research helps to illustrate the formal correspondences and dissimilarities between the Creed play and a Corpus Christi play that incorporates the Creed into its larger dramatic frame. A Creed play must find discrete historical or iconographic scenes to demonstrate each article (thus articles 7, 11, and 12, although all are associated with the eschaton, must be represented by three separate events); the Corpus Christi play of credal design, since it is not separated into twelve pageants, need not. Furthermore, since the

Chester Farsure	Corpus Christi Pageants
And I beleeve, through Godes grace, such beleeffe as Holy Church hasse— that Godes bodye granted us was to use in forme of bread.	?
And I beleeve, with devotyon, of synne to have remission through Christes blood and Passion, and heaven when I am dead.	?
And I beleeve, as all wee mon, in the generall resurrection of ych bodye, when Christe ys [bowne] to deeme both good and evell.	Last Judgment?
And I beleve, as all wee maye, everlastinge liffe, after my daye, in heaven for to have ever and aye, and so overcome the devyll.	Last Judgment?

Creed actually comprises more than twelve credenda of faith, a single article could sometimes be represented in such a cycle by more than one episode or pageant, and one pageant sometimes could represent more than one article.

Thus, to return to Chester, articles 1 and 2, as Anderson has suggested, could both easily have been represented by one play of Creation. Article 3 is represented by the Nativity pageant. Christ's Passion, Crucifixion, Descent into Hell and Resurrection (articles 4 and 5) were throughout Chester's history dramatized in three separate pageants, one of them made up of two discrete parts. Article 6 is represented in the Ascension pageant. Articles 7, 11, and 12 (Last Judgment, Resurrection of the Body, and Eternal Life) are all dramatically presented in the pageant of Doomsday. Article 8 (the Holy Spirit) is represented in the Pentecost pageant. Thus in the Chester cycle, all the articles, and indeed all the separate credenda, of the

Apostles' Creed are dramatically figured forth—all, that is, but articles 9 and 10: *Credo in Sanctam Ecclesiam Catholicam, Sanctorum Communionem, Remissionem Peccatorum.*

In the light of the foregoing discussion of the York Creed play, it is easy to see why neither of these two articles is obviously figured forth in any of Chester's pageants: they are articles of faith grounded not in biblical narrative but rather in the abstract concepts of the church's identity and power. To represent these articles, a play must in all likelihood have been allegorical or iconographic in design, although its actions could possibly have been inspired by Scripture or by apocryphal tradition. I believe that this is precisely the case in Chester, and that only in these terms can one account for the aforementioned features of Chester's Resurrection pageant—namely, the sacramentalism of Christ's Testament, Peter's role as the first to believe in Christ's Resurrection, and Christ's appearing before Peter to forgive him. In brief, I propose that these three features dramatically authenticate articles 9 and 10 of the Apostles' Creed: belief in the Holy Catholic Church, the Communion of Saints, and the Remission of Sins.

That Peter was the human symbol of Christ's church was a truth so familiar to a medieval audience that the slightest dramatic pressure was necessary to reinforce that identification. Christ himself makes that identification explicit in the closing episode of Pagina XVIII, as he accords Peter the power to grant remission of sins when Peter is in "soveraynty." Peter calls to Christ:

> A, lord, mercy I aske thee
> with full hart, knelinge on my knee.
> Forgeve me my trespase.
> My faynt flesh and my fraylty
> made me, lord, falce to be,
> but forgevenes with hart free
> thou graunt me through thy grace. [H]

And with "crosse-staffe in his hand" (R), Christ responds:

> Peter, so I thee beheight
> thou should forsake me that night,
> but of this deed thou have in sight
> when thou hast soverainty.

Thinke on thyne own deed today,
that flesh is frayle and fallinge aye;
and mercifull be thou allway
as now I am to thee.

Therfore I suffered thee to fall
that to thy subjects hereafter all
that to thee shall cry and call
then may have minning.
Sithen thyself fallen hase,
the mere inclyne to graunt grace.
Goe forth! Forgeven is thy trespase.
And have here my blessinge. [H]

What we have in this episode should now be quite apparent.
It may indeed be, as Prosser claims, a dramatic call to repentance,
but it is something else as well. Working close to received traditions,
the Chester playwright in this exchange has incorporated articles 9
and 10 into his Resurrection pageant. Whereas Peter in the York
Creed play held the key to heaven (symbol of papal and ecclesiastic
power), here Christ with "crosse-staffe in his hand" reveals to Peter
his ordained future as the church's rightful father. And rather than
by the dramatic story of the woman taken in adultery, article 10 in
Chester is validated by Christ's explaining to his first apostle that he
had "suffered" Peter to sin so that when in his "soverainty" Peter
would more mercifully remit the sins of his "subjects." In this context, it is only appropriate that Peter alone among Christ's followers
should have believed in Christ's Resurrection before having seen his
resurrected Lord. Thus, through a novel etiological myth the Chester
playwright has succeeded in dramatizing these two nonhistorical
articles. His most impressive accomplishment is that these articles of
faith are sacralized within the context of scriptural history, as Christ
ordains and blesses the institution of the holy Catholic church and
the remission of sins on the very day of his Resurrection to life.

This evidence I trust is sufficient proof of Chester's unique credal
design, but I have yet to account for the unusual nature of Christ's
Resurrection Testament. Here is the lyric in full:

Earthlye man that I have wrought,
awake out of thy sleepe.

213

Earthly man that I have bought,
of me thou take noe keepe.
From heaven mans soule I sought
into a dungeon deepe;
my deare lemmon from thence I brought,
for ruth of her I weepe.

I am verey prynce of peace
and kinge of free mercye.
Whoe wyll of synnes have release,
one me the call and crye;
and yf they will of synnes sease,
I grant them peace trulye
and thereto a full rych messe
in bread, my owne bodye.

I am verey bread of liffe.
From heaven I light and am send.
Who eateth that bread, man or wiffe,
shall lyve with me withowt end.
and that bread that I you give,
your wicked life to amend,
becomes my fleshe through your beleeffe
and doth release your synfull band.

And whosoever eateth that bread
in synne and wicked liffe,
he receaveth his owne death—
I warne both man and wiffe;
the which bread shalbe seene instead
the joye ys aye full ryffe.
When hee ys dead, through fooles read
then ys he brought to payne and stryffe.

Two critics have attempted to account for the heavy eucharistic emphasis of this lyrical address: J.W. Robinson suggests that Christ's Testament here is affectively akin to the rite of the Mass,[22] and Rosemary Woolf feels that the lyric successfully brings "to a close the Passion sequence which began with the Last Supper."[23] I believe that Christ's Resurrection Testament must be understood in light of the Chester cycle's interpretation of *Sanctorum Communionem*, the second part of the ninth article of the Apostles' Creed. The history of this phrase, incorporated into the Creed sometime in the late fourth century, is complex and fascinating: the question of its meaning has generated numerous theories and controversies, both medieval and modern.[24] For the purposes of this study, however, it will be necessary only briefly to consider three major (and often overlapping) interpretations of *Sanctorum Communionem* that found their way into late Middle English catechetical works.

The first medieval interpretation understood *Communionem* in general apposition to *Ecclesiam* and *Sanctorum* as a masculine noun. Thus the Communion of Saints signifies the communal society of Christian believers, the mystical fellowship in heaven, in purgatory, and on earth who truly followed Christ's teachings. This interpretation can be found in the *Cursor Mundi*'s farsure of the Creed:

> hali kirk is al were rede
> a geddering of alle cristen lede.
> than is this point for to say.
> we that liuen in cristin lai.
> In alle that trauth we agh at bow
> that hali kirke is wonte at trow.
> to haue with santis communing.
> this is a point of our trowing.[25]

A second interpretation understood *Communionem* in very loose apposition to *Ecclesiam* and interpreted *Sanctorum* as neuter rather than masculine. Thus the phrase posits belief in a communion in holy things, or in the sacraments. This interpretation is found in a number of Middle English works and is neatly expressed in Archbishop Thoresby's *Catechism:*

> That is communyng and felawred of al cristen folk,
> that communes to-gedir in the sacraments
> and in othir hali thinges that falles til halikirk.[26]

A third interpretation, and one extremely popular in Middle English farsures of the Creed, is most important in determining with precision the nature of Chester's credal design. In this tradition, article 9 is seen as constituting two separate credenda paratactically conjoined. *Sanctorum Communionem* was understood to represent, or symbolize, one sacrament alone, the sacrament of the eucharistic Host. An example of this tradition can be found in *The Lay Folks' Mass Book*, which farses the concluding articles of the Apostles' Creed as follows:

> wel I trow in tho holi gost,
>   and holi kirc that is so gode;
> And so I trow that housel es
>   bothe flesshe & blode;
> of my synnes, forgyfnes,
>   If I wil mende;
> vp-risyng als-so of my flesshe,
>   and lyf with-outen ende.[27]

It would be difficult to prove conclusively which of these three interpretations Chester adopted were it not for Chester's own verse farsure of the Creed recited by the apostles in Pagina XXI. The quatrain interpreting article 9 is spoken by Matthew:

> And I beleeve, through Godes grace,
> such beleeffe as Holy Church hasse—
> that Godes bodye granted us was
> to use in forme of bread.

Here Matthew clearly interprets the Communion of Saints as meaning the eucharistic Host, and in fact subordinates belief in the holy Catholic church to the church's belief in the transubstantiation of Christ's flesh. Matthew's emphasis upon the Eucharist is a corollary to the emphasis in the Resurrection play upon the sacramental identity and powers of Christ's Blessed Body, and proves conclusively that Chester dramatically validates every general article and indeed every separate credendum of the Apostles' Creed.

Chester is obviously more than a Creed play in disguise. The religious truths it supports include more than the twelve articles, and the episodes central to the cycle's credal design are shaped to do much more than simply to dramatize a single article of faith. But as one rhetorical strategy in a complexly structure cycle, the sacralization of the Apostles' Creed intensifies Chester's consistent emphasis upon the need to recognize the power and authority of Christ's truth. The need for steadfast faith is no more urgently invoked than in the cycle's remaining plays, at the center of which

Antichrist challenges, parodies, and magically reenacts the mysteries and miraculous events upon which Christian faith is founded. As we shall see, the royal representatives of humankind in the Antichrist play are duped by Christ's arch-parodist, and although their true faith is finally restored with demidivine assistance, they die for their belief. The cycle concludes, in the play of Doomsday, by illustrating for an audience living at history's penultimate moment that believing in the articles of Christian faith is not enough: to these beliefs must be added the works of corporal mercy if humankind, through Christ's mercy, is ever to gain salvation.

III

The foregoing discussion reveals that, had the Warwickshire priest alluded to Chester rather than to Coventry, we should concur with his assertion that the Corpus Christi play proved each article of the Creed to "be true and of authority." However, one significant question remains: when, in its two-hundred-year history, did the Chester cycle incorporate the dramatic innovations necessary to make actual its potential credal design? This question unfortunately may remain unanswerable, despite my attempts in Chapter 2 to detail all discernible stages of the cycle's growth. As we have seen, the medieval dramatic records from Chester are far from complete; the Early and Late Banns—each revised at least once—often offer inconclusive evidence; and the possible stylistic indicators of different authors' work are never totally reliable. Nevertheless, it is worth at least suggesting certain moments during Chester's development when such innovations could likely have taken place.

It is possible that Chester's credal design was never added to the cycle at all but rather was an integral part of the play's original form, when it was performed stationarily on Corpus Christi Day. (The York Creed play we know was in existence early in the fifteenth century; this play could possibly have preceded the York cycle in composition, and may perhaps even have influenced the Chester cycle's design at its inception.) However, it should be noted that the Chester play of Corpus Christi throughout the fifteenth century was considerably shorter and less complex in design than the later, sixteenth-century play it was to become—the Whitsun cycle. Thus it would appear quite likely that the two pageants most crucial to the play's credal design, the Resurrection and the Pentecost pageants, were likewise simpler and briefer in the cycle's early years—so that they included neither Christ's Testament, nor Christ's dialogue with Peter, nor the apostles' creation of their creed.

A second possibility is that the finishing touches of Chester's credal design were the work of that redactor who according to F.M. Salter "scattered revisions and interpolations throughout the cycle" between 1467 and 1488.[28] Because of his consistent use of cross rhyme (Salter believes) traces of this redactor's work can be seen in Paginae I, III, VII, X, XI, XVIII, and XXIII. The lines written in cross rhyme in Pagina XVIII, the Resurrection, are 9-12, 154-85, 266-69, and 278-81. None of these passages appears significant except Christ's Testament (ll. 154-85). But as I have noted in Chapter 2, Salter not only was inaccurate and prejudiced in his early dating of these cross-rhyme passages, but also was quite credulous in assuming that these passages all had to be the work of a single hand. It should be noted in addition that Christ's Testament is metrically distinct from the other cross-rhyme passages: whereas they are composed all in tetrameters, the quatrains of Christ's lyric address alternate tetrameter and trimeter lines ($a^4 b^3 a^4 b^3$). Even if the cross-rhyme redactor existed and were the composer of Christ's Testament, however, there is no evidence that he also authored the two other episodes important to the cycle's credal design—Christ's meeting with Peter and the apostles' formation of their creed—for both of these episodes are composed in Chester's traditional tail rhyme.

A third possibility is that the scenes crucial to completing Chester's credal design were added to the cycle early in the sixteenth century— more precisely, between 1505 and 1532 (the *termini a quo* and *ad quem* of the Early Banns' composition and revision) when the play of Corpus Christi Day was moved to Whitsuntide and amplified for its three-day performance. The imposition of a credal design upon the expanded cycle at this time would seem a perfectly appropriate way of honoring the play's new liturgical surroundings, with the apostles' creation of their creed at Pentecost emphasizing the significance of the Whitsun revelations.

A final possibility is that the revisions were made some time even later in the cycle's history, perhaps between the compositions of the original (1548-61) and revised (1561-72) versions of the Late Banns. Inconsistencies in the manuscripts of the Late Banns and in the manuscripts of the Resurrection pageant confirm that an attempt was made to redesign the structure of Pagina XVIII. Manuscripts HR of Pagina XVIII contain intact the play's concluding dialogue between Christ and Peter, but manuscripts HmAB break off before the dialogue begins. All manuscripts of the Late Banns allot to Pagina XIX (rather than to Pagina XVIII) Christ's "often speeche to the woman ["women" in RB] & his desiples Deere," and manuscript R of the Late Banns alludes to Christ's "Appearances" to his disciples in Pagina XIX, while manuscripts AB have "appearance."[29] Salter writes: "Is it not obvious that the author of the Late Banns lifted one hundred lines out of XVIII and dropped them into XIX? He must have done it in such a way, however, that the copyists misunderstood him, with the result that BDW [HmAB] omit the lines altogether, and HR give them to us in their original position."[30]

In Salter's judgment, the author of the Late Banns was also the last reviser of the cycle, working on the plays for the 1575 performance in response to state pressures demanding that the plays be corrected and amended. But we know now that the Late Banns were revised no later than 1572, and that whoever it was who may have revised certain quatrains in the Late Banns into rhyme-royal stanzas may well not have been that dramatist responsible for the rhyme-royal passages in the cycle itself. It is nevertheless possible that the Late Banns do contain information pertinent to dating the cycle's credal design. The Banns' pageant descriptions, for example, maintain a curious balance concerning the traditional integrity of Paginae XVIII and XXI, by allowing that the Resurrection play is "Not altered in menye poyntes from the olde fashion" and by urging that the Pentecost play be performed "in good order ... as hathe bine allwaye."[31] That the Resurrection play may have been revised very late in its history is a possibility given further support by the stanza lengths of the Late Banns descriptions: the Resurrection is accorded a rhyme-royal ("revised") stanza description, while the apparently unchanged Pentecost pageant is described in an "unrevised" quatrain. Thus on the one hand it could be argued that this evidence of a possible revision of Pagina XVIII indicates a late attempt to impose a credal design upon the cycle. On the other hand, however, this flurry of perhaps aborted revisings (be they additions, excisions, or exchanges of episodes) may all simply be further evidence of the several vain attempts made late in the cycle's career to palliate the increasing Protestant criticism of the plays.

My own general guess is that Chester's credal design was accomplished late rather than early—in the sixteenth century and not before. I base my intuition primarily upon internal evidence: the patent artistic subtlety with which articles 9 and 10 are incorporated into the *mythos* of Chester's Resurrection play. The credal design of the Chester cycle is so subtle that only the most perceptive in the audience are likely to have discerned the deep structure of Pagina XVIII. Why the privacy of intent, the seeming semiallegorical veil so foreign, for instance, to the purposes of the York Creed play, which was instituted to bring knowledge of the Creed "to the ignorant"? One explanation may be that the author, recognizing that his interpretations of *Ecclesiam Catholicam* and *Sanctorum Communionem* were both inimical to the state and to Protestant dogma, purposefully disguised these interpretations beneath the play's surface. In other words, Chester's Romish interpretation of these credenda was accomplished during those years when the reforming spirit excised from the other cycles (as well as from Chester) many of their Marian elements, scotched passages alluding to the Mass and the Eucharist, and generally attempted to suffocate the ancient "papistical" tradition of the Corpus Christi plays. Since the city of Chester is famous for its resistance against pressures to "correct" its cycle, it could be argued that this ingenious dramatist accomplished his semiprivate triumph only when that Protestant distrust of the plays reached its mid-century apex during the reign of Edward VI (1537-53). Or, perhaps a bit less valiantly, he composed the cycle's credal design during the cautious reassertion of the old plays' performances under the more sympathetic but brief reign of Mary (1553-58).[32]

But the other likely occasion in the sixteenth century when the cycle could have realized its credal structure is, in my present opinion, the more plausible guess: that occasion is the play's shift to Whitsuntide, circa 1519. During this shift the cycle was amplified in many ways: three new pageants were added, and as many as twelve other pageants were expanded by the addition of new episodes. It is clear that during the course of these amplifications a single playwright was able to work on several pageants at once (the *Stanzaic*

Life reviser being the most prominent example), and thus a single imagination could at this time have been responsible for integrating into Chester all the new elements necessary to complete the cycle's credal design. As I have already noted, the apostles' institution of their creed on Pentecost is an apt dramatic way of celebrating the cycle's new liturgical surroundings. In addition, the dramatic incorporation of the Apostles' Creed is an interpretive innovation perfectly consonant in style with the other pieces of didactic self-exposition added to the cycle during the Whitsun shift (see Chapter 2). Furthermore, Chester's credal design could in fact be attributed to the influence of its major dramatic competitor, the Coventry play of Corpus Christi. Lawrence Clopper has suggested that one major reason for Chester's shift to Whitsuntide and to a three-day performance on moving wagons was to rival Coventry technically, "in spectacle, in mechanical contrivances, in sheer theatricality";[33] we could add now that Chester may also have sought to rival Coventry formally, as another cycle which proved each article of the Creed to "be true and of authority." It must be conceded, however, that not only is there no external evidence in support of this conjecture, but the most reliable register of pageant amplifications during the Whitsun shift offers neutral commentary at best: that is, the two pageants crucial to the cycle's credal design—the Resurrection and the Pentecost—are both accorded "original" quatrain descriptions by the Early Banns.

Nevertheless, if one insists as I do that the shift to Whitsuntide was the occasion when Chester's credal design was in all likelihood accomplished, it would appear that the subtlety of that design remains a legitimate critical problem. In a form of drama which is normally understood to be public, propagandistic, and "naive," what point was there in incorporating designs so clever that they were well beyond the understanding of the "lewed" spectator? This question, I think, must be answered first by simply pointing out that these subtleties do in fact exist in Chester, all of them apparently additions made during the Whitsun shift. I am thinking specifically of the stage icon of the *arcus in nubibus* with which the "Noah" concludes; the comic, "fallen," and camouflaged *figurae* of the Eucharist in "The Shepherds"; and of course the ninth and tenth articles of the Creed as they are incorporated into "The Resurrection."

221

But the second point is that none of the "lewed" spectators, if they carefully attended each of these pageants, would ever be excluded from a pageant's primary meaning: these plays remain public celebrations of fundamental Christian truths. In addition, the truths alluded to by these subtle designs—that is, the future crucifixion of Christ, the celebration of the Eucharist, and the recitation of the Creed—will all be straightforwardly dramatized elsewhere in the cycle. Thus what is revealed in these designs is the work of a theological imagination which felt the need to achieve an artistic perfection for his personal satisfaction. Accordingly, we must conclude that the discovery of Chester's credal design has illustrated how this ingenious playwright, without in any way injuring the cycle's traditional form, was able to redesign his city's famous play for his own aesthetic and religious edification as well as for that of the most discerning members of his audience.

8

Reformations in the
Dramatic Image:
Paginae XXII-XXIV

While examining Chester's Old Testament pageants, I proposed three general models useful in understanding the larger designs of the individual cycles: the cycle seen as a dramatic *summa* of the primary tenets of Christian belief, the cycle as a dramatic interpretation of salvation history, and the cycle as an oblique projection of Everyman's spiritual education. Chester's unique design as a dramatic *summa* has been fully revealed by the end of its Resurrection Group: the twelve articles of the Apostles' Creed are the basic credenda of faith certified by the entire cycle. But Chester's dramatic realizations of these two other general models, because each is predicated not only upon time but upon the completion of time, have yet to be fully revealed. Chester's vision of the providential design of history will be defined completely only as its mimesis of history ends, like a tragedy or a comedy or some other form of dramatic action. Likewise, that human image reflected throughout history and intimately bound up with the audience's perceptions of itself will be defined most distinctly in the fullness of time, becoming a more prominent dramatic concern as the cycle's temporal designs grow increasingly complex.[1] Near the ending of each cycle, that is, the plays' temporal perspective shifts and then splinters. At a certain moment in each of the cycles, the world of biblical history has suddenly leaped "over" the audience into a biblical world of the future. This future world, closest in time to the audience yet nearly coincident with the end of time, is a dramatic world which, as it were, offers no future: the viewers, habituated by past pageants

223

to looking "forward," are forced finally to look elsewhere—"up" toward eternity, "back" over history, or "into" their own present spiritual conditions. The effect of these various shifts in time and perspective was surely meant to be edifying as well as disquieting: ideally each viewer will discover in the final designs of history an image of his own state of spiritual ill- or well-being.

That the Chester dramatist was unusually interested in the dramatic implications of the end of time is suggested by his having included not one but three pageants associated with the Eschaton. The temporal perspective of this unique Eschatological Group shifts in each pageant. The first offers, of all things, a series of prophecies predicting future events; the second offers a series of actions parodically iterating the past events of Christ's life; the third centers upon that moment in time where time gives way to eternity. Chester's dislocations of its "standard" dramatic representations of time helps its eschatological pageants emphasize, even as history comes to an end, their metahistorical concerns. These concerns center upon the viewers, upon their perceived relationship to the human image projected in the entire play, and upon the play's responsibilities as an indirect and imperfect image both of its audience and of eternal truth. It may be recalled from Chapter 7 that I suggested three heroes could be discerned within the Chester cycle. One collective hero, the apostles, has disappeared after achieving spiritual perfection; a second hero, Christ, has proved his perfection and will reappear at the cycle's end, in the "Last Judgment." Between the disappearance of one and the reappearance of the other, there is a dramatic moment when a third heroic potential may emerge. This moment belongs to the audience. Falling between time past and the end of time, this hiatus is the audience's Garden of Gethsemane. Like Christ's sleeping disciples in the Garden, many of the viewers may sense little of the spiritual wonder of this pause at the center of time. Others, however, may feel called upon to test their strength and to measure their faith before facing that final trial inevitably awaiting them.

That the Chester playwright chose to exploit this "empty" space is not surprising—we have seen him elsewhere amplify potential dramatic moments completely passed over by other playwrights. What is surprising, however, is the dramatic image he has chosen to

224

fill this void. As a preparation for the Last Judgment, two traditional dramatic images may have presented themselves immediately:
one a preacher-figure, such as the Expositor or Christ himself, who
in a sermonic address could exhort the audience to good works and
purer faith; the other a *Humanum Genus* character who in a morality-
play interlude could figure forth the psychological struggles and
moral choices of the viewers. Both of these the playwright has rejected—one a straightforward image of Christian wisdom and the
other a straightforward image of the Christian audience. Rather,
what the playwright offers is an image unique in English medieval
drama. It is Antichrist, that fiendish parody of Christ himself, who
takes the stage and takes the place of the audience's expectations.
Precisely why the Chester dramatist chose to include this blasphe-
mous charlatan we will probably never fully understand. But several
reasons immediately suggest themselves. Consider first this analysis
by Paul Zumthor of the ritual dynamics of medieval French drama:

> Ritualizing pity, feigning the tortures of Jesus or the martyr-
> dom of a saint, the actor occasionally faints with actual fatigue,
> real pain. Assuming a scapegoat role in addition to that of his
> costume, the actor takes on the latent violence of the people for
> whom he dies. A desymbolized one-way pseudocommunication,
> *this* alone *is*, reducing to naught our sufferings and sin [sic].
> With a "profane" theme the effect is analogous to the spiritual
> one, since all history lies in God's hands and serves only to make
> plain His transcendence.[2]

If I understand Zumthor's analysis, the purgative effect of the
French actor-martyr may be compared to that of Antichrist, even
though Chester's scapegoat is obviously a comic rather than a tragic
figure. Greeted by the Chester audience with hoots and jeers, dupli-
cating and parodying the miracles of Christ in his own foreshortened
career, this bombastic artificer may have successfully grounded those
anxieties raised earlier in the cycle by his truthful counterpart, thus
"reducing to naught our sufferings and sin." But if this comic purgation were Antichrist's full dramatic purpose, his appearance in
Chester would indeed be limited to a "desymbolized one-way
pseudocommunication." On the contrary, I believe that the Antichrist drama was intended on several levels to serve as a symbolic

225

two-way communication between the audience and the entire play. This can be inferred in part from the way Antichrist presents to the viewers a terribly distorted image of what they themselves would wish to be. That is, God at the creation made man in his image and then at the Incarnation took upon himself the image of man, so that all Christians thereafter might strive to unite these two images in themselves. At history's penultimate moment, the viewers of the Chester cycle would be expected most earnestly to recall the design of their past lives and to resolve to be more nearly perfect imitators of Christ's. Yet it is precisely at this moment that the Chester dramatist offers to his audience a horrid dramatic image which is a nearly perfect *literal* imitation of Christ's life. The significance of this dramatic image as part of the education of Christian history requires further exploration.

Also requiring further exploration is Antichrist's significance as a parodic image of drama itself, of the masterfully deceptive techniques employed by the entire cycle. If Zumthor's pious actor could purge his audience by identifying completely with Christ, this impious Antichrist, by identifying himself as the complete actor, may somehow have been intended as a purgation of the play itself as an artistic image. At least it must be seen that Antichrist's life is a careful simulation of the life of Christ presented by the cycle: he performs miracles, gathers his disciples, utters sermons, cites prophecies, resurrects the dead, convinces the world he is the Son of God, allows himself to die, is buried, and is resurrected. The strategies he uses to verify his spiritual identity are similar to the rhetorical strategies employed throughout the cycle: he convinces his doubting Thomases of the veracity of his claims by performing before their eyes a series of "empirical" proofs. How then does this profane pretender differ from the actor who pretends to be Christ? How does the artifice of one differ from the art of the other? The Chester viewers were probably not much troubled by such matters. Antichrist's art, they knew, was evil; the playwright's art, they assumed, was good. One was a powerful form of diabolical deception; the other was an edifying image outlining the way to salvation. But the critical issues posed by Chester's end-of-the-world juxtaposition of Christ and Antichrist were not that simply resolved, else that long-standing debate in the West between the iconoclasts and the iconodules would have been an empty exchange. In England, the more voluble side of this debate were the iconoclasts, who from the Lollards of the fourteenth century to the sixteenth-century Puritans argued that man-made images of God were at best ambiguous and misleading, at worst the works of the devil. In his study of this debate in England, John Phillips notes:

> The iconoclasts made their histories not in a broad confluence of intellectual currents, but in the exceedingly narrow channels that lay between God and the Devil—between salvation and hope of Heaven, or eternal damnation. Asserting the *a priori* virtue of God's handiwork as superior to man's was apparently the only aesthetic judgement a right-thinking Puritan could safely make. Outside such boundaries—themselves the proper province of religious dogma—lay the temptations of the world of artifice. Artifice was perilous not only because it might be merely extraneous to furthering the work of God—but because it might also be the work of the Devil or of Antichrist himself. The Antichrist was periodically awaited in a form not perfect—but *nearly* perfect. The subversion by Antichrist of man would be accomplished through acceptance, because of man's fallible perception, of works of *seeming* virtue and beauty.[3]

The Chester playwright, by incorporating into his own artistic world that character traditionally held to be the author of immoral artifice, was at the very least making a symbolic gesture in the direction of this aesthetic debate. In fact, I believe he was doing more. By using the imagery and language of drama itself, he figures forth both sides of this debate, holds them in tension, and finally achieves a dramatic resolution with the assistance of his own audience. The essential issues he raises are those concerned with the nature and power of the dramatic image, the kind of sacred reality it may contain, and the effects—good or evil—it could have on its viewers. Just as the Schoolmen could advance an aesthetic argument only by taking a stand on certain related psychological and theological issues, so in Chester's Eschatological Group this evaluation of the dramatic image is only one of several final judgments being made. Thus, not merely because of Antichrist's penultimate place in Christian history is it appropriate that these issues be raised most forcefully at this time.

227

Coming at the end of the cycle's last day of performance, these concluding pageants offer a retrospective assessment of the entire cycle—as an interpretation of salvation history, as a projection of Christian education, and as a powerful and potentially dangerous form of art. They also offer a final assessment of the viewers, testing in a number of unexpected ways their powers of imagination, perception, and moral judgment. Most important, these tests are all by way of preparing the viewers for their own days of doom, a dramatic image of which the cycle offers as its concluding pageant. As the viewers measure their Christian image against that image projected of them by the "Last Judgment," they not only are judging their own spiritual worth but are resolving for themselves that long-standing debate about the value of Christian art. If in response to the play they reform their lives to a life of consistent Christian virtue, they will have proved that Christian art is indeed a moral force leading the way toward salvation.

I

Pagina XXII, the Shermen's pageant, is called by both the Early and Late Banns "Prophets of Antichrist," but the Harley List of Companies gives it a more accurate general title, "Prophets of Doomsday." That this pageant opens a new and final chapter of the history of Christian salvation is evidenced immediately by its nonhistorical setting and "undramatic" character: four scriptural prophets appear in ceremonial sequence to express their visions of the end of time, each vision in turn is glossed by the Expositor, who then recounts in his own voice the fifteen signs of the Day of Doom. The pageant's unlocalized setting, in addition to its limitation of action and gesture, emphasizes the power and importance of these utterances as they loose the imagination into an awesome phantasmagoria of the end of the world. First to appear is Ezechiel, who describes his dream of a "feild" full of "bones fell" which are brought to life by the Holy Ghost; the Expositor explains that his vision was of the future "daye of doome" when the saved and damned will return in the flesh to be judged. Zacharias describes his vision next: from between two silver mountains four chariots came, drawn by horses of red, black, white and "dyvers hewe." The Expositor explains that the hills represent

Enoch and Elias, "that as good sylver shalbe aye / stydfast men and trewe," and suggests that the horses "may lickned bee / to sayntes of foure maners of degree": the red to martyrs, the white to "such that neyther night nor daye / dreeden death nothinge," the black to preachers, and the "skewed" to the "Jewes and paynims" who will be converted finally by the two prophets. Next, Daniel describes his magnificent dream of four beasts rising from the sea, the last sporting ten horns on its head: the smallest of the horns grows large, speaks "great wordes," consumes three of his fellows, and the rest bow down in abeyance to him. The Expositor interprets the horn as the Antichrist, who shall reign over the world three and a half years. The last of the visionary prophets is "Johannes Evange-lista," who, ravished to heaven, saw two prophets sent by God as "chandelours of great light" to destroy his enemies; the beast "from beneath" comes and kills them, but after three and a half days they rise and ascend to heaven. The Expositor explains that the prophets are Enoch and Elias, the beast with "the devilles power" is the Anti-christ. Pagina XXII closes then with the Expositor's description in eighty lines of the "xv signes" of the coming Day of Doom. These signs constitute a series of horrendous cosmic cataclysms whose dire magnitude clearly presages the end of the known world: seas rise "agaynst kinde"; fish yell and roar "hideouslye"; the waters of the world burn; trees bleed; all buildings fall to the ground; earthquakes reduce the hills to sand; madmen run from their caves; the dead rise from their graves; the stars fall, shooting fire; all humankind dies and rises again; everything is then consumed by fire, so that on the final day "made shalbee / neewe yearth, neewe heaven, through Goddes postee."

Criticized by one scholar as having been "rapidly conceived and executed,"[4] this relatively brief pageant (340 lines) is in my judg-ment an unusual success, for it transforms the tenor of the cycle entirely, while attempting to shift the audience toward a radically new attitude. Having just witnessed the comforting reduction of world history to twelve articles of Christian faith, the audience is forced immediately to confront a visionary horror-land of nearly limitless scope. Although these visions are themselves quite dreadful, the pageant appears designed to exercise fully the audience's imagina-tive powers: prompted by words alone, they find their imaginations

229

effortlessly giving shape to prodigies more wonderful than any stage-craft could ever have realized. This contrast itself suggests something of the limitations (and power) of the dramatist's art. However, the first clear sign that the Chester playwright may be manipulating his viewers—by exploiting their imaginative wonder and their dramatic anticipations—is the slight trick with which he concludes the pageant. Apparently the prophesied holocaust is not (yet?) to be performed, for the Expositor in his very last line suddenly announces the coming of Antichrist: "Hee comes! Soone you shall see!" This last-minute redirection of dramatic expectation, as the anticipated dramatization of the general Armageddon is suddenly preempted by the Antichrist, is one of many surprises, large and small, which dominate the cycle's last pageants. Once accepted, the idea of an Antichrist play appears a reasonable compromise—half-way between a totally undramatic play like "The Prophets of Doomsday" and a play whose ending-of-the-world subject is so dramatic that any stage production of it risks unintended self-parody. Thus as entertaining theater and as a way of forestalling the final Judgment, a pageant about this master charlatan makes good sense. But it would have to be unusually brilliant drama to match the imaginative powers of Scripture as just recited (and *not* dramatized) by the prophets and the Expositor. What stage image Antichrist could be expected to assume not even the most erudite in the audience could confidently predict. Theological tradition held that the Antichrist might appear in his revealed role as *Antichristus apertus* (perhaps like some horrid beast or humanoid monster) or he might appear in his disguised role as *Antichristus mysticus* (perhaps like some contemporary human figure or like Christ himself returning to earth as he had prophesied); or he might double his duplicity by assuming both roles, appearing at one and the same time as both *Antichristus apertus* and *Antichristus mysticus*.[5] Whatever form he has assumed, as he first pops up on stage, is therefore bound to be a delight, a disappointment, and a surprise: a surprise because there was no predicting his image, a disappointment because that single image could not possibly match the many imagined of him, and a delight because he reintroduces us to the fast-moving world of dramatic images themselves. Therefore, at the moment between this sudden announcement of Antichrist and his actual stage appearance, what we are offered is a rather complex interplay between three imaginative worlds: that of the words of Scripture, that of the mind of the audience, and that of the physical actualization on stage. This interplay, we shall see, is the overture to Chester's concluding "dramatic" study of the power and the limits of drama itself.

With Antichrist's first appearance in the Dyers' pageant, it is obvious that he is hardly a frightful cosmic beast rising from the vasty deep. Rather, his human form and the prolix rant of his first Latin declamation place him within that general dramatic tradition of the bombastic boaster, thus preparing the audience for at least a quasi-comic treatment of the world's last evil king. "Descendi praesens rex," he claims in two long stanzas plagiarized from the more controlled self-definitions offered by God and by Christ earlier in the cycle, "pius et perlustrator, / princeps aeternus vocor, Christus, vester salvator." These farcical claims to true messiahship are made even more ridiculous as Antichrist moves into the vernacular, citing the scriptural testimonies of "Moyses, Davyd, and Esaye" as proof of his divinity, despite the counterprophecies given in the preceding pageant. Four kings then enter, listen to Antichrist's assertions that he is the Son of God, and confess that they would believe his claims if they could see his divinity certified in "a signe that wee may see." Antichrist immediately performs a number of miracles before their eyes, accomplishing in an instant the greatest wonders of Christ's entire ministry. He then raises men from the dead and before the astonished kings he himself dies; they bury him, and then he dramatically rises from the grave, exclaiming, "I ryse! Nowe reverence dose to mee / God glorified greatest of degree" (H). Now convinced of his authenticity, the four kings bow before him and offer him sacrifice. In grateful recognition of their belief, Antichrist sends them the Holy Ghost: "Dabo vobis cor novum et spiritum novum in medio vestri." He further rewards them with gifts, promising them the kingdoms of the world if they remain steadfast in their faith.

At this moment Antichrist appears at the height of his power, having converted to his side all the representatives of humankind. In heaven, Enoch and Elias now resolve that "With this champion we must chide." They come to earth, confront the four kings, and exclaim that Antichrist is an imposter of the true Son of God: "Hee calles himselfe 'Christe' and 'Messye'. / Hee lyes, forsooth, apertlye."

With Antichrist standing before them, and with the memory of his many miracles just performed, the kings are understandably confused. But they resolve that if these two men who call themselves prophets can expose Antichrist "by prooffes of disputacon" and thus "doe him downe," they will confess their error, reconvert, and willingly die if need be "in hope of salvatyon." What follows is a long disputation of over two hundred lines between the prophets and Antichrist, filled with theological assertions and *ad hominem* attacks. Although Antichrist at one point refuses to believe in the Trinity and then quite illogically claims that he is God's son, the battle rages evenly and the prophets' arguments have no success in "doing down" their adversary either by sound logic or bitter abuse. Although the prophets are more restrained than Antichrist, the debate seems destined to become an endless flyting match, until, nearly at their wits' end, the prophets demand that their adversary offer them proof of his divine powers. Accordingly, Antichrist calls forth the men he had resurrected, and demands:

> Come eate and drynke, that men may see,
> and prove me worthye of deitee;
> so shall we stynt all stryffe.

But before offering them the bread that will prove their resurrection in the flesh, the prophets break and bless it, in the name of "on God and persons three." At the moment the bread is consecrated, Antichrist's hoax is exposed, for the eucharistic wafer shines so brilliantly before the "dead" men's eyes that they scream to have it taken away: "That prynt that ys upon hit pight, / hit puttes me to great feere." The four astonished kings recognize that they had been deceived "with sorcerye, wytchcraft, and nygromancye," and praying to Christ for forgiveness they prepare to die "for Christes love omnypotent, / in cause that ys rightwyse." Their martyrdom is quickly realized: in a rage, Antichrist draws his sword, crying "A, false faytures, turne you nowe?" and in one fell swipe kills them all—Enoch, Elias, and the four repentant kings. The concluding episode, which dramatizes Antichrist's death and the triumph of the martyred prophets, converts the up-and-down events of the pageant into the dramatic form, finally, of a joyful comedy. With the death of Enoch and Elias, Antichrist's reign of three and a half years comes to an end, and Michael appears with sword in hand, reviling him for his sins. As Antichrist is cut down, he calls out for help. Two demons rush in on cue, grab his corpse "by the toppe" and "by the tayle," and cart it off with relish and dispatch to its place of uneasy rest: "Yea, by the heeles in hell shall hee henge / in a dungeon deepe." Then the two prophets, miraculously and quite unexpectedly, "resurgent" (H). They praise the power and the glory of God, and are then led off to "heaven-blysse" by Michael as the angel sings, "Gaudete justi in domino."

I have offered this full summary of the Chester "Antichrist" to suggest its complete success as "high drama." With no earlier Antichrist play available as model, the Chester playwright has managed nevertheless to create a theatrical tour de force, a spectacular play of speed, suspense, and surprise. As evidenced in Antichrist's stage antics—his leapings, resurrectings, dying, self-resurrecting, killings, and second death—the play is a melee of dramatic activity, of histrionic to-ings and fro-ings, ups and downs. The counterplot, although more dignified in its movement, is equally active in its descendings from heaven, deaths, killing, resurrectings, and ascendings back to heaven. In no other Chester pageant are so many people killed; in no other pageant is there such hypermobility on stage. If, as I believe, this pageant is in part a definition of Chester's concerns about the powers of Christian art, there could hardly be a better showpiece in defense of drama's ability to entertain. Not all critics, however, have agreed about the pageant's dramatic sophistication. In his introduction to the twelfth-century Latin Tegernsee *Ludus de Antichristo*, John Wright criticizes the Chester playwright for his "misplaced sense of the dramatic" as seen in the "long and blustering theological disputation between Antichrist and the two Prophets."[6] My immediate response is that the Chester dramatist placed this disputation at the very center of his pageant to epitomize the entire play's disputatious nature. In other words, what saves the play from the senseless giddiness of farce are the several serious concerns that are touched upon time and again by the play's dialectical structure. As the pageant's plot twists and turns, arriving at one unexpected complication after another, a series of implicit questions are raised concerning the powers in this world of truth and falsehood, good and evil. Antichrist may be a fraud, yet his magic is real; the four kings are good, but they are weak in discerning the truth; truth, represented by the two prophets, cannot defeat fraud by using exclusively human powers; even when exposed by a higher power, fraud has the power to kill; the only power that in fact can kill fraud is the power of God himself. A brilliant comedy, the play is also a study in levels and degrees of power, with Antichrist managing to "up the ante" at each turn but the last. The pageant's central disputation could have been nothing else than a "long and blustering" debate because those traditional "human" techniques of exposing spiritual untruth—scriptural citings, Scholastic reasoning, rhetorical persuasion, and personal abuse—are one-by-one proved ineffectual. In the power struggle of the entire pageant, truth finally triumphs, but in a way it is never allowed to anywhere else in the cycle. That is, it is necessary finally that Michael come with sword in hand, as the comedy's *angelus ex machina*, because his superhuman strength alone has the power to "do down" the adversary. The play thus concludes fortunately as a triumphant Christian comedy; yet it also concludes with a pathetic reminder of human impotence, as the four good kings remain lying dead on the stage.

Chester's two Antichrist pageants significantly enrich the cycle's vision of salvation history and its vision of the education of the Christian spirit. Rather than neatly leaping from the Creed to the Last Judgment, Chester has chosen to represent in compressed form the tortuous pattern of the intervening years. Whatever simple design history may seem to have assumed at the end of Chester's Resurrection Group is now radically complicated by the up-and-down mayhem of Antichrist's reign. And whatever complacency the viewers may have felt about their role in the immediate future and their preparedness for final things should be dispelled by the potency of Antichrist's deceptions and by the fate of those four representatives of humankind. Not that the viewers are themselves meant to feel impotent at the pageant's end. Quite the contrary. A sense of personal power has been granted to the spectators from the very beginning of the Eschatological Group. They have been reminded of the power of their own imaginations to concoct wonders more varied than ever could appear on stage; they have seen certain "wonders" performed on stage which obviously, from one angle, are merely bits of theatrical quack-magic; and they have participated in a playful power-struggle where collectively they have managed to "do down" the stage charlatan himself. However, they must have recognized some time or other that this stage charlatan is merely a comfortably comic distortion of the real thing, of that powerful parody of Christ who will indeed succeed in duping all of human-kind. Thus for all their "play," these pageants offer a serious warn-ing. In the future, those traditional articles of Christian belief and those traditional ways of knowing Christ will all prove tragically inadequate. Thomas's skepticism, once used by the cycle to chastise the viewers for their less than perfect faith, serves now as a virtue not only to be emulated but to be extended: even those five senses that Thomas finally trusted in will prove to be unreliable. These Antichrist pageants do not, like a didactic Doomsday sermon, tell the audience how to prepare for the end, but they do manage to exercise all those human faculties needed for the trials ahead—imag-ination and reason, faith and doubt, the emotions and the senses. Thus if these pageants are the viewers' Garden of Gethsemane, they are hardly an agony of self-doubt, a bitter study of human weakness. Rather, they constitute an unpainful series of therapeutic exercises, a kind of psychological *agon* and dialectic of mind and spirit. The histrionic ups-and-downs, the back-and-forth manipulations of time and dramatic expectation, the now-you-see-it / now-you-don't tricks of Antichrist collectively bring into play nearly all the powers of human discrimination. Chester cannot guarantee that these powers will be sufficient to "do down" any future Antichrist. But through these dramatic exercises the viewers should be better prepared to face their future trials and to confront the dramatic image of their own Last Judgment.

To interpret Pagina XXIII in this way—as a preparatory exercise for the spiritual trials ahead—is to offer a "moral defense" for a play which a majority of viewers (and readers) may have perceived as nothing other than theatrical fun-and-games. In a perceptive study of this pageant, Leslie Howard Martin in fact concludes that Chester's comic treatment of the Antichrist "provides merely an antic inter-lude before the inevitable triumph of righteousness in *The Last Judgment*."[7] My "moral defense" may therefore be wrong; it is equally possible that Martin's "antic interlude" interpretation is wrong. But I would like to believe that both are at least somewhat right, not only because of the various levels of response the play surely prompted among its viewers, but because I am persuaded that the play's multiplicity of possible meanings is in fact one of its central thematic concerns. That this pageant should wish to call attention to itself as a dramatic image is not very surprising. I have observed in earlier chapters how Chester has occasionally interpreted its own dramatic scenes as "signes" and "tokenings" inspired by the power, and reflecting the history, of sacred truth. Differing from these in its higher degree of semiotic self-awareness, what makes Pagina XXIII unique is that it appears to doubt its own validity as truly Christian art. As an image which can only pretend to be inspired by the power and pretend to reflect the history of sacred truth, the play may possibly be no more than an idle frivolity or a dangerous hoax. Antichrist's sped-up ministry is a burlesque inversion of Christ's life, his "carnal" magic a profanation of the inspiration of the Holy Ghost. The show-within-a-show of Antichrist's career may just as easily be construed as a burlesque of the cycle itself—which has just completed its own sped-up version of Christ's life, employing the "magic" and "fraud" of theatrical deception.

In the eyes of certain late medieval English iconoclasts, all such dramatic deceptions had the devil's (and Antichrist's) blessings for several good reasons. One was that the devil saw these images as "empty" fictions distracting the Christian viewer from the moral responsibilities of real life; on such grounds not only the "Antichrist" but the entire Chester cycle would have to be judged as "merely an antic interlude." Another reason plays such as the Chester cycle were the devil's delight, the iconoclasts argued, was they succeeded all too well as pseudosacred images. Appealing to the "carnal" imagination of fallen man, these plays were so powerfully realistic that the viewer was transformed into an idolator, worshiping the carnal sign itself rather than the spiritual truth it signified. As a master craftsman of images, the Chester playwright would naturally seem to belong to the other party. One would expect him to agree with Thomas Netter and other anti-Lollardists who argued that Christ gave his blessing to images by the very act of his own Incarnation:

The Jews did not, therefore, fashion distinct images of things, because, in the prevailing darkness, everything was shadowy, and they saw nothing distinctly. But we Christians, having knowledge of Christ, cast out old shadows and, because we have been transformed in His image, praise images.[8]

In these few words Netter has succinctly given expression to that "incarnational" defense of images which had been a central apologetic in Christian aesthetics for centuries. By assuming the image of natural man, Christ had to a degree sacramentalized both nature and man and had endowed all images with potential spiritual significance. Because man had been radically reformed by Christ when in human guise, man-made images of Christ should ideally effect a similar spiritual reformation in man. Just as it was Christ in carnal form who reformed fallen man, so it was the carnality of the artistic image, its power of appealing to the five senses, that was held by apologists to be its special educative strength. Of course artistic images of Christ were not sacred in the way that the sacraments were. Yet, as Bishop Reginald Pecock argued, since the sacraments are "seable rememoratijf signes" of Christ's life and death, signs that "ben mor lijk to Crist and to his passioun, than ben the sacramentis whiche Crist ordeyned" must surely also be "leeful, expedient, and profitable."[9]

This sacramental analogy could serve as a defense of the way Christ in the cycle and the cycle itself both use "sacred" signs to lead their doubting Thomases from the shadows of confusion to the clarity of perfect belief. In Chester Pagina XIX, the "Emmaus and Thomas," this process of signification is most succinctly dramatized. The pageant opens in consternation, as Lucas and Cleophas try to comprehend that "mystie thinge" of Christ's reported Resurrection. Christ then suddenly appears before them, but remains unrecognized because he has assumed the guise of a pilgrim. Sitting with them, Christ tries to verify the Resurrection by citing "holy wrytt"; failing this, he breaks bread with his companions, and then suddenly vanishes. As Lucas and Cleophas later report, they did not recognize Christ until the moment of his disappearance: "our wyttes were so knytt / that him we might not knowe." What unknit their wits was the evidence of the consecrated bread which, when broken, suddenly reveals Christ ("By breakinge the breade I knewe his face / but nothinge there before") even as Christ suddenly disappears. It is not until Christ's final appearance before all his disciples, however, that this process of gradual revelation reaches its climax. Disguised neither in the robes of a pilgrim nor "behind" the Sacrament, Christ offers his naked, wounded body as absolute physical proof of his Resurrection, and Thomas finally believes: "My God, my lord, my Christ, my kinge! / Nowe leeve I withowt weeninge."

This sequence of gradual revelation—moving from the "general report" of Christ's Resurrection, to Christ's appearance in disguise, to "holy wrytt," to Christ seen "through" the Sacrament, and finally to Christ himself—is a process of empirical intensification employed in various ways by all the cycles. As the viewers are led more deeply into the dramatic frame, they are expected finally to accept the physical, tactile images offered as proof of the realities displayed. Thomas's intensely moving response as he touches his Savior's side should thus evoke an equally deep feeling of belief and love among the spectators themselves. But as the iconoclasts from the fourteenth century through the sixteenth angrily argued, what has evoked this "belief" and "love" is merely a sign, a powerful piece of artistic deception, an illusion. Is this not idolatry? And is it not likely that those most thrilled by the power and verisimilitude of the stage image of Christ will be those least apt to reform their lives at the play's end? Such were some of the charges leveled against the English cycles by the Lollard "Tretise on Miraclis Pleyinge":

> For Crist seith that folk of avoutrie sechen siche syngnys, as a lecchour sechith signes of verrey love, but no dedis of verrey love; so sithen thise myraclis pleyinge ben onely syngnis of love withoute dedis, thei ben not onely contrarious to the worschipe of God, that is bothe in signe and in dede, but also thei ben gynnys of the devvel to cacchen men to byleve of Anti-Crist . . . Not he that pleyith the wille of God worschipith hym, but onely he that doith his wille in deede worschipith hym.[10]

Where, in the midst of this long and tortuous debate, does the Chester playwright actually stand? As a human artisan fabricating "sacred" images, does he see his own art as a projection of Antichrist's art, or as a projection of Christ's? Does he see the reception

238

of his plays by his viewers as morally and spiritually positive, or negative, or neutral? These kinds of questions—so troublesome to a number of medieval artists and poets—the Chester playwright raises, albeit indirectly, in his Antichrist pageant. But because much of their resolution depends upon the viewers themselves, he seems to answer them only in part, leaving to his audience a considerable amount of freedom and responsibility. The essential choice they are given is neatly framed by the Antichrist pageant's counterposing two kinds of "magic" against which its own illusionistic signs may be measured. As Brother Linus Lucken has noted, one of Chester's few unique additions to the Antichrist legends was the specification of the eucharistic Host as the power which exposed Antichrist's fraud.[11] A perfect opposition between two signifying forces is thus established. On the one hand there is the magic of Antichrist—powerful, evil, and fraudulent; on the other hand there is the magic of Christ—powerful, good, and true. The choice to be made between these two is obvious. But where, between these two, is the signifying power of the dramatic image to be placed? Surely, it is much less than either of these, and far removed from both: neither powerfully good nor powerfully evil, neither totally false nor totally true. Rather, its "ontology" seems to be closest to that of the four poor kings. Like them, it can easily be swayed in one direction or the other. Compared to the powers of Christ and Antichrist, its "regal" powers are minuscule. Its desires can readily be obeyed, but they can just as easily be disobeyed. Always vulnerable, it can be exterminated just as easily as were the four kings. Of course, we should not be so naive as to accept this "humility trope" as the playwright's final word in defining his art. But the image it projects of a modest, well-meaning, and "innocent" craft could take much of the bluster out of any iconoclastic attack.

Chester's implicit aesthetic position, extrapolated here from a quite limited part of a single pageant, is one which would appear to grant to the viewers an extraordinary freedom in judging the value and meaning of the dramatic images they behold. It appears in fact to suggest that these images, ethically as well as spiritually, remain nearly neutral in meaning until the viewers invest them with their own perceived significance. But like so much else in the Antichrist pageant, what appears here to be Chester's aesthetic position

239

is a slight trick, a half-transparent disguise for something much more substantial behind it. Not surprisingly, the Chester dramatist proves eventually to be quite confident of the spiritual integrity of his craft, and worried only slightly about his drama's lack of absolute moral autonomy over its viewers. In order to give voice to the opposite aesthetic, to pass then through a neutral position, and to identify his viewers finally with his own position, the Chester playwright uses in this pageant the sort of stratagem which can be found generally in a number of literary works. "Literature," Geoffrey Hartman has pronounced, "is a kind of loyal (though not always legal) opposition which opens the sacred to scrutiny, and so at once profanes and purifies it."[12] What the Chester "Antichrist" has managed to do is to hold up to dramatic scrutiny several sacred images at once, and through the course of the pageant to "profane" and then to "purify" each of them. The first image is quite obvious: if Christ in the cycle has ever appeared less than perfect, the comic profanations of his arch-parodist have by the end of the pageant certainly reestablished Christ's spiritual perfection. More subtly, Antichrist may succeed also in purifying that human image both projected and addressed by the cycle: his literal imitation of Christ's life offers a negative exemplum, warning that it is the spirit of Christ's life which his followers should think first of emulating. But the level of "purifying profanation" I find most interesting is that of the drama itself. By a brilliant stroke, the Chester dramatist in conceiving his unique Antichrist pageant has, as it were, conceded everything to the iconoclasts. Not only does he appear to agree with their charges that Antichrist is the master of the dramatic image, but he "verifies" these charges within his own play by transforming Antichrist himself into a dramatic image. Then by casting Antichrist as the cycle's supreme scapegoat and arch-buffoon, the play manages (assisted by the raucous participation of its audience) to "do down" its own adversary. What survives after this comic purgation is the dramatic world intact, purified by its self-profanation, its identity and value as a "sign" now to be judged in context with that other surviving and more sacred sign, the sacrament of the eucharistic Host.

The "Antichrist" of course is not the only pageant in Chester which might be studied as an implicit *ars dramatica*, but as the brilliant centerpiece of a group of plays all concerned with the purpose and end of art its unusual degree of self-analysis calls for a special kind of critical assessment. This assessment is one of the many judgments that are made or need to be made as the cycle reaches its end. As we have noted, the "Antichrist" has realized in a number of unexpected ways the anticipations of the preceding pageant's Doomsday prophecies. In its turn, the pageant with which the cycle concludes, "The Last Judgment," fulfills in a number of unexpected ways the anticipations established by both pageants immediately preceding it. Its dramatization of final things is not that series of phantasmagorical catastrophes predicted by the prophets, nor is Christ's final role (as one might expect) the perfect antithesis to Antichrist's. Nevertheless, in a way which is aesthetically satisfactory and morally just, "The Last Judgment" fulfills the dramatic promise of all that precedes it, bringing the argument of Christian history to a perfectly balanced conclusion. At the same time, it resolves with much greater clarity than the "Antichrist" the aesthetic debate concerning the power and purpose of the stage image. In contrast to the helter-skelter pandemonium of the "Antichrist," "The Last Judgment" defines an aesthetic made beautiful by its very simplicity—steadily cadenced, handsomely balanced, and supremely moving. Furthermore, in this final response to the iconoclasts' charge that dramatic images are at best merely "signes of verrey love" far removed from "dedis of verrey love," Pagina XXIV does something unique in the Chester cycle. At the very end it reforms the entire cycle by converting its dramatic image into an urgent moral imperative directed at the viewers. If in response to this powerful appeal the viewers reform their lives to "dedis of verrey love," they will prove not only that these are beautiful images faithful to Christian truth, but that they are a moral force leading toward salvation. To understand the various resolutions achieved in this concluding pageant, I will begin first by simply describing its action from beginning to end.

II

Pagina XXIV, the Websters' "The Last Judgment," is a simple and powerful pageant arranged in formal episodes suggestive of the procedures of a high-court of law. Christ the judge is first to enter.

He reveals his conviction that human history must now end, and opens his tribunal:

> It ys full youre syns I beheight
> to make a reckoninge of the right.
> Nowe to that doome I will mee dight
> that dead shall dulye dread.

The tribunal itself is arranged so that the defendants can assess their own lives and thereby infer the nature of their own judgments. As the angels blow the trumps of doom, the first group of defendants appears. A pope, emperor, king, and queen describe to their judge the sins they had committed on earth, their acts of contrition, and their just pains and penitence in purgatory. Their narratives constitute an array of sins. The pope confesses that he violated the trust of his office; the emperor admits that in his life he "coveted ryches and renowne"; the king confesses, "meethought to thee I had no neede, / so wronge the world me wyled"; and the queen acknowledges that she gave her life to "All that might excyte lecherye— / perrelles and precyouse perrye." Yet each of these sinners, at the penultimate moment in life, repented, and that repentence, coupled with their sporadic acts of mercy and with their sufferings in purgatory, assures them that they may hope for salvation. Thus "Rex Salvatus" concludes his confession:

> But lord, though I were synfull aye,
> contrytion yett at my last daye
> and almes-deedes that I dyd aye
> hath holpen me from hell.
> But well I wott that ylke waye
> that Abraham went wynde I maye,
> for I am purged to thy paye,
> with thee evermore to dwell.

The first group of defendants is followed immediately by a second, whose sins were unseasoned by any acts of mercy or contrition. The confession of these sinners, whose numbers exceed that of the first group, serves as an explicit call to repentance and as exemplary condemnations of all the sins of the flesh. As pope, emperor, king, queen, justice, and merchant list their many crimes, they recognize that they are beyond Christ's mercy. The pope confesses

242

to the "sylvyr and symonye" that ruled his life; the emperor admits to "manslaughter," "covetousnes," "Misbegotten money," "traytor-ouse tornes," and "false doomes"; the king and queen confess that they had lived for "languowre," "Lecherye," and "covetousenes"; the justice acknowledges, "To reave and robbe relygion, / that was all my devotyon"; and the merchant confesses:

> Ofte I sett upon false assyce,
> rayvinge poore with layinge myse.
> Falsely, by God and saintes Hyse
> a thousand tyme I sware. [H]

The lamentations of each of these sinners include an explicit homily against the temptations of the flesh. The queen, for instance, cries out against the things which have brought her to her present plight:

> Fye on pearles! Fye on prydee!
> Fye on gowne! Fye on guyde!
> Fye on hewe! Fye on hyde!
> These harrowe me to hell.
> Agaynst this chance I may not chyde.
> This bitter bale I must abyde.
> Yea, woe and teene I suffer this tyde,
> noe lyvinge tonge may tell.

The power of this episode derives in part from the many lament-able exclamations of "Alas!," from the many tempting everyday sins which led the defendants to their sufferings in purgatory, and from the perfect egalitarianism of the tribunal itself. Although each of the defendants had enjoyed considerable power, he has now no recourse but to expose completely the faults and failures of his life.

The confessions and the subsequent judgment of the defendants in this pageant would appear to be sufficiently powerful to effect in the viewer a deep sense of guilt and an immediate resolution to repent. But like the Last Judgment pageants in the other cycles, Chester exacerbates that guilt by Christ's final address to human-kind. At the end of the lamentations of the damned, Christ descends from his heavenly scaffold and stands *quasi in nube*, surrounded by angels who display the attributes of his Crucifixion, *cum cruce, corona spinea, lancea, aliisque instrumentis, omnia demonstrantes* (H). Then, in a ten-stanza speech addressed to all who behold him, he reviews the acts of love and the patience with which he had tolerated man's constant "wyckednes" in history: his creating man "Of yearth," his assuming human form, his dying for their sins "on the roode-tree," and his ascending to his Father to beg a boon,

> that hee of you should have mercye
> and more gracyous be therebye
> when you had synned horryblie,
> not takinge vengeance to soone.

Then, as a demonstration of the enormous suffering he patiently underwent to try "thee to recover in this case / into my companye," Christ exposes his side, and allows his wounds to bleed again as a reminder of the anguish of his Passion. As *emittet sanguinem de latere eius*, Christ excoriates mankind for its willingness to "doe amys":

> Behould nowe, all men! Looke on mee
> and see my blood freshe owt flee
> that I bleede on roode-tree
> for your salvatyon.
>
> Howe durst you ever doe amys
> when you unthought you of this,
> that I bleede to bringe you to blys
> and suffered such woo.
> Me you must not white, iwysse,
> though I doe nowe as right ys.
> Therefore eych man reacon his,
> for ryghtwysenes must goo.

Christ's address here differs considerably from the address he gave at the moment of his Resurrection. Whereas the speech of the resurrected Christ was delivered as a compassionate act of consolation, offering proof of the spiritual redemption to be found in his presence in the Blessed Sacrament, here at the Last Judgment Christ's testament is a bitter reproof of humankind for their scant faith and vicious nature. The baleful testimony of Christ's bleeding side, the further signs of his suffering in the instruments of his Crucifixion, and his imploring questions addressed to sinful man, constitute a powerful and profound call to repentance. This final vision of Christ as the crucified sufferer was clearly constructed to effect in the audience a withering sense of guilt, shame, and personal remorse.

The judgment of that guilt follows immediately: its enactment is simple, its significance straightforward. The *Salvati* beg to be saved. Christ calls them before him and grants their wish because, he explains, while on earth they gave him clothing, meat, and drink, and harbored him against the cold. They confess they have no memory of these acts of mercy, so Christ explains:

> Yes, forsoothe, my freindes deare,
> such as poore and naked weare,
> you cladd and fedd them both in feere
> and harbored them alsoe.

Because of their general acts of corporal mercy, the *Salvati* are saved, and are led by the two angels to Christ's right hand. The judgment of the *Damnati*, however, is preceded by the appearance before Christ of two advocates from hell who plead their case against the six remaining defendants. Demon Primus and Demon Secundus argue that since the defendants served them while on earth, they deserve to be in their thrall forever. Since "on good deede...have they not to shewe," they must needs be damned in "great torment" and "in bitter bale to brenne" (H). Christ agrees:

> Loe, you men that wycked have benne,
> what Sathan sayth you heren and seene.
> Rightuouse doome may you not fleene,
> for grace ys put awaye.

Although "my sweete mother deare / and all the sayntes that ever were" prayed for the souls of those assembled, Christ explains, they are beyond the hope of salvation, because in their lives they failed to minister unto Christ when he was sick, hungry, and desolate. The *Damnati* complain that had they known Christ was among them and in need they would have succored him. So Christ must again explain the acts of corporal mercy:

> Naye! When you sawe the leaste of myne
> that on yearth suffered pyne,

245

with your rychesse you would not ryne
ney fulfill my desyre.
And syth you would nothinge enclyne
for to helpe my poore lyne,
to mee your love yt was not fyne.
Therefore, goe to the fyre!

And the *Damnati* are led off by the two devils to hell-pit. With
this absolute separation of the saved and damned, the pageant's
action comes to an end. But the drama of the cycle does not close
until Matthew, Mark, Luke, and John take the stage and address the
viewers. In a stanza each, the four evangelists testify to the truth of
the preceding dramatized events, the veracity of the words spoken
by Christ, and the necessity of preparing now for the Final Judgment.

What is immediately striking about this final pageant is how different it is from all that has preceded it. Whereas almost every
dramatic event to this point has involved a sense of forward-moving
historical action, here all has finally come to perfect rest. Rather like
a cathedral mural or bas-relief the meaning of which is defined in
large part by its symbolic arrangements in space, "The Last Judgment" is an almost stationary dramatic tableau. The dynamics of
this paradoxically powerful pageant therefore derive not from any
interchange or movement between characters on stage but from the
intense emotional currents between the stage scene and the viewers
themselves. For in this final pageant the viewers cannot avoid seeing
both an image of final things and an image of their own spiritual
conditions. In addition, this pageant turns the forward motion of the
cycle in a new direction: whereas all the "historical" plays have
shown us what we are obliged to believe, this play shows us now
what that belief obliges us to do. Finally, "The Last Judgment"
brings to conclusion all those issues—historical, theological, moral,
and "dramatic"—that I have been discussing in the course of this
study. To untangle some of these, I shall consider first the issue that
has been of foremost concern in this chapter: the debate on dramatic
images.

Coming after the nearly "empty" dramatic staging of the prophecies of Doomsday and the richly ambiguous imagery of the Antichrist pageant, "The Last Judgment" offers two clearly defined

aesthetic positions through its two distinctly different sets of stage images. On the one hand there are the semiallegorical figures of the saved and damned souls, who appear to define a conservative aesthetic which would be acceptable to all but the most uncompromising Puritan. No one could be expected to see these ahistorical figures as literally true: rather, they are metaphoric projections of the spiritual and moral condition of all humanity. On the other hand, there is Christ's direct appeal to the viewers' belief in his bleeding body, a dramatic gesture defining in an extremely powerful way the incarnational aesthetic which the iconoclasts so distrusted. Thus one form of dramatic characterization in Pagina XXIV implicitly endorses a kind of morality-play image of abstract spiritual types; the other endorses an iconic and perhaps even sacramental equation of art with sacred Reality. Where does Chester's self-defining aesthetics finally stand? Part of the final answer comes from the four evangelists themselves. At the end of the cycle, as they remark upon the foregoing dramatized events, none certifies the verisimilitude of Christ's stage image, but they are quite insistent upon verifying the scriptural accuracy of his words, "all that ever my lord sayth here." This final shift in focus helps to undercut any vestigial impression that Christ's stage image had somehow been a literal representation of his Person. The fullest positive answer, however, comes from Christ himself in the last speech he gives in the play. As with the *Salvati*, Christ must explain to the *Damnati* that throughout their lives on earth he had been in their midst, living within reach of all their senses. As "the leaste of myne," he had been in constant need of their loving attention. But the *Damnati*, literalists to the end, complain that had they only seen Christ, then "have harbored thee we would." They fail, that is, to understand how Christ on earth has assumed the form of a multitude of images in order to appeal to and to express the spiritual needs of all humankind. The aesthetic moral therefore is that one does not search for a single truthful image of Christ, but rather finds in all human images representations of Christ's truth. In the end, then, Chester's aesthetic debate is smoothly resolved because its two seemingly opposite sets of stage images prove to be unified. The abstract moral types and the literal stage image of Christ prove to be equally true as images because they are both images of Christ. They are also both equally true as images because they are both projections of the spiritual and moral condition of all humanity.

If this chapter's discussion of Chester's philosophy of images seems to have manipulated the significance of the concluding pageants far in the direction of theoretical aesthetics, my response is that—as with Dante's poetics—Chester's implied aesthetics is part and parcel of its moral and theological vision. Theologically, Chester offers at the very end of the cycle an interpretation of Christ as radically new as the seemingly heretical aesthetics offered by "The Coming of Antichrist." As noted earlier, the three other English cycles typically present Christ as a human, vulnerable, and compassionate friend of man. Chester, however, has consistently defined Christ as the divine king—aloof, powerful, and even severe. Thus it is perfectly in keeping that Christ should appear in the last pageant in the role of the just judge, announcing calmly and firmly that "Righteouse doome may you not fleene, / for grace ys put awaye." What is surprising, however, is that in the middle of this judgment Christ should suddenly expose his naked body, bleeding for all who wish to behold, to prove the tenderness and depth of his love for humankind. Here, unexpectedly, is the "immediate" Christ of human pity and sorrow, his wounds hypersensitive to every hateful or indifferent act committed against his Person. Having chosen not to include an "Appeal" in its dramatization of the Passion, why does Chester include this dramatic "Appeal to Man" in its interpretation of the Last Judgment? The answer may in part lie in the playwright's awareness of how easily the cycle's conservative "nominalist" Christology could be misinterpreted at the very end. Philosophically, the cycle's unswerving insistence upon Christ's divine otherness could be seen as an expression of an extreme form of skeptical fideism, suggesting that God is *deus absconditus*, a hidden God untouched by human concerns. Psychologically, Christ's absolute self-sufficiency could possibly evoke in some believers a feeling of spiritual redundancy, indifference, or despair. So, to conclude the cycle with dramatic proof of Christ's tender concern for our every human gesture toward him is to resolve these potential problems, uniting unequivocally the divine and human spheres and embracing every viewer as an individually significant actor in the drama of Christian salvation. Because each of our actions is registered with such effect on Christ's Person, we can only feel it right that Christ finally put mercy aside on Judgment Day: were he on that day anything less than perfectly just, he would be less than Christ. Equally as gratifying, however, is the revelation that although both the saved and damned souls judge themselves according to their "negative" sins, Christ mercifully chooses to judge them by their "positive" acts of corporal mercy. Most gratifying of all, however, is our recognizing at the play's end that this is but a dramatic image of the Last Judgment and that we are living still in the historical Age of Mercy. What could therefore be more merciful than Christ's now asking us to discharge our debt to him by means immediately within our reach, and what could be more just than our now succoring those among us who are hungry, thirsty, naked, sick, and shelterless? Thus those two seemingly opposite divine virtues, mercy and justice, prove to be unified in the person of Christ.

While bringing to final resolution these various concerns—theological, moral, and aesthetic—the Chester playwright also had to fashion an appropriate conclusion to his two basic dramatic models: the cycle's vision of the education of Christian Everyman, and its vision of the design of salvation history. These two models are closely interrelated, for every spiritual advance made by history should ideally effect a similar advance in the growth of the human spirit. But the designs of these two have never been identical, primarily because history's greatest leaps forward have been the heroic accomplishments of Christ alone—with his followers proving very much to be his followers as they meander, backslide, and fitfully progress behind him. As part of that abstraction called Everyman, the Chester viewers have participated fully in this drama of Christian education, finding themselves often "ahead" and sometimes "behind" Everyman's spiritual progress. But rather like Everyman in the play of that name, the Chester viewers' sudden confrontation with God's direct judgment of them is a moment long-promised but nevertheless disturbing and potentially threatening. At this moment the Chester dramatist could have tried to convert his cycle into a happy religious comedy, but only by sacrificing the evolving "argument" of his two basic dramatic models. Or he could have converted his cycle into a religious tragedy, with his audience

249

learning suddenly that all but a very few of them are beyond the pale of hope. What the Chester playwright obviously had to achieve at his conclusion was some kind of balanced design in his evocations of hope and fear. The reason he had to do so is succinctly defined by John the Baptist at the beginning of the N-Town Passion play:

The pathe that lyth · to this blyssyd · enherytawns
Is hope and drede · copelyd be conjunccyon
Be-twyx these tweyn • may be no dysseuerawns
Ffor hope with-outyn drede • is maner of presumpcion
And drede · with-owtyn hope • is maner of dysperacion
So these tweyn must be knyt be on Acorde.[13]

The Chester playwright counterbalances his images of hope and his images of dread in a number of ways at the end of his cycle. The Eschatological Group opens this ending with a series of dreadful prophecies of an undiscriminating destruction of all things; but what is eventually dramatized is a perfectly tranquil apocalypse, an even-handed and personal weighing of every human soul. Similarly, the Antichrist promises to be the most dreadful monster of history; but in dramatic fact he proves little more than a comic, long-winded magician. Not that each image of dread in Chester is eventually undercut or purged. At the cycle's end Chester tips the scale in the other direction as the six damned souls are marched off to perdition, while only four are led to eternal bliss. The Last Judgment is clearly a most solemn matter to be feared by all. But the imbalance in the numbers of saved and damned souls may be offset by the viewers' discovery of how easy their own salvation should be: through penitence and their daily acts of corporal mercy, they may hope eventually to gain admission to heaven on the day of doom. Thus, as in the other cycles, Chester's dramatic world ends not with a bang or whimper but with what Rosemary Woolf has called an "unexpected ambivalence."[14] Neither a perfect comedy (as might have been hoped) nor a perfect tragedy (as might have been feared), history ends as history. That is, it ends in perfect equipoise: Mercy and justice are unified, Christ and the devil are in agreement, good and evil are cleanly divided. Paradise, at the end of time, has been regained by some; but most have not regained it because of those many intractable and careless human characteristics that the uneven

250

course of history has so fully dramatized. History concludes in an intermediate state of "unexpected ambivalence" for another good reason as well: the viewers are part of that history, and have yet to define for themselves the final design of their own lives. So even though Chester closes with the harmony of historical order, it has warned its viewers that they must yet progress through the dreadful and demanding chaos of Antichrist's reign before arriving at the justice of their own Day of Doom.

In analyzing Chester's design of salvation history, I have chosen to include the viewers' involvement as part of that design. Likewise, I find it unavoidable to include the viewers within the cycle's design of the education of the Christian Everyman. This education has in most ways been quite straightforward. As the spirit of Everyman advances from Creation to Doomsday, the viewers reexperience the major events of history, they relearn the fundamental tenets of Christian belief, and they are reminded of the primary importance of their own daily acts of corporal mercy. Because this education is conveyed to them through the medium of the dramatic image, they are also invited to learn how to interpret Christian images imaginatively, spiritually, and morally. Christ is clearly one of the cycle's major recurring images: he appears normally as *Christus apertus* (Christ revealed), but at the cycle's end he retrospectively reveals his historical omnipresence as *Christus mysticus*, in human "disguise." An image of equal importance is that of Everyman, or *Humanum Genus*: this image is not "revealed" until the Last Judgment (in the *Salvati* and *Damnati*) but its various stage expressions are to have been recognized throughout the cycle. As individual Christians free to determine the course of their own lives, the viewers have been free to interpret these stage images of Christ and of themselves in various ways. But as the dramatic images of "The Last Judgment" make perfectly clear, each choice they make has been a moral act of the will. For as men and women made in the image of God, the Chester viewers have had the responsibility to discover in the images of the Chester cycle their own moral essence and spiritual value. This self-discovery should have effected, then, at one and the same time, a reformation of both sets of images in the direction of God. Such a theory of the reformation of images may seem to be based upon an ideal aesthetic psychology, but there is nothing radically new

251

about it. In a study entitled "Iconography and Philosophy in the Crucifixion Window at Poitiers," Robert Grinnell has extrapolated a comparable medieval theory of image interpretation:

An image himself, [man's] function is to convert other images into moral symbols, completing in this manner the moral possibilities of existence. This process is accomplished through the agency of man's free will, so that just as the mind constructs things as images in cognition, and in a real sense contributes its own essence to that construction, so the will accedes to that identification in a similar process of construction, contributing a moral essence to the image of cognition as its culminating actualization. The capacity, on the one hand, of mind to construct images, and on the other the capacity of images to *be* constructed and to be endowed freely with moral value constitutes the very nature of man as an image of God, and endows him with a certain metaphysical value from which nothing can be detracted. The character of those choices or constructions will determine his moral value, and such is the miraculous nature of this ability that the consequences of these choices...will accomplish a conversion of man...from an image of God to a similitude of God.[15]

Much of Grinnell's thesis conforms to the theory of images implicit in Chester's closing plays. But to those psychological faculties Grinnell mentions should be added one more that is of primary significance in the world of the dramatic image: this is the faculty of memory. As a series of ephemeral images made dramatically real on only widely separated occasions, the Corpus Christi plays had naturally to be concerned with the viewers' lasting recollection of their action and meaning. Because that memory was bound to be highly selective and "inordinately" influenced by the last few images it perceived, the way each cycle draws to a close was an extremely important matter. Had the Chester cycle concluded at Pentecost, for example, it is quite possible that the Apostles' Creed would have been recalled as the cycle's dominating theme. Had it ended with the Antichrist, the cycle could have been remembered as powerful "high drama." And had it closed (as it does) with the weighing of souls, the morality-play ambience of the Last Judgment was bound to redefine the meaning of prior dramatic actions. All of these levels of interpretation are an important part of the Chester cycle and have contributed to an enriched and "retrospective" understanding of its significance. Having understood this, however, we can now understand how essential it was that Christ's last "Appeal to Man" be placed where it is. The "thematics" of the Creed, the "dramatics" of the Antichrist, and the "morality" of the Judgment are all unified in the dramatic image of Christ himself. As he recalls again the major events of the cycle, emphasizing in his review that exchange of pain and love which is his memory of the past, Christ raises the experience of the cycle to its highest emotional point. As symbol, sacrament, icon, and image, with his naked flesh exposed and the attributes of his Passion surrounding him, Christ becomes the cycle's most memorable image. In conclusion, it seems only appropriate that the final meaning of a play called Corpus Christi should be embodied in the flesh of the Savior.

While examining each of Chester's twenty-four pageants, we have discovered that Chester is a rich and complex cycle controlled on various levels by a number of distinctive designs. The shadow-to-image hermeneutics of the Old Testament pageants, the Nativity Group's metaphoric projections of sacramental ritual, the conservative nominalism of the Ministry, the benign strategies of the Passion, the credal design of the Resurrection Group, the artistic self-scrutiny of the final plays: these are but a few of Chester's unique designs. Because these designs have been so carefully coordinated and so unobtrusively integrated into the dramatic action, it is tempting to believe that one highly sophisticated playwright had to be responsible for the finished achievement of the entire Chester cycle. If this is true, we should honor this genius properly by electing to call him the Chester Master. Yet even as we appreciate Chester's many distinctive features, we must recall in how many ways and how often Chester's major configurations and concerns have paralleled those of the other English cycles. These parallels are most powerfully felt at the very end. Like York, Wakefield, and N-Town, the Chester cycle concludes its dramatization of salvation history with the achieved balance of the Last Judgment and with the powerful dramatic image of the bleeding body of Christ. Like its dramatic sisters, Chester reveals in its closure an overriding moral concern for its viewers—in whom, ideally, there has been effected a liberation from past sins and a determination to love God and all who have been made in his image. Like them, Chester has revealed itself a masterwork of Christian art directed unequivocally toward a single end: the salvation of humankind.

Notes

Introduction

1. Richard Axton, *European Drama of the Early Middle Ages* (Hutchinson, 1974).
2. Walter E. Meyers, *A Figure Given: Typology in the Wakefield Plays* (Duquesne University Press, 1969).
3. Richard J. Collier, *Poetry and Drama in the York Corpus Christi Play* (Archon, 1978).
4. Alan H. Nelson, *The Medieval English Stage* (University of Chicago Press, 1974).

One

1. Lynn White, Jr., "Natural Science and Naturalistic Art in the Middle Ages," *The American Historical Review* 52 (1947): 429–30.
2. For studies of the origins of the Feast, see W.J. O'Shea, *New Catholic Encyclopedia* (1967), s.v. "Corpus Christi," pp. 345–47; C. Lambot, "L'Office De La Fête-Dieu. Aperçus Nouveaux Sur Ses Origines," *Revue Bénédictine* 54 (1942): 61–123; L.M.J. Delaissé, "A La Recherche Des Origines De L'Office Du Corpus Christi Dans Les Manuscrits Liturgiques," *Scriptorium* 4 (1950): 220–39; James L. Monks, *Great Catholic Festivals* (Henry Schuman, 1951), pp. 77–79.

In 1317 the *Festum Eucharistiae* was declared a principal feast in Canterbury, and in 1318 an entry in *Historia Monasterii Sancti Petri Gloucestriae* notes: "Anno Domini Millesimo trecentesimo decimo octavo incoepit festivitas de Corpore Christi generaliter celebrari per totam ecclesiam anglicanam." See Hardin Craig, *English Religious Drama of the Middle Ages* (The Clarendon Press, 1955), pp. 127-28.

3. The definitive study of the history of the Roman Mass remains Josef A. Jungmann, *The Mass of the Roman Rite: Its Origins and Development*, trans. Francis A. Brunner, 2 vols. (Benziger Brothers, 1951-55); see especially 1: 103-41.

4. An ample review of this allegorical exegesis of the Mass—often known as the Amalarian tradition—is to be found in O.B. Hardison, Jr., *Christian Rite and Christian Drama in the Middle Ages: Essays in the Origin and Early History of Modern Drama* (Johns Hopkins Press, 1965), pp. 35-79.

5. Jungmann, 1: 108.

6. The one notable exception is Hardison (pp. 35-79), who views the Mass as sacred drama.

7. Becon's criticism is quoted by Adrian Fortescue in *The Mass: A Study of the Roman Liturgy*, 2d rev. ed. (Longmans, Green, 1917), p. 342.

8. See Jungmann, 1: 116.

9. For a definition of the familial love expressed by the primitive Mass, see Richard Peter McKeon, *Thought, Action, and Passion* (University of Chicago Press, 1954), p. 41.

10. Craig, p. 129.

11. The medieval and modern forms of the Corpus Christi procession are described by Monks, pp. 81-92. For an interesting contemporary account, see Alan H. Nelson, "A Pilgrimage to Toledo: Corpus Christi Day 1974," *Research Opportunities in Renaissance Drama* 17 (1974): 123-29.

12. In addition to the studies of the feast by Lambot, Delaissé, Monks, and O'Shea, see Jerome Taylor, "The Dramatic Structure of the Middle English Corpus Christi, or Cycle, Plays," in *Medieval English Drama: Essays Critical and Contextual*, ed. Jerome Taylor and Alan H. Nelson (University of Chicago Press, 1972), pp. 150-52; and Clifford Davidson, "Thomas Aquinas, the Feast of Corpus Christi, and the English Cycle Plays," *Michigan Academician* 7 (1974): 103-10. For the readings of the feast itself, see Saint Thomas Aquinas, *Opera Omnia*, vol. 15 (Musurgia, 1950), pp. 233-38.

13. Browe, *Die Verehrung der Eucharistie im Mittelalter* (M. Hueber, 1933), p. 98 ff.

14. Hardison, p. 79.

15. Kolve, *The Play Called Corpus Christi* (Stanford University Press, 1966), p. 49.

16. Although the belief that the English Corpus Christi plays evolved out of the Corpus Christi processions has been challenged by Merle Pierson in "The Relation of the Corpus Christi Procession to the Corpus Christi Play in England," *Transactions of the Wiscon-*

sin Academy of Sciences, Arts, and Letters 18 (1915): 110–65, and by Craig, pp. 134–38, that belief is generally accepted by most critics as a reasonable assumption still in need of historical proof. See, for instance, Nelson, *The Medieval English Stage*, pp. 11–14.

17. For a critical study of those dramatic structures which existed prior to the formation of the cycles, see Axton, *European Drama*.

18. See Edouard Dumoutet, *Le Désir de Voir L'Hostie* (Beauchesne, 1926). For a historical study of the theology of eucharistic adoration, see Darwell Stone, *A History of the Doctrine of the Holy Eucharist*, 2 vols. (Longmans, Green, 1909), esp. 1: 242–313.

19. In England well before the institution of the Feast of Corpus Christi, for instance, there were Palm Sunday processions where the Host enclosed in a reliquary was carried outside the church, and there were similar processions inside the church during Holy Week. See Monks, p. 82.

20. See Woolf, *The English Mystery Plays* (Routledge and Kegan Paul, 1972), pp. 54–76.

21. My definition of sacred actions has been influenced somewhat by the analysis of metaphoric actions in James Fernandez, "The Mission of Metaphor in Expressive Culture," *Current Anthropology* 15 (1974): 119–33.

22. For a full study of this late medieval empiricizing imagination, see J. Huizinga, *The Waning of the Middle Ages*, trans. F. Hopman (E. Arnold, 1927). One should note, however, that the expressions of this imagination were considerably less extreme in England than they were in the Netherlands and in France.

23. J.K. Campbell, *Honour, Family and Patronage* (The Clarendon Press, 1964), pp. 347–48.

24. One well-known example of these early paraliturgical rites is the Winchester *Visitatio Sepulchri*, contained in St. Ethelwold's *Regularis Concordia* for English Benedictine monasteries, ca. 965–75. This and many related texts are printed in Karl Young, *The Drama of the Medieval Church*, 2 vols. (The Clarendon Press, 1933), 1: 249 ff.; text and translation are found in David Bevington, *Medieval Drama* (Houghton, 1975), pp. 27–28. Axton (pp. 65–67) considers this *Visitatio* a play, but C. Clifford Flanigan, in his perceptive study of early liturgical drama, insists that such early "dramatic" activities remained ritual. See Flanigan, "The Roman Rite and the Origins of the Liturgical Drama," *University of Toronto Quarterly* 43 (1974): 263–84.

25. For a clear analysis of the crucial distinctions between symbolism and allegory, see M.D. Chenu, *Nature, Man, and Society in the Twelfth Century*, trans. Jerome Taylor and Lester K. Little (University of Chicago Press, 1968), pp. 99–145.

26. For remarks on the significance of sight in the late Middle

Ages, see Huizinga, p. 284, and Judson Boyce Allen, *The Friar as Critic: Literary Attitudes in the Later Middle Ages* (Vanderbilt University Press, 1971), p. 127. A very lucid study of the metaphysics of sight in the late medieval aesthetic is found in Theresa Coletti, "Spirituality and Devotional Images: The Staging of the Hegge Cycle" (Ph.D. diss., University of Rochester, 1975); the first chapter, "Images, Vision, and the Religious Imagination," is especially useful.

27. For a study of these miracles of the Host and their effect on late medieval drama, see Leah Sinanoglou, "The Christ Child as Sacrifice: A Medieval Tradition and the Corpus Christi Plays," *Speculum* 48 (1973): 491–509.

28. *Thomas Aquinas: Selected Writings*, ed. and trans. M.C. D'Arcy (J.M. Dent and Sons, 1939), p. 39.

29. *The Chester Mystery Cycle*, ed. R.M. Lumiansky and David Mills, EETS, S.S. 3 (1974), p. 377. This is the first and only instance where I will cite the page number of a quotation from a cycle. Because both pageant and speaker will always be identified, and because none of the pageants is very long, any quotation can be found easily and quickly enough so that its page number, I feel, need not be given. In citations from Middle English texts, thorn and yogh have been regularly replaced by their modern orthographic counterparts: *th*; and *y, gh, s,* or *z*.

30. See Allen, pp. 54–116.

31. For the progress of nominalism in later medieval thought, many works could be recommended. See especially Gordon Leff, *Paris and Oxford Universities in the Thirteenth and Fourteenth Centuries* (John Wiley and Sons, 1968); Meyrick H. Carré, *Realists and Nominalists* (Oxford University Press, 1946); Carré, *Phases of Thought in England* (The Clarendon Press, 1949); and Heiko A. Oberman, *The Harvest of Medieval Theology: Gabriel Biel and Late Medieval Nominalism* (Harvard University Press, 1963). For an examination of the relevance of nominalism specifically to the Chester cycle, see Chapter 5 of this study.

32. See G.R. Owst, *Preaching in Medieval England* (Cambridge University Press, 1926); and Owst, *Literature and Pulpit in Medieval England,* 2d rev. ed. (Basil Blackwell, 1966).

33. See, for example, the fifteenth-century collection of English Mass-books for the laity entitled "Langforde's Meditations in the Time of the Mass," in *Tracts on the Mass*, ed. J. Wickham Legg (Harrison and Sons, 1904).

34. Two exemplary studies which incorporate the widening audience as part of their examinations of late medieval art are Erwin Panofsky, *Early Netherlandish Painting* (Harper, 1971), and E.W. Tristram, *English Wall Painting of the Fourteenth Century* (Routledge and Kegan Paul, 1955).

35. Cf. Nelson, *The Medieval English Stage*, pp. 1-14.

36. For a discussion of anachronistic time in the Corpus Christi play, see Kolve, pp. 101-23.

37. The accepted "truth" of apocryphal legend is discussed by F.P. Pickering in *Literature and Art in the Middle Ages* (University of Miami Press, 1970), p. 224 ff.

38. See *Ludus Coventriae; or The Plaie Called Corpus Christi*, ed. K.S. Block, EETS, E.S. 120 (1922; reprint ed., 1960), pp. 348–49.

39. This position has been supported by Martin Stevens in "Illusion and Reality in the Medieval Drama," *College English* 32 (1971): 448–64. Stevens does not deny that the play at moments may have been illusionistic, but contends that the play normally calls attention to itself as a theatrical artifice.

40. Kolve, p. 30.

41. For one study of the role of affective piety in the late medieval graphic arts and in the Corpus Christi plays, see J.W. Robinson, "The Late Medieval Cult of Jesus and the Mystery Plays," *PMLA* 80 (1965): 508–14.

42. Anne Righter, *Shakespeare and the Idea of the Play* (Chatto and Windus, 1962), pp. 23, 20.

43. Mircea Eliade, *Cosmos and History*, trans. Willard R. Trask (Harper, 1959), pp. 73–92.

44. In partial support of this contention is Robert Edwards's remark that "if ritualistic elements are present in early medieval drama, they may be present because the dramatist hinges the acceptance of his drama to the recognition of these elements." See his "Techniques of Transcendence in Medieval Drama," *Comparative Drama* 8 (1974): 160.

45. See Clifford Davidson, "The Realism of the York Realist and the York Passion," *Speculum* 50 (1975): 270–83.

46. Adolph E. Jensen, *Myth and Cult among Primitive Peoples*, trans. Marianna Tax Choldin and Wolfgang Weissleder (University of Chicago Press, 1963), p. 41.

47. In this respect the Corpus Christi play falls into the generic category R.G. Collingwood defines as "magical art": "a representation where the emotion evoked is an emotion valued on account of its function in practical life, evoked in order that it may discharge that function, and fed by the generative or focusing magical activity into the practical life that needs it" (*The Principles of Art* [The Clarendon Press, 1938], p. 68).

48. Northrop Frye, *Anatomy of Criticism: Four Essays* (Princeton University Press, 1957), p. 282; see also J.W. Robinson, "Late Medieval Cult," p. 513.

49. A thousand days of pardon from Pope Clement and forty days of pardon from the bishop of Chester were granted to "euery person resortyng in pecible manner with gode devocion to here & se

the [Chester Corpus Christi plays] frome tyme to tyme asoft as they shalbe plaied within this Citie." This entry is to be found in Lawrence M. Clopper, Jr., ed., *Chester, Records of Early English Drama* (University of Toronto Press, 1979), p. 28.

50. Too often the deliberate profanation of the sacred in late medieval art has been seen simply as a sign of the dissolution of the medieval "world picture." See, however, Huizinga, pp. 264-322, and Mikhail Bakhtin, *Rabelais and His World*, trans. Helene Iswolsky (MIT Press, 1968). Of special significance is Bakhtin's analysis of the ways on the Continent the Feast of Corpus Christi incorporated into its own celebration profanations of the eucharistic Host (pp. 229-30).

51. See Flanigan.

52. David Scott Kastan discusses the completeness of historical time in the Corpus Christi plays in contrast to the partiality of time in Renaissance drama in "The Shape of Time: Form and Value in the Shakespearean History Play," *Comparative Drama* 7 (1974): 264.

53. See Kolve, pp. 101-4.

54. See Mary H. Marshall, "Aesthetic Values of the Liturgical Drama," in *Medieval English Drama*, ed. Taylor and Nelson, pp. 28-43.

55. For a lucid survey of medieval scriptural exegesis, see Beryl Smalley, *The Study of the Bible in the Middle Ages* (The Clarendon Press, 1941).

56. See Fortescue, pp. 200-205.

57. For a survey of the procession, see M. Lyle Spencer, *Corpus Christi Pageants in England* (Baker and Taylor, 1911), pp. 61-82. For a clear discussion of the histories of the ecclesiastic and civic processions at York, see Alexandra F. Johnston, "The Procession and Play of Corpus Christi in York after 1426," *Leeds Studies in English* 7 (1973-74): 55-62; and Douglas Cowling, "The Liturgical Celebration of Corpus Christi in Medieval York," *Records of Early English Drama Newsletter* 2 (1976): 5-9. The changing relationship of the procession to the play in Chester will be noted in Chapter 2 of this study.

58. For general studies of the Mass, see Young, 1: 15-43, and Hardison, pp. 35-79; for general studies of the Corpus Christi play, see Arnold Williams, *The Drama of Medieval England* (Michigan State University Press, 1961), pp. 55-141, and Kolve.

59. The most recent complete editions of these four cycles are *York Plays*, ed. Lucy Toulmin Smith (1885); *Ludus Coventriae, or the Plaie Called Corpus Christi*, ed. K.S. Block; *The Towneley Plays*, ed. George England and Alfred W. Pollard, EETS, E.S. 71 (1897); *The Chester Mystery Cycle*, ed. Lumiansky and Mills. Unless otherwise noted, I will be quoting from these editions of the four cycles in the remainder of my study.

60. Woolf, p. 306.

Two

1. At this point, I prefer that the terms "Gothic" and "Romanesque" as applied to dramatic style remain less than fully defined. For the use of these terms by others, see Glynne Wickham, "The Romanesque Style in Medieval Drama," in *Tenth-Century Studies*, ed. David Parsons (Phillimore Press, 1975), pp. 115–22, and Waldo F. McNeir, "The Corpus Christi Passion Plays as Dramatic Art," *Studies in Philology* 48 (1951): 601–28. For an examination and definition in this study of Chester's dramatic style, see Chapter 5, "Christ's Neo-Romanesque Ministry."

2. Stephen Spector, "The Genesis of the N-Town Cycle" (Ph.D. diss., Yale University, 1973).

3. For a complete description of each of these manuscripts, see Lumiansky and Mills, eds., *The Chester Mystery Cycle*, pp. ix–xxvii.

4. Clopper, *Chester*, pp. 240–47.

5. For a thorough study of the Rogers' Breviary and its various versions, see Lawrence M. Clopper, Jr., "The Rogers' Description of the Chester Plays," *Leeds Studies in English* 7 (1973–74): 63–94. The texts may also be found in Clopper, *Chester*, pp. 232–54, 320–26, 351–55, and 433–36.

6. The Early Banns are transcribed in Clopper, *Chester*, pp. 31–39.

7. The Newhall Proclamation is transcribed in Clopper, *Chester*, pp. 27–28.

8. For transcriptions and a discussion of all the Chester lists and banns, see "The Lists and Banns of the Plays," in *The Trial and Flagellation with Other Studies in the Chester Cycle*, ed. W.W. Greg (Oxford University Press, 1936), pp. 121–71. The Harley 2104 List is transcribed in Clopper, *Chester*, pp. 22–23.

9. The Harley 2150 List of Companies is transcribed in Clopper, *Chester*, pp. 31–33.

10. Oscar L. Brownstein, "Revision in the 'Deluge' of the Chester Cycle," *Speech Monographs* 36 (1969): 55–65.

11. Bernice F. Coffee, "The Chester Play of *Balaam* and *Balak*," *Wisconsin Studies in Literature* 4 (1967): 103–18.

12. Hans-Jürgen Diller, "The Composition of the Chester *Adoration of the Shepherds*," *Anglia* 89 (1971): 178–98.

13. The other studies of this sort have tended to be concerned with Pagina V. See David Mills, "Two Versions of Chester Play V: 'Balaam and Balak'," in *Chaucer and Middle English Studies in Honour of Rossell Hope Robbins*, ed. Beryl Rowland (Allen and Unwin, 1974), pp. 366–71; and Clopper, "The Structure of the

Chester Cycle: Text, Theme and Theatre" (Ph.D. diss., Ohio State University, 1969), pp. 14–63, 243–81. See also D.S. Bland, "The Chester Nativity: One Play or Two?" *Notes and Queries* 10 (1963): 134–35.

14. Several years ago, using two of Chester's pageants (VIII and IX) as my base-texts, I attempted such a study with the computer. My hope was that—as with similar studies of the epistles of Paul, the *Federalist Papers*, and *The O'Ruddy*—a sensitive computer program would help discover the existence of dual authorship. But despite the outpourings of impressive-looking lists of statistics and graphs seemingly laden with hidden significance, the pilot project proved a fascinating failure. For an intelligent and informative history and analysis of the use of statistics and the computer in such areas, I recommend Robert Wachal's Ph.D. dissertation, "Linguistic Evidence, Statistical Inference, and Disputed Authorship" (University of Wisconsin, 1966).

15. Lawrence M. Clopper, Jr., "The History and Development of the Chester Cycle," *Modern Philology* 75 (1978): 219–46. Professor Clopper's work in the field of Chester's dramatic records has been exemplary. Were it not for his research and documentation, I am certain I would not have endeavored to write this chapter. My indebtedness, especially to his "History and Development" monograph, is beyond measure.

16. F.M. Salter, "The Banns of the Chester Plays," *Review of English Studies* 15 (1939): 432–57; 16 (1940): 1–17, 137–48.

17. Salter, *Mediaeval Drama in Chester* (University of Toronto Press, 1955), p. 122, n. 36.

18. E.K. Chambers, *The Mediaeval Stage*, 2 vols. (The Clarendon Press, 1903), 2: 352.

19. E.K. Chambers, *English Literature at the Close of the Middle Ages* (The Clarendon Press, 1945), p. 25.

20. Salter, *Mediaeval Drama*, pp. 36–42.

21. Craig, pp. 169–70.

22. Clopper, "The Rogers' Description," p. 73.

23. Glynne Wickham, *Early English Stages, 1300 to 1660*, 3 vols. (Routledge and Kegan Paul, 1959–81), 1: 145.

24. The originator of this tradition in the criticism of the Chester cycle may have been Rupert Morris, in *Chester in the Plantagenet and Tudor Reigns* (1893), p. 303. Morris writes: the plays "had an ecclesiastical origin, and were played at first, no doubt, in Latin, within the Abbey Church by the monks and clerks attached to the Minster, as a means of popular instruction in Sacred History and Religious doctrine." Morris founds his thesis on his apparently inadvertent misreading of the Newhall Proclamation.

25. The turning point in this debate appears to have been Kolve's *The Play Called Corpus Christi*; see especially pp. 33–42.

26. This theory was apparently first espoused by Heinrich Gottfried Ungemach who, in *Die Quellen der fünf ersten Chester Plays* (A. Deichert, 1890), attempted to prove, by the use of parallel passages, Chester's indebtedness to French drama. The theory has yet to expire, for even quite recently Woolf has written in *The English Mystery Plays* that "it seems clear that the Old Testament sequence (and perhaps more) was rewritten towards the end of the fifteenth century by an author who modelled his plays upon those in the *Mystère du viel testament*" (p. 306). For a review of many of the older arguments, see Craig, pp. 170-78, where he confidently concludes, "we may be sure that the Chester plays were translated and adapted from the French."

27. The most balanced study of this question is Albert C. Baugh's "The Chester Plays and French Influence," in *Schelling Anniversary Papers* (Century, 1923), pp. 35-63. Baugh concludes, after listing those passages in Chester most likely influenced, that it is "probable" that "somewhere in the development of the Chester cycle the influence of the French dramatic tradition was felt." But in fact several episodes Baugh selects from Chester as being close to French models are episodes—as we shall see in this chapter—taken from the long English poem *A Stanzaic Life of Christ*.

28. In his praiseworthy early work, "Studies in the English Mystery Plays" (Ph.D. diss., Yale University, 1892), Charles Davidson suggests that the Chester plays were indeed the work of a translator; however, he believes his dramatic models were not French, but English and "in part Anglo-Norman, as the cycle of the Parish Clerks of London probably was" (p. 131). Woolf (*The English Mystery Plays* [p. 338]) and Nelson (*The Medieval English Stage* [p. 172]) both find plausible the early London plays' influence on the northern cycles.

29. Clopper, *Chester*, pp. 353-54.

30. For a discussion of the possible relationships between the Chester plays and the Midsummer Show, see Nelson, *The Medieval English Stage*, pp. 165-68, and Axton, *European Drama*, pp. 182-87.

31. Chambers, *English Literature at the Close of the Middle Ages*, p. 26. In light of other speculations which envisage the early Chester play as more of a Passion play, Chambers's further observations are worth noting: "The appearances and speeches of the *Expositor* indicate that the primitive play contained at least a Noah, an Abraham, a *Prophetae*, with Moses, Balaam and Balak, and Balaam's Ass, a Nativity, which was given on a second day and brought in the *Magi* as well as Octavian and Sibylla, and a Prophets of Doomsday. Probably it had also both a Doomsday itself and an Antichrist. The *Expositor* does not appear in the extant texts of these, but he foretells them. There is nothing to suggest any treatment in the primitive play of the missionary life of Christ or of the Passion and

its sequels up to Pentecost.... The whole emphasis of the primitive play seems to have been on prophecies of the coming of Christ and of the Last Judgement."

32. Salter, *Mediaeval Drama*, p. 45.

33. Axton, p. 184.

34. For recent studies of the Franciscan aesthetics, see Judson Boyce Allen, *The Friar as Critic*; David L. Jeffrey, *The Early English Lyric and Franciscan Spirituality* (University of Nebraska Press, 1975); and John V. Fleming, *An Introduction to the Franciscan Literature of the Middle Ages* (Franciscan Herald Press, 1977). For the "Franciscan" qualities of Corpus Christi, see Allen, p. 127; for the possible influence of the friars, or of their aesthetic, on early vernacular drama, see David L. Jeffrey, "Franciscan Spirituality and the Rise of Early English Drama," *Mosaic* 8 (1975): 17–46.

35. Clopper, *Chester*, pp. 6–7.

36. These guild entries are all to be found in Clopper, *Chester*, pp. 1–23. See in addition Clopper, "History and Development," p. 243.

37. Clopper, "History and Development," p. 222.

38. Clopper, *Chester*, pp. 26–27.

39. Salter, "Banns," 16: 4.

40. Clopper, "History and Development," pp. 222–23.

41. Salter, "Banns," 16: 5, 15: 451; Clopper, "History and Development," pp. 223, 228–29.

42. Salter assumed "it may be postulated that, lacking evidence to the contrary, wherever eight lines or more, rather than the usual four, are accorded in the Early Banns to the description of a play, a new play has been inserted in the cycle or an old one divided" ("Banns," 15: 451). Clopper, however, sensibly adds that "revised" descriptions in the Early Banns could indicate not only a pageant's having been inserted or divided, but its having been revised as well ("History and Development," p. 227, n. 26).

43. "History and Development," p. 225.

44. Greg, *Trial and Flagellation*, p. 170.

45. Clopper, *Chester*, pp. 23–24.

46. Ibid., p. 25, and "History and Development," p. 228.

47. Nelson, *The Medieval English Stage*, p. 156.

48. For a fuller discussion of the empirical evidence of this shift, see Clopper, "History and Development," pp. 221–31.

49. Strictly speaking, the Chester cycle is not written in tail rhyme ($a^4 a^4 b^3 c^4 c^4 b^3$). But Chester's dominant scheme ($a^4 a^4 a^4 b^3 c^4 c^4 c^4 b^3$) has been called tail ryme (rime couée) for over fifty years; to change terminology now would only create confusion.

50. Salter, "Banns," 15: 452–53; 16: 15 and passim.

51. For a review of these critical assumptions, see Alexandra F. Johnston's Ph.D. dissertation, "The Christ Figure in the Ministry

Plays of the Four English Cycles" (University of Toronto, 1964), pp. 242-53.

52. Salter, "Banns," 15: 445, n. 2.

53. *A Stanzaic Life of Christ*, ed. Frances Foster, EETS, O.S. 166 (1926), p. xiv.

54. Robert H. Wilson, "*The Stanzaic Life of Christ* and the Chester Plays," *North Carolina Studies in Philology* 28 (1931): 413-32; however, Wilson believes that this dramatist was constructing the Chester cycle in its original form—by adding *Stanzaic Life* episodes to a preexisting play which was "very likely in French." The only other scholar even to have guessed the time of the *Stanzaic Life*'s influence is Craig, who suggests in *English Religious Drama* (p. 198) that the revisions "came into being at some time before 1467."

55. For a complete documentation of these dates, see Clopper, *Chester*, pp. 1-23.

56. Hans Utesch, *Die Quellen der Chester-Plays* (Kieler Tagespost, 1909), pp. 57-61.

57. Cf. *A Stanzaic Life of Christ* (ll. 7801-8108) and Jacobus de Voragine, *The Golden Legend of Jacobus de Voragine*, trans. Granger Ryan and Helmut Ripperger (Longmans, Green, 1941), pp. 221-23.

58. Cf. Foster, *A Stanzaic Life of Christ*, pp. xli-xlii, and Wilson, p. 414.

59. That the Chester "Christ among the Doctors" is a complete rewriting of the York play, rather than a conflation of its influence and a preexisting Chester play on the same subject, is an implicit assumption in Greg's study "'Christ and the Doctors' and the York Play" in *The Trial and Flagellation*, pp. 101-20.

60. For the best of the Chester time-studies, and a review of others, see Ruth Brant Davis, "The Scheduling of the Chester Cycle Plays," *Theatre Notebook* 27 (1972): 49-67. See, in addition, Clopper, "The Staging of the Medieval Plays of Chester: A Response," *Theatre Notebook* 28 (1974): 65-70.

61. For proof of Brome's influence on Chester (rather than vice versa) and an account of their aesthetic differences as well, see J. Burke Severs, "The Relationship between the Brome and Chester Plays of *Abraham and Isaac*," *Modern Philology* 42 (1945): 137-51. Woolf's estimation that "the Chester author [may have] pared down a version of the Brome play to fit his own preference for a severer style" (*The English Mystery Plays*, p. 151) is, I believe, precisely correct.

62. Paul Pival has been responsible for defining these pageants (as well as Paginae XI, XII, and XIII) as "analogically" rather than "causally" unified, in "Staging as Projection of Imitated Action in the Chester Cycle" (Ph.D. diss., University of Wisconsin, 1973). It is in fact worth wondering whether all five pageants Pival defines

according to this structure (I would include Pagina II, as well) were added or amplified for the Whitsun shift.

63. If Paginae IV and V were not the work of the same redactor, then the thesis I propose in Chapter 3 is obviously jeopardized. It is all well and good to say one must accept the final draft of a cycle as the finished and unified work; but clearly in cases where quite subtle principles are said to be underlying the entire cycle, at some point it is necessary that a single intelligence have been responsible for such designs, rather than the chance eventualities of piecemeal accretion.

64. Salter, "Banns," 16: 1.

65. W.W. Greg, *Bibliographical and Textual Problems of the English Miracle Cycles* (Alexander Moring, 1914), p. 113.

66. Diller establishes a much more sensitive set of criteria for distinguishing one kind of verse-form from another. See in addition Spector's "Genesis of the N-Town Cycle," which employs several criteria, including stanza-forms, in an impressive attempt to reconstruct the composition of the N-Town plays.

67. In his "Banns" article (15: 445) Salter writes: "Anyone who reads these [rhyme-royal] passages will undoubtedly agree that they are all the work of one man late in the sixteenth century."

68. For convincing proof of the integrity of these two episodes as parts of their respective pageants, as well as for an illuminating analysis of the signification patterns of the entire Chester cycle, see John McGavin's Ph.D. dissertation, "Signs and Related Didactic Techniques in the Chester Cycle of Mystery Plays" (University of Edinburgh, 1981).

69. The Cain and Abel episode of Pagina II is not mentioned in the Early Banns; "Noah" existed in an earlier version (see Brownstein's article, and the conclusion of this chapter); the "Woman Taken in Adultery" is not mentioned in the Early Banns; the blind man, Chelidonius, is not mentioned in either Early or Late Banns, or in the List of Companies; Pagina XIV, the Shoemakers' play, was changed somewhat later in the sixteenth century, so it is difficult even to guess what it was like before the Whitsun shift.

70. Woolf, *The English Mystery Plays*, p. 56.

71. Kolve, pp. 33–56.

72. Clopper, *Chester*, p. 239. An analysis of the feasibility of the Breviary's account of the processional production used at Chester is found in Davis.

73. The cycle in fact may have been given even less frequently, for proof of performance has survived, from the cycle's later years, only for the years 1532, 1546, 1561, 1567, 1568, 1572, and 1575, and possibly 1550 and 1554. See Clopper, "*The Chester Plays*: Frequency of Performance," *Theatre Survey* 14, no. 2 (1973): 46–58.

74. Clopper, *Chester*, p. 97.

75. Ibid.

76. Ibid., p. 104.

77. Ibid., p. 110.

78. This is Clopper's conjecture, because the Midsummer Fair would have been in progress at the abbey gates: see "History and Development," p. 235, n. 48.

79. Cf. Clopper, however, who in "History and Development" asserts that "The content, the shape, and the techniques of production which we associate with the plays at Chester, therefore, are early sixteenth century rather than medieval in date" (p. 231). The problem, of course, is determining when the Middle Ages "stopped" and when it was that the medieval religio-aesthetic was replaced by its Renaissance counterpart.

80. Harold Gardiner, *Mysteries' End: An Investigation of the Last Days of the Medieval Religious Stage* (Yale University Press, 1946), pp. 47–48.

81. For a full account of the Shoemakers' pageant as well as all the relevant primary evidence, see Clopper, "History and Development," pp. 232–33.

82. Salter, however, argues that the rhyme-royal revisions of the Late Banns (which were carried out, he believes, for the 1575 performance) do indicate that changes were made in the cycle itself; see "Banns," 15: 444–49. Clopper believes that these stanzas were probably revised, as well, and that they may, at least in some cases, indicate play revisions; see "History and Development," pp. 236–38.

83. The Harley List of Companies is the only document to mention Moses and the woman of Canaan; it also calls the Shermen's pageant "profettys Afore the day of dome," rather than "Prophets of Antichrist"; the Late Banns mention a number of characters not mentioned by the Early Banns: Cain and Abel, Melchisedec, the midwives, the doctors (Christ in the temple), and Enoch and Eli. See Clopper, *Chester*, pp. 31–32, 240–49.

84. Clopper, *Chester*, p. 241.

85. Ibid., p. 240.

86. Ibid.

87. Ibid., p. 245.

88. This is not meant to imply that these manuscripts and their relationships have not been meticulously and intelligently analyzed. The recent EETS edition of the Chester cycle, edited by Robert Lumiansky and David Mills, is a careful and extraordinarily helpful piece of scholarship; one looks forward eagerly to the publication of their second volume. See also the Bibliography given in that edition (pp. xli–xliii) for past editions and analyses of the play manuscripts and of parts of them. In my own, occasional, and amateur editing, I have heeded Salter's advice (*Trial and Flagellation*, p. 45): "For the

linguistic and mechanical basis of his text, an editor will do well, as Greg advises, to follow D [Hm], not only because D is by a year the oldest manuscript, but also because the scribe of D shows little tendency to emend on his own. The antiquarian knowledge of James Miller, however, the scribe of H, will often yield important clues that are worth following up."

89. See R.M. Lumiansky and David Mills, "The Five Cyclic Manuscripts of the Chester Cycle of Mystery Plays: A Statistical Survey of Variant Readings," *Leeds Studies in English* 7 (1973–74): 95–107.

90. Phillip C. McCaffrey, "Historical Structure in the Chester Old Testament Pageants: The Literary and Religious Components of a Medieval Aesthetic" (Ph.D. diss., University of Pennsylvania, 1972), p. 212. Woolf has also warned against what she calls "archaeological diggings" into the cycles, in *The English Mystery Plays*, pp. 305–6.

91. The differences between the dramatic offerings of the Group MSS and the H MS are discussed, briefly, by Lumiansky and Mills in *The Chester Mystery Cycle*, pp. xxviii–xxix.

92. Coffee, pp. 103–18. David Mills's study of the Cappers' play (see n. 13 above) is perceptive, but apparently was unable to take into account similar studies done by Clopper, Pival, and McCaffrey.

93. Clopper, *Chester*, p. 105.

94. Brownstein, passim.

95. *European Drama*, p. 186.

96. Salter, "Banns," 16: 11–13.

97. R.M. Lumiansky, "Comedy and Theme in the Chester *Harrowing of Hell*," *Tulane Studies in English* 10 (1960): 5–12.

98. *The Medieval English Stage*, p. 167.

99. The best account of the decline of medieval, and especially English, drama remains Gardiner's *Mysteries' End*. It should be noted, however, that even well before the shift in attitudes in the late sixteenth century, there were occasions when the plays were laughed at in unintended ways. The York "Fergus" play, for example, dramatized the doubting Jew's loss of his hands as he touched the Virgin's bier; in 1431 the Masons complained that this episode tended to cause laughter rather than devotional awe. See Kolve, pp. 130–31.

100. Despite its intent, this chapter has hardly managed to define, in any objective way, what a "unified" cycle is, nor has it proved that the Chester cycle is itself unified. I have relied upon a common-sense understanding of certain basic principles of order in discussing, mainly from the "outside," Chester's structural development; but to prove its dramatic, historiological, and thematic unity is a task which can be accomplished only through close, "internal," analysis of every pageant in the entire cycle. In his book *The Medieval Theatre*

(St. Martin's, 1974), Glynne Wickham confidently asserts that "The script of an English Corpus Christi Cycle was dramatically structured on a doctrinal basis with as clearly defined a beginning, middle and end as any Greek tragedy" (p. 74). This grand claim promises considerable edification in all the "architectural" principles upon which the cycles were built, but what follows is merely a weak piece of ancillary support: "the epic dimensions and episodic character of the narrative were buttressed against disintegration and collapse by constant typological cross-referencing."

Three

1. For a helpful review of some of these iconographic traditions, see Clifford Davidson and Nona Mason, "Staging the York *Creation, and Fall of Lucifer*," *Theatre Survey* 17 (1976): 162-78.

2. *The Holkham Bible Picture Book*, ed. W.O. Hassall (Dropmore Press, 1954), fol. 2. See in addition G. McN. Rushforth, *Medieval Christian Imagery* (The Clarendon Press, 1936), pp. 149-52; M.D. Anderson, *Drama and Imagery in English Medieval Churches* (Cambridge University Press, 1963), pp. 141-42.

3. See Rhoda-Gale Pollack, "Angelic Imagery in the English Mystery Cycles," *Theatre Notebook* 29 (1975): 124-39.

4. The iconography of the circular movement of the angels is discussed by Oscar G. Farmer in *Fairford Church and Its Stained Glass Windows*, 8th ed. (Harding and Curtis, 1965), pp. 27-29.

5. Although God's intention to "see this blesse in every tower" suggests that the set design of Pagina I represented the traditional vision of heaven as a towered castle, S.F. Crocker fails to include such a construction under "Buildings of Various Sorts" in "The Production of the Chester Plays," *West Virginia University Studies* 1 (1936): 77-8.

6. For a brief discussion of the hymns in Pagina I, see Nan Cooke Carpenter, "Music in the Chester Plays," *Papers on English Language and Literature* 1 (1965): 196-97. See in addition John Stevens, "Music in Mediaeval Drama," *Proceedings of the Royal Musical Association* 84 (1958): 81-95, and JoAnna Dutka, "Music and the English Mystery Plays," *Comparative Drama* 7 (1973): 135-49.

7. For a brief discussion of gilded masks in medieval drama, see Anderson, *Drama and Imagery*, pp. 164-65.

8. For a representative analysis of the symbolism of light and darkness, see Hugh of Saint-Victor, *Hugh of Saint Victor on the Sacraments of the Christian Faith*, trans. Roy J. Deferrari (The Mediaeval Academy of America, 1951), pp. 14-16.

9. *The Later Genesis*, ed. B.J. Timmer, 2d rev. ed. (Scrivner Press, 1954): lines 409-41.

10. An analysis of the fallen angels' pride and envy is offered by Saint Thomas Aquinas, *Basic Writings of Saint Thomas Aquinas*, 2 vols., trans. Anton C. Pegis (Random House, 1945), 1: 587–88.

11. Lightbourne's name apparently derives from "lighber," or "lightber" (light-bearer), a translation of Lucifer, as in the Middle English *Genesis and Exodus:*

> Wisdom the made ilc thing of noght,
> Quuat-so-euere on heuone or her is wrogt,
> Ligber he sridde a dere srud,
> An he wurthe in him-seluen prud,
> An wid that pride him wex a nyth,
> That iwel weldeth al his sith.

The Middle English Genesis and Exodus, ed. Olaf Arngart (C.W.K. Gleerup, 1968), p. 61.

12. Woolf, *The English Mystery Plays*, p. 107.

13. Anselm of Canterbury, *Truth, Freedom, and Evil*, ed. and trans. Jasper Hopkins and Herbert Richardson (Harper, 1967), p. 124.

14. As a specific form of drama, Pagina I is closely related both to the Doomsday pageants in the cycles and to the English morality plays. In the clarity of its moral definitions, Pagina I is like the Last Judgment plays, where the *salvati* and the *damnati* are divided and judged for eternity. These Last Judgment pageants, in their turn, as David J. Leigh has noted, are related to the moralities: both offer a "symbolic representation by means of allegory of nonhistorical events directly related to the moral lives of their audience." See Leigh, "The Doomsday Mystery Play: An Eschatological Morality," in *Medieval English Drama*, ed. Taylor and Nelson, p. 272. Of all the opening pageants in the cycles, only Chester's has made of central concern "fre arbitracion"—a theme Merle Fifield finds preeminent in all the English moralities. See Merle Fifield, *The Rhetoric of Free Will: The Five-Action Structure of the English Morality Play* (University of Leeds Press, 1974).

15. Clopper, *Chester*, p. 33.

16. Woolf has argued (but hardly proven) the influence of the Apostles' Creed upon the structure of the cycles, in *The English Mystery Plays*, pp. 59–61.

17. For a discussion of "postfiguration" in early Renaissance drama, see Murray Roston, *Biblical Drama in England* (Faber, 1968), pp. 69–78.

18. This paraphrase is adapted from Henri de Lubac, *The Sources of Revelation*, trans. Luke O'Neill (Herder and Herder, 1968), p. 99.

19. The best study of medieval exegetical attempts to resolve this problem is de Lubac's *The Sources of Revelation*.

20. *The Holkham Bible Picture Book*, fol. 3v.

21. See de Lubac, *The Sources of Revelation*, pp. 38–39.

22. John Dennis Hurrell, "The Figural Approach to Medieval Drama," *College English* 26 (1965): 598-604; Kolve, *The Play Called Corpus Christi*, pp. 57-100; Meyers, *A Figure Given*; Gardner, *The Construction of the Wakefield Cycle.* For studies which reveal some limitations of typology in the interpretation of medieval drama, see Arnold Williams, "Typology and the Cycle Plays: Some Criteria," *Speculum* 43 (1968): 677-84; D.W. Robertson, Jr., "The Question of 'Typology' and the Wakefield *Mactacio Abel*," *American Benedictine Review* 25 (1974): 157-73; and William F. Munson, "Typology and the Towneley Isaac," *Research Opportunities in Renaissance Drama* 11 (1968): 129-39.

23. Meyers, p. 8.

24. Rosemary Woolf, "The Effect of Typology on the English Mediaeval Plays of Abraham and Isaac," *Speculum* 32 (1957): 825.

25. Chester's double allegiance can be demonstrated further by contrasting it with the noncyclical play which influenced it, the Brome "Abraham and Isaac." (For proof of Brome's influence on Chester, rather than vice versa, see Severs, "The Relationship between the Brome and Chester Plays of *Abraham and Isaac*.") Chester retains in a distilled form the naturalism of Brome's characterization; it includes only the most necessary anachronistic reminders (the two cries to Mary and the one to Christ); and it makes consistent Abraham's figural correspondences with God. Abraham in Brome, by contrast, exclaims his heart "brekith on twain" as often as it breaks "on thre."

The dramatic counterpoint of figure and fulfillment is less evenly balanced in the Abraham plays of the other English cycles. Isaac in Wakefield is never made aware that it was God and not his father who had willed his death, so that at the close of the pageant Isaac is still fearful, lest his father again, inscrutably, raise his sword in anger. N-Town veers far in the other direction: Isaac is so righteous and obedient, he pleads so incessantly for his own death, and his father's fumblings are so protracted that the pageant's melodrama may possibly have tested the limits even of a fifteenth-century audience's love of the pathetic. The York version sacrifices the whimsical innocence of a youthful Isaac for literal typological symmetry: Isaac is thirty years old. But this exacting parallel, a rather doubtful advantage in any case, breaks down badly at the pageant's end as Abraham rejoicingly leads his son from the sacrificial to the marriage altar: Isaac is to marry Rebecca, his father explains, in order to multiply the seed that God has just blessed.

26. One possible answer to this question has been tendered by Phillip McCaffrey in "The Didactic Structure of the Chester 'Sacrifice of Isaac'," *Comitatus* 2 (1971): 16-26, where he argues that all three episodes are interrelated both "causally" and "symbolically."

However, Paul Pival, Jr., defines Pagina IV as an "analogically-unified" play rather than a "causally-unified" one in "Staging as Projection of Imitated Action in the Chester Cycle": "Each pageant in the Chester Cycle...may be classified as 'causally-unified' or 'analogically-unified.' Causally-unified pageants utilize plots whose episodes are causally linked; analogically-unified pageants link their episodes through *exempla* or figures" (p. 42).

27. *The Catholic Encyclopedia* (Robert Appleton, 1907–12), s.v. "Exegesis."

28. Chambers, *English Literature at the Close of the Middle Ages*, p. 27.

29. For the various traditional interpretations of the Cain story in the Middle Ages, see Oliver F. Emerson, "Legends of Cain," *PMLA* 21 (1906): 831–929. Although it is safe to assume that the Chester audience automatically saw Cain's offering as an analogue to Christian tithing, it is notable that, of all the pageants dramatizing the offerings of Cain and Abel, only Chester's fails to call these oblations tithes.

30. For the reasons that I prefer the H MS version of Pagina V to that of the Group MSS, see pp. 66–67.

31. See P.E. Dustoor, "The Origin of the Play of 'Moses and the Tables of the Law'," *Modern Language Review* 19 (1924): 462, which argues that the giving of the law is an episode in the cycles "directly traceable to the liturgical and homiletic material of the Lenten season."

32. For a careful study of the *processus prophetarum* and the principles according to which each of the English cycles has integrated the prophets into its dramatic frame, see Robert A. Brawer, "The Form and Function of the Prophetic Procession in the Middle English Cycle Play," *Annuale Medievale* 13 (1972): 88–124.

33. For representative studies stressing the "prophetic principle" of the cycle plays, see E. Catherine Dunn, "Lyrical Form and the Prophetic Principle in the Towneley Plays," *Mediaeval Studies* 23 (1961): 80–90, and Paul Strohm, "The Dramatic and Rhetorical Technique of the Chester Mystery Plays" (Ph.D. diss., University of California, Berkeley, 1966), pp. 15–52.

34. Kolve, pp. 57–100.

35. Woolf, *The English Mystery Plays*, p. 64.

36. Kolve (p. 120) includes this tripartite division of history in his chart illustrating the variety of ways medievals divided up the history of Christian salvation. The "three laws" concept had by the fifteenth century become a commonplace idea, one often mentioned by writers and preachers in passing but, to my knowledge, never explored as fully as it was by Hugh of Saint-Victor.

37. Hugh of Saint-Victor, *Sacraments of the Christian Faith*, pp. 182–204.

38. Joseph Allen Bryant, Jr. "Chester's Sermon for Catechumens," *JEGP* 53 (1954): 399–402.

39. Woolf, *The English Mystery Plays*, pp. 156–58.

40. Erich Auerbach, *Mimesis: The Representation of Reality in Western Literature*, trans. Willard R. Trask (Princeton University Press, 1953), pp. 143–73.

41. Peter Comestor, "Historia Scholastica" in *Patrologia Latinae*, vol. 198, ed. J.P. Migne, cols. 1053–1721.

42. Medieval linguistic turnings on the Hebrew semipun on "ish" (man) and "ishshah" (woman) took various forms. See, for example, Comestor, col. 1071. Part of the traditional EVA/VAE/AVE trope is found in *The Middle English Genesis and Exodus* (p. 60):

> Adam abraid, and sag that wif;
> Name he gaf hire dat is ful rif:
> Issa was hire firste name,
> Thor-of thurte hire thinken no same;
> Mayden, for sche was mad of man,
> Hire first name thor bi-gan.
> Sithen ghe brocte us to woa,
> Adam gaf hire name eua.

For other plays on Eve's name, see Arnold Williams, *The Common Expositor* (University of North Carolina Press, 1948), pp. 87–88. Early English literary interpretations of the Fall story have been fully reviewed by John Evans in *Paradise Lost and the Genesis Tradition* (The Clarendon Press, 1968), pp. 143–216. Also see J.B. Trapp, "The Iconography of the Fall of Man," in *Approaches to Paradise Lost*, ed. C.A. Patrides (Edward Arnold, 1968), pp. 223–65.

43. The Norwich Grocers' Play B is edited by Norman Davis in *Non-Cycle Plays and Fragments*, EETS, S.S.1 (1970), pp. 11–18.

44. Saint Augustine, *The City of God*, trans. Marcus Dods (Modern Library, 1950), p. 380.

45. Gower's analysis of the effects of division is presented in the Prologue to *Confessio Amantis*. See *The Complete Works of John Gower*, 4 vols., ed. G.C. Macaulay (The Clarendon Press, 1899–1902), 2: 31–32:

> Division, the gospell seith,
> On hous upon another leith,
> Til that the Regne al overthrowe:
> And thus may every man wel knowe,
> Division aboven alle
> Is thing which makth the world to falle,
> And evere hath do sith it began....
> And who so drawth into memoire
> What hath befalle of old and newe,
> He may that werre sore rewe,

Which ferst began in Paradis:
For ther was proeved what it is,
And what desese there it wroghte;
For thilke werre tho forth broghte
The vice of alle dedly Sinne,
Thurgh which division cam inne
Among the men in erthe hiere,
And was the cause and the matiere
Why god the grete flodes sende,
Of al the world and made an ende
Bot Noë with his felaschipe,
Which only weren saulf be Schipe.

46. Comestor's "Historia Scholastica" is in fact more explicit than Chester:

Et non invento simili sibi, *immisit*
Deus soporem in Adam, non somnum,
sed exstasim in qua creditur supernae
interfuisse curiae. Unde et evi-
gilans propthetavit de conjunctione
Christi et Ecclesiae, et de diluvio
futuro, et de judicio per ignem
ibidem cognovit, et liberis suis
postea idicavit. [col. 1070]

47. John E. Bernbrock, in "Notes on the Towneley Cycle *Slaying of Abel*," *JEGP* 62 (1963): 317–22, convincingly argues that the Wakefield interpretation of Cain and his crime was an ingenious dramatic rendering of all the qualities of character and action listed in Saint Ambrose's *De Cain et Abel*. The "mythic density" of the Chester pageant is in a way supported by negative evidence: the fact that no exegetical tract has been discovered as a major source for its design. After reviewing numerous medieval interpretations of the Cain story, Bennett A. Brockman, in "Cain and Abel in the Chester *Creation*: Narrative Tradition and Dramatic Potential," *Medievalia et Humanistica*, n.s. 5 (1974): 169–82, is forced to conclude: "If anything about this play is clear, it is that Cain is of compelling interest as a man caught up in a predicament which he has devised but scarcely understands, and which destroys him utterly. His suffering and the suffering that he causes—those human realities which cannot be negated by appeal to abstract realities—form the play's irreducible center."

48. See Jean Daniélou, *From Shadows to Reality*, trans. Wulstan Hibberd (Burns and Oates, 1960), pp. 69–112, and Don Cameron Allen, *The Legend of Noah; Renaissance Rationalism in Art, Science, and Letters* (University of Illinois Press, 1949).

49. Nelson, "'Sacred' and 'Secular' Currents in *The Towneley Play of Noah*," *Drama Survey* 3 (1964): p. 399.

50. Brownstein, pp. 55–65. In Chapter 2, it will be recalled, I suggested that these stanzas may have been added in the mid-sixteenth century, influenced in their inception by the Midsummer Show.

51. The most precious and ingenious discoveries of typological patterns in a Noah pageant have been Gardner's, pp. 39–48. See also David Bevington, who of the Wakefield Noah asserts that Noah is "a type of Christ" and that "the ark represents the true Church," in Bevington, *Medieval Drama*, p. 290.

52. James W. Earl, in "Typology and Iconographic Style in Early Medieval Hagiography," *Studies in the Literary Imagination* 8 (1975): p. 17, expresses clearly the near identity of the Harrowing and the Eschaton: "When the English homilistic Aelfric tells us that at the Harrowing of Hell Christ led the souls of the saved first to their bodies, and then to Paradise, we are given a keen insight into the nature of Christian historiography. The harrowing and the *eschaton* are hardly distinguishable theologically; and it is the theological significance of an historical event which is its real essence from the vantage of eternity, and in the typological vision of history."

The problem of the nature of the salvation accorded the ancient just immediately after the Harrowing is discussed by Ralph V. Turner in "*Descendit Ad Inferos*: Medieval Views on Christ's Descent into Hell and the Salvation of the Ancient Just," *Journal of the History of Ideas* 27 (1966): 173–94.

53. *The Holkham Bible Picture Book*, p. 72. Hassall's commentary is worth quoting at some length: "The bowing tree has not been noticed as an incident in the legend of Noah, but it exactly illustrates the words of Venantius Fortunatus' hymn in the Mass of the Presanctified, *Crux Fidelis inter omnes arbor una nobilis*. The lines which begin *Flecte ramos* are translated in *The English Hymnal*, No. 96:

> Bend thy boughs, O Tree of Glory!
> Thy relaxing sinews bend,
> For awhile the ancient rigour
> That thy birth bestowed suspend...
> Thou alone wast counted worthy
> This world's ransom to uphold,
> For a shipwrecked race preparing
> Harbour, like the Ark of old.

...There is a verbal, pictorial and mystical antithesis between the fatal bow (*arc*) of destruction bent for Lamech, and the vital bow of the Tree of Salvation bent for the good carpenter making the ark (*la arke*). Both are arches (*arcus*), and so is God's heavenly bow of promise. The three arches are like a window which allows rays of light to illumine the rood which they forefigure, and typify the

275

whole of the Old Testament, whose four thousand years of preparation are represented by the four weeks of Advent" (*The Holkham Bible Picture Book*, p. 72).

It is a curious coincidence that Chester's interpretation of the *arcus in nubibus* is in fact faithful to the original Old Testament understanding of God's bow: "The symbolism of the bow—the Hebrew word is always used of a weapon, never of an arc—goes back to the idea that the lightnings are the Lord's arrows (cf. Pss. 7:13; 18:14; Hab. 3:11), shot from his bow (cf. Ps. 7:12; Hab. 3:9), which is laid aside when his wrath is sated.... A possible source of his [the author's] imagery is the representation of the Babylonian creation myth... that Marduk's bow which he had used against Tiamat was set in the heavens as a constellation" (*The Interpreter's Bible*, 12 vols. [Abingdon-Cokesburg Press, 1952], 1: 551–52).

54. See Michael Swanton, ed., *The Dream of the Rood* (Manchester University Press, 1970), pp. 18–20.

55. Pickering, *Literature and Art*, pp. 285–307.

56. Translation by Pickering, pp. 303–4.

57. See Pickering, p. 305.

58. Sister Jean Marie, "The Cross in the Towneley Plays," *Traditio* 5 (1947): 331–34.

59. Kolve, p. 122.

60. Auerbach's interpretation of the "verticality" of Christian time is one of the most lucid expositions of this concept. See "Figura" in *Scenes from the Drama of European Literature*, trans. Ralph Manheim (Meridian, 1959), esp. pp. 58–59.

61. De Lubac, p. 144.

62. Although the basic comparative techniques of typology are rather simple, the variety of interpretive levels that may be employed to contrast the New with the Old makes typology in practice a complex of hermeneutical systems. As a consequence, typology as an exegetical "system" is difficult to define. For studies of this and related problems, see the articles and checklist published in *Studies in the Literary Imagination* 8, no. 1 (1975).

63. In *Mankind*, for example, the central figure—like Adam—must toil with a spade; and like God in the garden, Mercy cries out to sinful man, "Ubi es?" *Piers Plowman*, which opens with Lucifer's revolt and closes awaiting the Antichrist, is a complex interweaving of world history with the life of the individual Christian. The dramatic conflation of the history of the individual with the history of his race is graphically represented in the plates accompanying Thomas Chaundler's sixteenth-century humanistic "drama," the *Liber Apologeticus de Omni Statu Humanae Naturae*, ed. and trans. Doris Shoukri (Modern Humanities Research Association, 1974). Preceding the text of the play, these illustrations epitomize its major

events: *Humanum Genus* falls like Adam from paradise; clothed in the skins of beasts he is given a scourge and spade by God, who promises him future forgiveness because he acknowledged his error and repented. After Christ's Incarnation, *Humanum Genus* matures in faith under the rule of the four cardinal virtues; and although he is fearful of Death, as he dies he conquers Death and is then triumphantly restored to the heavenly throne from which he had originally fallen.

In the Mons Passion, there is in fact a character called *Humain Lignaige* who represents all of mankind throughout history: see *Le Livre de Conduite du Régisseur et Le Compte des Dépenses pour le Mystère de La Passion Joué à Mons en 1501*, ed. Gustave Cohen (Oxford University Press, 1925). In the English cycles, there is obviously no single character representing mankind; rather, each viewer is granted the freedom of choice to discover himself represented by any of the characters or any of the stages of salvation history.

64. For a more detailed analysis of the significance of "Jewish" characters in Chester, see Lawrence M. Clopper, Jr., "The Principle of Selection of the Chester Old Testament Plays," *Chaucer Review* 13 (1979): 272-83.

65. R.W. Southern, "Aspects of the European Tradition of Historical Writing: 2. Hugh of St. Victor and the Idea of Historical Development," *Transactions of the Royal Historical Society*, 5th ser., 21 (1971): 169.

66. Taylor, "The Dramatic Structure of the Middle English Corpus Christi, or Cycle, Plays," in *Medieval English Drama*, ed. Taylor and Nelson, p. 155.

Four

1. Gilbert Murray, "Excursus on the Ritual Forms Preserved in Greek Tragedy," in *Themis: A Study of the Social Origins of Greek Religion*, ed. Jane Harrison (1927; reprint ed., World, 1967), pp. 341-63.

2. Flanigan, "The Roman Rite and the Origins of the Liturgical Drama."

3. See Young, *Drama of the Medieval Church:* for the *Officium Pastorum*, 2:3-28; for the *Officium Stellae*, 2:29-101; for the *Ordo Rachelis*, 2:102-24. Selected Christmastide Latin dramas and their translations are included in Bevington, *Medieval Drama*, pp. 51-72, 178-201.

4. However, Thomas Campbell has cogently argued that, as the Gospel reading for the Sunday within the Christmas octave, the Purification story (Luke 2:33-40) is an integral part of the Christmas

liturgy. See his "The Nativity in the Medieval Liturgy and the Middle English Mystery Cycles" (Ph.D. diss., Indiana University, 1972), p. 38.

5. Paul E. Kretzmann, *The Liturgical Element in the Earliest Forms of the Medieval Drama*, The University of Minnesota Studies in Language and Literature, no. 4 (University of Minnesota, 1916), p. 73.

6. For a full study of music in the entire cycle, see Carpenter, "Music in the Chester Plays."

7. However, for a sensitive study of the four cycles' Nativity groups' relationships to the Christmas liturgy, see Thomas Campbell, "The Nativity."

8. For the influence of Bonaventuran psychology on the cycles, I am very much indebted to Coletti, "Spirituality and Devotional Images."

9. Frye, *Anatomy of Criticism*, p. 164.

10. For studies of the Chester cycle's indebtedness to the *Stanzaic Life*, see Foster, *A Stanzaic Life of Christ*, pp. ix-xliii, and Wilson, "The *Stanzaic Life of Christ*."

11. Wilson, p. 426; Samuel B. Hemingway, ed., *English Nativity Plays* (Henry Holt, 1909), p. 221.

12. For a graphic depiction of this scene, see "Die Weissagung der Tiburtinischen Sibylle" (Plate 1) in Ernst Günther Grimme, *Unsere Liebe Frau* (DuMont Schauberg, 1968).

13. Ranulph Higden, *Polychronicon Ranulphi Higden Monachi Cestrensis*, 9 vols. (Longman, 1865-86), 4: 295-99.

14. Craig, *English Religious Dramas*, p. 186.

15. Eleanor Prosser, *Drama and Religion in the English Mystery Plays* (Stanford University Press, 1961), p. 90.

16. Elder Olson, *Tragedy and the Theory of Drama* (Wayne State University Press, 1961), p. 47.

17. Victor Turner, *The Ritual Process: Structure and Anti-Structure* (Cornell University Press, 1969), p. 177.

18. Ibid.

19. The scriptural verse to which the playwright alludes is Ezekiel 5:5: "This is Jerusalem. I have set her in the midst of the nations and the countries round about her." The notion of an *axis mundi*, a concept understood fully by medieval thinkers, is analyzed by Mircea Eliade in *Cosmos and History: The Myth of the Eternal Return*, trans. Willard R. Trask (Harper, 1959), pp. 12-14.

20. Stanley J. Kahrl, *Traditions of Medieval English Drama* (Hutchinson University Library, 1974), p. 56.

21. It seems quite extraordinary that no article has yet been written that is concerned exclusively with the Chester Shepherds' play. However, there are two studies which discuss at some length the symbolism of Pagina VII: Margery M. Morgan, "'High Fraud':

278

Paradox and Double-Plot in the English Shepherds' Plays," *Speculum* 39 (1964): 676–89; and Kolve, pp. 161–66.

22. Jacobus de Voragine, *The Golden Legend of Jacobus de Voragine*, trans. Granger Ryan and Helmut Ripperger (Longmans, Green, 1941), p. 3.

23. Woolf, *The English Mystery Plays*, p. 186.

24. The most impressive of these studies is Leah Sinanoglou, "The Christ Child as Sacrifice: A Medieval Tradition and the Corpus Christi Plays," *Speculum* 48 (1973): 491–509.

25. See Ursula Nilgen, "The Epiphany and the Eucharist: On the Interpretation of Eucharistic Motifs in Mediaeval Epiphany Scenes," trans. Renate Franciscono, *Art Bulletin* 49 (1967): 311–16, esp. 315.

26. Young, 2:9.

27. Sinanoglou, p. 497.

28. Saint Aelred's *Sermon II* (*P.L.* CXCV, col. 227), translated by Sinanoglou in "The Christ Child," p. 495.

29. J.W. Robinson, "The Late Medieval Cult," p. 513.

30. Erwin Panofsky, *Early Netherlandish Painting*, 2 vols. (Harvard University Press, 1953), 1: 140–43.

31. The *Digby Mary Magdalene* has been edited most recently by Bevington in *Medieval Drama*, pp. 687–753.

32. Kolve, pp. 8–32. My hunch that the foodstuffs for the feast were obvious, artifical stage-properties is not supported by the Painters' records for 1574/75, where real food seems to have been bought for the performance. See Clopper, *Chester*, pp. 106–8.

33. In the Wakefield *Secunda Pastorum*, the figure of the unsuccessful trickster-magician, Mak, appears to play with the "illusion" of the sacramental mystery of the Incarnation.

34. Alan W. Watts, *Myth and Ritual in Christianity* (Beacon Press, 1968), p. 128.

35. Saint Bonaventure, *De Reductione Artium ad Theologiam*, ed. and trans. Emma Thérèse Healy (The Franciscan Institute, 1955), p. 31.

36. For an illuminating discussion of the importance of sight in Bonaventure's writings and in the cycles, see Coletti, especially Chapter 1.

37. See, for example, Hugh of Saint-Victor's discussion of music as the natural proportioning of love in his *Didascalicon*, trans. and ed. Jerome Taylor (Columbia University Press, 1961), p. 69.

38. The comic structure of the shepherds' inner pilgrimage to Christ can be contrasted with the tragic procession of Bosch's "Haywain" altarpiece. The play and the painting both employ "fallen" and disguised eucharistic symbols (the hay in Bosch's procession, David Jeffrey has argued, is a profanation of the sacramental wafer), and both employ music symbolically (according to Jeffrey, the

279

"celestial" lovers atop the haywagon who read a musical score under an angel's guidance represent the "harmony of communion"). Yet whereas in the altarpiece procession the physical (hence spiritual) proportions of the human figures grow more grotesque as they move from left (Eden) to right (hell), in the Chester pageant confusion and disfiguration give way to harmony, enlightenment, and salvation. See David L. Jeffrey, "Bosch's 'Haywain': Communion, Community, and the Theater of the World," *Viator* 4 (1973): 311–31.

39. David L. Jeffrey, "Franciscan Spirituality," p. 24.

40. The allegorical significance of these gifts has been examined by Lawrence J. Ross in "Symbol and Structure in the *Secunda Pastorum*," in *Medieval English Drama*, ed. Taylor and Nelson, pp. 177–211.

41. *De Imitatione Christi*, ed. John K. Ingram, EETS, E.S. 63 (1893), p. 266.

42. Young, 2: 21.

43. Carpenter, p. 203.

44. Young, 2: 4, ff.

45. For the importance of light and music in the Christmas Vespers, see Thomas Campbell, pp. 34–37; for the significance of music in the Corpus Christi Mass, see Jeffrey, "Bosch's 'Haywain'," p. 327.

46. It is therefore clear that at least in the Chester Shepherds' play we need not "wrestle with the uncombinable antimonies" and "immiscible juxtapositions" which so troubled A.P. Rossiter in the *Secunda Pastorum*; see Rossiter, *English Drama from Early Times to the Elizabethans* (Hutchinson University Library, 1950), p. 72.

47. See pp. 44–45 of this study.

48. "Quae in nostris cordibus digno debet splendore clarescere, ut rerum gestarum ordinem non solum credendo, sed etiam intelligendo veneremur." See *Breviarium ad Usum Insignis Ecclesiae Sarum*, ed. Francis Procter and Christopher Wordsworth, 3 vols. (Academiae Cantabrigiensis, 1879–86), 1: 333.

49. Craig, p. 188.

50. Bevington, p. 189.

51. Foster, *A Stanzaic Life of Christ*, pp. 68–70; see also pp. 54–56 of this study. For a study of the history of the Magi's gifts, see Winifred Sturdevant, *The "Misterio de los Reyes Magos": Its Position in the Development of the Mediaeval Legend of the Three Kings* (Johns Hopkins Press, 1927), esp. pp. 16, 65, 80–84.

52. Foster, *A Stanzaic Life of Christ*, p. 65.

53. For a review of Sepet's theories concerning the dramatizations of "la voix de l'Église," see E. Catherine Dunn, "Voice Structure in the Liturgical Drama: Sepet Reconsidered," in *Medieval English Drama*, ed. Taylor and Nelson, pp. 44–63.

54. *Non-Cycle Plays and Fragments*, ed. Norman Davis, pp. 90–105.

55. Axton, *European Drama*, p. 167.

56. Roston, *Biblical Drama in England*, pp. 24–25. For a balanced study of the role of Herod in medieval drama, see David Staines, "To Out-Herod Herod: The Development of a Dramatic Character," *Comparative Drama* 10 (1976): 29–53.

57. See Thomas Campbell, pp. 37, 171–75.

58. Bevington, p. 71.

59. Young, 2: 106.

60. Ernst R. Curtius, *European Literature and the Latin Middle Ages*, trans. Willard R. Trask (Pantheon, 1953), p. 428.

61. *The Digby Plays*, ed. F.J. Furnivall, EETS, E.S. 70 (1896), pp. 1–23.

62. See Wilson, pp. 420–21.

63. See Greg, *The Trial and Flagellation*, pp. 101–20.

64. See Campbell, pp. 38, 43; see also Watts, pp. 127–28.

65. E. Catherine Dunn, "Popular Devotion in the Vernacular Drama of Medieval England," *Medievalia et Humanistica* 4 (1973): p. 57.

Five

1. For the definition of these three dramatic requirements, I am indebted to Robert A. Brawer, "The Dramatic Function of the Ministry Group in the Towneley Cycle," *Comparative Drama* 4 (1970): 166–76.

2. As readers of medieval drama criticism will undoubtedly recognize, this "standard explanation" is in fact a conflation of several types of arguments, each with its own evaluative system: what I have attempted to do is to distill without critical comment the commonly held assumption that the plays all gradually developed "away" from their scriptural and liturgical sources.

3. Craig, *English Religious Drama*, p. 191.

4. McNeir, "The Corpus Christi Passion Plays," p. 610.

5. These marginal citations may be found in *The Chester Plays*, ed. Herman Deimling and J. Matthews, EETS, E.S. 62, 115 (1893, 1916), pp. 217–65.

6. *Interpreter's Bible*, 8: 438.

7. Craig, p. 177.

8. Erwin Panofsky, *Gothic Architecture and Scholasticism* (World, 1957), pp. 9–10.

9. Josef Pieper, *Scholasticism: Personalities and Problems of Medieval Philosophy*, trans. Richard and Clara Winston (Pantheon, 1960), p. 131. For a much fuller study of the propositions pre-

sumably condemned by Tempier and the climate surrounding them, see Etienne Gilson, *History of Christian Philosophy in the Middle Ages* (Random House, 1955), pp. 387–427.

10. For some general studies of nominalism, see n. 31 in Chapter 1 of this study. A collection of essays especially pertinent to this chapter is Charles Trinkaus and Heiko A. Oberman, eds., *The Pursuit of Holiness in Late Medieval and Renaissance Religion* (E.J. Brill, 1974).

11. Heiko A. Oberman, "Some Notes on the Theology of Nominalism," *Harvard Theological Review* 53 (1960): 51–56.

12. See especially Giles Constable, "The Popularity of Twelfth-Century Spiritual Writers in the Late Middle Ages," in *Renaissance Studies in Honor of Hans Baron*, ed. Anthony Molho and John A. Tedeschi (Northern Illinois University Press, 1971), pp. 3–28, and "Twelfth-Century Spirituality and the Late Middle Ages," in *Medieval and Renaissance Studies*, no. 5, ed. O.B. Hardison, Jr. (University of North Carolina Press, 1971), pp. 27–60. Constable also notes that many other eleventh- and twelfth-century writers were considered important in the fifteenth century: he lists Amadeus of Lausanne, Anselm, Bruno of Cologne, Elizabeth of Schönau, Hildegard of Bingen, Hugh of Fouilloy, Innocent III, Joachim of Flora, John of Fécamp, Peter Damiani, and Peter the Venerable.

13. See Heiko A. Oberman, *Forerunners of the Reformation* (Holt, 1966).

14. Woolf, *English Mystery Plays*, p. 233.

15. Alan H. Nelson, "The Temptation of Christ; or, The Temptation of Satan," in *Medieval English Drama*, ed. Taylor and Nelson, p. 222. See also David L. Wee, "The Temptation of Christ and the Motif of Divine Duplicity in the Corpus Christi Cycle Drama," *Modern Philology* 72 (1974): 1–16.

16. Nelson, "The Temptation of Christ."

17. See Oberman, "Some Notes on the Theology of Nominalism," p. 64.

18. Prosser, *Drama and Religion*, pp. 119–46.

19. Ibid., p. 104.

20. For this perception I am indebted to Paul Pival, "Staging as Projection of Imitated Action," pp. 67–70.

21. Pieper, p. 141.

22. Gordon Leff, *Medieval Thought: St. Augustine to Ockham* (Penguin, 1958), p. 289.

23. Ibid., p. 290.

24. Ibid., p. 298.

25. Johnston, "The Christ Figure," p. 217. David Mills, in "Approaches to Medieval Drama," distinguishes the four cycles according to their different thematic emphases: "The concentration

upon grace in *Ludus Coventriae*, upon the fulfillment of divine purpose in *Chester*, upon human foible in *York* and vital sin in *Towneley*" (*Leeds Studies in English*, n.s. 3 [1969], p. 60, n. 14).

26. Woolf, *The English Mystery Plays*, p. 233.

27. Prosser, p. 118.

28. Ibid.

29. Oberman, in *The Harvest of Medieval Theology* (Harvard University Press, 1963), traces this debate from the early church up through Biel, pp. 361-406.

30. Ibid., p. 64.

31. Ibid., pp. 44-47.

32. Ibid., p. 265.

33. Ibid., p. 267.

34. Oberman, "Some Notes on the Theology of Nominalism," p. 55.

35. Kathleen M. Ashley, "Divine Power in Chester Cycle and Late Medieval Thought," *Journal of the History of Ideas* 39 (1978): 387-404. Although Ashley hardly mentions the three Ministry pageants, I am nevertheless very much indebted to her study of divine power in Chester as a nominalist *topos*.

36. For an application of some of these nominalist tenets to part of one cycle, see Clifford Davidson, "The Realism of the York Realist and the York Passion."

37. "The Neo-Romanesque: Rustication or Revival?" is the full title of the address McGrath gave to the Dartmouth College Medieval University Seminar in the spring of 1976. The address was read from notes, and has not been written out fully, or published. My quotations are taken from McGrath's lecture notes.

Six

1. Julian of Norwich, *Revelations of Divine Love*, trans. Clifton Wolters (Penguin, 1966), p. 63.

2. One leaf, containing about sixty-five lines, is lost from the York "Last Supper" pageant; it is possible that the institution of the Christian Eucharist was dramatized in this missing section.

3. McNeir, "The Corpus Christi Passion Plays," p. 236.

4. Kolve, *The Play Called Corpus Christi*, p. 199.

5. Ibid., p. 189.

6. It appears that Pagina XVI throughout its history was considered one play made up of two sections, the "Trial and Flagellation" and the "Crucifixion"; the two sections were the responsibility of different guilds, which together cooperated in performing one

long play called the "Passion." For further information, see Clopper, "History and Development," p. 237, n. 55.

7. H differs from the other manuscript versions of the Passion in a number of ways, most of them minor; however, some variations are significant, such as the Group MSS's inclusion of Peter's denial, and H's inclusion of two further stanzas in Mary's *planctus*. Because no single MS version appears "pure," I will occasionally quote stanzas from H. For further evidence of the differences among the MSS versions, see the notes to Paginae XVI and XVIa in Lumiansky-Mills, as well as Appendix Ic and Appendix IIc.

8. See Arnold Williams, *The Characterization of Pilate in the Towneley Plays* (Michigan State College Press, 1950).

9. See Robert A. Brawer, "The Characterization of Pilate in the York Cycle Play," *Studies in Philology* 69 (1972): 289–303.

10. The term "crypto-Christian" is taken from McNeir, p. 612, n. 28; for a full study of the York Passion plays, see J.W. Robinson, "The Art of the York Realist," *Modern Philology* 60 (1963): 241–51.

11. See *The Middle-English Harrowing of Hell and Gospel of Nicodemus*, ed. William Henry Hulme, EETS, E.S. 100 (1907), and *The Apocryphal New Testament*, ed. and trans. Montague Rhodes James (The Clarendon Press, 1924), pp. 94–146, esp. pp. 99–100.

12. See Robinson, "The Late Medieval Cult of Jesus."

13. McNeir, p. 622.

14. Rose Jeffries Peebles, *The Legend of Longinus in Ecclesiastical Tradition and in English Literature, and Its Connection with the Grail* (J.H. Furst, 1911), pp. 136–37.

15. Craig, *English Religious Drama*, p. 192.

16. See Jerome Taylor's distinction between simple and complex art in "Critics, Mutations, and Historians of Medieval English Drama: An Introduction to the Essays That Follow," in *Medieval English Drama*, p. 16, n. 23.

17. The *tortores* dance, a spiritual reversal of the angels' joyful circumambulation of their Creator (seen for instance in Chester's first pageant—"nine orders of great beautye... walke aboute the Trenitie"), ultimately, albeit unwittingly, parodies the apostles' dance about Jesus as described in the apocryphal *Acts of St. John*:

> He gathered all of us together and said:
> Before I am delivered up to them,
> let us sing an hymn to the Father,
> and so go forth to that which lieth before us.
> He bade us therefore make as it were a ring,
> holding one another's hands,
> and himself standing in the midst he said:
> Answer Amen unto me.
> He began then to sing an hymn and to say:

Glory be to thee, Father.
And we, going about in a ring, answered him: Amen.

Translation from Maria-Gabriele Wosien, *Sacred Dance: Encounter with the Gods* (Avon, 1974), p. 28. For medieval spiritual applications of the dance, one might consult Jeffrey, *The Early English Lyric and Franciscan Spirituality*, pp. 133–41; for the influence of dance on medieval drama, see Axton, *European Drama*, pp. 47–60.

18. At least two critics in addition to myself consider these appeals by Christ to be close to ritual. Robinson in "The Late Medieval Cult" writes that the audience at these moments is "in some kind of communion" and "the dramatic experience is thus temporarily transformed into what is really a religious rite" (p. 513). And Thomas J. Jambeck, in "The Dramatic Implications of Anselmian Affective Piety in the Towneley Play of the Crucifixion," *Annuale Mediaevale* 16 (1975), writes that Christ's address occurs within "an eternalized moment wherein the spectators are invited to recognize that they too are mysteriously implicated in the ignominious death of their creator" (p. 112).

19. Clopper, *Chester*, p. 388.

Seven

1. Peter Stuart Macaulay, "The Play of the Harrowing of Hell as a Climax in the English Mystery Cycles," *Studia Germanica Gandensia* 8 (1966): 134.

2. Clifford Davidson, "From *Tristia* to *Gaudium*: Iconography and the York-Towneley *Harrowing of Hell*," *American Benedictine Review* 28 (1977): 263.

3. For reasons discussed in Chapter 2, the Alewife-epilogue found in the Group MSS is not here considered as part of the Chester "Harrowing of Hell."

4. *The Middle-English Harrowing of Hell and Gospel of Nicodemus*, ed. Hulme.

5. For commentaries upon the place of the Harrowing within salvation history, see Chapter 3, n. 52, of this study.

6. These dynamics in liturgical drama are intelligently exemplified in the Fleury *Visitatio*, where testimony progresses toward various kinds of evidence, where the Marys and later the Magdalene turn to the audience to share their state of partial conviction, and where at the end Christ appears "undisguised" before the audience as the Lord (*in similitudinem Domini*), and the choir sings the "Te Deum."

7. For a study of some of the popular motifs which helped shape these dramatic imperatives, see Sinanoglou, "The Christ Child as Sacrifice"; for a study of the peregrini episodes as treated in medieval literature and commentaries, see F.C. Gardiner, *The Pilgrimage of Desire: A Study of Theme and Genre in Medieval Literature* (E.J. Brill, 1971).

8. In all four English cycles, the bread Christ breaks with Luke and Cleophas is at least implied to be the eucharistic Host. In Wakefield, for instance, Cleophas exclaims: "I had no knawlege it was he, / Bot for he brake this brede in thre."

9. Although unlike the other three cycles York does not have a Resurrection Testament (wherein Christ directly addresses the audience), it may once have had. See Greg, *Bibliographical and Textual Problems*, p. 74, n. 1. Cf. Woolf, *The English Mystery Plays*, p. 406, n. 15.

10. Prosser, *Drama and Religion*, p. 160.

11. For a study of this lyric genre, see Rosemary Woolf, *The English Religious Lyric in the Middle Ages* (The Clarendon Press, 1968), pp. 44-60. Carleton Brown and Rossell Hope Robbins in *The Index of Middle English Verse* (Columbia University Press, 1943) list over sixty lyrics of the "Appeal of Christ to man"; none closely resembles Chester's Resurrection lyric. W.W. Greg was the first to suggest that the Chester Resurrection Testament was an independent poem, in *Bibliographical and Textual Problems*, pp. 74-75. Also see Woolf, *The English Mystery Plays*, p. 407, n. 19.

12. Various Middle-English versions of Christ's appearances are discussed by Prosser, pp. 147-78, 215-19.

13. Jerome Taylor argues the direct influence of the feast on the structure of the Corpus Christi plays in "The Dramatic Structure of the Middle English Corpus Christi, or Cycle, Plays," in *Medieval English Drama*, pp. 148-56.

14. For text and translation of the Fleury *Visitatio Sepulchri*, see Bevington, *Medieval Drama*, pp. 39-44.

15. For the influence of homiletic traditions on the English cycles, see Prosser, *Drama and Religion*, and Owst, *Literature and Pulpit*, pp. 471-547.

16. The numerical perfection of twelve (in contrast to eleven) is made explicit in *York Plays*, p. 465:

> For parfite noumbre it is none,
> Off elleuen for to lere,
> Twelue may be a-soundir tone,
> And settis in parties seere.

17. Woolf, *The English Mystery Plays*, p. 286. Woolf adds: "Possibly there has been some botched rewriting but, certainly as we read it now, the scene presents a piece of theological and literary fumbling."

18. *A Hundred Merry Tales, and Other English Jestbooks of the Fifteenth and Sixteenth Centuries,* ed. P.M. Zall (University of Nebraska Press, 1963), pp. 115–16, tale 56.

19. Anderson, *Drama and Imagery*, p. 40. See in addition G. McN. Rushforth, *Medieval Christian Imagery* (The Clarendon Press, 1936), pp. 337–43, and Clifford Davidson, *Drama and Art* (Medieval Institute, 1977), pp. 119–21.

20. Alexandra F. Johnston, "The Plays of the Religious Guilds of York: The Creed Play and the Pater Noster Play," *Speculum* 50 (1975): 55–90; for a study of the Mercers' pageant, see Johnston and Margaret Dorrell, "The Doomsday Pageant of the York Mercers, 1433," *Leeds Studies in English*, n.s. 5 (1971): 29–34.

21. Johnston, "Creed Play," p. 68.

22. Robinson, "The Late Medieval Cult," p. 513. In an otherwise excellent study, Robinson erroneously (I believe) suggests that all the cycles' Passion and Resurrection Testaments of Christ are "more or less interchangeable."

23. Woolf, *The English Mystery Plays*, p. 407, n. 19.

24. The most thorough study of interpretations of this tenet of faith is Emilien Lamirande, *The Communion of Saints,* trans. A. Manson, *The Twentieth Century Encyclopedia of Catholicism*, vol. 26, sec. 2 (Hawthorn Books, 1963).

25. *Cursor Mundi*, ed. Richard Morris, EETS, O.S. 68 (1878): p. 1436.

26. *The Lay Folks' Catechism*, ed. Thomas Frederick Simmons and Henry Edward Nolloth, EETS, O.S. 118 (1901): p. 24. See in addition *Dan Michel's Ayenbite of Inwyt*, ed. Richard Morris, EETS, O.S. 23 (1866): p. 14.

27. *The Lay Folks' Mass Book*, ed. Thomas Frederick Simmons, EETS, O.S. 71 (1879): pp. 20–22. Simmons's notes on this article are informative: see pp. 225–28. For a mixture of these interpretations, see "The Belief" of Lambeth MS 853, in *"Hymns to the Virgin and Christ," "The Parliament of Devils," and Other Religious Poems*, ed. Frederick J. Furnivall, EETS, O.S. 24 (1867): pp. 102–3.

28. Salter, "The Banns," 16: 15.

29. Clopper, *Chester*, p. 246.

30. Salter, "The Banns," 15: 446.

31. Clopper, *Chester*, pp. 245–46.

32. Although I no longer hold to this opinion (which I defended in the 1976 article from which this chapter derives), I consider it still a possibility that Chester's credal design was a cleverly disguised retort to Protestant criticism. The Protestant response to the traditional interpretations of the Communion of Saints is succinctly dramatized in *Pierce the Ploughman's Crede*, ed. Walter W. Skeat, EETS, O.S. 30 (1867): pp. 30–31. When the late fourteenth-century *Crede* was printed in 1553, the last year of the reign of Edward VI,

five original lines farsing the Communion of Saints were suppressed:

And in the [sacrament] also • that sothfast God on is,
(Fullich his fleche & his blod) • that for vs dethe tholede.
. . . For Christ seyde it is so • so mot it nede worthe;
Therfore studye thou nought theron • ne stere thi wittes,
It is his blissed body • so bad he vs beleuen.

The lines forged in the 1553 edition to replace those lines excised are:

The communion of sayntes • for soth I to the sayn;
And for our great sinnes • forgiuenes for to getten,
And only by Christ • clenlich to be clensed;
Our bodies again to risen • right as we been here,
And the liif euerlasting • leue ich to habben; Amen.

33. Clopper, "The History and Development," p. 246.

Eight

1. Since I have discussed in Chapter 3 the many complexities of the cycle's interpretation of Old Testament time, it can be seen that the further removed scriptural time is from the "center," the greater the artistic task may be in presenting it. This, however, does not mean that a dramatic interpretation of the time of the Gospels is a straightforward and simple matter. In the Gospel pageants, the fullness of time both has and has not come: the aoristic world of the Gospel narratives seems most often to hover in dramatic time somewhere between the present and present perfect.

2. Paul Zumthor, "From Hi(story) to Poem, or the Paths of Pun: The Grand Rhétoriqueurs of Fifteenth-Century France," trans. Annette and Edward Tomarken, *New Literary History* 10 (1979): 238.

3. John Phillips, *The Reformation of Images: Destruction of Art in England, 1535-1660* (University of California Press, 1973), p. xi.

4. Linus Urban Lucken, *Antichrist and the Prophets of Antichrist in the Chester Cycle* (The Catholic University of America Press, 1940), p. 137.

5. For a discussion of the distinctions between *Antichristus apertus* and *Antichristus mysticus*, see John Block Friedman, "Antichrist and the Iconography of Dante's Geryon," *Journal of the Warburg and Courtauld Institutes* 35 (1972): 108-22, and R.E. Kaske, "Dante's 'DXV' and 'Veltro'," *Traditio* 17 (1961): 185-254. An excellent general study is Richard Kenneth Emmerson, *Antichrist in the Middle Ages: A Study of Medieval Apocalypticism,*

Art, and Literature (University of Washington Press, 1981). Emmerson's book appeared after the completion of this chapter.

6. John Wright, *The Play of Antichrist* (The Pontifical Institute of Mediaeval Studies, 1967), p. 63.

7. Leslie Howard Martin, "Comic Eschatology in the Chester *Coming of Antichrist*," *Comparative Drama* 5 (1971): 165–66.

8. Thomas [Netter] Waldensis, *Doctrinale Antiquitatum Fidei Catholicae Ecclesiae*, ed. B. Blanciotti, 3 vols. (1757–59), 3: 939. This passage is translated by W.R. Jones in his very useful article "Lollards and Images: The Defense of Religious Art in Later Medieval England," *Journal of the History of Ideas* 34 (1973), 44. For this quotation and for several others cited in this chapter, I am indebted to Coletti, "Spirituality and Devotional Images."

9. Reginald Pecock, *The Repressor of Over Much Blaming of the Clergy*, ed. Churchill Babington, 2 vols. (Longman, Green, Longman and Roberts, 1860), 1: 163.

10. *Reliquiae Antiquae*, ed. Thomas Wright and James Orchard Halliwell (William Pickering, 1843), 2: 46–47.

11. Lucken, p. 68.

12. Geoffrey Hartman, "Structuralism: The Anglo-American Adventure," *Yale French Studies* 36, 37 (1966): 167.

13. *Ludus Coventriae*, p. 230.

14. Woolf, *The English Mystery Plays*, p. 299.

15. Robert Grinnell, "Iconography and Philosophy in the Crucifixion Window at Poitiers," *Art Bulletin* 28 (1946): 193.

Bibliography
of Cited Works

Drama Texts

Bevington, David. *Medieval Drama*. Boston: Houghton, 1975.

The Chester Mystery Cycle. Edited by R.M. Lumiansky and David Mills. EETS, S.S. 3. London: Oxford University Press, 1974.

The Chester Plays. Edited by Herman Deimling and J. Matthews. EETS, E.S. 62, 115. London: Kegan Paul, Trench, Trübner and Co., 1893, 1916.

The Digby Plays. Edited by F.J. Furnivall. EETS, E.S. 70. London: Kegan Paul, Trench, Trübner and Co., 1896.

Le Livre de Conduite du Régisseur et Le Compte des Dépenses pour le Mystère de La Passion Joué à Mons en 1501. Edited by Gustave Cohen. London: Oxford University Press, 1925.

Ludus Coventriae; or The Plaie Called Corpus Christi. 1922. Reprint. Edited by K.S. Block. EETS, E.S. 120. London: Oxford University Press, 1960.

Non-Cycle Plays and Fragments. Edited by Norman Davis. EETS, S.S. 1. London: Oxford University Press, 1970.

The Towneley Plays. Edited by George England and Alfred W. Pollard. EETS, E.S. 71. London: Kegan Paul, Trench, Trübner and Co., 1897.

Wright, John, trans. *The Play of Antichrist*. Toronto: The Pontifical Institute of Mediaeval Studies, 1967.

York Plays. Edited by Lucy Toulmin Smith. Oxford: The Clarendon Press, 1885.

Young, Karl. *The Drama of the Medieval Church*. 2 vols. Oxford: The Clarendon Press, 1933.

Other Primary Sources

Anselm of Canterbury. *Truth, Freedom, and Evil: Three Philosophical Dialogues*. Edited and translated by Jasper Hopkins and Herbert Richardson. New York: Harper, 1967.

The Apocryphal New Testament. Edited and translated by Montague Rhodes James. Oxford: The Clarendon Press, 1924.

Aquinas, Saint Thomas. *Basic Writings of Saint Thomas Aquinas*. 2 vols. Translated by Anton C. Pegis. New York: Random House, 1945.

_____. *Opera Omnia*. 25 vols. New York: Musurgia, 1950.

_____. *Thomas Aquinas: Selected Writings*. Edited and translated by M.C. D'Arcy. London: J.M. Dent and Sons, 1939.

Augustine, Saint. *The City of God*. Translated by Marcus Dods. New York: Modern Library, 1950.

Bonaventure, Saint. *De Reductione Artium ad Theologiam*. Edited and translated by Emma Thérèse Healy. St. Bonaventure, N.Y.: The Franciscan Institute, 1955.

Breviarium ad Usum Insignis Ecclesiae Sarum. 3 vols. Edited by Francis Procter and Christopher Wordsworth. Cambridge, England: Academiae Cantabrigiensis, 1879–86.

Chaundler, Thomas. *Liber Apologeticus de Omni Statu Humanae Naturae*. Edited and translated by Doris Shoukri. London: Modern Humanities Research Association, 1974.

Comestor, Peter. "Historia Scholastica." Vol. 198. *Patrologia Latinae*. Edited by J.P. Migne. Paris: By the Editor, 1844–64.

Cursor Mundi. Edited by Richard Morris. EETS, O.S. 57, 59, 62, 66, 68, 99, 101. London: Kegan Paul, Trench, Trübner and Co., 1874–93.

Dan Michel's Ayenbite of Inwyt. Edited by Richard Morris. EETS, O.S. 23. London: N. Trübner and Co., 1866.

Gower, John. *The Complete Works of John Gower*. 4 vols. Edited by G.C. Macaulay. Oxford: The Clarendon Press, 1899–1902.

Higden, Ranulph. *Polychronicon Ranulphi Higden Monachi Cestrensis*. 9 vols. Edited by Joseph Rawson Lumby. London: Longman, 1865–86.

The Holkham Bible Picture Book. Edited by W.O. Hassall. London: Dropmore Press, 1954.

Hugh of Saint-Victor. *Hugh of Saint Victor on the Sacraments of the Christian Faith*. Translated by Roy J. Deferrari. Cambridge, MA: The Mediaeval Academy of America, 1951.

_____. *Didascalicon: A Medieval Guide to the Arts*. Translated and edited by Jerome Taylor. New York: Columbia University Press, 1961.

A Hundred Merry Tales, and Other English Jestbooks of the Fifteenth and Sixteenth Centuries. Edited by P.M. Zall. Lincoln, NE: University of Nebraska Press, 1963.

"Hymns to the Virgin and Christ," "The Parliament of Devils," and Other Religious Poems. Edited by Frederick J. Furnivall. EETS, O.S. 24. London: Kegan Paul, Trench, Trübner and Co., 1867.

De Imitatione Christi. Edited by John K. Ingram. EETS, E.S. 63. London: Kegan Paul, Trench, Trübner and Co., 1893.

Jacobus de Voragine. *The Golden Legend of Jacobus de Voragine.* Translated by Granger Ryan and Helmut Ripperger. London: Longmans, Green, 1941.

Julian of Norwich. *Revelations of Divine Love.* Translated by Clifton Wolters. Harmondsworth, England: Penguin, 1966.

"Langforde's Meditations in the Time of the Mass." *Tracts on the Mass.* Edited by J. Wickham Legg. London: Harrison and Sons, 1904.

The Later Genesis. Edited by B.J. Timmer. 2d rev. ed. Oxford: Scrivner Press, 1954.

The Lay Folks' Catechism. Edited by Thomas Frederick Simmons and Henry Edward Nolloth. EETS, O.S. 118. London: Kegan Paul, Trench, Trübner and Co., 1901.

The Lay Folks' Mass Book. Edited by Thomas Frederick Simmons. EETS, O.S. 71. London: N. Trübner and Co., 1879.

The Middle English Genesis and Exodus. Edited by Olof Arngart. Lund: C.W.K. Gleerup, 1968.

The Middle-English Harrowing of Hell and Gospel of Nicodemus. Edited by William Henry Hulme. EETS, E.S. 100. London: Kegan Paul, Trench, Trübner and Co., 1907.

Peacock, Reginald. *The Repressor of Over Much Blaming of the Clergy.* 2 vols. Edited by Churchill Babington. London: Longman, Green, Longman and Roberts, 1860.

Pierce the Ploughmans Crede. Edited by Walter W. Skeat. EETS, O.S. 30. London: Kegan Paul, Trench, Trübner and Co., 1867.

Reliquiae Antiquae. Edited by Thomas Wright and James Orchard Halliwell. 2 vols. London: William Pickering, 1843.

A Stanzaic Life of Christ. Edited by Frances A. Foster. EETS, O.S. 166. London: Oxford University Press, 1926.

Waldensis, Thomas [Netter]. *Doctrinale Antiquitatem Fidei Catholicae Ecclesiae.* Edited by B. Blanciotti. Venice: 1757–59.

Scholarly Studies

Allen, Don Cameron. *The Legend of Noah; Renaissance Rationalism in Art, Science, and Letters,* appearing in *Illinois Studies in Lan-*

guage and Literature, vol. 33, nos. 3–4. Urbana, IL: University of Illinois Press, 1949.

Allen, Judson Boyce. *The Friar as Critic: Literary Attitudes in the Later Middle Ages*. Nashville: Vanderbilt University Press, 1971.

Anderson, Mary D. *Drama and Imagery in English Medieval Churches*. Cambridge: The University Press, 1963.

Ashley, Kathleen M. "Divine Power in Chester Cycle and Late Medieval Thought." *Journal of the History of Ideas* 39 (1978): 387–404.

Auerbach, Erich. *Mimesis: The Representation of Reality in Western Literature*. Translated by Willard R. Trask. Princeton: Princeton University Press, 1953.

_____. *Scenes from the Drama of European Literature*. Translated by Ralph Manheim. New York: Meridian, 1959.

Axton, Richard. *European Drama of the Early Middle Ages*. London: Hutchinson, 1974.

Bakhtin, Mikhail M. *Rabelais and His World*. Translated by Helene Iswolsky. Cambridge, MA: MIT Press, 1968.

Baugh, Albert C. "The Chester Plays and French Influence." *Schelling Anniversary Papers*. New York: Century, 1923.

Bernbrock, John E. "Notes on the Towneley Cycle *Slaying of Abel*." *Journal of English and Germanic Philology* 62 (1963): 317–22.

Bland, D.S. "The Chester Nativity: One Play or Two?" *Notes and Queries* 10 (1963): 134–35.

Brawer, Robert A. "The Characterization of Pilate in the York Cycle Play." *Studies in Philology* 69 (1972): 289–303.

_____. "The Dramatic Function of the Ministry Group in the Towneley Cycle." *Comparative Drama* 4 (1970): 166–76.

_____. "The Form and Function of the Prophetic Procession in the Middle English Cycle Play." *Annuale Medievale* 13 (1972): 88–124.

Brockman, Bennett A. "Cain and Abel in the Chester *Creation*: Narrative Tradition and Dramatic Potential." *Medievalia et Humanistica* 5 (1974): 169–82.

Browe, Peter. *Die Verehrung der Eucharistie im Mittelalter*. Munich: M. Hueber, 1933.

Brown, Carleton, and Robbins, Rossell Hope. *The Index of Middle English Verse*. New York: Columbia University Press, 1943.

Brownstein, Oscar L. "Revision in the 'Deluge' of the Chester Cycle." *Speech Monographs* 36 (1969): 55–65.

Bryant, Joseph Allen, Jr. "Chester's Sermon for Catechumens." *Journal of English and Germanic Philology* 53 (1954): 399–402.

Campbell, J.K. *Honour, Family, and Patronage; A Study of Institutions and Moral Values in a Greek Mountain Community*. Oxford: The Clarendon Press, 1964.

Campbell, Thomas. "The Nativity in the Medieval Liturgy and the Middle English Mystery Cycles." Ph.D. dissertation, Indiana

University, 1972.

Carpenter, Nan Cooke. "Music in the Chester Plays." *Papers on English Language and Literature* 1 (1965): 195–216.

Carré, Meyrick H. *Phases of Thought in England.* Oxford: The Clarendon Press, 1949.

_____. *Realists and Nominalists.* London: Oxford University Press, 1946.

The Catholic Encyclopedia. New York: Robert Appleton, 1907–12.

Chambers, E.K. *English Literature at the Close of the Middle Ages.* Oxford: The Clarendon Press, 1945.

_____. *The Mediaeval Stage.* 2 vols. Oxford: The Clarendon Press, 1903.

Chenu, M.-D. *Nature, Man, and Society in the Twelfth Century; Essays on New Theological Perspectives in the Latin West.* Translated by Jerome Taylor and Lester K. Little. Chicago: University of Chicago Press, 1968.

Clopper, Lawrence M., Jr., ed. *Chester. Records of Early English Drama.* Vol. 3. Toronto: University of Toronto Press, 1979.

_____. *"The Chester Plays:* Frequency of Performance." *Theatre Survey* 14, no. 2 (1973): 46–58.

_____. "The History and Development of the Chester Cycle." *Modern Philology* 75 (1978): 219–46.

_____. "The Principle of Selection of the Chester Old Testament Plays." *Chaucer Review* 13 (1979): 272–83.

_____. "The Rogers' Description of the Chester Plays." *Leeds Studies in English* 7 (1973–74): 63–94.

_____. "The Staging of the Medieval Plays of Chester: A Response." *Theatre Notebook* 28 (1974): 65–70.

_____. "The Structure of the Chester Cycle: Text, Theme and Theatre." Ph.D. dissertation, Ohio State University, 1969.

Coffee, Bernice F. "The Chester Play of *Balaam and Balak.*" *Wisconsin Studies in Literature* 4 (1967): 103–18.

Coletti, Theresa. "Spirituality and Devotional Images: The Staging of the Hegge Cycle." Ph.D. dissertation, University of Rochester, 1975.

Collier, Richard J. *Poetry and Drama in the York Corpus Christi Play.* Hamden, CT: Archon, 1978.

Collingwood, R.G. *The Principles of Art.* Oxford: The Clarendon Press, 1938.

Constable, Giles. "Twelfth-Century Spirituality and the Late Middle Ages." In *Medieval and Renaissance Studies*, no. 5. Edited by O.B. Hardison, Jr. Chapel Hill: University of North Carolina Press, 1971.

_____. "The Popularity of Twelfth-Century Spiritual Writers in the Late Middle Ages." In *Renaissance Studies in Honor of Hans*

Baron. Edited by Anthony Molho and John A. Tedeschi. DeKalb, IL: Northern Illinois University Press, 1971.

Cowling, Douglas. "The Liturgical Celebration of Corpus Christi in Medieval York." *Records of Early English Drama Newsletter* 2 (1976): 5-9.

Craig, Hardin. *English Religious Drama of the Middle Ages.* Oxford: The Clarendon Press, 1955.

Crocker, S.F. "The Production of the Chester Plays." *West Virginia University Studies: Philological Papers* 1 (1936): 62-86.

Curtius, Ernst R. *European Literature and the Latin·Middle Ages.* Translated by Willard R. Trask. New York: Pantheon, 1953.

Daniélou, Jean. *From Shadows to Reality; Studies in the Biblical Typology of the Fathers.* Translated by Wulstan Hibberd. London: Burns and Oates, 1960.

Davidson, Charles. "Studies in the English Mystery Plays." Ph.D. dissertation, Yale University, 1892.

Davidson, Clifford. *Drama and Art.* Kalamazoo, MI: Medieval Institute, 1977.

_____ . "From *Tristia* to *Gaudium*: Iconography and the York-Towneley *Harrowing of Hell.*" *American Benedictine Review* 28 (1977): 260-75.

_____ . "The Realism of the York Realist and the York Passion." *Speculum* 50 (1975): 270-83.

_____ . "Thomas Aquinas, the Feast of Corpus Christi, and the English Cycle Plays." *Michigan Academician* 7 (1974): 103-10.

Davidson, Clifford, and Mason, Nona. "Staging the York *Creation, and Fall of Lucifer.*" *Theatre Survey* 17 (1976): 162-78.

Davis, Ruth Brant. "The Scheduling of the Chester Cycle Plays." *Theatre Notebook* 27 (1972): 49-67.

Delaissé, L.M.J. "A La Recherche Des Origins De L'Office Du Corpus Christi Dans Les Manuscrits Liturgiques." *Scriptorium* 4 (1950): 220-39.

Diller, Hans-Jürgen. "The Composition of the Chester *Adoration of the Shepherds.*" *Anglia* 89 (1971): 178-98.

Dumoutet, Edouard. *Le Désir de Voir L'Hostie et les Origines de la Dévotion au Saint-Sacrement.* Paris, Beauchesne, 1926.

Dunn, E. Catherine. "Lyrical Form and the Prophetic Principle in the Towneley Plays." *Mediaeval Studies* 23 (1961): 80-90.

_____ . "Popular Devotion in the Vernacular Drama of Medieval England." *Medievalia et Humanistica* 4 (1973): 55-68.

Dustoor, P.E. "The Origin of the Play of 'Moses and the Tables of the Law'." *Modern Language Review* 19 (1924): 459-62.

Dutka, JoAnna. "Music and the English Mystery Plays." *Comparative Drama* 7 (1973): 135-49.

Earl, James W. "Typology and Iconographic Style in Early Medieval

Hagiography." *Studies in the Literary Imagination* 8 (1975): 15–46.

Edwards, Robert. "Techniques of Transcendence in Medieval Drama." *Comparative Drama* 8 (1974): 157–71.

Eliade, Mircea. *Cosmos and History: The Myth of the Eternal Return*. Translated by Willard R. Trask. New York: Harper, 1959.

Emerson, Oliver F. "Legends of Cain, Especially in Old and Middle English." *PMLA* 21 (1906): 831–929.

Emmerson, Richard Kenneth. *Antichrist in the Middle Ages: A Study of Medieval Apocalypticism, Art, and Literature*. Seattle: University of Washington Press, 1981.

Evans, John M. *Paradise Lost and the Genesis Tradition*. Oxford: The Clarendon Press, 1968.

Farmer, Oscar G. *Fairford Church and Its Stained Glass Windows*. 8th ed. Bath: Harding and Curtis, 1965.

Fernandez, James. "The Mission of Metaphor in Expressive Culture." *Current Anthropology* 15 (1974): 119–33.

Fifield, Merle. *The Rhetoric of Free Will: The Five-Action Structure of the English Morality Play*. Leeds: University of Leeds Press, 1974.

Flanigan, C. Clifford. "The Roman Rite and the Origins of the Liturgical Drama." *University of Toronto Quarterly* 43 (1974): 263–84.

Fleming, John V. *An Introduction to the Franciscan Literature of the Middle Ages*. Chicago: Franciscan Herald Press, 1977.

Fortescue, Adrian. *The Mass: A Study of the Roman Liturgy*. 2d rev. ed. London: Longmans, Green, 1917.

Friedman, John Block. "Antichrist and the Iconography of Dante's Geryon." *Journal of the Warburg and Courtauld Institutes* 35 (1972): 108–22.

Frye, Northrop. *Anatomy of Criticism: Four Essays*. Princeton: Princeton University Press, 1957.

Gardiner, F.C. *The Pilgrimage of Desire: A Study of Theme and Genre in Medieval Literature*. Leiden: E.J. Brill, 1971.

Gardiner, Harold. *Mysteries' End: An Investigation of the Last Days of the Medieval Religious Stage*. New Haven: Yale University Press, 1946.

Gardner, John. *The Construction of the Wakefield Cycle*. Carbondale, IL: Southern Illinois University Press, 1974.

Gilson, Etienne. *History of Christian Philosophy in the Middle Ages*. New York: Random House, 1955.

Greg, Walter Wilson. *Bibliographic and Textual Problems of the English Miracle Cycles*. Reprinted from four articles appearing in *The Library*. 3d ser. 5 (1914). London: Alexander Moring, 1914.

_____ . *The Trial and Flagellation with Other Studies in the Chester Cycle*. London: Oxford University Press, 1936.

Grimme, Ernst Günther. *Unsere Liebe Frau. Das Bild Mariens in der Malerei des Mittelalters und der Frührenaissance*. Cologne: DuMont Schauberg, 1968.

Grinnell, Robert. "Iconography and Philosophy in the Crucifixion Window at Poitiers." *Art Bulletin* 28 (1946): 171-96.

Hardison, O.B., Jr. *Christian Rite and Christian Drama in the Middle Ages: Essays in the Origin and Early History of Modern Drama*. Baltimore: Johns Hopkins Press, 1965.

Hartman, Geoffrey. "Structuralism: The Anglo-American Adventure." *Yale French Studies* 36, 37 (1966): 148-68.

Hemingway, Samuel B., ed. *English Nativity Plays*. New York: Henry Holt, 1909.

Huizinga, J. *The Waning of the Middle Ages*. Translated by F. Hopman. London: E. Arnold, 1927.

Hurrell, John Dennis. "The Figural Approach to Medieval Drama." *College English* 26 (1965): 598-604.

The Interpreter's Bible: The Holy Scriptures in the King James and Revised Standard Versions. 12 vols. Edited by George A. Buttrich et al. New York: Abingdon-Cokesbury Press, 1951-57.

Jambeck, Thomas J. "The Dramatic Implications of Anselmian Affective Piety in the Towneley Play of the Crucifixion." *Annuale Mediaevale* 16 (1975): 110-27.

Jean Marie, Sister. "The Cross in the Towneley Plays." *Traditio* 5 (1947): 331-34.

Jeffrey, David L. "Bosch's 'Haywain': Communion, Community, and the Theater of the World." *Viator* 4 (1973): 311-31.

_____ . *The Early English Lyric and Franciscan Spirituality*. Lincoln, NE: University of Nebraska Press, 1975.

_____ . "Franciscan Spirituality and the Rise of Early English Drama." *Mosaic* 8 (1975): 17-46.

Jensen, Adolph E. *Myth and Cult among Primitive Peoples*. Translated by Marianna Tax Choldin and Wolfgang Weissleder. Chicago: University of Chicago Press, 1963.

Johnston, Alexandra F. "The Christ Figure in the Ministry Plays of the Four English Cycles." Ph.D. dissertation, University of Toronto, 1964.

_____ . "The Plays of the Religious Guilds of York: The Creed Play and the Pater Noster Play." *Speculum* 50 (1975): 55-90.

_____ . "The Procession and the Play of Corpus Christi in York after 1426." *Leeds Studies in English* 7 (1973-74): 55-62.

Johnston, Alexandra F., and Dorrell, Margaret. "The Doomsday Pageant of the York Mercers, 1433." *Leeds Studies in English*, n.s. 5 (1971): 29-34.

Jones, W.R. "Lollards and Images: The Defense of Religious Art in Later Medieval England." *Journal of the History of Ideas* 34 (1973): 27-50.

Jungmann, Josef A. *The Mass of the Roman Rite: Its Origins and Development.* 2 vols. Translated by Francis A. Brunner. New York: Benziger Brothers, 1951-55.

Kahrl, Stanley J. *Traditions of Medieval English Drama.* London: Hutchinson University Library, 1974.

Kaske, R.E. "Dante's 'DXV' and 'Veltro'." *Traditio* 17 (1961): 185-254.

Kastan, David Scott. "The Shape of Time: Form and Value in the Shakespearean History Play." *Comparative Drama* 7 (1974): 259-77.

Kolve, V.A. *The Play Called Corpus Christi.* Stanford: Stanford University Press, 1966.

Kretzmann, Paul E. *The Liturgical Element in the Earliest Forms of the Medieval Drama.* The University of Minnesota Studies in Language and Literature, no. 4. Minneapolis: University of Minnesota, 1916.

Lambot, C. "L'Office de la Fête-Dieu. Aperçus Noveaux Sur Ses Origines." *Revue Bénédictine* 54 (1942): 61-123.

Lamirande, Emilien. *The Communion of Saints.* Translated by A. Manson. Twentieth Century Encyclopedia of Catholicism, vol. 26. New York: Hawthorn Books, 1963.

Leff, Gordon. *Medieval Thought: St. Augustine to Ockham.* Harmondsworth, England: Penguin, 1958.

_____. *Paris and Oxford Universities in the Thirteenth and Fourteenth Centuries: An Institutional and Intellectual History.* New York: John Wiley and Sons, 1968.

Lubac, Henri de. *The Sources of Revelation.* Translated by Luke O'Neill. New York: Herder and Herder, 1968.

Lucken, Linus Urban. *Antichrist and the Prophets of Antichrist in the Chester Cycle.* Washington, DC: The Catholic University of America Press, 1940.

Lumiansky, R.M. "Comedy and Theme in the Chester *Harrowing of Hell.*" *Tulane Studies in English* 10 (1960): 5-12.

Lumiansky, R.M., and Mills, David. "The Five Cyclic Manuscripts of the Chester Cycle of Mystery Plays: A Statistical Survey of Variant Readings." *Leeds Studies in English* 7 (1973-74): 95-107.

Macaulay, Peter Stuart. "The Play of the Harrowing of Hell as a Climax in the English Mystery Cycles." *Studia Germanica Gandensia* 8 (1966): 115-34.

McCaffrey, Phillip C. "The Didactic Structure of the Chester *Sacrifice of Isaac.*" *Comitatus* 2 (1971): 16-26.

_____. "Historical Structure in the Chester Old Testament Pageants:

The Literary and Religious Components of a Medieval Aesthetic." Ph.D. dissertation, University of Pennsylvania, 1972.

McGavin, John. "Signs and Related Didactic Techniques in the Chester Cycle of Mystery Plays." Ph.D. dissertation, University of Edinburgh, 1981.

McGrath, Robert C. "The Neo-Romanesque: Rustication or Revival?" Address presented at the Dartmouth College Medieval University Seminar, Hanover, NH: Spring 1976.

McKeon, Richard Peter. *Thought, Action, and Passion*. Chicago: University of Chicago Press, 1954.

McNeir, Waldo F. "The Corpus Christi Passion Plays as Dramatic Art." *Studies in Philology* 48 (1951): 601–28.

Martin, Leslie Howard. "Comic Eschatology in the Chester *Coming of Antichrist*." *Comparative Drama* 5 (1971): 163–76.

Meyers, Walter E. *A Figure Given: Typology in the Wakefield Plays*. Pittsburgh: Duquesne University Press, 1969.

Mills, David. "Approaches to Medieval Drama." *Leeds Studies in English* n.s. 3 (1969): 47–61.

_____ . "Two Versions of Chester Play V: 'Balaam and Balak'." *Chaucer and Middle English Studies in Honour of Rossell Hope Robbins*. Edited by Beryl Rowland. London: Allen and Unwin, 1974.

Monks, James L. *Great Catholic Festivals*. New York: Henry Schuman, 1951.

Morgan, Margery H. "'High Fraud': Paradox and Double-Plot in the English Shepherds' Plays." *Speculum* 39 (1964): 676–89.

Morris, Rupert Hugh. *Chester in the Plantagenet and Tudor Reigns*. Chester: By the author, 1893.

Munson, William F. "Typology and the Towneley Isaac." *Research Opportunities in Renaissance Drama* 11 (1968): 129–39.

Murray, Gilbert. "Excursus on the Ritual Forms Preserved in Greek Tragedy." In *Themis: A Study of the Social Origins of Greek Religion*. Edited by Jane Harrison. 1927. Reprint. Cleveland: World, 1967.

Nelson, Alan H. *The Medieval English Stage: Corpus Christi Pageants and Plays*. Chicago: University of Chicago Press, 1974.

_____ . "A Pilgrimage to Toledo: Corpus Christi Day 1974." *Research Opportunities in Renaissance Drama* 17 (1974): 123–29.

_____ . "'Sacred' and 'Secular' Currents in *The Towneley Play of Noah*." *Drama Survey* 3 (1964): 393–401.

New Catholic Encyclopedia. New York: McGraw-Hill, 1967–74.

Nilgen, Ursula. "The Epiphany and the Eucharist: On the Interpretation of Eucharistic Motifs in Mediaeval Epiphany Scenes." Translated by Renate Franciscono. *Art Bulletin* 49 (1967): 311–16.

Oberman, Heiko A. *Forerunners of the Reformation: The Shape of*

Late Medieval Thought. New York: Holt, 1966.

_____ . *The Harvest of Medieval Theology: Gabriel Biel and Late Medieval Nominalism.* Cambridge: Harvard University Press, 1963.

_____ . "Some Notes on the Theology of Nominalism." *Harvard Theological Review* 53 (1960): 47–76.

Olson, Elder. *Tragedy and the Theory of Drama.* Detroit: Wayne State University Press, 1961.

Owst, Gerald Robert. *Literature and Pulpit in Medieval England.* 2d rev. ed. Oxford: Basil Blackwell, 1966.

_____ . *Preaching in Medieval England.* Cambridge: The University Press, 1926.

Panofsky, Erwin. *Early Netherlandish Painting: Its Origins and Character.* 2 vols. Cambridge, MA: Harvard University Press, 1953.

_____ . *Gothic Architecture and Scholasticism.* New York: World, 1957.

Peebles, Rose Jefferies. *The Legend of Longinus in Ecclesiastical Tradition and in English Literature, and Its Connection with the Grail.* Baltimore: J.H. Furst, 1911.

Phillips, John. *The Reformation of Images: Destruction of Art in England, 1535–1660.* Berkeley, CA: University of California Press, 1973.

Pickering, Frederick Pickering. *Literature and Art in the Middle Ages.* Coral Gables, FL: University of Miami Press, 1970.

Pieper, Josef. *Scholasticism: Personalities and Problems of Medieval Philosophy.* Translated by Richard and Clara Winston. New York: Pantheon, 1960.

Pierson, Merle. "The Relation of the Corpus Christi Procession to the Corpus Christi Play in England." *Transactions of the Wisconsin Academy of Sciences, Arts, and Letters* 18 (1915): 110–65.

Pival, Paul John, Jr. "Staging as Projection of Imitated Action in the Chester Cycle." Ph.D. dissertation, University of Wisconsin, 1973.

Pollack, Rhoda-Gale. "Angelic Imagery in the English Mystery Cycles." *Theatre Notebook* 29 (1975): 124–39.

Prosser, Eleanor. *Drama and Religion in the English Mystery Plays: A Re-evaluation.* Stanford, CA: Stanford University Press, 1961.

Righter, Anne. *Shakespeare and the Idea of the Play.* London: Chatto and Windus, 1962.

Robertson, D.W., Jr., "The Question of 'Typology' and the Wakefield *Mactacio Abel*." *American Benedictine Review* 25 (1974): 157–73.

Robinson, J.W. "The Art of the York Realist." *Modern Philology* 60 (1963): 241–51.

_____ . "The Late Medieval Cult of Jesus and the Mystery Plays." *PMLA* 80 (1965): 508–14.

Rossiter, A.P. *English Drama from Early Times to the Elizabethans. Its Background, Origins and Developments.* London: Hutchinson University Library, 1950.

Roston, Murray. *Biblical Drama in England from the Middle Ages to the Present Day.* London: Faber, 1968.

Rushforth, Gordon McNeil. *Medieval Christian Imagery.* Oxford: The Clarendon Press, 1936.

Salter, F.M. "The Banns of the Chester Plays." *Review of English Studies* 15 (1939): 432–57; 16 (1940): 1–17, 137–48.

_____. *Mediaeval Drama in Chester.* Toronto: University of Toronto Press, 1955.

_____. "The 'Trial and Flagellation'." *The Trial and Flagellation with Other Studies in the Chester Cycle.* London: Oxford University Press, 1935.

Severs, J. Burke. "The Relationship between the Brome and Chester Plays of *Abraham and Isaac.*" *Modern Philology* 42 (1945): 137–51.

Sinanoglou, Leah. "The Christ Child as Sacrifice: A Medieval Tradition and the Corpus Christi Plays." *Speculum* 48 (1973): 491–509.

Smalley, Beryl. *The Study of the Bible in the Middle Ages.* Oxford: The Clarendon Press, 1941.

Southern, R.W. "Aspects of the European Tradition of Historical Writing: 2. Hugh of St. Victor and the Idea of Historical Development." *Transactions of the Royal Historical Society*, 5th ser., 21 (1971): 159–79.

Spector, Stephen. "The Genesis of the N-Town Cycle." Ph.D. dissertation, Yale University, 1973.

Spencer, M. Lyle. *Corpus Christi Pageants in England.* New York: Baker and Taylor, 1911.

Staines, David. "To Out-Herod Herod: The Development of a Dramatic Character." *Comparative Drama* 10 (1976): 29–53.

Stevens, John. "Music in Mediaeval Drama." *Proceedings of the Royal Musical Association* 84 (1958): 81–95.

Stevens, Martin. "Illusion and Reality in the Medieval Drama." *College English* 32 (1971): 448–64.

Stone, Darwell. *A History of the Doctrine of the Holy Eucharist.* 2 vols. London: Longmans, Green, 1909.

Strohm, Paul. "The Dramatic and Rhetorical Technique of the Chester Mystery Plays." Ph.D. dissertation, University of California, Berkeley, 1966.

Studies in the Literary Imagination, vol. 8, no. 1, 1975.

Sturdevant, Winifred. *The "Misterio de los Reyes Magos": Its Position in the Development of the Mediaeval Legend of the Three Kings.* Baltimore: Johns Hopkins Press, 1927.

Swanton, Michael, ed. *The Dream of the Rood.* Manchester: Manchester University Press, 1970.

Taylor, Jerome, and Nelson, Alan H., eds. *Medieval English Drama: Essays Critical and Contextual*. Chicago: University of Chicago Press, 1972.

Trapp, J.B. "The Iconography of the Fall of Man." *Approaches to Paradise Lost*. Edited by C.A. Patrides. London: Edward Arnold, 1968.

Trinkaus, Charles, and Oberman, Heiko A., eds. *The Pursuit of Holiness in Late Medieval and Renaissance Religion*. Studies in Medieval and Reformation Thought, vol. 10. Leiden: E.J. Brill, 1974.

Tristram, Earnest William. *English Wall Painting of the Fourteenth Century*. London: Routledge and Kegan Paul, 1955.

Turner, Ralph V. *"Descendit Ad Inferos:* Medieval Views on Christ's Descent into Hell and the Salvation of the Ancient Just." *Journal of the History of Ideas* 27 (1966): 173–94.

Turner, Victor W. *The Ritual Process: Structure and Anti-Structure*. Ithaca, NY: Cornell University Press, 1969.

Ungemach, Heinrich Gottfried. *Die Quellen der fünf ersten Chester Plays*. Erlangen: A. Deichert, 1890.

Utesch, Hans. *Die Quellen der Chester-Plays*. Kiel: Kieler Tagespost, G.m.b.H., 1909.

Wachal, Robert. "Linguistic Evidence, Statistical Inference, and Disputed Authorship." Ph.D. dissertation, University of Wisconsin, 1966.

Watts, Alan W. *Myth and Ritual in Christianity*. Boston: Beacon Press, 1968.

Wee, David L. "The Temptation of Christ and the Motif of Divine Duplicity in the Corpus Christi Cycle Drama." *Modern Philology* 72 (1974): 1–16.

White, Lynn, Jr. "Natural Science and Naturalistic Art in the Middle Ages." *The American Historical Review* 52 (1947): 421–35.

Wickham, Glynne. *Early English Stages, 1300 to 1600*. 3 vols. London: Routledge and Kegan Paul, 1959–81.

_____. *The Medieval Theatre*. New York: St. Martin's, 1974.

_____. "The Romanesque Style in Medieval Drama." *Tenth-Century Studies*. Edited by David Parsons. London: Phillimore Press, 1975.

Williams, Arnold. *The Characterization of Pilate in the Towneley Plays*. East Lansing, MI: Michigan State University Press, 1950.

_____. *The Common Expositor: An Account of the Commentaries on Genesis, 1527–1633*. Chapel Hill, NC: University of North Carolina Press, 1948.

_____. *The Drama of Medieval England*. East Lansing, MI: State University Press, 1961.

_____. "Typology and the Cycle Plays: Some Criteria." *Speculum* 43 (1968): 677–84.

Wilson, Robert H. "The *Stanzaic Life of Christ* and the Chester Plays." *North Carolina Studies in Philology* 28 (1931): 413-32.

Woolf, Rosemary. "The Effect of Typology on the English Mediaeval Plays of Abraham and Isaac." *Speculum* 32 (1957): 805-25.

_____ . *The English Mystery Plays*. London: Routledge and Kegan Paul, 1972.

_____ . *The English Religious Lyric in the Middle Ages*. Oxford: The Clarendon Press, 1968.

Wosien, Maria-Gabriele. *Sacred Dance: Encounter with the Gods*. New York: Avon, 1974.

Zumthor, Paul. "From Hi(story) to Poem, or the Paths of Pun: The Grands Rhétoriqueurs of Fifteenth-Century France." Translated by Annette and Edward Tomarken. *New Literary History* 10 (1979): 231-63.

Index

305